Leadership in the Prophetic Literature with Special Reference to Eighth Century BCE Prophets

Biblical Hermeneutics Rediscovered

The Series as the name suggests will focus on Biblical Hermeneutics, i.e., literary works concerned with methods of interpreting the Old and New Testaments of Bible via different stream of topics like Literature & Poetry, Indigenous Philosophizing, Ethical response towards Ecology, Health & Healing, Science & Technology, Feminist Theology, Sociological approach towards Human Rights, Law & Politics, Arts, History of Ideas, Ancient Civilizations, Cultural Contiguity, Religious Cosmologies & Mysticism, Appraisal of various Theologians, World Peace & Harmony, Global Capitalism, Network Marketing, Cybertheology, Population & Demographics, Epigraphic Studies, Contextualized Education, and many others. We welcome a Mss. on any topic/s mentioned, whether they are original works, scholarly monographs, collections of conference papers, revised dissertations, or translations of historical documents. Through the Series we, the Publishers, are striving to put forward published works that may help Institutions, Academic Bodies, Researchers, Scholars and the World at large in furthering their respective knowledge and understanding on the concerned subject. We welcome your comments on our efforts and further suggestions on how we can enshrine new ray of analysing & explaining the written Texts through our upcoming books.

Biblical Hermeneutics Rediscovered - 35

Leadership in the Prophetic Literature with Special Reference to Eighth Century BCE Prophets

A. Abeni Patton

Christian World Imprints

First Published in 2020 by

Christian World Imprints
Christian Publishing & Books from India
C-3, Wazirpur Industrial Area
Delhi-110052
cwidelhi2017@gmail.com
www.ChristianWorldImprints.com
Phone: +91 11 41526079

ISBN: 978-93-5148-474-5 (HB)
ISBN: 978-93-5148-475-2 (PB)

Printed in India.

Contents

Acknowledgement

First and above all, I praise God, the almighty for providing me this opportunity and granting me the capability to proceed my research successfully. This research has been one of the most significant academic challenges I ever had to face. Without the support, patience and guidance of the following people, this research would not have been completed. It is to them that I owe my deepest gratitude.

The research has been a rich and valuable experience, enhanced by the fellowship, encouragement and support of the Principal, Dean of Doctoral Studies, faculty, staff and students at Union Biblical Seminary, Pune.

I would like to express my special appreciation and thanks to my supervisor Prof. Paulson Pulikottil Ph.D who undertook to act as my supervisor despite his many other academic and professional commitments. His wisdom, knowledge and commitment to the highest standards inspired and motivated me.

I am indebted to the Baptist Theological College for their generous funding, which removed financial concerns from my decision to embark on this journey. The South Asian Theological Research Institute (SATHRI) provided further support during my research.

I take this opportunity to sincerely acknowledge my colleagues, my friends and my well wishers (too many to list here but you know who you are!) for providing support and friendship that I needed.

A special thanks to my family. Words cannot express how grateful I am to my mother and father, who have always supported, encouraged and believed in me, in all my endeavours. And to all my siblings and in-laws for all of the sacrifices that you've made on my behalf. Your prayer for me was what sustained me thus far.

May God bless you all.

This book in its original form is the thesis submitted to the Senate of Serampore College, towards the D.Th degree and is published with written permission. The candidate is responsible for the title, contents and opinions expressed in it. The title of the dissertation has been reframed to the present title for the purpose of publication. The candidate is accountable for framing the topic, methodology applied, arguments in place to support the propositions, the materials consulted and the conclusions arrived at.

Abbreviations

Reference, Academic Journals handbooks

AB	Anchor Bible
ABD	Anchor Bible Dictionary
ABQ	American Baptist Quarterly
AER	American Ecclesiastical Review
AHR	American Historical Review
AJA	American Journal of Archaeology
AJSL	American Journal of Semitic Languages and Literature
AJT	American Journal of Theology
ASOR	American Schools of Oriental Research
ATR	Anglican Theological Review
ANET	Ancient Near Eastern Texts Relating to the Old Testament
AThR	Anglican Theological Review
Arch	Archaeology
ABW	Archaeology in the Biblical World
AJT	Asia Journal of Theology
BiBh	Bible Bhashyam
BHS	Biblia Hebraica Stuttgartensia
BA	Biblical Archaeologist
BAR	Biblical Archaeology Review
BibInt	Biblical Interpretation
BR	Biblical Research
BTB	Biblical Theology Bulletin
BDB	Brown, F., S. R. Driver, and C. A. Briggs
BTF	Bangalore Theological Forum
CTJ	Calvin Theological Journal
CJT	Canadian Journal of Theology

CBQ	Catholic Biblical Quarterly
CHR	Catholic Historical Review
CJ	Concordia Journal
CTM	Currents in Theology and Mission
CTR	Criswell Theological Review
CGR	Conrad Grebel Review
CBC	Cambridge Bible Commentary
Dir	Direction
DDSR	Duke Divinity School Review
EvQ	Evangelical Quarterly
ExAud	Ex auditu
GTJ	Grace Theological Journal
HTR	Harvard Theological Review
HTS	Harvard Theological Studies
HAR	Hebrew Annual Review
HUCA	Hebrew Union College Annual
IB	Interpreter's Bible
IDB	The Interpreter's Dictionary of the Bible
IDBSup	Interpreter's Dictionary of the Bible: Supplementary Volume
IBS	Irish Biblical Studies
ITQ	Irish Theological Quarterly
Interpt	Interpretation
IJT	Indian Journal of Theology
IJS	Indian Journal of Spirituality
Jeev	Jeevadhara
JBQ	Jewish Bible Quarterly
JBL	Journal of Biblical Literature
JFSR	Journal of Feminist Studies in Religion
JNES	Journal of Near Eastern Studies
JAOS	Journal of the American Oriental Society
JSOT	Journal for the Study of Old Testament
JRL	Journal of Religious Leadership
JETS	Journal of the Evangelical Theological Society
JTS	Journal of Theological Studies
JTSA	Journal of Theology for Southern Africa
JHS	Journal of Hebrew Scriptures
JNSL	Journal of Northwest Semitic Languages
JITC	Journal of the Interdenominational Theological Centre
NIDOTTE	New International Dictionary of Old Testament Theology and Exegesis
NIDB	New International Dictionary of the Bible
NIB	The New Interpreter's Bible

NBD	New Bible Dictionary
OTA	Old Testament Abstracts
OTS	Old Testament Studies
Pre	Presbyterion
PT	Political Theology
ResQ	Restoration Quarterly
RevExp	Review and Expositor
RSR	Religious Studies Review
SJT	Scottish Journal of Theology
Semeia	Semeia
SJT	Southwestern Journal of Theology
SA	Studia Antiqua
TDOT	Theological Dictionary of the Old Testament
TLOT	Theological Lexicon of the Old Testament
TWOT	Theological Wordbook of the Old Testament
ThTo	Theology Today
TynBul	Tyndale Bulletin
ThR	Theological Review
TAJT	The Asia Journal of Theology
UCA	Union College Annual
VT	Vetus Testamentum
VTSup	Vetus Testamentum Supplements
Vid	Vidyajyoti
VTr	Voice of Tradition
WBC	Word Biblical Commentary
WW	Word & World
WTJ	Westminster Theological Journal

Books of the Bible (OT)

Abbreviations	Book
Gen	Genesis
Exod	Exodus
Lev	Leviticus
Num	Numbers
Deut	Deuteronomy
Josh	Joshua
Judg	Judges
I Sam	I Samuel
I Sam	II Samuel
I Kgs	I Kings
II Kgs	II Kings

I Chron	I Chronilces
II Chron	II Chronicles
Ezra	Ezra
Neh	Nehemiah
Ps	Psalms
Prov	Proverbs
Isa	Isaiah
Jer	Jeremiah
Lam	Lamentations
Ezek	Ezekiel
Dan	Daniel
Hos	Hosea
Joel	Joel
Amos	Amos
Mic	Micah
Nah	Nahum
Zech	Zechariah
Mal	Malachi
Non-Cananical	Book
I Macc	I Maccabees
II Macc	II Maccabees

Ancient Versions
LXX – Septuagint
MT - Masoretic Text
Syr - Syriac Peshitto
Tg - Targum
Vg – Vulgate

Bible
NRSV - New Revised Standard Version
General
BCE - Before Common Era
cf – Compare
ed (s) - Editor (s)
e.g. - For example
et al - And others
i.e - That is
MS (S) - Manuscript (s)
AWA - Ancient West Asia
OT - Old Testament
BHS - Biblia Hebraica Stuttgartensia

Introduction

1. Elaboration of the Problem

In ancient Israel the kings or royals and priests held their own offices and were regarded as leaders of Israel. On the other hand, although the prophets carried out important leadership role that have not been fully recognised as leaders. They were the main critics of the priests and the kings/royals. Hence, this research focuses on the "leadership roles" of the prophets. The texts such as Amos 7:10-17; Isaiah 7:1-17; 39:1-8; Hosea 4:1-10; Micah 3:1-12; point towards such critique on the issues of leadership and power struggle.

Some of the issues that have to do with leadership identified in this study are:

- Conflict of Perspectives
- Nominality in Leadership
- Manipulation of Cult/Religion by the Priest and the King (elites).
- The Problem of Status—the Affluent versus the Poor
- Lack of Vision in Leadershi

1.1. Leadership: Conflict of Perspectives

The Bible frequently alludes to conflict involving the prophets' conflict with each other, conflict with priests, conflict with kings and with various other people with whom they interacted, or to whom they addressed their oracles. The Bible tends to view these conflicts almost exclusively in ideological terms. It is a question of truth, and of a prophet truly sent by God: true religion, prediction, reading of events, true understanding of religious norms and true discourse for a needy people. Conflict is something to be endured and suffered in the interest of a higher duty to one's holy calling.

The text Amos 7:10-17 is about the controversy between prophet Amos and priest Amaziah. The relationship between Amaziah and Amos could well be characterized as a conflict. The tension between them, also seems to have been the issue of the right to free speech in a Temple no matter how unpleasant the topic. The reality in the text is a conflict of perspectives. The central characters in this conflict are identified immediately. On the one side is Amos, prophet from the southern kingdom, and Yahweh, the God of Israel, who has sent Amos; on the other side is Amaziah, priest at the national shrine at Bethel, and the king Jeroboam II, to whom he reports. Amaziah's actions in this narrative make best sense against the phenomenon of bureaucrats who report prophecy to the king in the ancient world, which suggests that he is acting primarily as a royal official rather than simply a custodian of the cult. The two perspectives are that of the state and that of the prophet. Amos speaks of and to a covenant people whose ruler is understood to be in fact the LORD.

Amaziah's words present a view of the northern kingdom as a nation whose ruler is the king. Although, Amaziah is chief priest at the principal place where the LORD was worshipped in Israel; his total concern is not for the will and worship of the LORD but for the safety and preservation of the king and the state. He thus perceives Amos' oracles condemning the national life and announcing judgement on the king and people as a threat to the welfare of king and state rather than as words from the Lord. He sees Amos not as a messenger of the LORD but a conspirator against the king. Amos' and Amaziah's leadership perspectives are different from one another although both were religious leaders of their day. They have differences in their perceptions. Thus, they have divergent goals: Amaziah's concern is to safeguard the king and the state whereas Amos' concern is for the covenant people. The issue here is the authenticity of chosen leaders—Amos the prophet and Amaziah the priest.

We find a similar incident in Isaiah 39:1-8. Here, the conversation that took place between Isaiah, the prophet and Hezekiah, the king reveals two different types of leadership: on the one hand is a leader (king) who seeks favour from a superior power for his own benefit. On the other hand, is a leader (prophet) who cares for the covenant people and that who sees God as mighty and powerful above every powers.

Micah 3:1-12 and Hosea 4:1-10 further reveal the false leaders/rulers whom the prophets addressed as hypocrites. They seek for judgement and prophesy for price and money and lead the covenant people without knowledge of God and תּוֹרָה. An ethical/moral issue of the leaders is identified here.

Micah introduces them not with the word courts but the term heads of Jacob. Heads of Jacob stands for family representative heads or rulers. In Micah's view, the purpose of government is to be the guardian of justice. When justice is not guarded in society then law certainly breaks down. Against the prophets Micah also cries out (Mic 3:5-8). His basic complaint against the prophets is that they have a favourite sermon. In fact, it is a sermon with a one-word title. It is the word שָׁלוֹם. Micah says this message which only emphasizes the loving-kindness of God and does not come to grips with evil and with sin and with the necessity for straightening out your life, this kind of a message basically comes from those who are speaking for hire. That is, the position they enjoy through the financial support of others. In the day to come the false prophets have no revelation at all. He says false prophets are for profit, in contrast to himself. The true prophet speaks of justice. Micah is a true prophet because he distinguishes between the right and the wrong.

Another eighth century BCE prophet, Hosea revels that priests and prophets are called by God to be responsible for the whole of God's creation. They are responsible to maintain "faithfulness," "loving kindness" and "knowledge of God" in the land. However, priests and prophets actively rejected "knowledge of God" in favour of easy religious teachings and practices that assure their own prosperity and place in the society (Hos 4:10-12,18-19). They failed to be faithful leaders. The conflict here is priests and prophets understand that the Knowledge is mere intellectual comprehension, but for Hosea knowledge is not intellectual understanding alone but it is tied in with a right relationship with Yahweh. Thus, Hosea's leadership was unique and his whole life was symbolic, an object lesson of his message.

1.2. Nominality in Leadership

The role of the prophet and the place of justice within the prophetic message are not marginal matters for God's people but central to the life and leadership of the community. Justice and righteousness did not affect the moral life of ancient Israel merely as abstract concepts or covenant ideals. Community requires leaders who promote and embody the foundational concepts. It is clear that, of all the leadership roles in ancient Israel, the role of prophet is most unique and distinctive of Israel as God's covenant people. However, not all religious leaders of ancient Israel were genuine leaders. There was nominality in their leadership. There were leaders who sought power and position in all levels of society, Amaziah, the priest of Bethel and the unnamed priests and prophets in Hosea and Micah are examples. The question here is, rather, how a genuine prophetic leadership can be ascertained.

1.3. Manipulation of Cult/Religion by the Priest and the King (elites)

The priests of the state temple had a specific role in all activities of worship. They served as powerful officials of the king and exerted their economic and political power on all levels of society. They controlled the cultic practices and manipulated tithes, offerings and sacrifices. Bethel was the centre of the religious culture in the Northern kingdom of Israel during the eighth century BCE and Amaziah was its priest who supervised the sanctuary, or the temple of the kingdom. As the leading official in charge of the cult at the Bethel sanctuary, he stepped forward to oppose the prophet Amos from Judah. Being influential with the king, Amaziah attempted to silence the prophet by civil power. According to his own admission, Amaziah's highest overlord was the king of Israel. As the responsible official in charge, he banished Amos from the country.

The issue here is why and how leaders of the nation and servants of the LORD could (both the priest and the king) manipulate the cult in their own interest. Also, how prophetic leadership outstands this manipulation and exemplify true leadership.

1.4. The Problem of Status: The Affluent versus the Poor

The book of Amos mentions Amos as one who lived in Tekoa, south-east of Jerusalem, a small town in Judah and that he came from humble origins. According to the editorial introduction he was from "among the shepherds," and he says of himself: "Yahweh took me from following the flock" (Amos 7:15). Generally he is conceived as a shepherd and migrant labourer who during the harvest season was a dresser of sycamore trees, probably one who punctures the fruit so that it could ripen. He has lived and worked in the country, not in a city. He comes from his farming work to be a prophet to the people of Israel.[1]

On the contrary, Amaziah the priest lives in an urban area and holds an important position in Israel and is associated with the royal family. Thus he communicates directly with the king. As the chief priest of the temple, he tries to exercise his power and show his position to Amos. Bethel is a Royal Chapel and a National Cathedral, and people like Amos are definitely uninvited. Thus, Amaziah unequivocally commands Amos to leave Israel and to prophesy in Judah.

We see here that Amos' response is equally clear and addresses very specifically the issue Amaziah is raising. Amos heeds neither Amaziah's advice to leave the country nor his command to keep silent. He cannot obey the high priest's command to prophesy in Judah, for in Judah he is simply a farmer; his call as a prophet relates to the land of Israel. Amos' first statement in his response to Amaziah's order to return to Judah in Amos 7:14: "I am no prophet, nor a prophet's son; but I am a herdsman and a dresser of sycamore trees," has been in scholarship discussion.[2] The concern here is why social status becomes an issue for leadership?

---

1 Simon Cohen, "Amos *Was a* Navi," *HUCA* 32 (1961): 175-178; John D. W. Watts, "Amos, the Man," *Review & Expositor* 63 (1966): 387-392; T. J. Wright, "Amos and the Sycomore Fig," *VT* 26 (1976): 362-368; James Philip Hyatt, "Book of Amos," *Interpretation* 3 (1949): 338-348; James L. Mays, "Words about the Words of Amos: Recent Study of the Book of Amos," *Interpretation* 13 (1959), 259-272.

2 The profession exercised by Amos before being called to the prophetic ministry has received much attention. Early scholarship assumed that Amos was a poor manual labourer. The traditional understanding of Amos profession before his call has increasingly been challenged in much modern scholarship. Amos economic position is uncertain one way or the other. William Rainey Harper, *Amos and Hosea: Critical and Exegetical Commentary* (Edinburgh: T&T Clark, 1905), civ, James Luther Mays, *Amos: A Commentary* (London: SCM Press Ltd,

1.5. Lack of Vision in Leadership

Leadership requires vision—a complete understanding for the big picture of where the leader wants to be. It should be a clearly communicable picture of the future, steeped in value, and philosophy, as well as structure. A clear vision provides direction and establishes purpose. However, in Israelite society the leaders could not lead the people as they were supposed to be. For instance, during the eighth century BCE Israel, especially, in the time of Ahaz and his son Hezekiah kings of Judah, the nation encountered several political crises that demanded a right decision. In Ahaz's time, Judah was invaded by the forces of Syria and of Israel whose king, Pekah, kills 120,000 men of Judah in a single day (II Chron 28:5-8). The survival of Ahaz on this occasion does not prevent the return of his enemies and, in fear, he sends for help to Tiglath-Pilesar, the king of Assyria. It is at this critical time that Isaiah meets with Ahaz assuring him of Yahweh's protection and urging him to look to heaven for a sign that Judah would be delivered (Isa 7). The failure of Ahaz to obey the counsel of the prophet is the result of an unwillingness to recognise his dependence on Yahweh and a determination to resort to fleshly means. His allegiance with Assyria develops, and it becomes the occasion of introducing further idolatry into the land (II Kgs 16:10-16; II Chron 28:22-25). Ahaz's wrong decision leads the nation to a great disaster. Judah becomes a vassal state and has to give heavy annual tribute to Assyria. In a time of crisis he ought to listen to Yahweh, but he does not. The challenge is given to Ahaz, but his lack of vision shattered the opportunity.

Hezekiah is considered as a good king because he loved the Lord and followed His ways. However, at the end of his kingship, he loses his trust in God and seeks help from the Babylonian king. It is his simple selfishness, greed and lack of vision in leadership. J. Alec Motyer sees the book of Isaiah portraying Hezekiah as one of the most truly human of the kings. He depicts Hezekiah as someone "whose heart was genuinely moved towards the Lord but whose will was fickle" in the moment of trial.[3] In his view, Hezekiah finally fails his responsibilities as a servant of Yahweh because of pride born from a sense of royal accomplishment. The reception of messengers from Babylon by Hezekiah is the beginning of the end (Isa 39). This is the enemy that would carry Judah captive as Assyria had carried Israel. If self-love comes in and appropriates the treasures of the soul, all good is destroyed.

1969), 3-4; Joseph Blenkinsopp, *A History of Prophecy in Israel* (Philadelphia: Westminster Press, 1983); Gerhard F. Hasel, *Understanding the Book of Amos: Basic Issues in Current Interpretation* (Grand Rapids: Baker, 1991), 35; Francis Brown, S. R Driver and Charles A. Briggs, *Hebrew and English Lexicon of the Old Testament* (Oxford: Clarendon Press, 1972), 667; Hans W. Wolff, *Amos the Prophet: Man and His Background* (Philadelphia: Fortress Press, 1973), 118.

3 J. Alec Motyer, *The Prophecy of Isaiah: An Introduction and Commentary* (Leicester: IVP, 1993), 290.

What led Hezekiah to show the treasures to the Babylonians? The answer is pride at his wealth (Isa 39:2). Isaiah uses Hezekiah showing the ambassadors his riches and wealth to illustrate his pride. Many are too preoccupied with materialism and that often brings disaster. King Hezekiah trusted worldly power and materialism than God who is above all worldly powers and thus he lost everything at the end. The question which confronts us here is: is leadership to seek for power and security only or to serve the purpose of the people?

2. Importance of the Research

The study is to explore the concept of leadership in the prophetic literature, particularly from the eighth century BCE prophetic books. The concept of leadership is centred on tribal chief, military commander, kingship, palace official in royal context, and temple officials found in different administrative capacities. Hence, this research will help in formulating a concept that prophets of ancient Israel possessed leadership qualities. Leadership is not only centred within the royal context but anyone whom God chooses. The ancient Israelite prophets could be leaders.[4] Prophetic leadership rises from Hebrew tradition and is rooted in prophets' teachings and actions. Thus, the purpose of this research is to explore the prophetic leadership and relate to the prophetic ministry in today's churches.

3. Limitation of the Research

The proposed research will mainly focus on the eighth century BCE prophets. Analysis of Amos' preaching at Bethel (Amos 7:10-17) which possibly contributed to the criticism of Amos on cult (priest) and the King/royal policies; conversation between prophet Isaiah of Jerusalem and kings of Judah especially Ahaz and Hezekiah (Isa 7:1-17;39:1-8); conflicts with nominal/false priests and prophets (Hos 4:1-10; Mic 3:1-12); Israel's concept of leadership, and also background of the eighth century BCE Israel (Political, Social, Religious) will be critically analysed.

---

4 Except Isaiah who belonged to the king, the rulers, and the priests of Jerusalem (since Jewish tradition indicates that *Amoz* [the father of Isaiah] was the brother of King Amaziah. If that was so, then Isaiah would have been a member of Judah's royal house), Amos, Hosea and Micah were belonged to unrecognised family or social status, however, they responded to the "call of God" and thus become *prophets* with leadership qualities. Cf. J. Skinner, *The Book of the Prophet Isaiah, Chapters I-XXXIX* (ed. J. F. Kirkpatrick; Cambridge: University Press, 1896), xxii; George A. Buttrick, ed., *IDB* (Nashville: Abingdon Press, 1962); E. Clements, *Isaiah 1-39* (NCBC; ed. R. E. Clements; Grand Rapids: Wm. B. Eerdmans, 1980), 12.

4. Working Definition: Prophet as Leader (נָגִיד)

The Hebrew word נָגִיד is generally translated as prince, ruler, leader, and so on.[5] Books of Chronicles have repeated usage of this term to refer the leadership role.[6] In Daniel 9:25 מָשִׁיחַ נָגִיד refers to "the Anointed ruler/one." Kings were anointed with the holy oil. Therefore, נָגִיד, closely related to king and leadership, is given on the basis of election through anointing.[7] The term is not referred to prophets nor mentioned directly in the prophetic literature except in Isaiah 55:4 in reference to David.[8] The term נָגִיד however, is a synonymous title to refer to נֹקֵד "shepherd" and the prophets were addressed as נֹקֵד "shepherd."[9] Thus, prophets were also addressed as leaders in one way or the other.

5. Method of the Research

The study will be based on combination of several methodologies such as the sociological method in order to analyse the social and cultural aspects of the text. This method is a literary paradigm for approaching a text. The basic concept is that we are not only living in a literary and historical world but also in a social world. So this approach analyses the social and cultural dimensions of the text in order to clearly understand the chief aspects of public life, such as family, economy, government, ritual and religious practices.[10]

The sociological criticism helps to see whether the text characteristically acts as an advocate within a concentrated area that is, the vested interests economically, socially and politically. This method will help us to explore the real social situation of the eighth century BCE Israelite society. The advantage of this method is that

---

5 Hasel, "נגד (*ngd*)," in *TDOT* (vol. IX; ed. G. Johannes Botterweck et al; trans. David E. Green; Grand Rapids: William B. Eerdmans Publishing Company, 1986), 192; Kenneth T. Aitken, "נָגִיד," in *NIDOTTE* (vol. 3; ed. William A. VanGremeren; Carlisle: Paternoster Press, 1996), 20. The term נָגִיד has been used for leader than any other words.

6 It is used variously to denote a tribal chief (I Chron 12:27 [28]; II Chron 19:11), military commander in royal context (I Chron 13:1; 27:4), palace official (II Chron 28:7), or temple officials found in different administrative capacities (I Chron 9:20; 26:24; II Chron 31:12 cf. Jer 20:1). Cf. BDB (Oxford: The Clarendon Press, 1962), 617-618.

7 Aitken, "נָגִיד," in *NIDOTE*, 20.

8 Motyer, *The Prophecy of Isaiah*, 455 (Cf. Pss 18:43-44; 89:3-4; 15-37). Motyer states that the term נָגִיד is used thirteen times of the kings of Israel and Judah (of which seven refers to David)" who is the great king. It is also used to refer to kings such as Saul (I Sam 9:16; 10:1); David (I Sam 13:14; II Sam 7:8); Jeroboam (I Kgs 14:7); Bashan (16:2); Hezekiah (II Kgs 20:5). Hence the term נָגִיד refer to leader, commander and prince but also it refers to king or kingship. See Aitken, "נָגִיד," in *NIDOTE*, 20-21.

9 J. J. Gluck, "Nagid-shepherd," *VT* 13 (1963): 144-150. It is used as a complementary title which indicates the loving care to the weaker members of the flock, and characteristically used for the ideal leader.

10 Norman K. Gottwald, *The Hebrew Bible-A Socio-Literary Reading* (Philadelphia: Fortress Press, 1985), 26.

it complements other critical diachronic[11] and synchronic[12] methods by providing the specific cultural and social arrangements.

The diachronic study of Amos 7:10-17; Isaiah 7; 39:1-8; Hosea 4:1-10 and Micah 3:1-12 in its historical details through social settings and political settings is helpful to substantiate the text's origin, development and history as to reconstruct the meaning effectively (for instance form criticism, tradition-historical criticism and sociological approach). Further, synchronic study is taken into consideration in order to analyse the author, genre, and time period, technical or idiomatic usage, accompanying circumstances. The study will help us to analyse the concept of prophetic leadership to find a relevant message especially to our contemporary society.

6. Survey of the Previous Scholarship

6.1. Eighth Century BCE Prophetic Literature

6.1.1. Amos 7:10-17

The issues related in Amos 7:10-17 are: Amos' pre-prophetic vocation, particularly as it relates to the usage of the terms describing his previous profession, for instance: בוֹלֵס, שִׁקְמִים, בוֹקֵר, נֹקֵד; the nature of the relationship between the prophetic office and the state; Amos' own understanding of his status as a prophet; and Amos encounter/controversy with Amaziah, the priest of Bethel. A few scholars have attempted to address these issues.[13]

The issue of controversy that comes from the message of Amos was discussed by Paul R. Noble, and Ziony Zevit.[14] According to them, both Amos and Amaziah didn't see eye to eye. There was a personality conflict and even more—a conflict of ideas and of faith. Amos is creating trouble. Amaziah wanted him gone. He went to the king and said, "Amos is raising a conspiracy against you in the very heart of Israel. The land cannot bear all his words. For this is what Amos is saying: 'Jeroboam will die by the sword, and Israel will surely go into exile, away from

11 Diachronic approach evaluates the text in the light of historical development of a given text by means of taking the issues of authorship and historical setting of the text.

12 Synchronic approach means the method applied to biblical studies giving importance to text or text centred. Here all the non-historical aspects are taken together to explain or analyse the text.

13 To mention few: Terry Giles, "A Note on the Vocation of Amos in 7:14," *JBL* 111 (1992): 690-69; Jimmy J. Roberts, "A Note on Amos 7:14 and Its Context," *Restoration Quarterly* 8 (1965): 175-78; Åke Viberg, "Amos 7:14: A Case of Subtle Irony," *Tyndale Bulletin* 47 (1996): 91-114; Jack P. Lewis, "A Prophet's Son' (Amos 7:14) Reconsidered," *Restoration Quarterly* 49 (2007): 229-240; Lawrence Zalcman, "Piercing The Darkness At *Bôqēr* (Amos VII 14)," *VT* 30 (1980): 252-255.

14 Paul R. Noble, "Amos and Amaziah in Context: Synchronic and Diachronic Approaches," *CBQ* 60 (1998): 423-439; Ziony Zevit, "A Misunderstanding at Bethel Amos VII 12-17," *VT* 25 (1975): 783-90.

their native land.'" Amaziah is trying to get Amos on treason-speaking against the king.

Some of the scholars have discussed the meaning of Amos' surprising answer to Amaziah's command to leave Israel and to prophesy in Judah: "I am no prophet, nor a prophet's son" (Amos 7:14).[15] The majority of the scholars resolve the difficulty by stating that Amos is denying any association with Israel's prophetic movement.[16] Although, the different attempts at resolving the problem are interesting and sometimes even inspiring, they are not completely satisfactory. For example, the solutions proposed do not take into account the rhetorical nature of Amos' statement. Amos' answer is set into a confrontational context and is meant to settle the issue of his legitimacy.

Amos 7:10-17 revels two different kinds of leadership qualities that possess by Amaziah, the priest and Amos, the prophet. Amaziah is all about king and country, but not a word about God. Not a word about repentance. Just an accusation that Amos is someone trying to put the fear of God into people for personal profit. On the other hand, the humble leadership quality that possesses by Amos has been worth discussing.

6.1.2. Isaiah 39:1-8

Similarly a few scholars attempted to address the issues in the book of Isaiah about king Hezekiah and prophet Isaiah.[17] Generally scholars view Hezekiah as a favourable or a noble pious king. Chronicler (II Chron 32:30-32) also mentions Hezekiah as a good king. However, reading the narrative of Isaiah 39 in terms of the ethical demands of the book of Isaiah as a whole produces a negative judgement of Hezekiah's character. According to Peter R. Ackroyd, Hezekiah's illness and recovery in Isaiah 38 is "a type of judgement and exile" and as such

15 The expression "son of a prophet" does not refer to physical descent but designates one as a member of one of the prophetic guilds or bands (I Sam 10:5, 10; 19:20) whose members were - sometimes designated "sons of the prophets" (I Kgs 20:35; II Kgs 2:3, 5, 7, 15; 4:1, 38).

16 To mention few: Lewis, "A Prophet's Son (Amos 7:14) Reconsidered," 229-240; Mays, *Amos: A Commentary*, 137; H. W. Wolff, *Joel and Amos* (trans. Waldemar Janzen; ed. S. Dean McBride, Jr.; Philadelphia: Fortress Press, 1977), 313-15; G. M. Tucker, "Prophetic Authority: A form Critical Study of Amos 7:10-17," *Interpretation* 27 (1973): 423-34; Cohen, "Amos *Was* a Navi," 177; J. Morgenstern, "Amos Studies IV," *HUCA* 32 (1961): 295-350; J. Lindblom, *Prophesy in Ancient Israel* (Oxford: Basil Blackwell, 1962), 183.

17 Michael L. Barre, "Restoring the 'Lost' Prayer in the Psalm of Hezekiah (Isaiah 38: 16-17b)," *JBL* 114 (1995): 385-399; Vicki Hoffer, "An Exegesis of Isaiah 38: 21," *JSOT* 56 (1992): 68-84; Margaret Barker, "Hezekiah's Boil," *JSOT* 95 (2001): 31-42; Robert I. Vasholz, "Isaiah and Ahaz: A Brief History of Crisis in Isaiah 7 and 8," *Presbyterion* 13 (1987): 79-84; James M. Kennedy, "Yahweh's Strongman? The Characterization of Hezekiah in the Book of Isaiah," *Perspectives in Religious Studies* 31 (2004): 383-397; Peter R. Ackroyd, "An Interpretation of the Babylonian Exile: A Study of 2 Kings 20, Isaiah 38-39," *Scottish Journal of Theology* 21 (1974): 329-52.

parallels the story about the visiting Babylonians in Isaiah 39.[18] Ackroyd takes Hezekiah's restored health and continuing rule to point to the possibility of such a future restoration for the exiled community. Furthermore, in his opinion, the narrative about Hezekiah's exhibition of wealth before the Babylonian envoys in Isaiah 39 is not about a bad king, but a good one who made a momentary slip of judgement.

Similarly Christopher Seitz reads Isaiah 36-37 as the promotion of a high reputation for Hezekiah.[19] Seitz represents Isaiah 38 as augmenting and reinforcing Hezekiah's positive portrayal by showing that Jerusalem's deliverance derives from the king's obedience to and trust in Yahweh.[20]

Katheryn Pfisterer Darr and Marvin Sweeney describe Hezekiah as presenting a prototype of godliness in Isaiah.[21] Sweeney depicts Isaiah 39 as enhancing the alleged thematic praise of Hezekiah's loyalty so dramatically displayed in Isaiah 36-38.

Alec Motyer and Robert H. O'Connell present different interpretations of Hezekiah from the above views. Motyer affirms that Hezekiah finally fails his responsibilities as a servant of Yahweh because of pride born from a sense of royal accomplishment.[22] For Robert H. O'Connell, Isaiah 36-38 portrays Hezekiah as a promising ruler. Isaiah 39, however, depicts Hezekiah as ultimately disappointing any hopes about an ideal Davidic king.[23] On the whole, the book of Isaiah presents a characterization of Hezekiah that holds the king to the same responsibility of moral blindness and deafness that marks the entire nation. From the book of Isaiah's point of view, the fact is that Hezekiah is a bad king.

---

18 Ackroyd, "An Interpretation of the Babylonian Exile: A Study of 2 Kings 20 and Isaiah 38-39," 329-52.

19 Christopher R. Seitz, *Zion's Final Destiny: The Development of the Book of Isaiah: A Reassessment of Isaiah 36-39* (Minneapolis: Fortress, 1991), 75-81. Seitz sets his take on Hezekiah in the context of an attempt to establish the redactional priority of Isaiah 36-39 as it relates to II Kings 18:1-20:19. In Seitz's opinion, the older account is the book of Isaiah's, from which the deuteronomic historian draws for his own purposes. In Seitz's reading, the narrative of Isaiah 36-38 justifies Hezekiah from participation in the alliances with Egypt that Isaiah condemns in chapters 30 and 31.

20 Seitz, *Zion's Final Destiny,* 191.

21 Katheryn Pfisterer Darr, *Isaiah's Vision and the Family of God* (Louisville: Westminster John Knox, 1994), 216; idem, "No Strength to Deliver: A Contextual Analysis of Hezekiah's Proverb in Isaiah 37.3b," in *New Visions of Isaiah* (JSOTSup 214; eds. Roy F. Melugin and Marvin A. Sweeney; Sheffield: Sheffield Academic Press, 1996), 219-56; Marvin A. Sweeney, *Isaiah 1-39 with an Introduction to Prophetic Literature* (FOTL 16; Grand Rapids: Eerdmans, 1996), 486.

22 Motyer, *The Prophecy of Isaiah,* 290.

23 Robert H. O'Connell, *Concentricity and Continuity: The Literary Structure of Isaiah* (JSOTSup 188; Sheffield, England: Sheffield Academic Press, 1994), 140.

6.1.3. Hosea 4:1-10

Some of the issues in Hosea 4 have been addressed by few scholars namely Jack R. Lundbom, Jeffrey H. Hoffmeyer, R. Micahel Casto, and J. Carl Bosma.[24] The twofold division (Hos 1-3 and 4-14) of the book of Hosea is supported by majority of the scholars.[25] This belongs to the prophetic lawsuit and one of its sub-categories, the "court speech."[26]

The Book of Hosea consists of six cycles of prophetic speeches. Cycle A is 1:2-2:1; cycle F is 2:2-23; cycle C is chapter 3; cycle D is 4:1-6:3; cycle E is 6:4-11:11; and cycle F is 11:12-14:8. Most of these oracles are messages of God's judgement against sinful Israel.[27] Hosea 4 falls into the second major division of the book and belongs to cycle D of prophetic speeches. Cycle D includes prophetic judgement oracles (Hos 4:1-5:15a), God's promise of restoration (Hos 5:15b), and an exhortation to repent (Hos 6: l-3).

Scholars have long noted the literary unevenness inherent in the complexes of Hosea's oracles in Hosea 4-14.[28] Hosea 4:1-19 includes a compositional interweaving of individual oracles: (1) Hos 1-3; (2) Hos 4-10; (3) Hos 11-14; (4) Hos 15-16; (4) Hos 17-19. The identification of individual oracles within these larger units is informed primarily by changes in addressees, such as Israel and Ephraim or Judah, and by changes in prophetic speech types or forms and themes.

Graham I. Davies, however, opposes the practice of dividing these larger complexes into numerous individual oracles. He is convinced that Hosea's abrupt change in style and addressees in the course of his prophetic speeches is due to his taking "on the role of an *advocatus Dei.*"[29]

---

24 Jack R. Lundbom, "Contentious Priests and Contentious People in Hosea 4:1-10," *VT* 36 (1986): 53-70; Jeffrey H. Hoffmeyer, "Covenant and Creation: Hosea 4:1-3," *Review & Expositor* 102 (2005): 143-151; R. Michael Casto, "Conversing with the Text Application of Conversational Exegesis to Hosea 4:1-3," *Duke Divinity School Review* 40 (1975): 18-33; J. Carl Bosma, "Criation in Jeopardy: A Warning to Priests (Hosea 4: 1-3)," *Calvin Theological Journal* 34 (1999): 64-116. They have attempted to address the issues such as textual problems in Hosea 4, Literary Structure, covenant and creation: Israel's failures in its covenant with God have consequences for the natural world, controversial priest and prophets and their failures.

25 While most commentators agreed to this twofold division, a few scholars propose a threefold division of the book (Hos 1-3; 4-11; 12-14). These include James L. Mays, *Hosea* (OTL, Philadelphia: Westminster, 1969), and Hans Walter Wolff, *Hosea: A Commentary on the Book of the Prophet Hosea (*trans. Gary Stansell; Philadelphia: Fortress, 1974).

26 Douglas Stuart, *Hosea-Jonah* (WBC, vol. 31; ed. Bruce M. Metzger, et al; Nashville: Thomas Nelson Publishers, 1987), 72; C. Westermann, *Basic Forms of Prophetic Speech* (Philadelphia: Westminster, 1967), 199.

27 For a complete outline of the book and discussion of the portion of Hosea's cycled D see Charles H. Silva, "The Literary Structure of Hosea 1-3," *Bibliotheca Sacra* 164 (2007): 181; and idem, "The Literary Structure of Hosea 4-8," *Bibliotheca Sacra* 164 (2007): 291-306.

28 For example: Wolff, *Hosea,* 74-76.

29 Graham I. Davies, *Hosea* (NCBC; Grand Rapids: Eerdmans, 1992), 136.

Rhetorically, the significant moves are from the general to the specific and from the indefinite to the definite. In Hosea 4 the enormous burden which the prophet carries for his nation begins to be unloaded. Here, controversy is seen to be with the priests and the people; and the accusation is made against the priests.[30] According to J. Wellhausen, the priest is to stumble with the prophet.[31]

F. I. Andersen and D. N. Freedman in their commentary *Hosea* consider the words of Hosea 4:9a, "like the people, like the priest," thematic for the whole of 4: 1-7.[32] Hosea 4:1 addresses the king along with the priests and the people. The phrase "your people" in Hosea 4:4b denotes the king's people, the people of Samaria about whom Hosea has much to say in Hosea 10:5, 10, and 14. That Hosea 4 speaks also about Samaria's king (Hos 4:3, 7, 15). But here Hosea says that the king's people are acting either like controversial priests or like controversial people. Amos spoke about the city's excessively rich (Amos 4:1). Hosea's concern is with those who are excessive in their arguments and accusations. "You shall stumble" (Hos 4:5) is also addressed to the king. Thus our predisposition in oracles of judgement has been to pair priest with (false) prophet. Here, however, it is the king who will stumble with the (false) prophet. The sequence of speaking first to the king and then to the priest is one that deserves more attention. Here we find scholarship discussion on the leadership of the kings, priests and the false prophets, (the leadership that stumble their audience) and the comparative leadership between Hosea and his contemporary leaders (kings, priests and false prophets).

Hosea was a man of deep spiritual conviction who throughout his long ministry became progressively concerned for the reputation of Israel. According to Richard D. Patterson, Hosea's heartfelt concern over "Israel's spiritual complacency, religious syncretism, and critical position in relation to the major powers of the Ancient Near East" may be felt in the advancing flow of his messages.[33] Charles H. Silva states that in one of his prophetic oracles (Hos 4:4-10), Hosea accuses and condemns Israel's apostate priesthood: "the priests were especially guilty for which they would experience His justice and that He would reject them from being priests (cf. I Sam 15:23). The more the priests multiplied, the more they sinned against the Lord."[34] So, He would turn their glory into a shameful disgrace (Hos 4:7). Silva further asserts that the aphorism "like people, like priest" emphasizes that the priests were "just as punishable as the people" and

30 Stuart, *Hosea-Jonah*, 77.

31 J. Wellhausen, *Prolegomena to the History of Israel* (Edinburgh, 1885), 137.

32 Francis I. Andersen and David Noel Freedman, *Hosea: A New Translation with Introduction and Commentary* (Garden City/New York: Doubleday & Company, 1980), 320.

33 Richard D. Patterson, "Portraits from a Prophet's Portfolio: Hosea 4," *Bibliotheca Sacra* 165 (2008): 300.

34 Charles H. Silva, "The Literary Structure of Hosea 4-8," *Bibliotheca Sacra* 164 (2007): 291.

Hosea protests that they would be repaid for their terrible deeds (Hos 4: 9-10).[35] An exegetical study of the passage (Hos 4:1-10) will be dealt with which will throw light on the reasons for Hosea's protest against the priests.

6.1.4. Micah 3:1-12

Major issues in Micah have been discussed by the following scholars. Jennifer R. Berenson Maclean and Carol J. Dempsey focus on the questions of the book's coherence and its ethical message particularly on the usage of a variety of literary techniques, linguistic markers that set apart the passage from another, and the shift in forms.[36] Issues concerning corruption in cult/religious activities, false prophets, and unfaithfulness among religious leaders in Micah have been discussed by Rick Marrs, Joyce Rilett Wood, and Ehud Ben Zve.[37]

The passage (Mic 3:1-12) invites one to burst forth in fury against false prophets. According to Ralph L. Smith, this pericope is a judgement oracle (Mic 3:1-4, guilty rulers; 5-8 peace prophets; and 9-12 corrupted leaders and Zion's fall).[38] It focuses on the prophet's condemnation of his competitors. These prophets must have formerly been recipients of divine oracles. Micah implicitly recognizes that these prophets were not simply faking their oracles. One response to the problem of false prophecy is to seek criteria for distinguishing it from true prophecy. Hans Walter Wolff proposes five criteria: (1) A true prophet confronts sin and pronounces God's judgement on it; (2) a true prophet speaks only upon divine prompting; (3) a true prophet does not modify his message to gain approval of his audience; (4) a true prophet is ethically beyond reproach; (5) a true prophet is sent by God.[39] These are all theoretically good criteria, but only the first and the fourth are in any way independently verifiable. The important issue of "true verses false" prophets will be discussed in the second chapter.

Although, some scholars attempt to address various issues in the eighth century BCE prophetic literature, including issues of leadership and power

---

35 Silva, "The Literary Structure of Hosea 4-8," 291.

36 Jennifer R. Berenson Maclean, "Micah 3:5-12," *Interpretation* 56 (2002): 413-416; Carol J. Dempsey, "Micah 2-3: Literary Artistry, Ethical Message and Some Considerations About the Image of Yahweh and Micah," *JSOT* 85 (1999): 117-128. Cf. Kenneth Barker, "A Literary Analysis of the Book of Micah," *Bibliotheca Sacra* 155 (1998): 437-448; David G. Hagstrom, *The Coherence of the Book of Micah: A Literary Analysis* (Atlanta: Scholars, 1988), 13-22; Brevard S. Childs, *Introduction to the Old Testament as Scripture* (Philadelphia: Fortress, 1979), 431.

37 Rick Marrs, "Micah and the Task of Ministry," *Restoration Quarterly* 30 (1988): 1-16; Joyce Rilett Wood, "Speech and Action in Micah's Prophecy," *CBQ* 62 (2000): 645-662; Ehud Ben Zve, "Wrongdoers, Wrongdoing and Righting Wrongs in Micah 2," *Biblical Interpretation* 7 (1999): 87-100.

38 Ralph L. Smith, *Micah-Malachi* (WBC, vol. 32; ed. John D.W. Watts; Texas: Word Books, Publisher, 1984), 30-35.

39 Hans Walter Wolff, *Confrontations with Prophets* (Philadelphia: Fortress, 1983), 63-76.

struggle, however, the discussion on these issues still need to be addressed in the light of Amos 7:10-17; Isaiah 39: 1-8; Hoses 4:1-10 and Micah 3:1-12. On the other hand, in a broader perspective, a few scholars address the issues of leadership and power struggle in prophetic literature in general.

6.2. Prophetic Literature

6.2.1. Walter Brueggemann

Walter Brueggemann discusses the task of prophetic ministry in his book "The Prophetic Imagination."[40] He develops this thesis by analysing the theme of prophetic imagination in the Bible. He focuses especially on the achievements of leaders such as: Moses, Solomon, Jeremiah, Second Isaiah, and Jesus. Moses, the model prophet, seeks to establish a new community of faith characterized by an economics of equality, a politics of justice, and a religion of God's freedom. Solomon, however, promotes an economics of affluence, a politics of oppression, and a religion of immanence. In this way he restores the same type of imperial society that Moses had criticized in Egypt. Jeremiah, sensitive to the perceptions that Moses had articulated, grieved as the end of his country drew near. Second Isaiah, with his vision of God enthroned as king, gives fresh hope to a people despairing in exile. Jesus embodies the anguish of those rejected by the dominant culture, and at the same time he fulfils the prophetic tradition by proclaiming the new beginnings that God promised.

The refreshing approach in this book is its emphasis upon the nurturing and energizing work of the divinely inspired alternative consciousness. It does not stop with the prophets' judgement which serves to dismantle the generally accepted view of reality. Readers are helped to appreciate the up-building shepherding or pastoral role of prophetic ministry along with its characteristic biting critique.

Brueggemann also analyses leadership in his article "Ancient Israel on Political Leadership: Between the Book Ends."[41] Here, the author recounts Solomon as a leader who was committed to enormous success, specializing in wealth, grandeur security, and the wisdom to sustain that grand achievement. On the other hand, Josiah, the king of Judah is presented as a faithful leader who practised Torah Covenant. He resolved to keep the commandment of Sinai, and to practice policies in the political economy that were congruent with the theological passion rooted in the God of Sinai. The figures of Solomon and Josiah, in Deuteronomic construct, occupy the beginning and ending points in the narrative account of the dynasty. More than that, they are offered as nearly pure models of the exercise of leadership and the use of public power. Indeed, one may judge that these models

40 Walter Brueggemann, *The Prophetic Imagination* (Philadelphia; Fortress Press, 1978).

41 Walter Brueggemann, "Ancient Israel on Political Leadership: Between the Book Ends," *Political Theology* 8 (2007), 455-469.

are so pure as to be artificial and excessively choreographed. Nonetheless what is given in this interpretive tradition seeks to be instructive.

Through these leadership examples, Brueggemann argues that the role of the prophets was to evoke an "alternative consciousness" and establish an "alternative community" that would criticize the presuppositions of the dominant culture. It also helps to articulate the promise of new beginnings toward which the community of faith could move. In a similar way, he argues, the task of prophetic ministry today is to nurture the formation of an alternative community that seeks to recover its traditions of faith, resists the demands of a consumer-oriented society and anticipate the new future that God has promised.

6.2.2. Walther Zimmerli

Walther Zimmerli addresses issue of leadership in his book "Old Testament Theology in Outline."[42] According to him the task of leadership is one of the gifts of Yahweh to human kind. Ancient Israelite leaders namely Moses, Joshua, Judges and the Nazirites were charged with the task of leadership. Then leadership was assumed by the kings who were called the representatives of Yahweh. The priests and the prophets work alongside with the kings.

Zimmerli clearly has a special concern for the prophets; for it is here that he sees the divine address reaching its most profound point in the whole Old Testament history of revelation. In his preface, Zimmerli states his view that it is in Old Testament prophecy; in the confrontation between Yahweh and his people Israel achieves its "radical depths." If the Law represents the normative divine will, the prophets stand for the authentic word of God as heard through God's servants. The first thing the prophets do is uphold the claims of the Law to demonstrate Israel's complete inability to obey God's will. For example, when Elijah confronts king Ahab with his violation of the Decalogue in the episode with Naboth and his vineyard, the prophet functions as the authorized messenger of God who announces a sentence of death on Ahab: "Thus says the LORD: Have you killed, and also taken possession?" You shall say to him, "Thus says the LORD: In the place where the dogs licked up the blood of Naboth, dogs will also lick up your blood." (I Kgs 21:19). Zimmerli identifies Elijah's role here as "the guardian of the divine law" whose preaching results in the pronouncement of a death-dealing curse arising out of the transgression of the law.

6.2.3. Bruce Birch

Bruce Birch discusses the issue of leadership in his article "Reclaiming Prophetic Leadership."[43] According to him the church requires the development of a theology of leadership, which she needs to learn from prophetic leadership of

42 Walther Zimmerli, *Old Testament Theology in Outline* (trans. David E. Green; Edinburgh: T&T Clark Ltd, 1978).

43 Bruce C. Birch, "Reclaiming Prophetic Leadership," *Ex auditu* 22 (2006): 10-25.

ancient Israel. He illustrates the role of prophet and the place of justice within the prophetic message. These are not marginal matters for God's people but central to the life and leadership of the community. The prophet was but one office of leadership. Prophetic commitment to covenant values places leadership on behalf of justice more prominently on the agenda of the church's leaders.

While trying to address the issues of leadership and power struggle in other prophetic literature, the above scholars however inadequately deals with the issues in the books of Amos, Isaiah (1-39), Hosea and Micah. Hence, the present study is an attempt to look at the motif of prophetic leadership that plays an important role in establishing an alternative community that would criticize the presuppositions of the dominant culture, particularly in the light of Amos 7:10-17; Isaiah 39:1-8; Hoses 4:1-10 and Micah 3:1-12.

Chapter 1

Emergence of Royal Leadership in Israel

Introduction

The emergence of monarchy is marked as one of the most significant events in Israel as it brought many changes in social, political, economic, and spiritual realms among the people of Israel. This chapter gives a historical and socio-political analysis of the people of Ancient Israel in Palestine. It is divided into three main sections: Pre-Monarchical Israel and its leadership, the emergence of monarchy in Israel, and uniqueness of the kingship in Israel.

1.1. The Consolidation of the Israelite Tribes

Israelites in Palestine existed as a mutually integrated tribal confederacy until the emergence of the monarchy. The OT tradition presents the Israelite community as a twelve-tribe association embedded in ethnic and kinship relations.

The origins of the Israelites tribes in the central highlands are understood by different scholars variedly. According to Norman K. Gottwald and W. F. Albright the separate ancestral traditions and Moses tradition were joined into one body of tradition which reflected the combined unity of the confederated tribes.[44] This in turn became the official and canonical tradition probably from the

44 The origins of Israelites in Palestinian highlands were preserved in traditions namely, "Ancestral traditions" and "Moses tradition" which were merged in a later time. For more details see Norman K. Gottwald, *The Bible and Liberation: Political and Social Hermeneutics* (New York: Orbis books, 1983), 28; Idem, *The Hebrew Bible in its social World and Ours* (Atlanta: Scholars Press, 1993), 223; W.F. Albright, *Archaeology and the Religion of Israel* (Baltimore: The John Hopkins Press, 1956), 99.

monarchial period. Niels Peter Lemche suggests that the reign of David provided the "terminus quo" for the emergence of a pan-Israelites ideology.[45] Most of the individual ancestral traditions were lost and later were replaced by the conceptions of a joint conquest of Palestine by Israel as a whole.[46] This section deals with social and political organization of the tribal confederation in Israel and the nature of its leadership.

1.1.1. The Social Organization of the Tribal Confederation

The fundamental form of social organization is tribal viz., the social relationships are organized according to a tiered system of kinship groups. An individual is a member of a family. Each family is a member of a larger family (extended family). In Joshua 7:14-18 the hierarchy of the three tiered system of בֵּית־אָב (father's house), מִשְׁפָּחָה (clan) and שֵׁבֶט (tribe) in Israelite community is clearly stated. In regard to the social organization of tribal Israel the smallest organizational unit is the בֵּית־אָב. However, according to Rober de Vaux and Gottwald, בֵּית־אָב includes the family head (father), his wife/wives and his sons, their wives and children and the servants.[47] Which explains that a group of several related families constituted מִשְׁפָּחָה the "clan." The clan is composed of a number of greater or lesser families which is inter-related by marriage. The מִשְׁפָּחָה is the most important form of social organization of a Tribe. Gottwald supposes that מִשְׁפָּחָה is not only refers to a group of related families but also to a more neutral characterization of a "protective association of extended families."[48] A group of clans formed a tribe. Tribe is the highest social unit in the tribal organization. A Tribe consists of many autonomous families who believe that they are descended from a common ancestor. The social organization of tribe was more looser than בֵּית־אָב and מִשְׁפָּחָה. The בֵּית־אָב and מִשְׁפָּחָה formed the real sphere of life for the individual, in which a person could expect solidarity, and solidarity could be required of the person.[49]

1.1.2. The Political Organization of the Tribal Confederation

The book of Judges presents that the tribal confederation as a body is without any organized government and lacking real political coherence. According to John Bright, "early Israel had none of the apparatus of state: neither central government,

45 Niels Peter Lemche, *Ancient Israel* (Sheffield: JSOT, 1988), 108.

46 Martin Noth assumes that Joshua 1-12 as a Benjaminite narrative and thereby asserts that the Benjaminite tradition was used as the basis for description of the combined Israelite conquest of the land west of the Jordan. Martin Noth, *The History of Israel* (London: SCM Press, 1987), 75-76.

47 Gottwald, *The Hebrew Bible,* 285-287; Robert de Vaux, *Ancient Israel: Its life and Institution* (London: Dorton Longman, 1961), 8.

48 Gottwald, *The Hebrew Bible,* 285-287.

49 Albertz, *A History of Israelite Religion in the Old Testament Period,* 73.

nor capital city, nor administrative machinery, nor bureaucracy."[50] It was a self-governing system. Political leadership among the tribes seems to have been clan or village oriented. In the tribal political economy, the family played a significant role and particularly the leader of the family had a significant role. Albertz opines that the political institution follows the tribal-regional divisions of society and he identifies two political bodies namely, "the elder/head of the family" and "the men of the city/tribe."[51] The elders carried out minor political business such as, settling conflicts among clans, administering the law and carried on negotiations.

1.2. Aspect of Leadership in Pre-monarchical Israel

This section will focus on the kind of leadership before the onset of the monarchy which includes role of judges, Amphictyonic theory, and chieftaincy.

1.2.1. Judges: Israel and its Leadership in the Judges Period

When Israel settled in Canaan there was no proper social organizational structure. The tribes of Israel were governed separately by charismatic leaders called judges who delivered the people from their enemies. Though they were called "judges" by the author (Judg 2:18) the noun is never used as a title for individuals. This suggests that the position was not an "office" but rather a function or responsibility to which individuals were appointed by Yahweh as need arose.[52] תּוֹרָה envisioned them functioning as one nation. However, Judges reveals a largely loose association of tribes, bound not so much by principle and outlook as by their occasional common enemies. There was no administrative connection to one another. Thus, when a tribe was threatened, it would be the responsibility of the judge of that respective tribe to address the threat utilizing the available members of the tribe. Judges speak of raising a judge when there was a problem. Regardless of the validity of the scholarly suggestion of Israel being organized on the analogy of the Greek "amphictyony," Israel's lack of organizational unity during this period is evident. There is no specific mention of Israel as a national unit in Judges. This is illustrated by the activities of the so-called major judges whose leadership was rather confined to a specific region or few tribal areas.[53]

Role of the Judge: What sort of leadership did the judges carry out during the period of Judges? Were they presented as political as well as religious leaders? What sort of political structure was envisaged? The term שָׁפַט "judge," or "govern,"

50 John Bright, *A History of Israel* (3rd ed.; Philadelphia: Westminster Press, 1972), 166.

51 Albertz, *A History of Israelite Religion in the Old Testament Period,* 72-73.

52 Alan J. Hauser, "Unity and Diversity in Early Israel Before Samuel," *Journal of the Evangelical Theological Society* 22 (1979): 289-303; Bright, *A History of Israel,* 167.

53 J. Maxwell Miller & John H. Hayes, *A History of Ancient Israel and Judah* (2nd ed.; Louisville, London: Westminster John Knox Press, 2006), 98-99.

suggests a prime activity of making legal decisions.[54] Judges 4 describes Deborah's involvement in judging. It is clear that the author means is that she was giving case decisions. Miller and Hayes note that she "involved in the settlement of disputes and the arbitration of justice."[55] Yet, according to the story which follows, she was also a military heroine. Therefore, the explanation of the verb שָׁפַט and the substantive שֹׁפֵט is to refer to the activity of the military heroes of the pre-monarchic period. The editor of the book of Judges believes that like Deborah, the rest of the judges, during this period were filled both a military and a judicial role. Thus, Judges were "judges" as well as warriors who were closely involved to military conflicts with the enemies. They led other warriors to the battlefield.

The description of the military leader as saviour ultimately points to Yahweh as the only saviour of Israel. Yahweh is the One who can raise a saviour for the people of Israel. Therefore, the primary roles of the judges are to save their people from their enemies, to rule the tribes as governors as their divinely sanctioned leaders, and to make decisions at critical situations namely, at battlefield, conflicts between the tribes, and so on.

The term "Charismatic leaders" is applied to the role of the judges as well since the judges had been directly raised by Yahweh to meet successive crises in Israel's affairs.[56] Although, charismatic leaders appeared in temporary alliances of tribes for defence against the enemies, they demonstrated the leadership role as fitting to the context. They were empowered by the "spirit of Yahweh." This form of leadership is regarded as having been acceptable to and understood by the Israelite community. The type of leadership is apparently viewed as a continuation of the functions exercised by Moses and Joshua during exodus.

In this sense the "judges" of the period of judges were figures of supreme authority. However, according to McKenzie, the judges were theologically idealized prototypes of the later kingship in the Deuteronomist formulation. He further assumes that the kingship of Israel resulted from the subsequent development of the Israelite belief of a charismatic leader: that the king is one upon whom the spirit rests permanently and the king in turn is the type of the Messiah.[57] The understanding here is that the "spirit of Yahweh" is the central thrust to show the continuity between the concept of a judge and a king in Israel. The Book of Judges shows that the judges exercised both civil and military power (Deborah

54 The root שפט can be linked with different Semitic languages, for example, in Mari texts appears: *sapatun* (verb), *sapitum* (participle), *septum* and *sapitutum* (abstract nouns). After detailed studies of each of the words scholars have concluded that the root word שפט denotes "some kind of administrative official within the tribal organization." Keith W. Whitelam, *The Just King: Monarchical Judicial Authority in Ancient Israel* (JSOTSupp 12, Sheffield: JSOT Press, 1979), 55.

55 Miller & Hayes, *A History of Ancient Israel and Judah,* 98; Donald A. Mekenzie, "The Judge of Israel," *VT* 17 (1967): 118-122.

56 Judg 3:10; 11; 29; 13:25; 14:6, 19; 15:14.

57 J. L. McKenzie, *The World of the Judge* (Englewood Cliffs, NJ: Prentice Hall, 1966), 16-17.

in Judg 4:4-24). The other role is proclamation at regular intervals of the law, specifically Israelite law.

1.2.2. Amphictyonic Theory

Martin Noth proposes the model of amphictyony for the organization of the tribes during judges' period.[58] Noth's theory, along with his reconstruction of the office of the judge of Israel (based on the lists in Judg 10:1-5; 12:7-15) as the main office of leadership for all Israel. It has come to dominate scholarly interpretation of Israel's early years in Palestine, with scholars assuming that Israel, while politically fragmented, was nevertheless religiously united during this era due to the role all twelve tribes played in the institution of the judge-led amphictyony. The amphictyony was founded at Shechem (Josh 24), that each tribe took a turn to lead the ceremony of the renewal of the covenant at Shechem.

This theory was widely accepted and many scholars had adopted Noth's basic position.[59] However, this has been subjected to strong critical criticism on the basis that nowhere in Judges is the tribal unity denoted as the confederacy of twelve tribes. The narratives of the major judges do not cover the whole country but only limited areas, mainly of Ephraim and Benjamin. The narratives always refer to a limited area or to a particular tribe where there is trouble from enemies. Bright remarks that Noth's hypothesis of amphictyony, however, is not redundant. The revised opinions contend that this religious confession was the dynamics of a uniting tribal confederacy.[60]

1.2.3. Chieftaincy

Some scholars argue that the historical period described by I Samuel 8-12 is part of the transitional period between tribal organization and a fully established monarchy in Israel. Flanagan in his essay "Chiefs in Israel," sees the reign of Saul and the early part of David's reign as the last stages of the chieftaincy in Israel. He feels that the chiefdom in Israelite's history stands between what he calls,

58 Noth, *The History of Israel,* 85-109. The term was adopted from the Greece and Italy for a loosely connected organization with a central cultic place and a common culture.

59 To mention few, Albright, Gerhard von Rad (he built his holy-war theory on the foundation of a presumed amphictyony). Mowinckel, Weiser and Muilenburg have presumed this organization, and Robert G. Boling has presumed its existence in his commentary, *Judges* (AB; Garden City, New York: Doubleday, 1975). Murray Newman has written an historical interpretation of Israel from Moses to David that revolves entirely around the idea of an amphictyony. *The People of the Covenant: A Study of Israel from Moses to the Monarchy* (Nashville: Abingdon, 1962). J. H. Hayes, "The Twelve-Tribe Israelite Amphictyony: An Appraisal," *Trinity University Studies in Religion* 10 (1975): 27-28. According to Noth, the minor judges served as the chief officials within the amphictyony; they were the revered depositories and interpreters of sacral law, whose word all Israel was bound to obey. Noth, *The History of Israel,* 103.

60 Bright, *History of Israel,* 163.

segmental society and coercive state. In order to make matters easier for the readers to understand, he adopts Renfrew's twenty points that qualify the characteristics of a chieftain society. And in doing so he makes a case of Saul and David that held very closely the characters of chiefdom. These include the Chief's authority that was rooted in skills of warfare, dancing, solidifying allegiances, and redistributing goods. These exhibit the chief's charisma and inspire confidence and a sense of solidarity in his followers.[61]

On the distinction between נָגִיד and מֶלֶךְ in the work of Alberch Alt, Flanagan expounds the two Hebrew words. נָגִיד, according to him, has a religious function while מֶלֶךְ "designated the office conferred by the peoples' acclaim" (political and religious functions embodied in a leader's reign).[62] Cross suggests that נָגִיד was a term used for the judges and מֶלֶךְ to David and Solomon. He concludes that מֶלֶךְ was a term properly ascribed only to David (although he was considered a נָגִיד initially) and the following kings of Israel. Flanagan's main contribution in his approach is his cross-cultural perspective of the understanding of the social-political factor in the origin of the kingship in Israel.

Frank S. Frick agrees with Flanagan's approach and uses the idea of a chieftaincy to sketch the society of Saul as a transitional stage from a segmentary society to a state. Frick sees the first two monarchs, Saul and David, as military leaders. He proposes three approaches for the understanding of the formation of the state: the conflict approach; the integrative approach, and the synthetic approach. The Conflict Theory describes how a group, sometimes against social background conflict between different populations, motivates the creation of government and administration in order to terminate social unrest and the threat. The integrative approach emphasizes the environmental influence on both geography and human. Here Frick acknowledges conflicts as factors but coordination and organization among the people are characterized as the main factors. The synthetic approach discloses multiple factors in state formation. These approaches stress different major social factors in the understanding of the social system. For instance, the view of the conflict approach is that internal or external conflict in a society forms a major social factor in the formation of a state. Frick argues that the state system is composed of various reaction systems that are preceded by pre-state polices. The significance of the inner dynamics of the Israelite society in relation to religion, according to him is "to a particular adaptive strategy or strategies on the part of the Israelites in their own distinctive

61 James W. Flanagan, "Chiefs in Israel," *JSOT* 20 (1981): 47-73. Unfortunately in Flanagan's discussion, he did not specify when the chieftaincy began among the Israelite. Hence, it is difficult to place the time of Saul and the early period of David's reign in order to recognize the role they played as the final chieftains among the people. Apparently, Flanagan implied that the Judges were chieftains.

62 Flanagan, "Chiefs in Israel," 67.

environmental situation/s."[63] His study provides a starting point to reconstruct a possible social structure of the Israelite monarchy.

1.3. Emergence of Monarchy in Ancient Israel

The growth of the monarchy in Israel marks a momentous event in the history of Palestine. The tribal confederacy encountered a gradual transition from a tribal organization to a monarchic organization. Biblical narratives picture the Philistine pressure as a major cause for the emergence of monarchy. Nevertheless, there are various socio-economic reasons which led to the transition. Furthermore, the transition to a monarchical system brought important changes in socio-economic life of the people of Israel. The two factors that contribute for the formation of monarchy in Israel are discussed in the following section.

1.3.1. External Factors

One of the specific factors for the formation of monarchy in ancient Israel is seen as the Philistines' military threats to Israel's existence. The Philistines were the sea people who migrated from Crete and Asia Minor. It is apparent that they came very close to subjugating Israel completely at the end of the period of the judges. They were a professional military class, well armed, and thoroughly trained, under a unified command. The Philistines were a much advanced force to reckon with. They had a much more organized system of governance and also had the vital advantage of metallurgy.[64]

This advantage proved vital because the Philistines overwhelmed and overran the Israelite's important religious and commercial towns and left them depleted. Gottwald remarks that "this highly unified military threat called forth a countervailing unified military defence on Israel's part."[65] Martin Noth argues that the external threats during the period of Judges were brief and geographically

---

63 Frank S. Frick, "Social Science Methods and Theories of Significance for the Study of the Israelite Monarchy: A Critical Review Essay," *Semeia* 37 (1986): 9-22.

64 They occupied and settled in the "Penta-polis" of the Canaanite reign and had an advanced material culture with a monopoly over iron. See, Noth, *The History of Israel,* 168; J. Maxwell Miller & John H. Hayes, *A History of Ancient Israel and Judah* (2nd ed.; Louisville, London: Westminster John Knox Press, 2006), 115; Roland de Vaux, Ancient *Israel: Its Life and Institutions* (trans. John McHugh; London: Darton, Longman & Todd, 1961), 94; idem, *The Early History of Israel: To the Period of the Judges* (trans. David Smith; London: Darton, Longman & Todd, 1971), 822; Bright, *A History of Israel,* 185; Charles F. Pfeiffer, *Old Testament History* (Grand Rapids, Michigan: Baker Book House, 1973), 244-246; Leon J. Wood, *Israel's United Monarchy* (Grand Rapids, Michigan: Baker Book House, 1979), 22; Anthony R. Ceresko, *The Old Testament: A Liberation Perspective* (Bangalore: St Paul Press Training School, 2009), 173-175; J. Barton Payne, *An Outline of Hebrew History* (Grand Rapids, Michigan: Baker Book House, 1954), 90; S. D. Anand Raj, "Crisis and Hope in the Emergence of Israelite Monarchy and its implication on the Present Indian Political Scenario," *BTF* 34 (2002): 19. Robert L. Chaney, "Systemic Study of the Israelite Monarchy," *Semeia* 37 (1986): 67.

65 Gottwald, *The Hebrew Bible: A Socio-Literary Introduction*, 319.

confined which could be handled locally.[66] However, the Philistine threat was different, since it challenged all of Israelite society over an extended period of time. Further, Israelites were surrounded by hostile forces around, namely, Ammon and Amalek, they took advantage of the situation and pressed the Israelites at the marginal areas of their settlement. This weakening state with the onslaught of the Philistines, with hostile neighbours threatened the very existence of the Israelites. Consequently, external pressure forced the Israelites to unite as a more singular state.

1.3.2. Internal Factors

Some scholars suggest that internal factors also contributed to the formation of monarchy in ancient Israel.[67] They observe that demographic intensification and agricultural surplus in the highlands added to the need of establishing a monarchy. Israel Finkelstein notes that the Iron Age I settlements in the central hill country between the early 12th and late 11th centuries from the eastern and central hill country to the western slopes as evidence of Israelite population expansion. He further evaluates that the growth of population in Israel prior to the monarchy compelled an expansion of the area of settlement into regions. This required a regional specialization of agricultural production (olive and wine in the west; grain and cattle in the east) which led to trade between the regions.[68] This apparently led to increasing social stratification and the rise of an advanced administration.

Similarly, Gottwald observes that because of various developments, namely, use of iron and plastered water cisterns enabled the expansion of agriculture in the hill country, rise in agricultural products, and population growth. With the

66 Noth, *History of Israel,* 165-168.

67 Chaney, "Systemic Study of the Israelite Monarchy," 61; Gottwald, *The Tribes of Yahweh,* 655-58; Keith W. Whitelam, "Retreating the History of Israel," *JSOT* 35 (1986): 61-62; Finkelstein, "The Emergence of Monarchy in Israel: The Environment and Socio-Economic aspects," 44-50.

68 Finkelstein, "The Emergence of Monarchy in Israel: The Environment and Socio-Economic aspects," 59. To support this hypothesis, Finkelstein demonstrates the archaeological data in Ephraim (since 1980). He demonstrates that in the earlier part of the Hebrew tribal confederation iron depots were discovered in huge junks in the North of Ephraim: the place where the Hebrews settled. However in the latter part, iron depots were discovered in the Western part (almost the double of what they found in the north). This perhaps triggered the Hebrew to the northern plains where they met hostile forces in a race to dominate the plains. Waldbaum supports this theory. He suggests that there was a possible growth of the use of Iron in the 11th century especially in the 10th century: A settlement process eventually. The settlement in these plains required agricultural intentions. Hence the nomadic nature completely dissolved into a permanent one. But this settlement required security because the Philistines in the west, Amalek in the south and Amnion to the east threatened the very existence of the Israelites. They required a central leadership (especially a military one) hence a centralized system, a monarchy was born. Waldbaum, Jane C. *From Bronze to Iron: Studies in Mediterranean Archaeology* 54 (Goteborg: P. Astrom, 1978).

growth in agricultural surpluses, there arose the need of advanced management and it gradually led to social changes, namely, organization beyond the family unit.[69]

Keith W. Whitelam and Frank S. Frick agree with Gottwald. Whitelam states that the internal pressure was due to the increase in population which led to competition for land and therefore, there was a need of a stabilized institution in order to meet their needs. Frank S. Frick pays special attention to agricultural risks, namely, droughts, climatic variability, crop failures and the like, which necessitated solutions beyond the family level probing a better organization.[70]

Another reason could be, since the various regions of the central hill country were not all equally fertile and productive and so the production varied whereby the accumulation of wealth also varied. In the process more wealthy Israelites subjected some of the less privileged people to service and in due course became local nobles and wealthy farmers who became the support city-state systems. These wealthy landholders wanted to control the centralized military leadership to achieve maximum economic and political influence. The disadvantaged agrarians hoped for a king who would intervene in restoration and protections.

Further, the pressure towards more centralized politics also derived from complaints, namely, growing economic and social inequality, breakdown of judicial system, civil strife and the like (I Sam 8:1-3; 22:1-2). Thus one reason could be a socio-political analytical picture emerges as a possibility for the emergence of monarchy in ancient Israel.

1.3.3. Appraisal of the Emergence of Monarchy in Ancient Israel

Scholars see the kingship as a result of the culmination of social, political and economic processes in Israel.[71] Generally, scholars agree that the kingship in Israel is not the result of any single factor, but a mixture of both external and internal factors. External factors: threat of the Philistines and the neighbouring kingdoms forced Israel to establish a strong administration in order to defend her nation. Also internal forces such as population pressure, agricultural development and inter-regional trade effected the forming of the monarchy in Israel. On the whole, they view the kingship as an advanced and indispensable political institution to guide the economy. They highlight inter-regional trade and contend that it

---

69 Gottwald, *The Tribes of Yahweh,* 655-56. The intensification of population owes to the agro-technological developments such as terracing, cistern hewing, use of iron tools etc., which proved very effective in cultivating highlands resulting agriculture surplus.

70 Keith W. Whitelam, "Recreating the History of Israel," *JSOT* 35 (1986): 61-62; Frick, *The Formation of the State in Ancient Israel: A Survey of Models and Theories,* 36.

71 Keith W. Whitelam, "king and Kingship," in *ABD* (vol. 4; ed. David Noel Freedman, at el; New York: Doubleday, 1992), 40-48; Gottwald, "The Participton of Free Agrarians in the Introduction of Monarchy to Ancient Israel," 77-106; Chaney, "Systemic Study of the Israelite Monarchy," 53-76; R. B. Coote and Frank S. Frick, *The Formation of the State in Ancient Israel: A Survey of Models and Theories* (Sheffield: Almond, 1985), 26-41.

eventually caused social stratification because not many people received direct benefits from trade. It was a specific labour group in Israel that benefited from trade. The distinction between the groups which accelerated trade was based on the need of people, and the ability to control labour so the majority of the people were unaffected by trade. Eventually inter-regional trade played a major role in the formation of a state.

The emergence of the state/monarchy in ancient Israel is thus internally as well as externally intelligible and plausible. Monarchy was formed because there was a large popular expression in favour of introducing a monarchy to rule over the previously decentralized Israelite tribal confederacy. The people of Israel were tired of its instability due to local tribal federation, which did not bring stability and security to its national existence. Therefore, establishment of the central power became the need of the hour. Certainly social, economic and political factors that compelled Israel to hope for the centralization of a state, which would result in the country's peace and security though it was a threat to theocracy. King and kingship in Israel is as a gift of Yahweh. Kingship reveals the highest leadership in Israel.

1.4. Royal Ideology in Ancient Israel in the Context of Ancient West Asia (AWA)

The divinity of kings in ancient Israel is open for discussion since its neighbouring nations considered king as their god. The popular belief is that kings in ancient Israel were elected or appointed by national God, but never is the king raised to the level of a god. He remained as a human, an Israelite among Israelites, but called by God to the office of ruling Israel on God's behalf. E. Jacob says, in AWA the king was a god, in Israel it was God who was king.[72] Roland de Vaux remarks that "if popular religion or the royal ideology had accepted such a divine character of the king, we should find traces of it in the prophets, who are anything but lenient towards unfaithful kings. They accused the kings of many crimes, but never of claiming divinity. Israel never had, never could have had, any idea of a king who was a god."[73] The royal ideology in ancient Israel differs from that of the AWA. The concept of the king as a sacred god and the son of the god are well attested in Egypt, Mesopotamia and Canaan.

1.4.1. Royal Ideology in Egypt

King in Egypt was regarded as divine and an incarnation of the gods. He was considered as god himself, manifested upon the earth in a human body in whom was incarnated one of the souls of the gods. He was believed to be the son of

72 E. Jacob, *Theology of the Old Testament* (New York: 1958), 238 (Lev 25:23). The fundamental thought is that Israel has the concept of Theocracy. De Vaux argues that "Israel is Yahweh's People and has no Other Master But Him." *Ancient Israel: Its Life and Institutions,* 99.

73 de Vaux, *Ancient Israel: Its Life and Institutions,* 113. Ezek 28:1-2,7,8-9; cf. Isa 14:13-14.

various gods. Egyptians thought that the king was formed by the gods in the queen's womb; he was attributed divinity, even before his birth.[74] Thus, he was raised to the level of gods. The king in Egypt has never been merely a representative or just an interpreter of the supreme god.

Ancient Egypt was also anchored on the divinity of kingship. Kingship in ancient Egypt saw the ruler or Pharaoh as an incarnation of what is believed as sacred. The Egyptians saw their king as god. He was viewed as the son of *Amon-Re*, the Sun god; who was the chief deity of the land. The king was also regarded as the intermediary of the gods. Thereby, all prayers, mediations and the divine blessings of the country were done through his person.[75] This great sun god, *Amon-Re*, of Egypt is praised as a creator god and as a king of the two lands (Upper and Lower Egypt). A prayer addressed to this great god reads:

> Hail to thee, Amon-Re, Lord of the Thrones of the Two Lands, presiding over Karnak over Upper Egypt: Unique in His nature like the fluid of the gods, the lord of truth and father of the gods. Who made mankind and created the beasts made herbage, and gave life to cattle.[76]

This great god *Re* was called "Lord of justice and order" who created the divine order of the world and the king was the executor of justice. King was considered the image of the gods and thus stood in the most intimate relationship with the divine; he played the role of mediator between heaven and earth. Heschel notes, in Egypt "the kings were regarded as gods, sacrifices were offered to them, and their worship was celebrated in special temples by special priests."[77] Egyptians, above all, saw the king as a being to be worshipped. They believed that the king was the exceptional being who had a privilege of knowing the gods. Thus, the king was the only person on earth who had access to the gods to acquire the divine knowledge. The king also functioned as a priest since he possessed priestly authority.

Egyptians further believed that the king was one who could bring well-being to the people by conquering chaos, especially the enemies, by combining social circumstances for order, by bringing unity in the society, and by conveying divine knowledge to govern society perfectly. The prime concept is that the king represented them as priest before the gods in the cults. Thus, the idea of the

74 Ivan Engnell, *Studies in Divine Kingship in the Ancient Near East* (Oxford: Basil Blackwell, 1967), 4.

75 William C. Hayes, "Daily Life in Ancient Egypt," in *Everyday Life in Ancient Times: Highlights of the Beginnings of Western Civilization in Mesopotamia, Egypt, Greece, and Rome* (Washington: National Geographic Society, 1961), 79; Abraham J. Heschel, *The Prophets* (New York: The Jewish Publication Society of America, 1962), 474; Engnell, *Studies in Divine Kingship in the Ancient Near East*, 4.

76 John A. Wilson, "Egyptian Hymns and Prayers," in *ANET* (3rd ed.; Princeton: Princeton University Press, 1969), 365.

77 Heschel, *The Prophets*, 474.

exaltation of the king revealed that the king is either a god among gods or the priest of priests.

1.4.2. Royal Ideology in Mesopotamia

Kingship in Mesopotamia was considered as an important institution in sustaining the affairs of the people. The relationship between god and people was more direct; they did not need any mediator. The king was not god. Though his position in the community entitled him to certain special privileges and favours like any other people, he had humbly sought the divine instructions for his life. The royal ideology transmitted a divinely sanctioned kingship. Mesopotamia accepted the fact that kingship came down from the gods, considered to be a gift and the king was regarded as a man-made divine.[78] However, the king was considered as submissive to the deity. Walther Zimmerli contends that in ancient Mesopotamia, "the king was viewed as a moral being, but the kingship was of heavenly origin, the king a figure of divine election."[79] Furthermore, Frankfort notes:

> Mesopotamia asserted that kingship, not the office holder was of superhuman origin. The Mesopotamia viewed their king as a mortal endowed with a divine burden. Royalty was not of human origin but added to society by the gods, the king was a mortal made to carry a superhuman charge which the gods could remove at any time to bestow upon another.[80]

The royal ideology in Mesopotamia saw the king as the chosen representative of the gods on earth. He was given responsibility to be the ruler of the city and was reported to have stood in a special relation to the gods. The ruler had the authority in his city, with its patron god, temple, and its economic properties such as land, flocks, herds, and buildings and the basic responsibility of the city ruler was to take care of gods' properties.

The king in Mesopotamia had three fundamental roles as the agent of the gods: He was the political leader, as high priest he was the cultic leader, and as warrior he was the military leader.[81] Similar to Israel, the Mesopotamian king ruled in the court of law and acted as the army commander and chief. In Babylon, the king had certain functions to fulfil during New Year's festival. Zimmerli notes that the chief role king played on New Year's festival was in the sacred marriage of the gods, which guaranteed the fertility, of the New Year, and in the great procession

78 G. Lieck, *The Babylonians: An Introduction* (London: Routledge, 2003), 80; M. Van de Mieroop, *The Ancient Mesopotamian City* (Oxford: Clarendon, 1997), 119-120; John Gray, "Canaanite Kingship in Theory and Practice," *VT* 2 (1952): 193.

79 Zimmerli, *Old Testament Theology in Outline*, 86-87.

80 H. Frankfort, *Kingship and the Gods* (Chicago: University Press, 1948), 295.

81 Marc Van de Mieroop, *The ancient Mesopotamian City* (Oxford: Clarendon, 1997), 119-120; W. G. Lambert, "Kingship in Ancient Mesopotamia," in *Kings and Messiah in Israel and the Ancient Near East: Proceedings of the Oxford Old Testament Seminar* (JSOT Supp. 270; ed. J. Day; Sheffield: Sheffield Academic Press, 1998), 55.

to the site of the celebration called the *bit akitu.* Here the king had more to do than merely give the sign for the great procession of the gods to begin.[82]

In Mesopotamia the king was also called "shepherd." The term "shepherd" demonstrates the basic role of the king. It is a symbolic description to denote the fundamental role of the king to bring wealth, based on agriculture, and protection from the enemies. The Mesopotamians believed that wealth and protection come from the gods through the divine sanction of the kingship of Mesopotamia; its royal ideology played a major role to legitimize the kingship as representative of the divine order in economic and political matters. Their belief is that only divinely sanctioned kingship could bring wealth and protection to the kingdom and its people. We find a good example of a failure king in the legend of Naram-Sin, son of Sargon.[83] Initially Naram-Sin was a successful warrior king but at the end he turned out to be the unfortunate king. Thus, it is believed unless the king is authorized by god he cannot function as king well.

1.4.3. Royal Ideology in Canaan

An important idea of the royal ideology in Canaan is found in Ugarit which shows a close relationship between kingship and priesthood. Canaanite kings generally possessed priestly authority and acted as priests. The Canaanite king has a special place in relation to god, since he is portrayed as son of *El.*[84] There is a special relationship between the ancestor of the ruling king and the patron god *El* (father-son relationship). The expression of father-son relationship is found in the *keret saga* (Krt A) as follows:

> The house of [a k]ing is *destroyed*, who had seven [bre]thren, Eight mother's sons. Keret in offspring is ruined, Keret is *undermined* of establishment. His lawful wife he did find. His legitimate spouse. He married the woman, and she "departed." *Flesh of kinship* had he: One-third died *in health,* One-fourth of sickness; One-fifth pestilence gathered unto itself, One-sixth *calamity;* ne-seventh thereof fell by the sword...(So) he enters his cubicle (and) weeps, *An inner chamber* and cries. His tears do drop like shekels to the ground. His bed is soaked by his weeping, and he falls asleep as he cries..... And in his dream El descends, In his vision the Father of Man. And he approaches asking Keret: "what ails Keret that he weeps, The beloved, Lad of El, that he cries? It is a kingdom like Bull his father's he desires, Or authority like the Father of Man's?"[85]

While Keret is in deep depression and agony of losing all of his belongings including his family, *El* appears to him as a comforter to promise wealth and

82 Zimmerli, *Old Testament Theology in Outline,* 87.

83 Van de Mieroop, *The Ancient Mesopotamian City,* 119; Oppenheim, "Babylonian and Assyrian Historical Texts," in *ANET,* 266, 268.

84 *El* is the chief god of the pantheon, who was addressed as king and creator of the humankind.

85 H. L. Ginsberg, "Ugaritic Myths, Epics, and Legends," in *ANET,* 143.

prosperity in his life again and demands a sacrifice from him. The story suggests that *El* communicated directly with *Keret* but wanted a sacrifice from him, a task that belongs to a priest.[86] In the text, the relationship between kingship and priesthood is highlighted.

In Ugarit, the concept of the king as the son of god and god himself is part of the royal ideology. The story of *Keret* further characterizes certain aspects of the kingship of Canaan. First, the relationship between the king and the god is seen in terms of a priestly king. Secondly, the king is seen as a son of god as well as god himself. Lastly, the story of *Keret* demonstrates the character of a king as successful if he achieves something for the well-being of the society and brings righteousness for the people. Although the king is considered as the son of *El*, it does not isolate him from the community; he remains a man, a Canaanite among Canaanites. Hence, the king was singled out from among the people and shouldered him with special responsibility, to be the protector of his country people. Canaanite king also maintains a close association or relationship with the community. The closeness of the king and the people is evidenced by the blessing of the gods as they say, "Be greatly exalted, [Keret], In the midst of the *community* of the land, In the number of *the population of the realm*."[87] This kind of expression emphasizes that the king is responsible to maintain peace and freedom in the land.

1.4.4. Summary

The royal ideology of the AWA is an essential part of the organization and the social system, since a kingdom is destined to have a king. The primary focus of the royal ideology is to exclaim the kingship as the centre of the whole society. The kingship would provide the apex point to combine all the social organizations. Thus, the royal ideology provides a religious, social, political foundation for the kingship to justify and to legitimatise the king's rule over his potential political enemies, as well as against social threats.[88] In the AWA, religion served as fundamental for formation of the royal ideology. The fact is no kingship had been sustained without the support of the religion. However, the relationship between religion and kingship is liable to be flexible, since each institution has its own divergent norms and even dissimilar from one culture to another. In the AWA, title of the kings demonstrates the specific case of the religious aspects in the royal ideology.

86 The *keret saga* of Canaanite text emerges that kingship is hereditary, it pass on father to son. See, Gray, "Canaanite Kingship in Theory and Practice," 196.

87 Ginsberg, "Ugaritic Myths, Epics, and Legends," in *ANET*, 146.

88 S. Pollock, *Ancient Mesopotamia: The Eden that Never was* (Cambridge: Cambridge University Press, 1999), 173; Keith W. Whitelam, "Israelite kingship: The Royal Ideology in its Opponents," in *The World of Ancient Israel: Sociological, Anthropological and Political Perspective* (ed. Clement; Cambridge: Cambridge university Press, 1989), 121.

1.4.5. Royal Ideology in Ancient Israel

In AWA kings were considered as representative of the gods to fulfil the divine order. Scholars argue that in ancient Israel, although an anointed king stood in a special relationship to Yahweh and was an exalted figure among people, the king is neither the son nor an incarnation nor a representative of God. He is the ruler appointed by God who must reign according to the will and the *mishpat* of God.[89] Though Israel has a specific understanding about the kingship, some scholars claim that in one way or the other some of the ideas about kingship of AWA sheds light on the understanding of kingship in Israel. For example, in Mesopotamia, the king is the representative of the god on earth to fulfil the divine order or command. In Egypt, the king is called the son of god. In Israel, the king is the adopted son of God and not his naturally born son (Ps 2).[90] Israel uses the term metaphorically denoting the divine choice of the king. In AWA contexts the kings were responsible to provide wealth to the people and also to give protection just as the shepherd did to his sheep. The same analogy is applied to the Israelite kings. Psalm 72 clearly mentions that the king is responsible to bring righteousness and peace.

In his book, *Ancient Near Eastern Thought and the Old Testament,* John H. Walton compares and contrasts the ancient Israelite concept of kingship with those of the surrounding nations and culture in the AWA. While noting similar ideas about the king's divine sonship and responsibilities, Walton nevertheless emphasizes some key differences between how kingship was viewed in Israel and how it was viewed elsewhere in the AWA. For instance, in AWA, there often was the concept that kingship was the creation of the gods given as a boon to humans.[91] This is quite obviously different than what is mentioned in OT, where Yahweh allows Israel to have a king (I Sam 8). Walton also points out that there is a clearly negative view of kingship presented in Deuteronomy 18. He further notes that archetypal humanity bears the image of God rather than this being distinctive of the king. The OT shows the Davidic king who was clearly human and clearly capable of a multitude of sins, he was nevertheless the representative of Yahweh to Yahweh's people.[92] Unlike the other kings of the AWA, who were often seen as divine in and of themselves, the Davidic king was clearly only human. Nevertheless, since he was to be Yahweh's representative to his people; he was to

89 However, some kings had failed to rule with justice. The kings had forgotten that ultimately the people were not theirs; the kingdom was not theirs; but the people and kingdom belonged to God and so they should lead as God wanted. They had forgotten that and paid the price. Heschel, *The Prophets*, 477.

90 Ps 2:7 "you are my son, today I have begotten you."

91 John H. Walton, *Ancient Near Eastern Thoughts and the Old Testament: Introducing the Conceptual World of the Hebrew Bible* (Grand Rapids: Baker, 2006), 280-284.

92 In Ps 2:7 the Davidic king is called Yahweh's son; and in II Sam 7:13-14 Yahweh tells David that his son, the Davidic king, will be a son to Yahweh.

reflect the image of God to his people through a faithful reign characterized by righteousness and justice.

Conclusion

Every transition had its own set of underlying tensions throughout the period of leadership that culminated in the displacement of the leader. Prior to the institution of kingship the tribes of Israel were governed separately by charismatic leaders called judges who delivered the people from their enemies but were united under a common theocracy in their obedience to God. These unique tribes had loose political ties through their beliefs, but no administrative connection to one another. Thus, when a tribe was threatened, it would be the responsibility of the judge of that respective tribe to address the threat utilizing the available members of the tribe. This system of the judges had worked in the past when Israel was threatened, but with the continual dominance of the Philistines, the Israelite populace realized that a more permanent mode of government was necessary. Moreover, it is also illustrated that the population grew in size and the land was not enough to accommodate all the people with their increasing agricultural surpluses. It is because of all these reasons that the people demanded for a king. Israelites then requested Samuel, the judge, the priest, and the prophet to anoint a king for them. Thus, kingship in ancient Israel evolved out of Samuel's mentorship of the tribes of Israel into Saul's transitionary kingship in which he played the role of a uniting leader but lacked the strong political and religious ties necessary to create an empire. The emergence of monarchy in Israel brought several changes to the tribal society and its leadership to which the researcher would probe into the next chapter.

Chapter 2

Leaders in Israel and Ancient West Asia
An Overview

Introduction

The quest for order in any society leads to leadership structures that are variously determined by different societies. Both AWA and the ancient Israel possessed hierarchies at all levels of society from the family to professional levels and the society as a whole. Embedded in the concept of leadership among the people is the significance attached to an interconnection of individual and communal welfare. Consequently, the well-being of the individual is inseparable from that of the community. This explains why utmost care is taken in the selection of leaders in ancient Israelite community, for responsibility must be ensured. The ethics of responsibility rather than that of individual rights are thus encouraged.

The justification for regarding rights as secondary to responsibility is to be linked to the requirements and implications of social life, which elevates communal well-being above individual comfort. The conviction being that the welfare of the individual is best guaranteed within that of the community. Several leadership positions could be identified in monarchical Israel. All of them perform various functions and satisfy different needs and aspirations of the people in the community.

The kings, the priests, and the prophets of Israel may have some similarities or parallels personalities with other Semitic religions and religious functionaries. Therefore, it is important to compare them with other types of people of ancient history who made similar claims. Thus, the purpose of this chapter is to explore the leadership concepts in both AWA and Israelite contexts, namely, royal leadership, priestly leadership, and prophetic leadership: different functions exercised by the leaders.

2.1. Royal Leadership

The kings and the royal officers hold a very important position in ancient Israelite society. They were the key leaders of the nation. Thus, the leadership authority (different responsibilities hold by the king and royal officers) that they exercised is important to study.

According to the biblical tradition, the monarchs who ruled during the period of United Monarchy in ancient Israel are: Saul, David, and Solomon. The period of United Monarchy is seen as a progressive transition from the tribal systems. Frick identifies three progressive states in the United Monarchy: the period of Saul and early days of David as an inchoate state; latter days of David as a typical state and the days of Solomon as a full blown state. In other words the kingship of Saul can be regarded as chiefdom; the kingship of David as a transition from a chiefdom to state and from the kingship of Solomon seen as a fully developed state.[93]

The kingship in ancient Israel (for example: David and Solomon) portrays the transition of the Israelite tribes to a monarchical administration. This transition had enormous significance upon the political and socio-economic life of the people of ancient Israel. The traditional tribal administration was replaced with the newly emerged bureaucracy of the state.[94] The new administrative government brought changes to the whole social structure of the state and had decisive effect on the tribal structure. It brought a destruction of the old solidarity of ancient Israel. Walter Bruggemann observes that monarchy brought a change from traditional to bureaucratic leadership, from tribal ordering to governmental districts.[95] This is very clearly expressed in I Samuel 8:1-22.

George E. Mendenhall describes this as the "paganization of Israel."[96] Robert Gnuse remarks that kingship brought a return to bronze-age paganism where the old oriental despotism revisited.[97] Bernard Lang notes that from the era of David and Solomon onwards there was a progressive canaanization of the economic

93 Frick, *The Formation of the State in Ancient Israel*, 69. Cf. Finkelstein, "The Emergence of Monarchy in Israel: The Environment and Socio-Economic Aspects," 47-48.

94 For example: The administration that David set up had a clear development of a class-based system consisting of recorders, scribes, priests, military commanders, and various other political appointments, who controlled the central government.

95 Walter Bruggemann, *A Social Reading of the Old Testament* (Minneapolis: Fortress Press, 1994), 23.

96 George E. Mendenhall, *The Tenth Generation: The Origins of the Biblical Tradition* (London: The John Hopkins University Press, 1973), 195-196.

97 Robert Gnuse, *You Shall not Steal: Community and Property in the Biblical Tradition* (New York: Orbis Books, 1985), 67-68.

system.[98] With the establishment of the Monarchy, a bureaucracy was created displacing the authority of the local tribal leaders. The Tribal Confederacy looked at the societies from "bottom up" whereas the Monarchy looked at the society from a top to down perspective. Solomon created social and political structures aimed at consolidating and securing a large complex nation under the firm, centralized control of the royal house. The enormous bureaucracy was the means through which "command economy" was administrated: the centralized political control of the production and distribution of goods.[99]

Under monarchy Israel became a state with taxing and conscripting power with a monopoly of force over and above its people. David established a strong standing army and also an empowered bureaucracy was set up to carry out these conscriptions. Most scholars view the census under David as mainly meant for extracting taxes, for conscription and to impose forced labour upon the people.[100] King David created the district administrative system in order to extract taxes and labour from the districts. During the reign of King Solomon, the state imposed forced labour and increased the taxes which increased more difficulty for the peasants. Consequently many were losing their inheritance through debt traps. Solomon divided Israel into twelve provinces, each of which had to supply provisions to the court for a month (I Kgs 4:7-19; 5:7). In this way the subjects of the state who were largely peasants and common people were given the burden to sustain the royal family and the kingdom apparatus.[101] Furthermore the rise of the new class of aristocracy widened the gap between the rich and the poor. Thus, we find the characteristics of monarchy in a centralized government and administration; comprise oppressive rule, power politics, compulsory military service, labour corps and a heavy burden of taxation.

It is also apparent that in various forms throughout the Israelite and Judean history, most of the monarchs have been corrupted in many ways, taking due advantage of their power and position. They were disobedient to the Word

---

98 Bernard Lang, "The Social Organization of Peasant Poverty in Biblical Israel," *JSOT* 24 (1982): 48.

99 George E. Mendenhall, "Ancient Israel's Hyphenated History," in *Palestine in Transition* (ed. D. N. Freedman and D. F. Graff; Sheffield: Almond Press, 1983), 94.

100 To mention few Gottwald, Ahlstrom, et al,.

101 The finality in Solomon's kingship occurred religiously and politically, but it took place at the cost of the people. The Israelites who desired so much to be united under a monarchy were finally given a true monarch and suffered under him. It is observed that what the Israelites had to pay in labour and wealth for Solomon's prosperity was regarded as plain oppression. While the nation of Israel had achieved the peak of political, economic, and military power they were not able to escape the tensions that came along with such things. Solomon was the culmination of the evolutionary process of the monarchy, a king just like the surrounding nations/cultures (the demand of the Israelite). As the kingship evolved within Israel, the consequences of their request for a king followed. As a people that went from tribes to an empire under evolving leaders, their final position placed them in oppression.

of Yahweh and disloyal to the Covenant. One of the main reasons is political instability that had brought the states into crisis. Perhaps a great deal of instability sprang from the fact that the monarchs were looking for their own interest, power, and fame with no respect of the Covenant and Torah. Political instability is like a chronic disease, which plunges the states into uncertainty and unstable future. In the history of the northern kingdom most of the kings enthroned themselves through bloody coups.[102] Political unrest is a result of self-centredness of the political leaders who desire to be in power at any cost.

Political instability in both Israel and Judah caused a downfall of the kingdoms. As a nation, Northern Israel was taken into captive and the kingdom was torn into pieces and later the same fate fell upon Judah. Throughout the monarchic leadership the society lost its moral and ethical values. The royal leadership illustrates that at all levels; corruption, greed, oppression and exploitation crept into the just society. The social sins, however, dispense justice, which had left bitterness behind and affected their relationship with Yahweh. Religiously, the sacred cord of right relationship with Yahweh was broken. The people failed to live up to the ethical standards and violated the covenantal codes.

In summary, the emergence of new leadership, administration, and organization brought significant changes in the Israelite society. The old tribal social organization being replaced with a new administration had economic implications. The state was re-organized into economic units to raise tribute for the sustenance of the kingdom. Since the dominant part of Israel's production was agricultural goods, the conscription of tribute was mainly agricultural goods which obviously had put the peasants in debt.

2.1.1. Functions/roles of the King

The general understanding is that kings in ancient Israel were appointed by Yahweh as representatives to carry out certain responsibilities for the country. They were the executive branch who was supposed to carry out the foreign policy as urged by the prophets and condition the life of the people upon the laws and ethics of the Torah. In the following section some of the important functions of

---

102 Omri (876-869 BCE) the army general ascended the throne in a violent manner and established his dynasty in North Israel. Later Jehu (842-814 BCE) assassinated the entire royal family of Jehoram (a descendant of Omri) in a bloody manner, and founded a new dynasty of five kings who successively occupied the throne for almost a century, nearly half of the time of North Israel's existence. With the death of Jeroboam II (one of Jehu's descendant), there was a sharp decline in the political power of Israel which was sapped from within by a rapid succession of palace revolutions and royal assassinations. The dynasty of Jehu and Jeroboam II came to an end when Zechariah son of Jeroboam II was assassinated by Shallum after a reign of six months. Albertz, *A History of Israelite Religion in the Old Testament Period*, 162; Schultz, *The Old Testament Speaks,* 198; Bruce K. Waltke, *An Old Testament Theology: An Exegetical, Canonical, and Thematic Approach* (Grand Rapids/Michigan: Zondervan, 2007), 695, 715-716, 731.

the king as a chief leader in military field, as an administrator of the nation, and as an important figure in religious sphere will be discussed. In all his functions the king was expected to act according to the will of God.

2.1.1.1. King as Military Leader

The people of Israel wanted the king to "go out before" them (I Sam 8:20), that is, to take the battles away from their cities or homes. They also wanted the king to "fight our battles" (I Sam 8:20) that is, to relieve them of the burden of answering a call to arms when Israel was threatened. Thus the king had the role of commander-in-chief of a professional standing army. For example, one of Saul's first noted acts of kingship is his military defeat of the Ammonites. Saul came through with a military victory to save Israel in its time of trouble. As Samuel J. Schultz notes that Saul was a warrior who led his nation in numerous military victories.[103] With the unification of Israel once again at Mizpah and the defeat of the foreign threat in times of trouble, Saul cemented his title as king. Soon after that, at the strategic location on a hill three miles north of Jerusalem, Saul fortified Gibeah to counteract the Philistine military superiority. The leadership role that Saul took had evolved from one of the tribal unification under God, the unification in times of need with Samuel, to the stage of total unification of the tribes under a monarch with Saul as their head. Similarly, when David came to power; he established himself as a strong military leader, by capturing Jerusalem and made it his royal capital.[104]

The king as the leader of the armies was a prominent motif in the literature and practice in the cultures of Ugarit, Philistia, Aram, Ammon, Moab, and Edom. The AWA institution of kingship as a permanent, administrative office occupied for life and with dynastic succession, lent stability to the nation, which would have thereby enabled it to meet military threats better. In AWA context, as warriors, the kings were to lead their nations in battle and protect the society from outside threats. The Mesopotamians believed that the king was a brave warrior, who led his army into war, who can conquer their enemies and subdue both the land and the people.[105] The king stressed his divine origin in royal inscriptions of his glorious victories over enemies. Keith C. Seele remarks that in Egypt, the king's military duties were of primary importance, thus the king even participated in recruiting and arming of troops and as a commander-in-chief led his troops into battle.[106] The kings worked for the expansion of the kingdom and concentration of the military power under men who were primarily warlords.

103 Samuel J. Schultz, *The Old Testament Speaks* (5th ed.; San Francisco: Harper Collins Publishers, 2000), 123.

104 Miller and Hayes, *A History of Ancient Israel and Judah,* 151.

105 Mieroop, *The Ancient Mesopotamian City,* 120.

106 Keith C. Seele, *When Egypt Ruled the East* (Chicago: The University of Chicago Press, 1957), 86.

The king also served for the unity of his people, encouraged the citizens to stand for the well-being of the community. The kings as warriors or military leaders not only led his countrymen into war with other nations but were also expected to conduct treaty arrangements with neighbouring cities and foreign countries for smooth running of the kingdom in order to protect their country people from foreign invasion. Thus, one sees the kings in both ancient Israel and AWA as conquerors, subduers of foreign lands, the bringers of peace and prosperity, through military campaigns.

2.1.1.2. King as Administrator

Soon after affirmation of his kingship, David focused on the political affairs and administration. He expanded the territory of Israel from the Sinai Desert and the Gulf of Eilat in the South and South-West to the Euphrates River in the north-east, and from the Mediterranean Sea in the west to the Syrian Desert in the east.[107] When Solomon succeeded David he fulfilled the role of king throughout the area by unifying the people under a strict administration. And the rest of the monarchs followed the same kind of administration. As administrators, the kings in ancient Israel had duties or responsibilities to be fulfilled:

(i) Kings passed judgement since the chosen king was expected to established justice in the land. The prime duty was to pass right judgement to all the citizens, particularly to the weaker sections, namely widows, orphans, and strangers. מִשְׁפָּט (justice) should be administered in public, at the gate of the town (Deut 21:19; Amos 5:10), in a holy place or a sanctuary (Exod 21:6; 22:7), the kings also gave judgements in the porch of judgement (I Kgs 7:7).[108] In Solomon's prayer at Gibeon this potential responsibility of kingship is supposed to have weighed heavily upon him for thus he prayed: "And give to your servant a hearing heart for judging לִשְׁפֹּט your people and to distinguish between good and evil;" (I Kgs 3:9) and he was commended by Yahweh for asking "to understand to hear מִשְׁפָּט" i.e. to hearken to matters of equity. One of his early cases was the two harlots' claim to the one living child. For his decision in this case he became famous: the Bible declares "And all Israel heard of the מִשְׁפָּט which the king had given שָׁפַט and they were in awe of the king, for they saw that wisdom of God was in him to do מִשְׁפָּט."[109] The Queen of Sheba praised him for his righteousness in doing מִשְׁפָּט (I Kgs 10:9).

In Isaiah's day when Uzziah became ill, his son Jotham was given the responsibility of "שָׁפַט 'judging' the people of the land" in addition to his duties as chamberlain (II Kgs 15:5). Thus in ancient Israel, it was the duty of the king to give relief to those who could not otherwise secure justice. מִשְׁפָּט was not just a function; it was a responsibility. Thus, the function of the God-fearing king was to

107 Bright, *A History of Israel*, 191-199.

108 De Vaux, *Ancient Israel: Its Life and Institutions*, 155.

109 I Kgs 3:28; II Sam 8:15; I Kgs 7:7 for Solomon's throne and hall of מִשְׁפָּט.

lead Israel in keeping covenant and to trust God for deliverance. As Gerald Eddie Gerbrandt states, the king was to lead Israel by being the covenant administrator; then he could trust Yahweh to deliver. At the heart of this covenant was Israel's obligation to be totally loyal to Yahweh.[110]

This kind of responsibility was also carried out by the AWA kings. In AWA, the king administered the god's territory and his people. As administrator and chief judge the king was to guarantee justice within the nation. The kings' primary role, as representatives of the people to the gods, was to establish justice in the community.[111] According to the law code (Hammurabi) the king is expected to create peaceful atmosphere in the land. The law expresses, the laws of justice, which Hammurabi, the efficient king, set up, and by which he caused the land to take the right way and have good government. He is expected to be the protector of the citizens from unjust social orders and to bring welfare to the people. As administrator of justice, the king should provide and ensure social justice to the weaker strata of society from being unfairly deprived of their due: the legal status, property rights, and economic condition. The idea was expressed by such phrases as "that the strong might not oppress the weak."[112] Weak ones here refer to orphans and widows, that justice to be done to them. A widow or an orphan need not necessarily be poor, but on the death of the head of a household there might be no one to defend their rights, especially their inheritance rights. The king, therefore, being the head of the household for the population as a whole intervened for the cause of the helpless ones. Thus, the king Hammurabi is remembered by the oppressed for whom he had done justice as the master who is like the father of a child to his people.[113] The law code of Hammurabi further mentioned:

> Lofty Anum, king of the Anunnaki (and) Enlil, lord of heaven and earth...named me to promote the welfare of the people... to cause justice to prevail in the land, to destroy the wicked and the evil that the strong might not oppress the weak, to rise like the sun over the black-headed (people), and to light up the land.[114]

This shows that the kings were expected to establish justice in the courts for the weaker section of the society. Clearer instruction to the king is seen in the admonition of Yassib, the son of Keret when Keret was unable to administer justice in the nation because of his severe illness. He says,

110 Gerald Eddie Gerbrandt, *Kingship According to the Deuteronomistic History* (Atlanta: Scholar Press, 1986), 102.

111 S. Mowinckel, *He That Cometh* (trans. G. W. Anderson; Oxford: Basil Blackwell, 1959), 47; Theophile J. Meek, "The Code of Hammurabi," in *ANET*, 164.

112. Meek, "The Code of Hammurabi," 164, 177.

113 Meek, "The Code of Hammurabi," 164.

114 Meek, "The Code Hammurabi," 164.

> Go unto thy father, Yassib;... Repeat unto Ke[ret the Noble]: List and incline [thine ear]. Thou hast let thy hand fall into mischief. Thou judgest not the cause of the widow, Nor adjudicat'st the case of the wretched. Having become a brother of the sickbed, A companion of the bed of suffering, Descend from the kingship-I'll reign; From thine authority-I'll sit enthroned. Yassib the Lad departs, Enters his father's presence, and lift up his voice and cries: Hearken, I pray thee, Keret the Noble! List and incline thine ear.[115]

This kind of reproach revealed that the kings were chosen to be the representative of the gods on the earth and thereby to administer for the well-being of the citizens. In fact, the king himself believed that his judicial functions for the well-being of the nation had been successfully completed when he declared "I established law and justice in the language of the land, thereby promoting the welfare of the people."[116] In the inscription of the new building dedication in tenth century BCE, Yehimilk, king of Byblos, is described as "a righteous king and an upright king before the Holy Hods of Byblos!"[117]

In Mesopotamian society, the king has always been regarded as the one who holds or controls political powers, including palace organization and made all decisions on his own. In order to bring peaceful atmosphere in the land and provide healthy living standard, the king "guaranteed the fertility of the land by digging and maintaining irrigation canals, provided justice."[118] In Egypt various legal documents and hymns tell that the king is the judge. For instance, the documents recorded during the reign of Thutmose III (ca. 1490-1436 BCE), tells of the appointment of the Rekh-mi-Re, the Vizier of Upper Egypt as "prophet of maat." Rekh-mi-Re declares that "I raised justice to the height of heaven."[119] The king in Egypt also has the authority to appoint or choose a vizier who works under him. The vizier administered according to the code of regulations. The office of the vizier was the administrative centre of the entire land. Seele explains that the vizier "sat at judgment in a special hall in which no other official was permitted to give a hearing or cause punishment to be administered. All administrative business had to pass through his hands. He gave judgement in boundary controversies, wrote reports to the king, and controlled the lists of recruits who were to 'accompany his majesty to the north and the south.'"[120] Furthermore, the kings were given the power to control their own nation and palace economy by controlling the main

115 Ginsberg, "Ugaritic Myths, Epics, and Legends," in *ANET*, 149.

116 Meek, "The Code of Hammurabi," 165.

117 Franz Rosenthal, "Canaanite and Aramaic Inscriptions," in *ANET*, 653.

118 De Mieroop, *The Ancient Mesopotamian City*, 118-120.

119 The goddess Maat was "Truth" or "Justice." In his capacity as the highest magistrate, Rekh-mi-Re was the priest of Maat). John A. Wilson, "Egyptian Documents," in *ANET*, 213.

120 Seele, *When Egypt Ruled the East*, 86.

sources and incomes of the neighbouring countries.[121] Thus, as an administrator the king is expected to do justice in all his responsibilities for the benefit of his county.

(ii) Israelite's kings were expected to maintain שָׁלוֹם "peace" in the land: to provide peace or "wholeness" with foreign nations as well as within the nation (social and mental peace-genuine peace and prosperity). This is one of significant proclamations of the prophets. According to Paul D. Hanson the term שָׁלוֹם describes the realm where chaos is not allowed to enter, and where life can be fostered free from the fear of all which diminishes and destroys. It is the duty or responsibility of the king to establish שָׁלוֹם in society. He further explains that שָׁלוֹם was God's doing, not something achieved by human resources.[122] Thus, in order to create שָׁלוֹם in society, the king is expected to be obedient to Yahweh and committed to the service of Yahweh and the nation. Perry B. Yoder argues that "God was depicted as sovereign ruler by virtue of justice, so was Israel's king obligated to rule justly.... Israel's prayer was that the king might be given God's righteous justice in order that he might implement a just social order where the strong would not oppress the weak. The result of such social justice will be shalom."[123] However, the prophets often declared that the kings failed to do one of their primary responsibilities, i.e., to provide peace and security among the people rather than foreign alignments or resistance to foreign rule. For instance, prophet Isaiah sought so diligently to instruct Judean kings in the way of trust in Yahweh which alone could ensure peace.[124]

(iii) The king had a specific responsibility towards the poor. More elaborated duty is mentioned in wisdom literature, particularly in Proverbs 31:1-9 where a king's mother urged her son to consider the wisdom of ensuring that his personal and public lives are cohesive, non-contradictory and reflective of personal discipline.[125] Here King Lemuel is called upon, specifically as king or leader of his community, to stand up for the poor (literally, "for the dumb," for those who

---

121 For instance, during the reigns of Shalmaneser III (860-823 BCE) and Adad-nirari III (810-783 BCE) the Assyrians controlled trade routes of Phoenicians, the Cilician silver mines, and the Hittite iron mines. Cf. David Nichols, "Ancient Near East 855-745 B.C," *Journal of the Evangelical Theological Society* 18 (1975): 244; Maxwell Miller J. & John H. Hayes, *History of Ancient Israel and Judah* (2nd ed. Louisville: Westminster John Knoz Press, 1982), 331-32.

122 Paul D. Hanson, "War and Peace in the Hebrew Bible," *Interpretation* 38 (1948): 345,348.

123 Perry B. Yoder, "Towards a Shalom Biblical Theology," *Conrad Grebel Review* 3 (1983): 48.

124 Hanson, "War and Peace in Hebrew Bible," 352 (Isa 7:9; 9:5-6; 11:1-9; 28:15; Jer 23:5-6; 33:15-16). Jonathan Paige Sisson, "Jeremiah and the Jerusalem Conception of Peace," *JBL* 105 (1986): 429-442.

125 By way of definition, wisdom constitutes something of a problem. According to J. L. Crenshaw there are varieties of viewpoints. His own definition is interesting, he says, "Wisdom is the quest for self-understanding in terms of relationships with things, people and the Creator." J Crenshaw, "Prolegomenon," in *Studies in Ancient Israelite Wisdom* (edited by J. Crenshaw; New York: Ktav, 1976), 3.

cannot speak for themselves). He is to be just. His role as a leader in public life is to be oriented towards others. The king cannot simply do what he wants as the people for whom he is responsible and depend on him for the fulfilment of their needs. C. H. Toy accepts this understanding of the text (Prov 31:6-7) when he says that there are two proper occasions for the use of alcoholic drinks: bodily suffering and mental distress.[126] It is difficult to justify the literal reading given in the other proverbs that warn of excess.[127] Here King Lemuel's mother says that if the king follows a dissolute lifestyle, then let everyone, especially those without hope, be given alcohol to appease their sad state of affairs. The point being made is that of a leader's example giving credibility to the "way of wisdom," which in this case is the way of sobriety.

The "two ways" is a recurring motif in Proverbs, and is sometimes seen as the hermeneutical key.[128] Equally important is the king's personal life in relation to his public office and task. The great virtue here is discipline or self-control. The king cannot allow himself excess to liquor, pleasure, or power. Drunkenness could lead to ill-advised decisions that may not be reversible. Becoming besotted with too many women could lead to undue influence-especially in cultures that use marriage to support economic bonds and military alliances. Neither drink nor women are prohibited. Both are referred to in the context of the social duties of the king. Both have potentially destructive results if abused. Proverbial wisdom literature, then, suggests that the king, as leader of his community, needed to be self-disciplined, to have integrity, to be compassionate, to be just, and to speak up for the poor.

2.1.1.3. King as Religious Leader

In ancient Israel when the king was chosen, he was sanctified by his anointing and adopted by Yahweh, is a sacred person and seems thereby to be empowered to perform religious functions. G.W. Ahlstrom points out that religion and religious policy were part of the king's duty and in fact he is the organizer of the cult.[129]

The king is mentioned several times in the formal prophetic books or historical books as the leader in acts of worship.[130] For instance, David was himself a distinguished religious leader, though denied the privilege of building

126 C. H. Toy, *International Critical Commentary on Proverbs* (Edinburgh T&T Clarke, 1977), 540; J. Crenshaw, "The Sage in Proverbs," in *The Sage in Israel and the Ancient Near East* (ed. J. G. Gammie and L. G. Perdue; Winona Lake Eisenbrauns, 1990), 207, seems supportive of this position too, saying of the Queen Mother "In her view, wine enables society's castaways (and perhaps condemned criminals) to forget their misery."

127 See for instance Prov 20:1; 23:20-21; 29-35.

128 R. van Leeuwen, "Liminality and Worldview in Proverbs 1-9," *Semeia* 50 (1990): 111-44.

129 G. W. Ahlstrom, *Royal Administration and National Religion in Ancient Palestine (*vol. 1; Leiden: E. J. Brill, 1982), 6.

130 De Vaux, *Ancient Israel: Its Life and Institutions,* 113. II Sam 24:25; 7:2-3; I Chron 22-29; I Kgs 5-8; 12:26-33; 8:17; II Kgs 22:3-7.

the Temple. As king of the Israelite empire, David did not fail to acknowledge God as the one who granted Israel military and materials prosperity (II Sam 22:1-51). Thus he, not content in Jerusalem being only the political capital of Israel, had the ark brought to Jerusalem as well. This act made Jerusalem a religious centre as well as political and placed David in the role of a religious leader.[131] The religious aspect that Saul lacked and attempted to make up for by offering the sacrifice himself is filled by David's actions in transferring the ark. This now placed the king of Israel in a position of military, political, and religious authority, granting him all the rights that kings of other empires in the AWA held and hold. Solomon was able to build the temple that David had wanted to, completing the religious authority of the king by moving the ark into the temple and designating it as the house of God.

Likewise, kings were responsible for the maintenance and the building of temples. For instance, King Josiah appointed three of his top officials to head the project of repairing the temple (II Chron 34:8b). The king to be sure, was an exalted figure, exercising considerable influence and power, the protector and guardian of the people.

Deuteronomistic historian emphasized that one of the primary duties of a king was to let the people to remain faithful to the covenant Yahweh had made with Israel. Although, kings were not regarded as priests, some of them were given opportunity to exercise a priestly function on special occasion and this is attested in the Scripture.[132] However, the conduct of worship was left to the priest. Scholars argue that kings who performed sacerdotal function were exceptional actions. Roland de Vaux affirms that "the part played by the king in the regulation and supervision of worship or the nomination of the clergy does not mean that he was himself a priest; it does not exceed the prerogatives which the head of State may have over the state religion."[133] Further Dommershausen notes that unlike the rest of the ancient near east-the king himself never claimed to be a priest in Israelite society.[134]

We may also note that reigning king had exceeded his authority in intervening in cultic matters in ancient Israel. Samuel and Saul were clearly in sharp antagonism on this subject, and Samuel rejected Saul's right to offer sacrifice (I Sam 13:8-15). Possibly Saul was endeavouring to establish his right to exercise

---

131 Bright, *A History of Israel,* 196; F. F. Bruce, *Israel and the Nations* (Grand Rapids: Wm. B. Eerdmans Publishing Company, 1963), 30.

132 Historian recorded that David's sons were priests (II Sam 6:18). When the ark was brought to Jerusalem David officiated as priest, dressed in the priestly linen *ephod* (II Sam 6:14), offering holocausts and communion sacrifices and blessing the people (II Sam 6:18). During the dedication of the Temple Solomon played priestly role (I Kgs 8:14,62). Josiah religious reform also can be cited as the example of the king who played priestly role (II Kgs 22-23).

133 de Vaux, *Ancient Israel: Its Life and Institutions,* 114.

134 Dommershausen, "כֹּהֵן," in *TDOT* (vol. 7; ed. G. Johannes, et al; trans. David E. Green; Grand Rapids; Michigan: William B. Eerdmans Publishing Company, 1995), 73.

cultic functions, as did the kings of other nations. The actions of Jeroboam I when he established his own priesthood in Israel, and officiated himself at the altar (I Kgs 12:26-33), called forth a strong prophetic protest (I Kgs 13:1-6). The bold statement of the Dtr Historian in Kings that "the Lord smote the king, so that he was a leper to the day of his death" (II Kgs 15:5) is augmented by the Chronicler, who notes that this punishment was because the king (Uzziah) "entered the temple of the Lord to burn incense on the altar of incense" (II Chron 26:16-21), in spite of the uncompromising rebuke of the priests whose authority and privileges were being usurped.

In the AWA contexts also religion was fundamental for forming the royal ideology.[135] Religion and the kingship were intrinsically related in the AWA. No kingship had been sustained without the support of its religion. However, the relationship between the kingship and the religion was likely to be flexible, since each institution had a different system of maintaining their government.[136]

In Egypt, Assyria and Phoenicia the kings represented the god on earth, and thus at times functioned or acted as priests, performing certain religious rituals. In Egypt the kings also possessed priestly authority, and are known as priest-king and wherein he acted as a priest and led religious affairs.[137] Seele remarks that an Egyptian king acted as high priest of the land, participate in the great religious festivals. The king personally conducted foundation and dedication ceremonies in the temples which he built for the gods, as well as other priestly functions.[138]

2.1.2. Functions/Roles of the Royal Officers

It takes a special state of mind to be royal officers. They also have specialist roles. As a royal officer, one should be responsible for the welfare and management of the community. The following section will discuss the designated functions or roles of the royal officers under David and Solomon's administration (II Sam 8:16-18=I Chron 18:15-17; II Sam 20: 23-26; I Kgs 4:1-6).

2.1.2.1. Military Leadership

Ancient Israelite society was led by the charismatic warrior-leaders (tribal fighters) which led to the formation of an organized army during early monarchy. The Book of Joshua reports that the twelve tribes that comprised the nation at the time of the conquest all supplied troops for battle through a general levy of able-bodied

135 J. N. Postgate, *Early Mesopotamia: Society and Economy at the Dawn of History* (London: Routledge,1992), 260.

136 K. W. Whitelam, "King and Kingship," in *ABD* (vol. 4; ed. D. N., Freedman, et al; New York: Doubleday, 1992), 40-48.

137 Thomas L. Leclerc, *Introduction to the Prophets: Their Stories, Sayings, and Scrolls* (New York: Paulist Press, 2007), 26; Heschel, *The Prophets*, 477-78; de Vaux, *Ancient Israel: Its Life and Institutions*, 1961), 113.

138 Seele, *When Egypt Ruled the East*, 85.

men of military age, apparently those twenty years of age and up.[139] They were the defenders of the nation. This type of militia continued through the period of the judges and into the early monarchy. Saul and David personally led their armies, at least for part of their reign.

David rose to power largely because of his military leadership, but then shared the responsibility with his commanders Abner and Joab. Sometimes David personally led the troops (II Sam 5:1-2,10:17-19), but more often sent them out with his commanders (II Sam 10:7; 18:3). In some cases, the texts record the troops as insisting that David would stay behind in order to stay out of danger (II Sam 18:3-4; 21:17). When David became king over twelve tribes, for the proper administration, he delegated to different persons as military officers. David assigned Joab over the professional army and Benaiah over the Kerethites and Pelethites (II Sam 8:16,18; 20: 23).

One of the duties/responsibilities of military officers (צָבָא) was "to go out to serve in the military" leading the troops.[140] The other duty was to organized professionals army into units of thousand, hundred, fifty and ten soldiers (II Sam 18:1). Each of the units is led by their respective officers, called the שַׂר (שָׂרִים) (leader/chief/captain).[141] These army played a great role in the field of military administration.[142] One of such groups was assigned to be in the royal palace. They were designated to be royal runners or messengers. They usually stand at the entrance to the palace and carry messages for the kings.[143] The commander of the army was one of the members of the palace, for whom he carried out civil as well as military tasks according to the circumstances. The armies carried out the service of the king which consisted of military as well as civil tasks for the economic well-being of the country.

---

139 Several texts state that men twenty years and older were considered of military age. See Num 1:3, 45; 26:2, 4; 14:29; Deut 2:16; and I Chron 27:23. G. E. Mendenhall suggests 20-45 years as the age for military service. George E. Mendenhall, "The Census Lists of Numbers 1 and 26," *JBL* 77 (1958): 60.

140 A. S. Van der Woude, "צָבָא," in *TLOT* (vol. 2; trans. Ernst Jenni and Claus Westermmann; Peabody/Massachusetts: Hendrickson Publishers, 1997), 1039; Tremper Longman III, "צָבָא," in *NIDOTTE* (vol.3.; ed. Willem A. VanGemeren; Carlisle/Cumbria: Paternoster Press, 1997), 733; John E. Hartley, "צָבָא," *TWOT* (vol. 2; R.Laird Harris, eds.; Chiccago: Moody Press, 1980), 750.

141 Gary G. Cohen, "שַׂר," in *TWOT*, 884; J. W. Wevers, "Army," in *IDB* (vol.1; George Arthur Buttrick, et al; NY/Nashville: Abingdon Press, 1962), 229.

142 Commanders over fifties (I Sam 8:12; Deut 1:15-17; II Kgs 1:9-14 and Isa 3:3). Commanders over tens (Deut 1:15-17 and Amos 5:3). Other titles also appear, but the information is not clear enough to determine how they fit into the overall structure. Walter Dietrich, *The Early Monarchy in Israel: The Tenth Century B.C.E* (trans. Joachim Vette; Atlanta: SBL, 2007), 191.

143 T. O. Hall, Jr, "Army," in *IDB* (Supp, vol.; ed. Keith Crim, et al; Nashville: Abingdon Press, 1962), 54; Gordon, *1 & 2 Samuel*, 297; Hertzberg, *1 & II Samuel*, 293.

Professionals army also served as royal bodyguard along with their military tasks.[144] Bodyguards were usually formed by the foreigners whose personal loyalty was totally committed to the kings, and less interested in the involvement of the national politics. They were also called foreign mercenaries but with "special responsibility for the person of the king."[145]

The issue that we noticed in military leadership was power struggle among the leaders. Power struggle among military leaders was never ending throughout Israelite monarchy. The conflict between army commanders took place for several reasons. For instance, while Abner son of Ner, had been the commander-in-chief of the army under the reigns of Saul (I Sam 14:50; 17:55) and Ishbaal (II Sam 2:8), David had already formed a new army whose members came from Judah (during Ishbaal's reign). There were two chief commanders in the army, one for Judah and one for Israel.

Abner was commander of the army of Israel, and Amasa son of Jether, was commander of the army of Judah (I Kgs 2:32). After David had established the monarchy, he took the co-ordination of these two armies under his control. He created a new office and put Joab, his faithful friend, in control of the army (II Sam 8:16). Later when Joab learned that Abner had been reconciled to David and David had let Abner go in peace, he sought and killed him (II Sam 3:22-27). It is clearly evident that the action of Joab was an attempt to revenge the death of his brother Asahel.[146] Keith W. Whitelam further remarks that the murder of Abner by Joab raises questions about the early monarchy and the administration of

144 Hall, Jr, "Army," in *IDB*, 54

145 Hans Wilhelm Hertzberg, *1 & 2 Samuel: A Commentary* (London: SCM Press Ltd, 1964), 293; de Vaux, *Ancient Israel*, 123. The origin of bodyguards is in question, since scholars suggest different interpretations. II Sam 8:18=I Chron 18:17; II Sam 20:23 mentioned or identified that royal bodyguards were Kerethites and Pelethites. They might have come to Palestine with the migrations of "Sea People." Robert P. Gordon, *1 & 2 Samuel: A Commentary* (Exeter: The Paternoster Press, 1986), 247. According to Kyle McCarter "the Cherethites have been plausibly identified as Cretans," most probably originated in Crete." Kyle McCarter, Jr. *II Samuel* (AB; Garden City/New York: Doubleday & Company, INC, 1984), 256. However, according to I Sam 30:14, Kerethites must refer to a tribal or ethnic group. The origin of the Pelethities is totally difficult to understand. McCarter, Jr. *II Samuel*, 256. Hans Wilhelm Hertzberg however notes that "'Pelethites' can only mean Philistines." Hertzberg, *1 & 2 Samuel*, 293. During the reign of David, Benaiah son of Jehoida was given responsibility over the Kerethites and the Pelethites. McCarter observes that David probably raised this private mercenary army while living in Ziklag (I Sam 27-31), near which was "the Negeb of the Cherethites (I Sam 30:14), presumably the homeland of the first of the two groups." McCarter, Jr. *II Samuel*, 256.

146 Keith W. Whitelam, *The Just King: Monarchical Judicial Authority in Ancient Israel* (JSOTSupp. 12, Sheffield: JSOT Press, 1972), 106. By killing Abner, Joab violated the covenant between the king and Abner, and the hospitality granted to Abner become invalid.

justice.[147] Abner's murder was the effective end of Eshbaal's kingship as a worthy military opponent of Judah.

When David received the title "king" over both Israel and Judah following the death of Abner and Eshbaal (II Sam 5:1-3).[148] Joab become in-charge over David's entire army; he was a strong and capable man. He apparently had a high respect for David, as David had for Joab. However, due to his revengeful attitude, he was replaced, and the same assignment was given to Amasa. When Joab noticed that the king had no confidence on him any longer, he was in disgrace, and out of rage (II Sam 17:25; 20:4-13) he murdered Amasa in Gibeon.[149] In both occasions Joab was guilty since he murdered them in the absence of war, when the king declared peace. Thus, throughout the reign of David and the rest of the monarchs in ancient Israel we see the manipulation of monarchical judicial authority and the conflict between the leaders (military officers).

The discussion shows that the commander of the regular army clearly held a position of great power. The texts recorded Abner and Joab as playing major roles in political affairs of the kingdom as well leading the army. They are shown taking part in the affairs of the royal family (II Sam 14), making a treaty (II Sam 3:12), making or crowning a new king (I Kgs 1:7, 19), carrying out killings for the king (I Kgs 28:34-4:4), rebuking the king (II Sam 19:5-8), and disobeying the king's express order (II Sam 18:5, 10-15; 19:13).

2.1.2.2. Royal Secretaries

Secretaries were the immediate representatives of the king, master of the palace. The texts II Kings 18:18, 37; Isaiah 36:3 record that Shebna, the royal secretary was one of the three officials sent by king Hezekiah to hold the discussion with Sennacherib's emissary for better relationship of the two nations. Sheva was also recognized as secretary in II Samuel 20:25. De Vaux remarks that king's private secretary and secretary of state were responsible for all correspondence, internal and external affairs.[150] They participated in all public affairs because they were the source of information to the royal court as well as to public. Secretaries handled the routine activities of the king and court and perhaps diplomatic correspondence as well. Hertzberg notes that secretary was responsible for the execution of written matters, including diplomatic correspondence.[151] During the reign of Joash the

---

147 Whitelam, *The Just King: Monarchical Judicial Authority in Ancient Israel*, 105. The manipulation of monarchical judicial authority has been seen throughout the reign of David.

148 Historical critics argue that David might have "arranged the murder of Abner," although the assassination of Eshbaal was unclear. James C. Vanderkam, "David Complicity in the deaths of Abner and Eshbaal," *JBL* 99 (1980): 534.

149 Hertzberg, *1 & II Samuel*, 373. At this time Joab was considered as a "commander of a detachment."

150 De Vaux, *Ancient Israel: Its Life and Institution*, 131.

151 Hertzberg, *1 & 2 Samuel*, 293.

royal secretaries were given responsibility of collecting the contributions given for the repair of the Temple.[152]

2.1.2.3. Recorder

Recorder was responsible for records (שָׁלוֹם) and documents of both economic and administrative affairs. According to II Samuel 20:24, Jehoshaphat son of Ahilud was recognized as recorder. Hertzberg notes that שָׁלוֹם "recorder is the most important figure in domestic politics at court; he is the spokesman who has to keep the king continually informed and to transmit his decisions."[153] שָׁלוֹם also means "one who reminds," thus in his duty he kept records and reminded the king of appointments and responsibilities. He may also have served as official herald for assemblies.[154] De Vaux remarks that the equivalent function of ancient Israelite royal recorder is found in the Egyptian scheme of titles: he who repeats, calls, announces.[155] In ancient Egyptian royal context the recorder played an important role, and he was considered as Pharaoh's herald. De Vaux further notes:

> He was in charge of the palace ceremonies and introduced people to audiences,... He reported to the king on what concerned the people and the country, but also passed on to the people the commands of their sovereign. He was the Pharaoh's official spokesman. When the Pharaoh went abroad, he accompanied him, watched over his person, and prepared quarters for each stage of the journey.[156]

The secretary and the recorder in ancient Israelite society were also regarded as high officials in royal palace. Like that of the ancient Egyptians, he was also considered the king's "Messenger," he was therefore entitled to receive all the officials' news and conveyed them to the kings.

2.1.2.4. Palace Administrator

Palace administrator's main responsibility was to carry out the ministry of negotiation with other nations. For example, Hezekiah sent three of his officers, namely, Eliakim the palace administer, Shebna the secretary, and Joah the recorder to negotiate with Assyrian field commander for a peaceful relationship between the two countries, and also he sent them to Isaiah, the then prophet to inform the current situation of Judah (Isa 36:3,22). Shebna was referred as a סכן "steward" in

---

152 De Vaux, *Ancient Israel,* 131. II Kgs 12:11; cf. II Chron 24:11. In the process of renovation/repairing of the Temple, the secretary Shaphan discovered the "Book of the Law." II Kgs 22:3, 8-10, 12; II Chron 34:15, 18, 20.

153 Hertzberg, *1 & 2 Samuel*, 293.

154 Leon J. Wood, *Israel's United Monarchy* (Rapids, Michigan: Baker Books House, 1979), 178.

155 De Vaux, *Ancient Israel: Its Life and Institution*, 132; cf. William F. Albright, *Archaeology and the Religion of Israel* (Baltimore: John Hopkins, 1953), 120.

156 De Vaux, *Ancient Israel: Its Life and Institution*, 132.

Isaiah 22:15, though the exact meaning is not clear in Hebrew, it associates with other semitic language. In Amarna letters *Zukinu* is a gloss on a term identifying the governor of the territory of Asshur as well as governor of the conquered countries. In Ugarit the term is identified with the chief officer under the king.[157] John N. Oswalt remarks that סכן is addressed as "the one who is over the house" and function as second to king.[158] Thus, the Ugaritic term "corresponds to the position held in Judah by Shebna, סכן (*soken*) and master of the palace."[159] Since Shebna held an important position in the royal leadership, prophet Isaiah singled out Shebna and pronounced the judgement oracle, that he was accountable to his role as a leader.

The three officials, secretary, recorder, and palace administrators held prominent leadership positions in the royal administration. They were diplomats (Isa 31:1), messengers, and representatives of monarchs.

2.1.2.5. Commander in Charge of Forced Labour

Forced labour in Israel was introduced during the time of David and he appointed Adoniram to take in charge for the work (II Sam 20:24). Initially, David imposed it on the defeated enemy (II Sam 12:31).[160] When Solomon resumed the administration, he strengthened the policy, since more men were needed for his several building projects. He appointed Jeroboam and put him in charge over the house of Joseph.[161] J. Alberto Soggin comments, "a characteristic element of the way in which the tribute was collected by the administrations of David and Solomon is that communities and individuals were conscripted for forced labour."[162] Scholars assume that it was in fact this burden laid on the Israelites which incited Jeroboam to revolt against the leadership of Solomon.[163] The prime duty of the officer was the distribution of the work, allotting daily works to different clans and tribes. The office of forced labour continued throughout the Israelite monarchical period.

---

157 De Vaux, *Ancient Israel: Its Life and Institution*, 131.

158 John N. Oswalt, *The Book of Isaiah 1-39* (Grand Rapids, Michigan: William B. Eerdmans Publishing Company, 1986), 418.

159 De Vaux, *Ancient Israel: Its Life and Institution*, 131. Azrikam, the Ephraimite and Elkakah were recognized as the officer in charge of the palace, and second to the king (II Chron 28:7).

160 De Vaux, *Ancient Israel: Its Life and Institution*, 141. Whether David treated the Ammonites as a slave or only imposed tax is not clear.

161 Jeroboam was certainly a talented individual, had leadership experience and no doubt possessed charisma. 1 Kings 11:28 informs us that he was a valiant warrior and even Solomon had recognized him as being "industrious;" hence he appointed him to a leadership position. De Vaux, *Ancient Israel*, 141-42.

162 J. Alberto Soggin, *An Introduction to the History of Israel and Judah* (3rd ed.; London: SCM Press, 1999), 91.

163 De Vaux, *Ancient Israel: Its Life and Institution*, 142.

2.1.2.6. District Officers

Solomon's extended administration policy is seen in I Kings 4:7-19 where he divided his kingdom into twelve districts reminiscent of the twelve tribes for administrative purposes. Gray, however, argues that the twelve districts suggest twelve months of the year but not the twelve tribes.[164] Each district was supervised by an appointed officer. Azariah, the son of Nathan, was given responsibility to administer over all the twelve district officers. Leon J. Wood notes that "these were established mainly for the purpose of taxation, with each district supplying provisions for the court one month per year, though there was no doubt other functions the districts served as well.[165] Thus, the purpose of appointing these officers was to supply the palace with food on a monthly rotation.[166] Taxation program was organized by David. The income from the taxes was not shown in any of the biblical records but perhaps David taxed people quite heavily.[167] De Vaux remarks that high taxation was common for the day as it is shown in Ugartic references.[168] I Kings 4:22, 23 record that Solomon lived and entertained lavishly. Hence, he extracted more taxes to enhance or support his living standard. Thus, the duties or the functions of the twelve officers were to supply provisions on a rotating monthly basis for the royal court and to provide barley and straw for the horses of Solomon's chariots and other horses, as well as food for the people (I Kgs 4:7, 27-28).

2.1.2.7. Elders/Counsellors

Elders in Israel comprised heads of the families in the clans, and the leading citizens of the place. The elder (זקן) is not only a person of advanced age, but also a man of distinct social grade and a responsible person (Isa 3:2; 9:15; Mic 4:9). The elders were the consulting body of the city, the nation, or the king respectively, and as such were considered "the wise" (cf. Ezek 7:26; Jer 18:18) and counsellors. They were addressed by the most prominent titles "the elders of the people" or "the elders of the country," and "the elders of the city." These members were given proper instruction on how to govern the community's affairs or settle the disputes.[169] Elders played a significant role in the daily lives of most Israelites. They sat at the village gate and discussed community matters. However, they were

164 John Gray, *I & II Kings: A Commentary* (London: SCM Press Ltd, 1964), 131.

165 Leon J. Wood, *Israel's United Monarchy* (Rapids, Michigan: Baker Books House, 1979), 287, 293.

166 Dietrich, *The Early Monarchy in Israel: The Tenth Century B.C.E.,* 194.

167 Wood, *Israel's United Monarchy*, 179.

168 De Vaux, *Ancient Israel: Its Life and Institutions*, 140.

169 Exod 23:1-3; 6-8 cf. Lev 19:15, 35. "They must not bear false witness nor follow the majority in defiance of justice, nor accept gifts; they must acquit the innocent and condemn the guilty." De Vaux, *Ancient Israel*, 153.

criticized by the prophets for failing in their duties miserably (Amos 5:10, 12, 15; Zach 8:16).

One of their cruel actions and great dishonesty is illustrated by the story of Naboth. Basing on the false witness of the Elders, action was taken (that Naboth was stoned to dead). De Vaux remarks that all municipal affairs are in the hands of the *zeqenîm*.[170] The writer of Deuteronomy referred to them as "men who take action under the laws."[171] This statement illustrates that the Elders' participation in decision making is valued. In ancient Israel the appointment of state judges did not negate the role of the town elders. Instead, he prefers to speak of complementary roles of the city elders and the royal judicial appointees.

In most of the AWA contexts, we find records of Elders' organization. For example, in Mesopotamia, Elders were regarded as representatives of the people, though they had no administrative function; Hittite's Elders managed all municipal affairs.[172]

2.1.2.8. Judges

In ancient Israel, the professional judges were appointed by kings in every town for the purpose of the proper management of the administration. The role of judicial courts had the function of maintaining justice based on the principle of entitlement: to safeguard the misinterpretation of justice; to judge justly between right and wrong; to declare the innocent and to help one gain justice; to protect the rights of the innocent in legal disputes over life and property; and to maintain pure justice in settling disputes (Amos 5:7, 12; Mic 7:3; Isa 3:2, 11, 13). However, eighth century BCE Prophets criticized the corrupt court systems (Amos 5:7, 10; Isa 1:23). Even the governmental and judicial officials, who were responsible for preserving justice, were contributing to what the prophet considered to be an ungodly social imbalance. The courts had become the very instruments of undermining justice (Amos 5:12; Isa 5:21). Hence, Amos singled out the judicial officials who "turn justice to wormwood" (Amos 5:7). He denounced the corruption of the judges who acquitted the guilty because of a bribe.

2.1.2.9. Appraisal

We are not very well informed about the administration of the leadership shared by different officers during Israelite's monarchy. There is no specific organized leadership structure. There are at least three lists of officers in Deuteronomist

---

170 De Vaux, *Ancient Israel: Its Life and Institution*, 69, 138.

171 Deut 19; 21:1-9, 18-21; 22:13-21; 25:5-10. When Saul died without a successor "David sent messages and gifts to the Elders of the different towns of Judah," appealing them to anoint him as a king. Jehu addressed himself to the Elders of Samaria (II Kgs 10:1, 5). Jezabel wrote to the Elders of Yizreel (I Kgs 21:8). De Vaux, *Ancient Israel: Its Life and Institution*, 138, 153 (I Sam 30:26-31).

172 De Vaux, *Ancient Israel: Its Life and Institution*, 138.

record (II Sam 8:16-18= I Chron 18:15-17; II Sam 20:23-26; I Kgs 4:1-6). The position or the rank of the officers keeps changing as it is shown in the lists of the officers. The list of officers in both places (II Sam 8:16-18; 20:23-26) may be due to the fact that when an editor removed II Samuel 21:1-14, he detached parts of its context as well, both before (the list of officials) and after the section.[173] Thus, Ackyrod thinks that the two different lists during the reign of David are simply variants, rather than reflections of different periods of David's reign.[174] Further, McCarter assumes that "the variants probably arose in the course of the final arrangement of the book."[175]

The above mentioned officers were the bureaucrats who controlled the function of the administration or central government. At the national level, political and economic power was administered by a very small group of people. The governing classes were: the royal family, the royal court, high civil, military officials, large landowners, wealthy merchants, leaders in the priesthood, and others. These are the bureaucrats who controlled the entire economic well-being as well as the legal and political viability of the rest of the country's inhabitants, who fell into a range of classes or professions with diminished status and power.

The study of "Royal Leadership in Israel" reveals that the kings in Israel were chosen by Yahweh as a representative, and to rule the people according to the purpose of Him. The first king of Israel, Saul failed to establish the central administrative government. David succeeded where Saul failed, and created a vast empire for Israel but was not able to control his own family, leaving Israel in the hands of Solomon, who is the strongest administrator and finally became the king that was modelled in other cultures. The finality in Solomon's kingship occurred religiously and politically, but it took place at the cost of the people. The Israelites who desired so much to be united under a monarchy were finally given a true monarch and suffered under him. While the nation of Israel had achieved the peak of political, economic, and military power they were not able to escape the tensions that came along with such things. Solomon was the culmination of the evolutionary process of the monarchy, a king just like the surrounding cultures. As the kingship evolved within Israel, so too did the consequences of their initial request. As a people that went from tribes to an empire under evolving leaders, their final position placed them in oppression.

173 The officers that appear in both lists are: Joab, Jehoshaphat, Zadok, and Benaiah. It is only an apparent exception that II Samuel 8:17 reads Ahimelech, son of Abiathar as priest, while II Samuel 20:25 has only Abiathar. In II Samuel 8:17 the names are transposed, since Ahimelech was the father, not the son, of Abiathar. The names of the scribes in the two lists are given as *Seraiah* in II Samuel 8:17 and as *Sheva* in II Samuel 20:25; the two seem to be variants of the same name. Smith, *The Books of Samuel,* 309, 372. The differences between the two lists consist of the mention of David's sons as priests in II Samuel 8:18, where II Samuel 20:26 has *Ira* and the appearance of *Adoram* as master of forced labour in II Samuel 20:24.

174 P. R. Ackroyd, *The Second Book of Samuel* (CBC; London: Cambridge, 1977), 46.

175 McCarter, *II Samuel,* 257.

The study also reveals that almost all the monarchs in Israel followed the system of administration instituted by the early monarchs. They followed the system of class-based society: consisting of recorders, scribes, priests, military commanders, and various other political appointments who were called bureaucrats; and the common people who served the royals officers and the kingdom. Most of the monarchs and the royal officials failed to exercise their functions and roles as they were supposed to be. Thus, all through the struggle of the history of Israel, we see prophets who tried to give advice and correct the monarchs and royal officials whenever it was needed.

Israel and AWA have some common understanding about king and his functions and responsibilities: kingship is intimately related to the religious realm of nation; kings were chosen by the deity; king and kingdom is the gift of God; the relationship between the God and the king is mutual and grounded on faith and trust; the king was chosen to establish peace and justice in the land; the king is represented the gods and God to provide wealth and protection to the people as their shepherd.

At the same time, Israelite concept of king and kingship (kingdom) is different from AWA. In Israel, the type of government before monarchy was "theocracy" in which God ruled over His people. Though Israel welcomed monarchy, the concept of "theocracy" is still instilled in the hearts of the people. The understanding is that God is the supreme King, and He chose the king in Israel, to be His representative to the people. Thus the king should rule the nation with truth, justice, and righteousness. The "kingship" in Israel is unique, in the sense that the "king" is not higher than the One who chose him, that is "Yahweh." Keeping this concept in mind the king acted as the loyal servant of his master in every responsibility that he performed. The king only executed the divine will as he was empowered by the "spirit of Yahweh." Therefore the king should know what the divine will is, and needs divine sanction for its execution on matters (I Sam 28:6; 30:8; II Sam 5:23-24).

2.2. Priestly Leadership

In this section we discuss the most ancient office of Israelite's society that is, the priestly office. Priestly office in ancient Israel was one of the most ancient and essential aspect of the Hebrew people and their covenant with God. Thus, any proper understanding of the Israelite necessarily includes an investigation into the role of the priests.

During the time of the ancestors (before Babylonian exile), the Hebrew people did not function by means of a special priesthood constituted of a divinely instituted family line. Usually the heads of the Hebrew household would perform what would later come to be recognized as properly priestly functions (i.e., such as the offering of sacrifice).[176] During the time of exodus, part of that covenant is

176 de Vaux, *Ancient Israel: Its Life and Institution*, 345.

a special priesthood with restrictions on who is included or can be admitted into that priesthood. Thus, in the following section the institution of the office of the priest, functions, and its leadership will be discussed.

2.2.1. *Etymology of* כֹּהֵן *(priest)*

The Hebrew word used exclusively in the OT for priest is כֹּהֵן, the Greek translates it as ἱερευς (*iereus*), it even refers to a non-Hebrew priest.[177] From the outset, however, we have difficulty in understanding what exactly כֹּהֵן means etymologically. Some scholars believe that it comes from Akkadian root *kanu* which means "bow down," "to do homage," and "worship."[178] In that case, the priest would be the one who would bow down before the divinity. However, other scholars see it as coming from a root word כון meaning "to be firm," or "to stand firm."[179] The priest, then, is the one who stands up before the divinity. Others think that it comes from a root *kahhen,* Syrian word which meant "bring abundance," "make happy," or "to make prosperous."[180] Fittingly, the priest would be one who brings blessings or abundance upon the people.

Priests in Ugarit were called *khnm* and those who serve under the high priest were called the *ngdm/qdshm.*[181] Ugaritic scholars point out that the *khnm* described in Ugaritic texts are not connected to the cult but are included in lists of administrative offices, sometimes connected with the palace.[182] Ugaritic texts refer to "sacrificers" with other terms, which implies that the *khnm* were not essentially or exclusively officiants at sacrifice. The term may refer to a purely administrative office.[183] Thus, according to Ugaritic understanding the priest is counted as one of the administrative officers who assists both in palace and temple.

---

177 Philip Jenson, "כֹּהֵן," in *NIDOTE* (vol. 2; ed. Willem A. VanGemeren, et al; Grand Rapids, Michigan: Zondervan, 1997), 600; Dommershausen, "כֹּהֵן," in *TDOT* (vol. 7; ed. G. Johannes Botterweck, Helmer Ringgren, and Heinz-Josef Fabry; trans. David E. Green; Grand Rapids, Michigan: William B. Eerdmans Publishing Company, 1995), 66. I kgs 4:5; II Sam 8:18; 20:26; I Chron 18:16, 17; de Vaux, *Ancient Israel: Its Life and Institution*, 345.

178 Dommershausen, "כֹּהֵן," in *TDOT,* 66; de Vaux, *Ancient Israel: Its Life and Institution*, 346.

179 Jenson, "כהן," in *NIDOTE,* 600; E. Gerstenberger, "כון," *TLOT* (vol. 2; ed. Ernest Jenni and Claus Westermann; trans. Mark E. Biddle; Peabody: Hendrickson Publishers, Inc, 1997), 602.

180 Dommershausen, "כֹּהֵן," in *TDOT,* 66.

181 Ringgren, "כֹּהֵן, *Kohen,*" in *TDOT,* 64. There must have been vowels in the pronunciation, but these were not written, and cannot be reconstructed. But this is more relevant to the discussion about the meaning of נֹקֵד "shepherds."

182 D. M. L. Urie, "Officials of the Cult at Ugarit," *PEQ* 80 (1948): 42-45; Antonine DeGuglielmo, "Sacrifice in the Ugaritic Texts," *CBQ* 17 (1955): 89-91; A. F. Rainey, "The Kingdom of Ugarit," *BA* 28 (1965): 122-24.

183 Urie, "Officials of the Cult at Ugarit," 45-47.

Ancient Egypt does basically have two common words for priest: *w'b,* "pure man," and *hmw-ntr* "servants of God," later translated as "prophet."[184] Thus, fittingly a priest is a servant of gods, a man with a pure heart, who can carry out the sacred duty of his god. Aelred Cody's extensive study of West Semitic origin of the word כֹּהֵן, helps him to find little insight into the role of the priest. Among Arabian sources, he finds the closest parallels to early Israelite priests to be the *sadin* rather than the *kahin* and concludes that if the priests of Yahweh were not called "*kohanim* when they arrived in Canaan... they adopted the Canaanite name which" applied to their office.[185]

Despite these differing explanations, scholars really do not know if it is either, any, or a combination of all these meanings which adequately describes the genealogical history of the word. Yet, it is helpful to note these various meanings since they seem to point to some aspect of the priest as he was seen in the OT. The above explanation shows that there is no universal meaning to the term "priest," but in brief a priest can be said to be the one performing daily rituals as well as rituals during certain holidays.

2.2.2. Formation/Origin of the Office of Priests in OT

The question of origin of priesthood in the OT is extremely complex.[186] The traditional understanding is that following the Exodus from Egypt, males of the tribe of Levi were assigned special religious responsibilities, and male descendants of Aaron were selected to serve as priests, and this kind of instituted hierarchy remained throughout the Israelite history.[187] Nevertheless, the history of

184 Ringgren, "כֹּהֵן, *Kohen*," in *TDOT* (vol. 7; ed. G. Johannes Botterweck, et al; trans. David E. Green; Grand Rapids/Michigan: William B. Eerdmans Publishing Company, 1995), 61; James, *An Introduction to Ancient Egypt*, 143.

185 Aelred Cody, *A History of Israelite Priesthood* (Rome: Pontifical Biblical Institute, 1967), 29.

186 Gerhard von Rad, *Old Testament Theology* (2 vols; trans. D. M. G. Stalker; New York: Harper & Row, 1962, orig. 1957), 1:241-49; Aelred Cody, *A History of Old Testament Priesthood* (Rome: Pontifical Biblical Institute, 1969); De Vaux, *Ancient Israel: Its Life and Institutions*, 345-405; Gary A. Anderson and Saul M. Olyan, eds., *Priesthood and Cult in Ancient Israel* (Sheffield: JSOT Press, 1991); Merlin D. Rehm, "Levites and Priests," in *ABD* (6 vols; David Noel Freedman, et al., eds; New York: Doubleday, 1992), 4:297-310.

187 This reflects an understanding that Levites descendants of the tribe of Levi were confined to serving as lesser temple functionaries, and were ambiguously priests. The other eleven tribes could not hold priesthood of any sort. Since priests were by definition holier than other (men), they were "holy" by heredity, rather than through ethical and spiritual qualities.

Though Moses consecrates the tribe of Levi to act as the priestly tribe of Israel, not all were allowed to perform the properly priestly functions. Thus there was a kind of hierarchy within the priestly class. The only Levites who could be legitimately called priests would be the direct descendants of Aaron (Exod 28:1,43; Num 3:10). And from among these priests were chosen the high-priest or the ruling priest who would govern over the other priests. The rest of the Levites then were not priests per se but were assistants to the priests. Leon J. Wood, *A Survey of Israel's History* (rev. David O'Brein; Grand Rapids, MI: Zondervan, 1986), 159.

Israelite priesthood could be traced back since the time of the patriarchs in the Pentateuch.[188] The account of Israel's genealogy found in the Pentateuch, as well as in the Deuteronomic History and Chronicles give evidences that it was the tribe of Levi "devoted by God" as "religious personnel" in the Israelite religious institution.[189] Moreover, they were further categorised according to their clans to hold certain responsibilities in the tabernacle. However, while dealing with the subject of priesthood in the OT, it is often elusive as there are issues regarding the strata in the priestly office. Leithart remarks that "in the Old Testament text, the *real* history of Israel's priesthood, and hence of Israel's religion, is one of continual strife between various self-interested priestly families and between temple priests jealous of their privileges and country Lévites seeking a piece of the sacrificial pie."[190] Hence, it is difficult to ascertain the origin of priestly office in OT.

Julius Wellhausen's threefold origin of priestly office is cited by Frank Moore Cross: i) An early age when there was no fixed, hereditary priesthood; ii) The age of the kings when a Levitical priesthood began to emerge dominant in Jerusalem, and iii) Post-exilic theocracy in which the Aaronides ruled supreme and Levites in general became hierodules.[191]

One of the basic questions is textual strands, Scholars have posited in the Pentateuch is a "priestly" source, (P) which emphasizes matters relating to the priests, temple, and ritual, and generally accepted to be the product of post-exilic period. Wellhausen, in his classic on source criticism, argues that the institution of priesthood in ancient Israel was entirely post-exilic.[192] Patrick D. Miller emphasizes that though there were influences of their AWA nations on the "head of priest," Wellhausen's hypothesis remains valid that it is of post-exilic origin.[193] However, some scholars have taken issue with this position and have concluded that pre-exilic traditions in "P" have historical validity.[194] Scholars emphasize that

188 The ancestors (Adam, Cain, Abel, Noah, Abraham, etc.), "invoked the god for himself without the help of a mediator." Theophile James Meek, *Hebrew Origins* (revised edition, New York: Harper & Row, 1960), 119. Moreover, in Exod 19:6, Yahweh declared to Israel as "for me a priestly kingdom and a holy nation" (NRSV), and it was this notion that the patriarchs were the priests as "the head of the family." John Howard Raven, *The History of the Religion of Israel* (Grand Rapids: Baker Book House, 1979), 81.

189 Exod 6:16-25; 18:3-4; Num 26:58; Josh 21:1; 22:13; 24:33; Judg 20:28; I Sam 7:1; 14:3; 22:9; II Sam 8:17; I Kgs 2:26-27; I Chron 6:1-8. Leon J. Wood, *A Survey of Israel's History* (rev. David O'Brein; Grand Rapids: Zondervan, 1986), 159.

190 Peter J. Leithart, "Attendants of Yahweh's House: Priesthood in the Old Testament," *JSOT* 85 (1999): 4.

191 Frank Moore Cross, *Canaanite Myth and Hebrew Epic: Essays in the History of the Religion of Israel* (Cambridge: Harvard University Press, 1973), 199.

192 Wellhausen, *Prolegomena to the History of Ancient Israel*, 121-52.

193 Partick D. Miller, Jr., "Wellhausen and the History of Israel's Religion," *Semia* 25 (1982): 69.

194 R. Abba, "Priests and Levites," in *IDB* (Vol. 3; New York: Abingdon Press, 1962), 876-89.

the priesthood changed from pre-monarchy, to monarchy, to post-exile. N. H. Snaith notes,

> There are many passages in the Old Testament which show that the Aaronic priestly caste of later days was a development from a very different state of affairs. Once, all Levites were priests and not the sons of Aaron only. Earlier still, it was not even necessary to be a Levite in order to be a priest. Any man could be a priest, provided that he had been properly consecrated.[195]

One can agree with Abba, who states that "origin and development" of priesthood "together with the relationship of priests and Levites, constitutes one of the major problems of OT scholarship."[196] The question of the relation between priests and Levites has long been a fundamental factor in the interpretation of the history of Israel.[197] One of the scholarships' discussions is the origin of the priesthood in Israel which is different, and not genuinely connected with the tribe of Levi. The priestly office during the time of David was further divided into twenty-four divisions (1 Chron 24:1-31) because of the outnumbering of the priests and Levites where each division served in turn for one week.[198] Therefore, it is important to bring about their origin and understand their different functions at the outset.

2.2.3. The Concept of Priestly Office in Israel and AWA

To understand the concept of priestly office in Israel it is important to define what was an Israelite priest? R. K. Duck defines Israelite priesthood as "a religious institution within which certain people were given particular and often exclusive rights, roles and responsibilities as mediators between the divine and human realms."[199] According to Todd Compton, priesthood in Israel was connected with sanctuary and temple, cult and ritual, holy and pure person serving as a mediator between God and human, was virtually always connected with a temple and performed ordinances connected with it-sacrifice, purification and prayer.[200] Therefore, it can be understood as a person who is specially chosen and assigned for religious purposes. According to Roland de Vaux, in ancient Israel, the

---

195 N. H. Snaith, "The Priesthood and the Temple," in *A Companion to the Bible* (ed. Thomas Walter Manson; New York: Charles Scribner's Sons, 1947), 418-43, 418; Cf. Raymond Abba, "Priests and Levites in Deuteronomy," *VT* 27 (1977): 257.

196 Abba, "Priests and Levites," 876.

197 G. E. Wright, "The Levites in Deuteronomy," *VT* 4 (1954): 325-330; J. A. Emerton, "Priests and Levites in Deuteronomy," *VT* 12 (1962): 129-138; R. Abba, "Priests and Levites in Deuteronomy," *VT* 27 (1977): 257-267.

198 Wood, *A Survey*, 159.

199 R. K. Duke, "Priest, Priesthood," *Dictionary of the Old Testament: Pentateuch* (ed. T. Densmond Alexander & David W. Baker; Leicester: InterVarsity Press, 2003), 646.

200 Todd Compton, "Kingdom of Priests: Priesthood, Temple and Women in the Old Testament and Restoration," *Dialogue* 36 (2003): 42.

priesthood was not a vocation but an office.[201] Therefore, an Israelite priest was born and not made. De Vaux further notes that "priest in ancient Israel were not 'ordained': they began their work without any religious rite conferring on them grace, or special powers. And yet a priest was made holy and sacred by virtue of his work."[202] Walther Zimmerli also remarks that ancient Israelite priesthood office is important because it is a "special office set apart by God to protect the boundaries at the place of the divine presence, to teach the people proper conduct with respect to the sacred realm, and to mediate the blessing promised from this realm."[203] Their main duties were to perform the cults and rituals in the temple and also to minister to the people of Israel by delivering the word of Yahweh and teaching Torah.[204] Therefore, the priest is understood as a person who is especially chosen by Yahweh and is assigned for religious purposes. Priests hold an honoured position and priesthood was restricted to the tribe of Levi.[205] It was the tribe of Levi "devoted by God" as "religious personal" in the Israelite religious institution.[206] However, they were further categorized according to their clans to hold certain responsibilities in the tabernacle. The descendants of Aaron were "declared to the priests" (Exod 28:1, 43; Num 3:10), while the Levites ("the other members of Levi's tribe") assisted them in the cultic rituals.[207] However, the office of the priests after the exile did not strictly follow the lineage of Aaron and Levi and the "pedigrees were assuredly mixed," which might also contribute to the differing regard for the Gentiles.[208] Levites were divided into three groups,[209] each filled different roles in the Tabernacle and later in the Temple services.

Religion was a central social institution and its temple was the centre of religious life in AWA. Various types of priesthood were found in AWA religious context, particularly in ancient Mesopotamia and Egypt. Priesthood was an essential highlight of Mesopotamian religion, which was hereditary and was divided into different classes with specialized functions. The chief priests were

201 De Vaux, *Ancient Israel: Its Life and Institution*, 346.

202 De Vaux, *Ancient Israel: Its Life and Institutions*, 347.

203 Zimmerli, *Old Testament Theology in Outline,* 98; De Vaux, *Ancient Israel: Its Life and Institutions,* 347-348.

204 Peter J. Leithart, "Attendants of Yahweh's House: Priesthood in the Old Testament," *JSOT* 85 (1999): 21.

205 Martha Himmelfard, A Kingdom of Priests: Ancestry and Merit in Ancient Judaism (Philadelphia: University of Pennsylvania Press, 2006), 1.

206 Leon J. Wood, *A Survey of Israel's History,* 159.

207 Wood, *A Survey*, 159; D. A. Hubbard, "Priests and Levites," in *NBD* (ed. I. H. Marchall, et al; Secunderabab: OM-Authentic Books, 2007), 956.

208 John Bright, *A History of Israel* (3rd ed.; London: SCM Press, 1981), 435-436.

209 The descendants of Gershon, or Gershonites, the descendants of Kohath, or Kohathites, and the descendants of Merari, or Merarites. Frank Moore Cross, *Canaanite Myth and Hebrew Epic: Essays in the History of the Religion of Israel* (Cambridge: Harverd University Press, 1973), 206.

at the head of the institution. The Mesopotamian priesthood included diviners, magicians, some of whom were women. Generally, the priests acted as scribes and teachers.[210]

However, in Egypt the system or structure was different from Mesopotamia. In contrast to Israel, there was no class of full-time professional priests and priestly office was not meant to be hereditary. In Egypt, since king was raised to the level of gods, "king was the only legitimate priest who could enter into association with the gods."[211] The Pharaoh would have the power to choose someone as priest from the society. Thus, the priests of ancient Egypt were unlike the priests found in other AWA societies. The priests were in charge of keeping order; they made sure that the people followed the rules made by the Pharaoh, who was venerated as god. So, rather than acting as holy figures, the priests were more like members of the local government. Many of the priests served in the temple for part-time and they would engage in another job, serving the state in different level. The priests were organized into four equally staffed groups, each group took its own turn to serve in the temple at the allotted time of the month and then return to their other job for three months and come back to serve in the temple.[212]

In Assyria, priests occupied a very high position in society. They were exempted from taxes and military services and they owned large portions of land and slaves which belonged to the temples. Various instructions of proper conduct were being given to the Hittite priest with regard to the shrine and sacred things, for instance, bodily cleansing, use of the food for offering to gods, guard duty and for sexual relations.[213]

2.2.4. Zadok and Other Priests

In Israel priestly office was hereditary except in the case of Zadok, who came to the priestly office through royal appointed by King David.[214] The origin of Zadok can be traced back to I Chronicals 12:28 "and Zadok, a brave young warrior,

---

210 Edwin A. Ahirika, "Priesthood in Israelite and Igbo Religions: A Comparison," *Bible Bhashyam: An Indian Biblical Quarterly* 27 (2001): 123.

211 Ringgren, "כֹּהֵן, *Kohen*," in *TDOT*, 61-62.

212 James, *An Introduction to Ancient Egypt*, 143.

213 Albrecht Goetze, "Hittite Instructions," in *ANET*, 207-210.

214 George Mendenhall, "The Monarchy," *Interpretation* 29 (1975): 155-170. The status of Zodak is in scholarship discussion for years, however, no conclusive decision about his background has taken place since the early narratives gives absolutely no information as to his background. No information other than that he was a court prophet.

Regarding the function, Martin A. Cohen says since priestly office is hereditary and Zadok came to office through royal appointment there is a difference in functioning, "Abiathar could command the loyalties of the people and the old guard leadership and through them could generate power. Zadok could not. His power came from the king and his loyalty to the monarchy was therefore assured. Martin A. Cohen, "The Role of the Shilonite Priesthood in the United Monarchy of Ancient Israel," *UCA* 36 (1965): 89.

with 22 officers from his family." Christian E. Hauer asserts that Zadok and the 22 officers defected to David in Hebron.[215] The other narrative also supports this incident that Zadok was a Jebusite priest of Jerusalem who, for reasons unknown, went over to the side of David prior to the capture of Jerusalem by the Hebrew army. His actions on behalf of David gained him a position of preferment which was enhanced during David's reign by steadfast loyalty (II Sam 15:24-29) and at David's decline by a judicious choice of factions (I Kgs 1:32-48; 4:4). He became "naturalized" as a Hebrew and came to be recognized as the eponymous head of a powerful faction within the Jerusalem priesthood.[216] The loyalty of Zadok to Davidic kingship is seen in the enthronement of Solomon to be the next king's heir. Abiathar the Shilonite supported Adonijah and Zadok supported Solomon. There appeared personal rivalry that led to the "cultic competition between the two priests."[217] In I Chornicals 6:8-15 there is evidence that the descendants of Zadok were the "chief priests" in Jerusalem "from Solomon till the exile."[218] Saul Olyan suggests three possible reasons for the origin of Zadok coming to the priesthood: (1) Zadok's company of 22 is much smaller than the larger units listed for the other tribes. Hence, this unit is independent of the others (2) Zadok's father's house is anonymous for some unknown reason (3) He is subordinate to the Aaronite leader.[219]

Then, as various priestly families came to hold control in different centres, it was the Zadokites, generally held to be of Jebusite origin, who took control of Jerusalem.[220] In this situation, Josiah's reform suddenly placed the Zadokites in a highly privileged position, because they alone were now recognized as legitimate. The country-priests, on the other hand, were deprived of their livelihood. This privileged (position) of the Zadokites was also a threatened position, however, because the country-priests, anxious to retain their livelihood, now pressed a priestly claim on a new basis, that of Levitical descent.[221] Thus, Josiah's reform produced a situation in which country-priests were pressing a *Levitical* claim

---

215 Christian E. Hauer, "Who was Zadok," *JBL* 82 (1963): 91-92.

216 Hauer, "Who was Zadok," 89-94; Saul Olyan, "Zadok's Origins and the Tribal Politics of David," *JBL* 101 (1982): 177-193; Miller and Hayes, *A History of Ancient Israel and Judah*, 178-179.

217 Saul Olyan, "Zadok's Origins and the Tribal Politics of David," *JBL* 101 (1982): 179.

218 Colin M. Wells, "Levites and Priests," in *ABD (*vol. 5; ed. David Noel Freedman; New York: Doubleday, 1992), 802.

219 Olyan, "Zadok's Origins and the Tribal Politics of David," 178-179.

220 H. H. Rowley, "Zadok and Nehushtan," *JBL* 58 (1939): 113-141; F. M. Cross, *Canaanite Myth and Hebrew Epic: Essay in the History of the Religion of Israel* (Cambridge/Massachusetts: Harvard University Press 1973), 208-220; de Vaux, *Ancient Israel: Its Life and Institutions*, 372-376.

221 Wellhausen, *Prolegomena,* 139. Scholars differ on the manner in which the different priestly families came to press such a claim. See Cody, *History of Israelite Priesthood*; Gunneweg, *Leviten*; Nielsen, *Schechem.*

to serve at the Jerusalem sanctuary, because the reform had deprived them of their living. There are two essential presuppositions of this view: (i) that the only meaningful distinction within the priesthood is that between Jerusalemite (Zadokite) and non-Jerusalemite priests; and (ii) that the non-Jerusalemite priests are to be associated with the priests of the "high-places" which Josiah destroyed (Deut 18:6-8 and II Kgs 23:8-9).

2.2.5. Structure of Priesthood in Israel

The priestly office constituted a threefold hierarchy of cultic officials- high priest, priest and Levite with different functions and privileges. They are as follows:

2.2.5.1. The High Priest

The title "high priest" was used only after the Babylonian exile.[222] Zimmerli remarks that the high priest, as an office, becomes fully developed in the post-exilic period.[223] Cody notes that during the monarchy, this title was not labelled to the temple personnel because the king was "representative of the people before God and as supreme moderator of the national cult, a role which left the head of the professional priests in a position to subordinate to inspire his being given such a title."[224] Therefore, the title seems to have been appropriated in the restored community as there was no king. During the second Temple period, the high priest held the position of "king like" as there was no monarchy and the Temple was the centre of the community.[225] Niehr explains that the "vassal king or governor" was equal with the high priest and they shared the political power together.[226] Therefore, the high priest was supreme in the civil as well as the ecclesiastical realm. The main duty of the high priest was the "operation of the cult" in the Temple and alongside he governed Judah as "a political entity."[227] James C. Vanderkam remarks that one of the functions of the high priests was "cultic role on the Day of Atonement when they entered the holy of holies and offered stipulated sacrifices."[228]

222 Abba, "Priests and Levites," 876; De Vaux, *Ancient Israel: Its Life and Institution*, 397; Aelred Cody, *A History of Israelite Priesthood* (Rome: Pontifical Biblical Institute, 1967), 176.

223 Zimmerli, *Old Testament Theology in Outline*, 95.

224 Cody, *A History of Old Testament Priesthood*, 176.

225 Abba, "Priests and Levites," 878.

226 Hebert Niehr, "Religio-Historical Aspects of the Early Post-Exilic Period," *The Crisis of Israelite Religion: Transformation of Religious Tradition* (ed. Bob Becking & Marjo C. A. Korpel; Leiden: Brill, 1999), 232.

227 Lester L. Grabbe, *An Introduction to Second Temple Judaism: History and Religion of the Jews in the Time of Nehemiah, Maccabees, Hillel and Jesus* (London: T&T Clark, 2010), 42.

228 James C. Vanderkam, *An Introduction to Early Judaism* (Grand Rapids/Michigan: William B. Eerdmans Publishing Company, 2001), 180.

The priestly office, during the second Temple, especially the high priest controlled the Jewish State.[229] Therefore, in this regard the high priest must have come directly to the duties outside the Temple and operated both religious and political roles. Joshua was the high priest during the time of restoration (Zech 3:6-10) and Haggai mentions him as the "high priest" along with Zerubbabel (governor of restored Judah), whereas, in Zechariah he takes the responsibility of the two.[230]

During the time of Ezra and Nehemiah, a lot of work on reformation of the cult is visible. They addressed issues of disobedience by the Jews pertaining to religious matters such as the induction of an Ammonite in the Temple by the high priest, disregarding the tithes of the Levites, desecration of the Sabbath, etc., as seen in Nehemiah 13.[231] These issues are likely to have been carried on in subsequent generations. One of the issues perhaps reflects the apostasy by the Jewish leadership around the Maccabean era. In order to resolve some of the issues Nehemiah formed a committee which was set over the temple treasury. Then the priests were given responsibility "in sole control of the financial affairs of the sanctuary, they were now forced to share that control with the Levites."[232] Along with the economic administration the "priests and Levites were entrusted with taking an inventory of and administering the treasure of silver, gold and precious cult objects brought to Jerusalem by Ezra and his entourage" (Ezra 8:33-34).[233]

There was a significant change in the office of the high priest during the reign of Antiochus (175 BCE) when Jason, the brother of the high priest Onias took over the office by "corruption" and introduced new elements of the Greek culture and religion "at the expense of traditional Jewish practices."[234] The office of the high priest deteriorated further when Menelaus took it over by "outbidding" Jason for the post, and selling the temple utensils to cover his costs.[235] Antiochus IV issued a decree in 167 BCE which forbade the Jews from practising their religious activities and ordered them to follow the customs of the Greek religion.[236] Thus, the cult became corrupted by the practices of religious syncretism and the cult officials were a central part in the disintegration of the cult.

---

229 Grabbe, *An Introduction to Second Temple Judaism*, 42.

230 R. J. Coggins, *Haggai, Zechariah, Malachi* (Sheffield: JSOT Press, 1987), 13.

231 Goldenberg, *Origins of Judaism*, 107.

232 Joachim Schaper, "The Temple Treasury Committee in the Times of Nehemiah and Ezra," *VT* XLVII (1997): 201.

233 Schaper, "The Temple Treasury Committee in the Times of Nehemiah and Ezra," 202.

234 II Macc 4:7b-10, 14-15.

235 II Macc 4:24-25.

236 I Macc1:41-50.

2.2.5.2. Priest

In Israelite society the priest was associated with the high priest and was responsible for the Temple's vessels as well as sacrificial duties of the altar. R.B.Y. Scott explains that one of the main responsibilities of priests was "to give instruction in religious matters as well as to officiate in the sacrificial cultus."[237] They were supported by the offerings given in the Temple such as first fruits of the field; first-born of animals; specified sacrificial dues; and a tenth of the people's tithes. Vanderkam also notes that "the priests were compensated for their work by receiving stipulated parts of many types of sacrifices, contributions, and a tenth of the tithes given to the Levites."[238] They mostly lived in the Temple and took care of the spiritual well-being of the people.

The priests were deported to Babylon during the exile, which made the remaining people in Jerusalem to request the Aaronite priesthood at Bethel to maintain the cultus at Jerusalem. Thus, the Zadokite priests who returned from Babylon could not regain their monopoly, but they gained power eventually and the Aaronites left to Samaria. The Zadokites reclaimed the priestly office by holding the "honourable Aaronic name."[239] Though the pre-exilic prophet like Jeremiah was generally critical of the Jerusalemite priesthood, yet during the exilic period Ezekiel "exalted" them as a plan for the new Jerusalem above the Levites.[240] Therefore, the Zadokites were the priests in Jerusalem after the exile. It is evident that the Zadokites were manipulating the Aaronite priesthood to gain status and position in the community as stated earlier that Temple was the centre of all the organizations and functions of the community.

2.2.5.3. Levite

The Levites were placed at the bottom in the structure/system. Rodney K. Duke remarks that the Levites enjoyed equal rights with the priests at the central sanctuary before they arrived at Jerusalem.[241] The Levites who went to Babylon did not anticipate of their return to Judah because they were considered low and usually served as "servants of the Temple."[242] They were further divided into different classes as singers (I Chron 25), gate-keepers (I Chron 26:1-9), other tasks around the Temple (I Chron 26:20-32).[243] They were supported by the tithes

---

237 R.B. Y. Scott, "Priesthood, Prophecy, Wisdom, and the Knowledge of God," *JBL* 80 (1961): 6.

238 Vanderkam, *An Introduction to Early Judaism,* 176.

239 Abba, "Priests and Levites,"874,879,884, 958; Todd Compton, "Kingdom of Priests: Priesthood, Temple, and Women in the Old Testament and in the Restoration," *Dialogue* 36 (2003): 42.

240 Wells, "Priests and Levites," 806.

241 Rodney K. Duke, "The Portion of the Levite: Another Reading of the Deuteronomy 18:6-8," *JBL* 106 (1987): 194.

242 Hubbard, "Priests and Levites," 958.

243 Cody, *A History of Old Testament Priesthood,* 186.

received in the Temple but they were deprived, therefore they left the Temple and went to their field in order to sustain themselves.[244]

The emergence of monarchy gave rise to a "uniform and structured priesthood" consisting of the high priest, and a "second priest" assisting them,[245] and keepers of the threshold.[246] Hence, Reuss asserts that the priestly lineage (e.g. Zadokites) and genealogy become important from the time of monarchy.[247] Accordingly, the history of Israelite priesthood can be summarized as a structure in which genealogy and hierarchy play a vital role in determining the position and roles of the temple officials.

2.2.6. Priestly Functions/Roles

The priests in OT times did not exalt themselves to the position but were appointed by God, and were subjected to the authority of Moses and the terms of the covenant. They had clearly defined roles and functions which differentiated them from the other Israelites. They performed the following functions:

2.2.6.1. The Priest and the Sanctuary

While priests in the OT had functions beyond temple and ritual, temple and temple-related ritual were central. Cody, writes that, "priestly duties and activities varied somewhat, but primary in the early period, and always basic, was the idea that a priest is a person attached to the service of God in a sanctuary, God's house."[248] Dommershausen, in his article on כֹּהֵן, lists as the priests' first function, guarding the sanctuary.[249] He further explains that the earliest priests were thus charged with guardianship of the sacred precincts and what went on there. Sacrifices are offered by the worshippers themselves, but the priests are permitted to take a portion of the offerings for their sustenance.[250] The priestly ministry is thus primarily an altar ministry. Ringgren, describing the priests in Solomon's temple, writes, "in the pre-monarchic period, the priest appears as the attendant of a sanctuary and a giver of oracles."[251] Since the priests were the guardian of the sanctuary, they were assigned guard duty within the Temple itself.[252] This kind of

244 Hubbard, "Priests," 958.

245 II Kgs 25:18; Jer 53:24; II Chron 19:11; 26:20; 30:10. Horst Dietrich Reuss, *Old Testament Theology* (vol. 2; Louisville: Westminster John Knox Press, 1996), 54.

246 II Kgs 23:4; 25:18; Jer 52:24. De Vaux, *Ancient Israel,* 379.

247 Reuss, *Old Testament*, 54.

248 Cody, "Priests and High Priest," 608; Bruce M. Metzger and Michael D. Coogan, eds., *The Oxford Companion to the Bible* (New York: Oxford University Press, 1993), 608-11.

249 Dommershausen, "köhen," 66-67.

250 Dommershausen, "köhen," 66-67. See also, de Vaux, *Ancient Israel: Its Life and Institution*, 348: "Every priest was chosen and installed to serve in a sanctuary."

251 Ringgren, *Israelite Religion,* 205. See Judg 17; 1 Sam 1-4; 7:1.

252 Duke, "Priests, Priesthood," 654; de Vaux, *Ancient Israel: Its Life and Institutions,* 348.

duty was instituted from the time of Exodus; Aaron's sons were assigned to guard the Tent.

In David's time there was an outnumbering of the priests and Levites and consequently they were divided into twenty-four divisions (I Chron 24:1-31) where each division served in turn for one week.[253] They organized into twenty-four guard rosters or shifts, each of which took its turn to serve in the Temple for a week at a time. Each of the groups served in the temple at least twice in a year.[254] When the ark was brought from Kirjath-jearim to Jerusalem, the Levites were separated into four classes- "those who assisted the priests in the work of the sanctuary; those who judged the legal class and kept the record as scribes; the gatekeepers of the sanctuary; and the musicians (I Chron 24-26)."[255] The priest's cultic duties were largely tied up with the sacred place and structure, the temple. It included animal sacrifice, burnt offerings, cereal, incense, first-fruit, and atonement sacrifice. It also included replacing the bread of the Presence of the Sabbath (Lev 24:8), dressing the lamps in the holy place (Exod 30:7), maintaining all the temple accessories, sounding the festal trumpets (Num 10:8, 10), and "blessing in the name of Yahweh" (Deut 10:8; 21:5; I Chron 23:13). During the week, all the priestly portions of the sacrifices brought to the Temple were distributed among the members of the guard (Deut 18:1-5). In this regard Dommershausen explains that priests were permitted to take a portion of the offerings for their sustenance.[256]

The priest put the prime emphasis on worship and fined joy in ceremonies and ritual observances. They were persons even emotionally involved in the service of God in a sanctuary. De Vaux states that in ancient Israel "every priest was chosen and installed to serve in a sanctuary."[257] The original concept of the priest as minister of God in the sanctuary was equivalent to that of a king's minister in the palace. It is generally understood that the priest was chosen and installed for the service of the sanctuary.[258] The OT identifies the priestly tribe of Levi was mainly set apart to attend to the sanctuary of Yahweh. This unique task, given to them by Yahweh, affected the entire lives of all of the Levites. There was a greater need to be ritually pure: for example, priests were not allowed to drink wine nor could they attend funerals (unless it was a close relative). The Torah forbade

253 Wood, *A Survey of Israel's History*, 159.

254 Vanderkam, *An Introduction to Early Judaism*, 182.

255 John Howard Raven, *The History of the Religion of Israel* (Grand Rapids/MI: Bakers Book house, 1979), 84.

256 Dommershausen, "כֹהֵן," in *TDOT,* 66-60. Priest Eli and his sons serve as priests at Shiloh; the sons are censured for taking the portions due them prematurely of time (I Sam 2:16-17). Abimelech, the priest of Nob, gives David some of the bread of the presence because he does not have any ordinary bread.

257 De Vaux, *Ancient Israel: Its Life and Institutions,* 348.

258 Jenson, "כֹהֵן," in *NIDOTTE,* 600

the priest to marry a divorcee or a "harlot," here including any woman with a promiscuous past (Lev 21:7, 3-15). Priests were also prohibited from coming in contact with the dead, for such contact imparted a forbidden degree of ritual impurity.[259] Moreover, this idea of being set apart for God was also shown in the fact that they received no land, for their inheritance was Yahweh. They wore special garments while entering a tabernacle to intercede for people.

Some of the basic functions of being ministers of the sanctuary included singing Psalms during Temple services, performing construction, looking after the furnishings, maintenance for the Temple, transporting the tabernacle, and performing other services.[260] During the First Temple period one of the emphases on the duty of the high priest was to maintain the physical structure of the Temple. Jehoash's (the king of Judah) instruction to the priests to use the donations made to the temple in order to maintain and repair its physical structure is clearly mentioned in II Kings 12:4 and 5.[261] According to the description of II Kings 12, the priests were responsible for the collection of donations from people towards the maintaining of the physical structure of the Temple and its high priest was responsible for the administration of these funds. The book of Ezra reports that the Levites were responsible for the construction of the Second Temple and also the translation and explanation of the Torah when it was publicly read.

2.2.6.2. Priest and the Divine Oracle

Another function of the priesthood was that of the communicator of the divine will, or the oracle. Especially in the early history of Israel, priests were sought in order to discover God's will (and this would apply to all Levites). One of the main ways the priest would seek out Yahweh's will was by use of the sacred lots, the Ephod and of the Urim and Thummin.[262] The use of these objects, however, was

259 Only in the case of the death of any of seven close relatives may a priest become ritually impure. These relatives include the priest's father, mother, brother, spinster sister, son, daughter, and wife (Lev 21:1-3). As priests cannot walk among the graves in cemeteries, it is customary to have the members of priestly families buried close to the road, so that their survivors can visit their graves. If a priest encounters a dead body and there is no one else to see to the burial, he is duty-bound to bury the body, even though it results in his becoming ritually impure. At funerals of anyone, the priests will generally remain outside the funeral chapel, for being under the same roof with the deceased would render them ritually impure. Cf. Henry McKeating, "Ezekiel 'Prophet like Moses'?" *JSOT* 61 (1994): 101.

260 Jenson, "כֹּהֵן," in *NIDOTTE*, 601.

261 In the parallel version of the story in II Chron 24, the priests are not given the charge to maintain the temple, but rather to collect money for the project (II Chron 24:5), a task that they, and the Levites, are in no hurry to perform. See the discussion of Sara Japhet, J *& II Chronicles: A Commentary* (OTL; London: SCM, 1993), 841-43.

262 Dommershausen, "כֹּהֵן," in *TDOT*, 67 (Num 27:21; Judg 17:5; Hos 3:4; I Sam 14:41; Ezra 2:63); Zimmerli, Old *Testament Theology in Outline*, 96; Thomas L. Leclerc, *Introduction to the Prophets: Their Stories, Sayings, and Scrolls* (New York: Paulist Press, 2007), 287; de Vaux, *Ancient Israel; Its Life and Institutions*, 349.

restricted to the high priest only.[263] The Ephod[264] refers to a number of different things. Two traditions in the Bible speak of the Ephod as a special part of a priest's clothing (Exod 29:5; Lev 8:7) while another tradition speaks of it as merely as an object used for consulting (the will of) Yahweh (I Kgs 20:13; 22:6; II kgs 3:11). While the two definitions might not necessarily be mutually exclusive it is plain to most scholars that the Ephod contained the Urim and Thummin.[265]

No one really seems to know what exactly the Urim and Thummin were. They may have been small stones or sticks. What is clear is that they seemed to work like lots. A person would ask the priest a question and the Urim and the Thummin would be cast to seek out Yahweh's answer.[266] Sigmund Mowinckel explains the usage of Urim and Thummim that, "the priest can mediate revelation through technical means; thus it was the priest who used the Urim and Thummim."[267] An example of their use can be found in I Samuel 14:36-42 when Saul consulted the priest and also Abiathar's use of Urim and Thummim to advise David in battle (I Sam 23).[268] After the reign of David, however, it seems that the use of the Urim and Thummin slowly disappeared. According to Dommershausen, "in postexilic Jerusalem there were no longer any priests capable of using Urim and Thummim, although it is likely that in individual cases priests answered inquiries in God's name, although without using special methods of divination."[269]

263 Wolf Baudissin, "Priests and Levites," *A Dictionary of the Bible* (Vol. IV; ed. James Hastings *et* al; Edinburgh: T&T Clark, 1947), 67; C. Van Dam, "Priestly Clothing," in *Dictionary of the Old Testament Pentateuch* (ed. T. Desmond Alexander and David W Baker; Illinois: InterVarsity Press, 2002), 634.

264 The ephod is to contain two stones on the shoulder pieces (I Sam 23:9-12). On these two stones were engraved the names of the twelve sons of Israel. Aaron was to wear these, "as stones of memorial for the sons of Israel," to bear "their names before the Lord on his two shoulders for a memorial" (Exod 28:6-14). To seek for such an oracle was called "to inquire of God." The oracle itself was regarded as an answer from God. It is narrated that Saul, during the war with the Philistines, brought with him a priest who wore the ephod with the oracle-stones and communicated oracles. David is said to have consulted the priestly oracle frequently and in different affairs. I Sam 23:2,4,9-12; 30:7-8; II Sam 2:1. Other examples of such oracle-giving Numbers 27:21; Judges 18:5-6; 20: 27-28; I Sam 22:10. The mention of the ark in Judges 20:27-28 is the result of a later enlargement of the original tradition; cf. also I Sam 14:18. Sigmund Mowinckel, "Cult and Prophecy," in *Prophecy in Israel: Search for an Identity* (ed. David L. Petersen; Philadelphia: Fortress Press, 1987), 82-83; Anthony Phillips, "David's Linen Ephod," *VT* 19 (1969): 485-487; Neville Tidwell, "Linen Ephod: I Sam 2:18 and II Sam 6:14," *VT* 24 (1974): 505-507.

265 De Vaux, *Ancient Israel: Its Life and Institutions,* 350.

266 H. H. Rowley, *Worship in Ancient Israel,* 1967, 66; Michael S. Moore, "Role Pre-Emption in the Israelite Priesthood," *VT* 46 (1996): 236.

267 Sigmund Mowinckel, "Cult and Prophecy," in *Prophecy in Israel: Search for an Identity* (ed. David L. Petersen (Philadelphia: Fortress Press, 1987), 74.

268 Klaus Koch, *The Prophets Vol. I: The Assyrian Period* (Philadelphia: Fortress, 1983), 17; de Vaux, *Ancient Israel: Its Life and Institution,* 352.

269 Dommershausen, "כֹּהֵן," in *TDOT,* 67. Cf. Jenson, "כֹּהֵן," in *IDOT&E,* 603.

In ancient Israel, casting of lots was practised in making decisions.[270] For instance: to select Saul as Israel's first King (I Sam 10:20-21), to fix responsibility on Jonah for the raging storm (Jonah 1:17), and presumably to determine the guilt of Achan at Jericho (Josh 7:16-21). Along with it, but not necessarily related to it, is the exclusivity of the priest as the one who oracles as Yahweh's instrument of choice to communicate His will to Israel. One might inquire of Yahweh about a sickness (I Kgs 14; II Kgs 18), a military situation (I Kgs 22; II Kgs 3), a lost animal (I Sam 9), or distress of a more religious kind (II Kgs 22). In spite of the many references to casting lots in the OT, nothing is known about the actual lots themselves. They could have been sticks of various lengths, flat stones like coins, or some kind of dice; but their exact nature is unknown. However, in all these cases, the intent was for the priest to reveal the future or to deliver a decision of the deity in a specified situation. Lot casting was also practised among AWA communities to decide right or wrong. There are many variations on the basic technique. In Mesopotamia, for instance, the objects of animals' bones and six-sided clay cubes were used to find out the answer yes or no.[271]

2.2.6.3. The Priest as a Teacher

Teaching the people the law of Yahweh is yet another responsibility of the priestly office. Several passages state that the priests were to be its teachers in both words and deed. For instance, in Leviticus 10:11; Numbers 27:21; Deuteronomy 33:10; Nehemiah 8:7, the priests were given responsibility to teach the people of Israel all the statutes of the LORD. The point of these references was that the survival of Israel depended on how well the people heeded the words of Yahweh which, in turn, depended on how well the priests taught the Torah to them in both theory and in practice. Further, in Deuteronomy, we read that the Levites will "teach His decisions to Jacob and His instructions to Israel" (Deut 26:3-4). This refers to the priestly office of teacher in the Hebrew nation which all Levites could participate in. This consisted in interpreting the law of the Lord and teaching it to the people. Usually this teaching office was performed within or around the temple area. One of the main ways the priest-teacher taught was by way of the Torah. They were the guardian of the Torah. One of their main responsibilities was to maintain the true doctrine and unity of faith.[272] These were short teachings on particular

---

270 Divination by means of the sacred lot is best attested as a priestly function. For detail discussions see: J. Lindblom, "Lot-casting in the Old Testament," *VT* 12 (1962): 164-78; Anne Marie Kitz, "The Hebrew Terminology of Lot Casting and its Ancient Near Eastern Context," *CBQ* 2 (2000): 207-214; E. Robertson, "The Urim and Tummim," *VT* 14 (1964): 67-74.

271 Leclerc, *Introduction to the Prophets*, 28; Anne Marie Kitz, "The Hebrew Terminology of Lot Casting and its Ancient Near Eastern Context," *CBQ* 2 (2000): 207-214.

272 Dommershausen, "כֹּהֵן," in *TDOT*, 67-68; Paul L. Schieber, "Priests Among Priests: The Office of the Ministry in the Light of the Old Testament," *Concordia Journal* 14 (1988): 220; RBY Scott, "Priesthood, Prophecy, Wisdom, and the Knowledge of God," *JBL* 80 (1961): 3. For instance, In Jeremiah 2:8, the prophet attacks the priests, and prophets who were supposed to

topics typically about a practical conduct and cultic worship or ritual purity.[273] Yet it is believed that the priest's teaching authority was not necessarily limited to interpreting the law or to determining ritual purity. One can see the influence of the priest's teaching in the very name of the Pentateuch: the Torah. Like the office of oracle, as the priesthood developed, the office of teacher slowly expanded to those who were not Levites.[274] They served as teachers (teach the knowledge of Yahweh) and judges, maintaining cities of refuge.

2.2.6.4. The Priest and Sacrifice

The priests offered sacrifices for the people of Israel. They were assigned to serve in the Temple and it was they who offered the different sacrifices brought by the people. De Vaux notes that "the offering of sacrifice is seen as the principal function of a priest."[275] There were different kinds of offerings that the people of Israel offered. For instances, burnt offerings, grain offerings, peace offerings, sin-offerings and trespass offerings. And it was the duty of the priests to offer sacrifices. Among the duties of the priests were offering the daily sacrifices each morning and evening and caring for the lamp and the incense burned in the Temple. Those priests with visible disabilities were not permitted to perform the sacrifices in the Temple.

In some sense, all Levites shared in this ministry, but only in degrees. On the lowest end, the non-priestly Levites would help in administration to the altar by doing basic and practical tasks such as transporting the animal sacrifices, or even slaughtering them. Only the priest, however, could perform those tasks which required some kind of necessary contact with the altar such as the sprinkling of the victim's blood or offering the incense.[276] Yet there were also tasks which only the high-priest could perform. This included the entering of the Holy of holies and blessing the people by pronouncing the name of Yahweh during the feast of יוֹם כִּפּוּר (Day of Atonement).[277]

Similar activities were being done by the priest in AWA context. It is understood that the priests were representatives of a society's universal-religion

be the guardians of the Torah; but they refused to learn from Yahweh and therefore cannot tell the people Yahweh's will. In Malachi 2:7, it is the duty of the priest to guard knowledge and proclaim Torah as messengers of Yahweh Sabbath. Ezekiel 44:23 says, "they [the priests] shall teach (Torah) my people the difference between the holy and the common, and show them how to distinguish between the unclean and clean."

273 De Vaux, *Ancient Israel: Its Life and Institutions,* 354.

274 By the time of Jesus, the teaching of the law had moved out of the temple into the synagogue and was performed mostly by the rabbis instead of the priests.

275 De Vaux, *Ancient Israel: Its Life and Institutions,* 355.

276 Jenson, "כֹּהֵן," in *NIDOTTE*, 602; Dommershausen, "כֹּהֵן," in *TDOT,* 69; Zemmerli, *Old Testament Theology in Outline*, 97.

277 For detail study see, Rav A. Soloff, "Yom Kippur: Cover up or Plea for Probation?" *Jewish Biblical Quarterly* 25 (1997): 86-89 (Lev 16:3-22).

concept. Thus, the priest officiated at religious services to national gods: the priest conducted annual rites; rites of passages; all rites connected with order within the community and with the rhythm of the entire life cycle. In Ugaritic sacrificial texts, most of the animals named belonged either to the category of sheep and goats, birds were also fairly frequently mentioned.[278] Priests in Assyria were engaged in exorcism, offered sacrifices to the deities, and performed ritual sacred marriages. In Egypt, priests functioned as judges and magistrates occasionally. Other related duties were: ritually magic services to the god of his temple and performing funeral rites for the dead.[279]

2.2.6.5. The Priest as Mediator

There are several roles that the priests undertook as religious leaders of the society. One of the roles played by the priests was being "mediators between gods and human" that marked them out as important and valuable members of society. The priests were to perform the task of mediation through cultic sacrifices. Philip Jenson notes this in the light of one single idea: the priest as mediator between God and human.[280] According to Todd Compton, a priest is an especially holy and pure person serving as a mediator between God and man, was virtually always connected with a temple and performed ordinances connected with it-sacrifice, purification, and prayer.[281] The mediation of sacrifices purged humans, drawing them closer to the realm of God, now centred in the sanctuary. The central element in Israel's life was worship at altars or sanctuaries overseen by priests.[282] The whole עֹלָה "burnt offering," חַטָּאָה "sin offering," אָשָׁם "guilt offering," and שְׁלָם "well-being/peace offering" even allowed Israelites to feast in the presence of God before the sanctuary.[283] The priesthood was an institution for mediation. The priest represented God before people when he conveyed God's message, when he gave an instruction and explained the Torah. Likewise the priest represented people before God, when he offered sacrifice for the sins of the individual, and burned incense upon the altar.[284] The priests stood before God in prayer and petitions for several reasons, for the needs of the individual and of the nation.

278 Dennis Pardee, "Divinatory and Sacrificial Rites," *Near Eastern Archaeology* 63 (2000): 234.

279 Ringgren, "כֹּהֵן, *Kohen*," in *TDOT*, 63.

280 Jenson, "כֹּהֵן," in *NIDOTTE*, 600.

281 Todd Compton, "Kingdom of Priests: Priesthood, Temple and Women in the Old Testament and Restoration," *Dialogue* 36 (2003): 42.

282 Fredrick C. Holmgren, "Priests and Prophets: Spirituality and Social Conscience," *Worship* 79 (2005): 306.

283 See the interpretation of sacrifices by G. J. Wenham, *The Book of Leviticus* (NICOT; Grand Rapids: Eerdmans, 1979), 47-112; D. R. Jones, "Sacrifices and Holiness," in *Sacrifice and Redemption* (ed. S. W. Sykes; Cambridge: Cambridge University Press, 1991), 9-21; R. Nelson, *Raising Up a Faithful Priest: Community and Priesthood in Biblical Theology* (Louisville: Westminster John Knox Press, 1993), 55-82.

284 De Vaux, *Ancient Israel: Its Life and Institutions*, 357.

Even in AWA context, the priests, being the mediators, were expected to know the will of gods, thus, they practised divination, casting lots, and interpretation of dreams in order to find out the will of gods for the people. Since they could find out the possible messages for the people in times of need, they remained popular leaders in the society.

2.2.6.6. The Priest as Judge

In each town in ancient Israel, judges were being appointed for the welfare of the society, however, in disputed cases, priests assisted as judges. Priests were responsible in settling the cases in Israelite society.[285] They functioned as judges, as Dommershausen puts it, "in disputed cases (lawsuits, manslaughter, bodily injury) they and the secular judges are to arrive at a ruling together (Deut 17:8-13; 21-5)."[286] II Chronicals 19:8 states, King Jehoshaphat appointed Levites, priests, and heads of families to disputed cases in Jerusalem. Also in Ezekiel 44:24 records that the priests are to conduct judgement when there are disputes in the land. The text (I Chron 26:30-32) clearly states that when David took over Transjordan, he appointed members of the Hebronite levitical families as his officials and they were sent out for all the work of Yahweh and for the king's service. From this, one can assume that the Levites not only officiated as priests but "as civil servants or judges," and as a "police force…who supervised all the affairs of Yahweh and the king on both sides of the Jordan."[287] Thus, one can conclude that priests and Levites participated in solemn legal proclamation throughout monarchy but the full involvement of the priests in legal transactions is probably best ascribed to the period when Israel ceased to be an independent state.

2.2.7. Appraisal

Priestly office was very ancient and the most prominent as far as the history of Israel is concerned. Yahweh explicitly revealed His will regarding the conduct of the priests and His regulations of their varied ministries (Lev 21; Num 18). From this instruction it is apparent that they were called into a high vocation and were expected to contribute to the development of the religious and civil life of the nation. However, a careful study of Leviticus 16:21 and Numbers 18 reveals that the priests were fallible men who had to strive for holiness in much the same way as their fellow Israelites. The study also reveals that priestly office experienced much instability in the course of history of Israel. Bruce K. Waltke remarks that "Israel's priesthood during the time of rule by warlords has failed to provide the nation the leadership it needs."[288] In fact the priests were considered as the teachers whose task was to teach the Torah to the people: the right living.

---

285 Duke, "Priests, Priesthood," 653.

286 Dommershausen, "כֹּהֵן," in *TDOT,* 69.

287 De Vaux, *Ancient Israel: Its Life and Institutions,* 133.

288 Bruce K. Waltke, *Old Testament Theology* (Grand Rapids, Michigan: Zondervan, 2007), 683.

According to David Wanefsky, "the priests were supposed to be the natural allies of the prophets in their fight against the immoral indulgences of the kings, their ministers, and the people. Unfortunately, however, the priest succumbed quickly under the pressure exerted by kings and people. They lined up on the side of those forces which promised a more abundant life."[289] The priests failed to perform their duties and, in effect, the people did not heed the law. This led to a sequence of ups and downs in the collective life of Israel that culminated in the judgement of God.

The study also shows that Hebrew priesthood was unduly influenced by the prophets' disparagement of mere cultic observance, and by the pictures of such unlovely characters as the sons of Eli and Amaziah, the priest of Bethel. In fact, it was the corruption of such priests and their failure to convey to the people the knowledge of God which was their duty to teach, and which became the chief point of prophetic criticism. The priests failed to do their due responsibility, to teach their household, and together they failed to teach the children of Israel to "know the Lord" (I Sam 2:12, 22-24; 3:18; II Chron 15:3). In this way the priests failed miserably in their leadership. Thus, corruption and decline of the priesthood became inevitable.

It is also understood that there were divisions in the priestly office in the OT times where confusion crept in. However, the discussion above makes it clear that the priests in the OT were specially anointed people assigned to carry out the responsibility of being the "intermediaries" between God and the people which is the most important function. The priests were practically associated with the temple and they carried out the tasks related to it such as sacrifice and prayer. The study also shows that priesthood was instituted under a covenant mediator. To the priests, Israel's tradition meant that Yahweh had chosen her to be a priestly kingdom and a continuing religious community and that he was ever-present at her shrines. The priests were concerned with the wisdom embodied in the traditional Torah; the keeping of the statutes and ordinances of Yahweh would give Israel a reputation among the nations as a wise and understanding people. The priests spoke of what among the nations as a wise and understanding people. Thus, Israel looked to its priests for instruction in knowledge of God through the story of his promises and saving deeds, and through their declaring the ethical obligations of his covenant and the requirements of his cult.

2.3. Prophetic Leadership

In ancient Israel, prophets did not hold any recognized leadership office (except court-prophets like Nathan and Gad) like the royals and the priests. However, they were the main critique of the priests and the royals with the interest of Israel's welfare. Their messages and writings occupy a large portion of the Hebrew

---

289 Rabbi David Wanefsky, *The Prophets Speaks to us Anew* (New York: Philosophical Library, 1952), ix.

Bible.[290] Thus, the prophets were unique among ancient Israelite leaders in that, unlike other functionaries, they claimed no personal part in the communication which they conveyed. The Prophets acted as leaders in the life of the people of Israel, because they were regarded by themselves as well as the people of their time. The following section is an attempt to study the leadership role carried out by the prophets in Israelite's society.

2.3.1. Etymological Survey

2.3.1.1. The term נָבִיא

There is no common agreement among scholars concerning the etymological background of the primary term for נָבִיא "prophet." Thus. the primary meaning of the word "prophet" still needs to be considered. Some scholars have tried to connect it with the Hebrew verb נבא, which means "to bubble forth," or "gush forth."[291] Others tried to connect the noun prophet to the Akkadian verb (the passive participle of a verb) *nabu'*, which means "to call," or "to announce," and in the prologue to his law code, the Babylonian king Hammurabi referred to himself as *nibit Enlil,* "one called by the god Enlil," it means a person designated for an important function in the society.[292] David L. Petersen also takes it in the passive sense as one who is called (by God) to a certain task.[293] Similarly, a "prophet" of the Lord is "one called" by God to serve as a deputy, a representative, an ambassador from the court of heaven-"one called" by God to be a spokesperson for God. He is a person who proclaims the words that God tells him (Jer 19:2). The prophet, as one who has been called, is a man and woman of vocation. Others take it in the active sense נָבִיא, as an announcer, a proclaimer of a message.[294] The verb

290 The division of the Hebrew Canon, the Prophets, falls into two sections; The former prophets-Joshua, Judges, Samuel and Kings, and the later prophets, which includes the Major and Minor Prophets.

291 Whether the Lord poured forth his word or the prophet poured them out like a spring. The ecstatic dimension in the prophetic experience was assumed in either interpretation. However, this view is technically unsound, and has nothing to commend it except that it tries to establish a basis for the idea that ecstasy is fundamental to all prophecy. Simon B. Parker argues against the relation of the possession trance and Israelite prophecy in "Possession Trance and Prophecy in Preexilic Israel," *VT* 28 (1987): 271-85. Cf. R. K. Harrison, *Introduction to the Old Testament* (Grand Rapids Wm B Eerdmans Publishing Co, 1969), 742; Joseph Blenkinsopp, *Sage, Priest, Prophet* (Louisville: Westminster, 1995), 124; Leon Wood, *The Prophets of Israel* (Grand Rapids Baker Book House, 1979), 60.

292 This has given rise to another form of explanation; the prophet has been called by deity (Exod 3:1-4, 17; Isa 6; Jer 1:4-19; Ezek 1-3; Hos 1:2; Amos 7:14-15; Jonah 1:1). Cf. Harrison, *Introduction to the Old Testament*, 742.

293 David L. Petersen, *The Prophetic Literature: An Introduction* (Louisville/London: Westminster John Knox Press, 2002), 6.

294 Harrison, *Introduction to the Old Testament*, 742; Leon Wood, *The Prophets of Israel* (Grand Rapids: Baker Book House, 1979), 60.

corresponding to the noun נָבִיא is *hithnabbe,* meaning "to prophesy."[295] Robert L. Wilson links נָבִיא with stereotypical prophetic behaviouristic patterns that might vary from group to group.[296] Interestingly, Max Weber compares the prophet to a *guru,* a charismatic man, who by his charisma internalized his teaching among his followers.[297] God authorized his messengers to pour forth the word. They were proclaimers, publishers, speakers, namely, of God and His secrets. They were charged with a burden, a word from Yahweh that they had no choice but to deliver.

The word "prophet" in Babylonian and Mari is *muhhu/muhhhutum,*[298] (fem. *Muhhutu*) in Assyrian *mahhu,* the word is derived from the root *mahu,* which means "to become crazy," "to go into a frenzy," "to go into trance."[299] In Mari inscription, there is another title for prophet, persons who are attested or engaged in prophetic activities are also called *apilu(m)* (fem. *äpiltu),*[300] *it comes from the root word apalu,* meaning "one who answers."[301] The etymology suggests that the "Answerer" gave oracles in response to the questions put to the god.[302] In Meri's

295 In Amos 7:12-16 the meaning of this word in the context pointedly indicates that Amos was prophesying when he was speaking God's message. In some instances the verb "to prophesy" involves the idea "to praise," as is apparent in I Chronicles 25:1-3. This may also have been the activity described in Numbers 11:25-29, I Samuel 10:1-13; 19:18-24; Jeremiah 26:20; Ezekiel 37:9-10. In none of these references is there any indication that a divine revelation occurred in which a new message from God was given to the participants.

In two references "to prophesy" may mean "to rave" or "to act violently" (I Sam 18:10 and I Kgs 18:29). In neither case is a message given, but violent activity is indicated. Leon J. Wood, "Ecstasy and Israel's Early Prophets," *Bulletin of the Evangelical Theological Society* 9 (1966): 125-37, points out that in all the references above, described that the prophetic message or activity is "not basically intellectual but emotional." Applying these secondary meaning of "praising" and "raving" to the basic idea of "speaking a message," Wood concludes that "to prophesy" in its full sense means "to speak fervently." Say Wood in his conclusion, "the prophet if he speaks in character as a true prophet spoke with emotion. He put his heart into his message. He proclaimed with strength. He did not recite words but preached a message." Cf. H. H. Rowley, "The Nature of Prophecy in the Light of Recent Study," *The Harvard Theological Review* 38 (1945): 1-38; Robert R. Wilson, *Prophecy and Society in Ancient Israel* (Philadelphia: Fortress Press, 1980), 136-38.

296 Robert R. Wilson, "Prophecy and Ecstasy: A Reexamination," *JBL* 98(1979): 321-37.

297 Max Weber, "The Prophet," in *Prophecy in Israel: Search for an Identity* (ed. David L. Petersen; Philadelphia: Fortress Press, 1987), 99-111.

298 *Muhhutum,* are sometime called cultic prophets, and prophetic activities were confined to the temple.

299 Wilson, *Prophecy and Society in Ancient Israel,* 103.

300 *apil(t)um* activities were mostly travelling from place to place. Nissinen, *Prophets and Prophecy in the Ancient Near East,* 6.

301 Nissinen, *Prophets and Prophecy in the Ancient Near East,* 6; Herbert B. Huffmon, "Prophecy in the Mari letters," *Biblical Archaeologist* 31 (1968): 107-8; Cf. Wilson, *Prophecy and Society in Ancient Israel,* 100-102.

302 Huffmon, "Prophecy in the Mari letters," 105.

context, prophets were considered as "servants of the gods whose words they proclaimed."[303] Thus, a prophet is a person who receives a message from someone superior and conveys that message to the people.

The etymological argument, however, is quite inconclusive, and we have no certainty as to the primary meaning of the root. For this, OT does provide information concerning the precise meaning of the term. Exodus 7:1-2 states, "The LORD said to Moses, See, I have made you like God to Pharaoh, and your brother Aaron shall be your prophet. You shall speak all that I command you, and your brother Aaron shall tell Pharaoh to let the Israelites go out of his land." These verses show that the prophets' function was as spokespersons for another, it makes the prophet a leader: Aaron spoke for Moses and Moses spoke for God (Exod 4:15-1). And both Moses and Aaron become leaders of Israelites. In other words, prophets were the one who were consider as mediators between God and the people, and God charged them to be leaders of His people.[304] This idea is conformed in Deuteronomy 18:15-22 where the prophet arising after Moses is one who will speak for God and becomes a leader. They stand between God and human-being with the responsibility of faithfully declaring to people the whole purpose of God.

2.3.1.2. The term for "Seer"

The two words רֹאֶה, and חֹזֶה, are synonyms. Both are translated as "seer."[305] It is difficult to establish any distinction in meaning. Some have argued that רֹאֶה emphasizes the ability to see by visions things the ordinary man could not see.[306] This individual may have been connected with the cult. On the other hand, חֹזֶה is thought to be the official diviner in the king's court.[307] Some have supposed that in the evolution of usage נָבִיא came to be the general term for the older expressions, רֹאֶה and חֹזֶה.[308] Others have proposed the two terms are rooted in regional differences, specifically that רֹאֶה belongs to the Ephramite literature while חֹזֶה belongs to the Judean tradition.[309] Petersen explains that רֹאֶה was a public and social figure, a man, who was fully integrated into the structures of Israelite

303 Nissinen, *Prophets and Prophecy in the Ancient Near East*, 16.

304 Dommershausen, "כֹּהֵן," in *TDOT*, 73; Victor H. Matthews, *Social World of the Hebrew Prophets* (Peabody: Hendrickson Publishers, Inc, 2001), 47.

305 For discussions of these terms see: *BDB*, 302, 909; Robert D. Culver, "*rō'eh*," in *TWOT*, 2:823-825; D. Vetter, "חֹזֶה," in *THAT*, 1:534-538; A. Jepsen, "chōzeh," in *TDOT*, 4:280-290; Rendtroff, *TDNT*, 6:809; Morris Jastrow, "*Rō 'eh* and *ḥōzeh* in the Old Testament," *JBL* 28 (1909): 42-56; H. M. Orlinsky, "The Seer in Ancient Israel," *Or Ant* 4 (1965): 153-174.

306 A. B. Davidson, *Old Testament Prophecy* (Edinburgh: T&T Clark, 1903), 82.

307 Jastrow, "*rō 'eh* and *ḥōzeh*," 50; Rendtroff, *TDNT*, 6:809.

308 Jastrow, "*Rō'eh* and *Hōzeh*," 51; Johannes Lindblom, *Prophecy in Ancient Israel* ((Philadelphia: Fortress, 1976), 94.

309 Wilson, *Prophecy*, 140, 254.

society, as in the case of Samuel.[310] Prophet Gad is called by David חֹזֶה (II Sam 24:11; Amos 7:12, Mic 3: 7), thus it is difficult to conclude concerning the role of a "seer" in the strict sense.[311] The title חֹזֶה is found mostly in Chronicles, where the חֹזִים are presented among the temple musicians.

2.3.1.3. The term "The Man of God"

The term אִישׁ הָאֱלֹהִים is translated "(the) man of God."[312] The term refers to individual males in a positive manner of whom stories were told of God's mighty acts through him, for example Samuel, Elijah and Elisha.[313] Matthijs J. De Jong states that "in the biblical traditions, 'man of God' is often synonymous with 'prophet'."[314] Some infer that the נָבִיא has the distinction of being called an הָאֱלֹהִים אִישׁ because he is one that was thought to be more closely related to God than other men. This means he has "divine qualities bestowed on him,"[315] which allow him to perform miracles, see the future, and proclaim it as God's messenger. Others see in the term no more than the English phrase "a holy man."

2.3.1.4. Summary

Scholars have sought in one way or another to connect all three (רֹאֶה, חֹזֶה, and אִישׁ הָאֱלֹהִים of these terms with נָבִיא. They connect with נָבִיא in contexts which suggest that the terms have the same meaning (I Sam 2:27; I Kgs 12:22; 13:1; 20:28).[316] The terms are considered "synonyms" which emphasize different prophetic functions. Several lines of evidence point to these conclusions:

(i) I Samuel 9:9 says that the term נָבִיא superseded the term רֹאֶה.
(ii) The translators of the Septuagint translated both רֹאֶה and חֹזֶה by the term *prophets*.
(iii) When the term אִישׁ הָאֱלֹהִים comes with a specific word from Yahweh, the context suggests the same meaning as נָבִיא (I Sam 2:27; I Kgs 12:22; 13:1; 20:28).

310 David L. Petersen, *The Roles of Israel's Prophets* (JSOT 17; Sheffield: JSOT, 1981), 38-40 (1 Chron. 9:22; 29: 29).

311 Lindblom, *Prophecy*, 89-90.

312 For discussions of this term see: N. P Bratisiotis, " 'îš," in *TDOT*, 1:222-235; J. Küblewein,"'îš," *THAT*, 1:130-138; Rendtorff, *TDNT*, 6:809; Raphael Hallevy, "Man of God," *JNES* 17 (1958): 237-244.

313 Koch Klaus, *The Prophets: The Assyrian Period* (London: SCM Press Ltd, 1982), 18; David, *The Roles of Israel's Prophets*, 40-50.

314 Matthijs J. De Jong, *Isaiah among the Ancient Near Eastern Prophets: A Comparative Study of the Earliest Stages of the Isaiah Tradition and the Neo-Assyrian Prophecies* (Boston: Leiden, 2007), 320.

315 Davidson, *Prophecy*, 79; Lindblom, *Prophecy in Ancient Israel*, 73.

316 Rendtorff, *TDNT*, 6:809.

(iv) In I Kings 13:18, though there is an obvious contrast between the older נָבִיא and the younger אִישׁ הָאֱלֹהִים, *the older prophet says, "I am also a prophet like you."*

(v) Though Amaziah calls Amos a חֹזֶה (Amos 7:12), his response (Amos 7:14) indicates that he regarded the terms as synonymous.

All of these terms, while giving some insight into the nature of prophecy, provide "no real aid to understanding the function or office of prophet."[317] The very existence of these different titles may suggest a period in Israel's history when there existed an uncertainty as to the identification of the prophetic roles. If Israel itself had trouble identifying the prophetic roles, it is not surprising that "there is a certain artificiality" in these distinctions of scholars or that the basis of these distinctions "is the conclusions of scholars rather than what is to be found in the pages of the Old Testament."[318] The inadequacy of the prophetic titles to produce a very coherent picture of prophecy in Israel forced scholars to turn to terms which for the most part do not occur in the literature at all. This "broadening the search for comparative material both geographically and chronologically" has resulted in hypothetical constructs which make attempt to describe prophecy largely by analogy.[319]

Scholars have used biblical and extra-biblical models in their attempts to develop an all- encompassing definition of prophecy. Thus, Davidson can define the prophet as "one who speaks to men for God," and then go on to argue that they are men of God, servants, messengers, interpreters, mediators, statesmen, revolutionists, counsellors, upholders of theocratic law, maintainers of law, etc.[320] Muilenburg, while arguing that the prophets stood in the tradition of Moses as covenant mediators, can speak of them as messengers, speakers for Yahweh, proclaimers of the law, apostles, and politicians.[321] The result is that each term emphasizes a particular aspect of prophetic activity.

2.3.2. Moses as Prophet

The first person whom the Bible calls a נָבִיא (prophet) was Abraham (Gen 20:7), but OT prophecy received its normative form in the life and person of Moses, who constituted a standard of comparison for all future prophets (Deut 18:15-19; 34:10). Every feature which characterized the true prophet of Yahweh in the

---

317 Hayes, *Introduction*, 261.

318 J. R. Porter, "The Origins of Prophecy in Israel," in *Israel's Prophetic Tradition: Essays in Honour of P. R. Ackroyd* (eds. Richard Coggins, Anthony Phillips and Michael Knibb; Cambridge: Cambridge University, 1982), 17. Wilson observes essentially the same thing in his discussion of "Seer," *Prophecy*, 140.

319 Blenkinsopp, "Prophecy," 324.

320 Davidson, *Prophecy*, 89.

321 James Muilenburg, "The 'Office' of the Prophet in Ancient Israel," in *The Bible in Modern Scholarship* (ed. J. Philip Hyatt; Nashville: Abingdon, 1965), 96.

classical tradition of OT prophecy was first found in Moses. He received a specific and personal call from God. The initiative in making a prophet rests with God (Exod 3:1-4:17; cf. Isa 6; Jer 1:4-19; Ezek 1-3; Hos 1:2; Amos 7:14-15), and it is only the false prophet who dares to take the office upon himself (Jer 14:14; 23:21). The primary object and effect of the call was an introduction into God's presence. This was the "secret" or "counsel" of the LORD (I Kgs 22:19; Jer 23:22; Amos 3:7).[322] The prophet stood before people, as a man and a woman who had been made to stand before God (I Kgs 17:1; 18:15).

Again, the prophetic awareness of history stemmed from Moses. When Isaiah makes his tremendous polemic against idolatry, one of his most potent contentions, that Yahweh alone is the author of prophecy and that the idols are at best wise after the event (Isa 45:20-22), stems directly from Moses and the Exodus.[323] The purpose of Yahweh sending Moses into Egypt was to interpret the great events which were to follow in the history of Israel. History became revelation. Moses was not left to struggle for the meaning of events as or after they happened; he was forewarned of events and of their significance by the verbal communications of Yahweh. So, it was with all the prophets. J. Kenneth Eakins remarks, "Moses became the faithful servant (*'eded*) of Yahweh" because he submit "to the leadership of God."[324] Israel always had a true awareness of history. They owed it to the prophets, and, under the LORD of history, the prophets owed it to Moses.

Likewise they owed to him their ethical and social concern. Even before his call Moses concerned himself with the social welfare of his people (Exod 2:11-17), and afterwards, as the prophetic lawgiver, he outlined the most humane and philanthropic code of the ancient world, concerned for the helpless (Deut 24:19-22) and the enemy of the oppressor (Lev 19:9-22).

Many of the prophets were found confronting their kings and playing an active, statesman's part in national affairs.[325] This was a function of the prophet which found its prototype in Moses, who legislated for the nation, and was even called "king" (Deut 33:5).[326] It is interesting that the first two kings of Israel were also prophets (I Sam 10:10-11; 19:32-24), but this union of offices did not

322 Hava Shalom-Guy, "The Call Narratives of Gideon and Moses: Literary Convention or More?" *JHS* 11 (2011): 5; Jimmie L.Nelson, "His Servants, the Prophets," *SJT* 24 (1981): 87; T. T. Crabtree, "The Prophet's Call-A Dialogue With God: As Seen In Jeremiah," *SJT* 4 (1961): 33-56; Robert R. Wilson, "Prophecy in Crisis: The Call of Ezekiel," *Interpretation* 38 (1984): 127.

323 Eugene H. Merrill, "Isaiah 40-55 As Anti-Babylonian Polemic," *Grace Theological Journal* 8 (1987): 3-18; Diana Lipton, "Bezalel in Babylon? Anti-Priestly Polemics in Isaiah 40-55," *JANES* 31 (2008): 62-84.

324 J. Kenneth Eakins, "Moses," *Review & Expositor* 74 (1977): 469.

325 For instance: Nathan (II Sam 12); Elijah (I Kgs 18); Amos (Amos 7:10-17); Isaiah (Isa 7).

326 Paitick D. Miller, Jr., "Moses my Servant," *Interpretation* 41 (1897): 248.

continue, and the Mosaic-theocratic role was prolonged by the association of the anointed king and the anointed prophet.

We also see in Moses that combination of proclamation and prediction which is found in all the prophets. This will concern us in greater detail presently, as a feature of prophecy at large. Moses established the norm here also, namely, that in the interests of speaking to the present situation the prophet often undertakes to enlarge upon events yet to come. It is this interlocking of proclamation and prediction which distinguishes the true prophet from the mere prognosticator. Even when Moses uttered his great prophecy of the coming Prophet (Deut 18:15-22) he was dealing with the very pressing problems of the relation of the people of God to the practices and allure ends of pagan cults.

Two other features characteristic of the prophets who were to succeed him are found in Moses. Many of the prophets used symbols in the delivery of their message (for example, Jer 19:1-13; Ezek 4:1-15). Moses used the uplifted hand (Exod 17:8-12), and the uplifted serpent (Num 21:8), not to mention the highly symbolic cultus which he mediated to the nation. And finally, the intercessory aspect of the prophetic task was also displayed in him. He was for the people to God, represented the people before God and brought their cases before God (Exod 18:19; Num 27:5) and on at least one notable occasion literally stood in the breach as a man of prayer (Exod 32:30-32; Deut 9:18 cf. I Kgs 13:6; II Kgs 19:4; Jer 7:16; 11:14).

Prophets are figures closely associated with the word of God. Moses is one with whom God spoke "face to face, clearly, and not in riddles" (Num 12:8), and God promises that when he raises up a prophet like Moses, "I will put my words in the mouth of the prophet" (Deut 18:15-18). The classic introduction to the words of the prophet is "Thus said Yahweh." Amos is to introduce his message with, "Now then hear the word of the Yahweh" (Amos 7:16). God tells Jeremiah to "say whatever I command you," and God then reaches out his hand and touches his mouth and says, "Now I have put my words in your mouth" (Jer 1:7,9). Later, Jeremiah says, "your words were found and I ate them, and your words became to me a joy and the delight of my heart" (Jer 15:16). We read of Jeremiah and Ezekiel that "the word of Yahweh came" to them (Jer 1:2,4; Ezek 1:3). When a prophet proclaims an "oracle," or "declaration," it is a "lifting up [of the voice]" (Isa 13:1; 15:1; 17:1). With such emphasis on the word of the Lord, the prophets are among the finest word of the Bible. They are as many poets as are the psalmists, and their use of imagery is second to none.

It is clear that God's sending of prophets to Israel is a privilege, the special provision of an extra opportunity for the people to hear what should already have been understood because of its inclusion in the law. There was a hope that just as the prophets of old spoke out for God and told of his intervention in human history, so in the future there would be a "prophet like Moses" who would be the precursor of the supreme intervention of God in his world, and perhaps even a prophet who could reflect God with no possibility of dilution or distortion (Deut 18:15). We might say that the entire story of the prophets, beginning with the death of Moses, is in search of another "prophet like Moses." The role is fulfilled by the prophets.

2.3.3. Who are Called Prophets?

To prove who is to be called a prophet is a difficult subject, since most of the ancient Israel's prophets refused to be addressed as נָבִיא "prophet." For example, several passages of the book of Isaiah the word נָבִיא is not applied to Isaiah himself. Rather it is usually applied to those in society whom Isaiah criticizes for leading people astray (Isa 9:15). Only in Isaiah 37:2; 38:1; and Isaiah 39:3, in the narrative portion that corresponds to II Kings 18-20, is Isaiah called a prophet. The designation never recurs in Isaiah 40-66.[327] John Barton suggests that those we call prophets were not prophets at all, but lay people "whose assumption of the prophet's mantle was just as much a ploy to command a hearing as was their use of forms of speech properly at home in the lawcourt, the diplomatic service, or the cult."[328] The title later attributed to them domesticated and regularized activities that were at the time when they spoke characterized by social protest and opposition. Amos and Micah similarly use the term only negatively (Amos 7:14; Mic 3:5, 6, 11) and never in relation to themselves.[329] It is safe to say that in the time of Isaiah and his colleagues a prophet was someone who presumed to speak for God, but not necessarily someone others believed was doing so. Only later, during and after the exile, did the term assume a more consistently positive meaning as the roll of those of bygone generations who were hailed as true prophets stabilized.

Another difficult issue in this discussion is discerning the true from the false prophets. In the history of Israel there is difficulty in discerning the true from the false prophets. According to biblical teaching, prophets were false when they misled people (Deut 13:2; 18:20; Jer 2:8; 23:27), when their morals were loose (Jer 23:14), or when they practised magic and divination (Isa 8:19; 14:14). Willem A. VanGemeren remarks, "false prophets belonged to the socially and religiously acceptable institution of 'professional' prophets who responded to the needs of their time. They operated from within the limited perspectives of their contemporaries. These prophets encouraged the people by giving concrete

327 In Isaiah 30:10 is actually חֹזִים, "visionaries," paralleling רֹאִים, "seers." These two terms, along with "man of God," served as synonyms for "prophet," though connotative distinctions are not precisely understood.

328 John Barton, *Oracles of God: Perceptions of Ancient Prophecy in Israel after the Exile* (London: Darton, Longman and Todd, 1986), 272.

329 See also Hoses 4:5, Amos' refusal of the designation in Amos 7:14, the overwhelming negativity in Jeremiah's oracles toward the prophets, beginning in Jeremiah 2:8, and in Ezekiel 13:2, the criticisms of prophets in Zephaniah 3:4, Lamentations 2:9, 14; 4:13, and the absence of the term altogether from Joel, Obadiah, Jonah, and Nahum.

solutions in crisis and by speaking comforting words based on their understanding of the Word of God."[330] The false prophets did not realize that they posed a threat to the prophets of God and that they deceived the people of God. The false prophets did not completely reject Yahweh and his way, but they were blind to God's greatness. They all had one goal: self, power, greed and self-justification.

The issues involved in this discussion are, how could a true prophet be distinguished from a false one? How could one judge between diametrically opposed messages of two seemingly genuine prophets? The problem is there is no firm set of criteria for distinguishing "true" from "false" prophets. Thomas W. Overhold notes that "the designation of these prophetic opponents as "false" rests solely upon the specific content of their message."[331] But, it is hard to measure by their messages because all prophets claim that they received message from Yahweh. For example, the prophet Hananiah spoke without obvious authority, for he came forward in the name of Yahweh (note the use of the messenger formula in Jer 28:2,11) and succeeded in handing Jeremiah an apparent initial defeat. Hananiah was no mere impostor, and it is clear that his "falsity" was not immediately obvious to Jeremiah. We can assume that he was conscious of a prophetic call, and we have no reason to doubt his conviction that he spoke Yahweh's word.

The curious thing is that considered apart from its historical context, there is nothing particularly "false" about Hananiah's message. Hananiah asserted that the fortunes of the city were about to be restored (Jer 28:2-4,10). In doing so, he stood firmly within the tradition of the prophet Isaiah, who was convinced that Zion would never fall (cf. Isa 1:7; 31:4; 33:17-22). This means that the problem to be faced here was not one involving the prophetic message in abstraction from its historical context. G. von Rad recognizes this when he interprets the confrontation between Jeremiah and Hananiah as raising the question of the correspondence between prophecy and history. Since for Israel, history was the place in which Yahweh's rule was recognizable.[332] This becomes the crucial issue in the matter of false prophecy. It is the historical context alone that makes an otherwise unobjectionable message "false." Hananiah was guilty of misreading Israel's election faith. It is certainly true that Yahweh has chosen this people and wills their salvation (cf. Deut 7:6; 20:4), but Hananiah had apparently forgotten that the covenant also carries with it definite obligations which the people must fulfil. He did not have the right perception and apparently failed to interpret the political events of his day as a punishment levelled by Yahweh against a sinful people.

---

330 Willem A. VanGemeren, *Interpreting the Prophetic Word* (Grand Rapids/Michigan: Zondervan, 1990), 59.

331 Thomas W. Overhold, "Jeremiah 27-29: The Question of False Prophecy," *JAAR* 35 (2967): 244.

332 Gerhard von Rad, *The Message of the Prophets* (New York: Harper & Row, 1967), 178-179.

Concerning the argument as to who a true prophet is? according to Joel 2:28-29, everyone will be able to prophesy, which would render prophets a "redundant entity." Not all who preach are prophets, and not all who prophesy are prophets. This leaves a question unanswered. If Micah, Amos, Isaiah and others like them were not prophets, what were they? There were those who obviously viewed their oracles as being from an authentic spokesperson of God, otherwise they would not have preserved their messages. Granted, there were those who engaged in נָבָא "prophesy" who were not considered prophets, such as Saul (I Sam 10:10). However, Saul's activity led the people to ask whether he was "among the prophets" since he himself was prophesying. Thus it is assumed that there is some validity in both theories.

The true prophets of Israel believed that God judges everyone because they believed God belongs to no one. Their call to repentance was a plea for the people to humble themselves in recognition of the absolute sovereignty of a God who loved them before they even loved God, and who redeemed them time and again from pits dug with their own hands. The God of the true prophets was- and is- a God of severe mercy, who judges and redeems because of who God is. When the true prophets of scripture chose to belong to God, a curious thing happened. In belonging to God, they were bound to their people, suffering on their behalf in what Abraham Heschel calls "prophetic pathos."[333] They spoke as they did because they cared as they did. They loved the people they served because they served the God they loved. This is where their concern for justice was born. In belonging to God, they also belonged to others that injustice became intolerable. Their strident words reflected this basic bonding.

Considering objections voiced by one prophet against another, we find a wide variety of statements which can be categorized as message-centered objections and person-centered objections. False prophets, Jeremiah says, proclaim deception or fraud: (Jer 14:14). How does one know this? It is seen in the words of Jeremiah 23:32: "It does not *profit* this people at all!" The false prophet proclaims the vision of his own mind (Ezek 13:1-2). Here again it is stressed that these prophets only pretend to speak the word of Yahweh. This kind of prophecy is often characterized as saying, "peace, peace" where there is no peace (Ezek 13:10; Jer 6:13,14; 8:11; 14:13; 23:17; 28:2-3, 11; Mic 3:5).

Babylonian Exilic community also witnessed the activities of false prophets. Ezekiel called activity of the errant prophets "whitewashing" and daubing of a wall. Jeremiah called it healing the wound of my people lightly (Jer 23:16-17). False prophets follow their own foolish spirit, and have seen nothing (Ezek 13:1-2). They complain against other prophets and deals with their morality. They engage in magic (Ezek 13:17-19), are lovers of money (Ezek 13:19; Jer 6:13), fail to expose iniquity (Lam 2:4), and engage in cover-up (Ezek 13:10; 22:28-31; Jer 6:13; 8:10). Hans walter Wolff points out that to the original Hebrew false

333 Abraham J. Heschel, *The Prophets* (New York: Harper & Row, 1962), 24-26.

prophet means "to cause some one to wonder about lost or to be drunk as to be incapable of going to the desired direction."[334] Truly, the prophets were leading the people to be false worshippers and worship Baal only.

In this scenario, Micah sharply criticized the prophets, who led the people into false religiosity and proclaimed the wrong message. In Micah 3:5-8, he accused them of leading the people astray (Mic 3:5). A Message of peace was proclaimed to those who filled their mouths, in fact, there would be no peace at all. However, the declaration was against those who did not respond.[335] The outcome of this was the terrible offence against God by commercializing His holy name. Therefore, in the same sense, James L. Mays also points out that "Money talked louder than God."[336]

Micah ironically recited the punishment against the false prophets, the outcome of their unethical and immoral behaviour against God. The irony of the situation is that darkness will rule over the false prophets. Micah used these words in the metaphorical sense, such as "night," "darkness," "sun going down," and "the day shall be black" to express the silent of God. God will remain silence as the consequence of the failure of the prophets to maintain covenantal justice and trust in the society.[337] Yahweh's judgements, announced by Micah, continued with the same ironic language. He called the prophets הֹזֶה and קֹסֵם, which is an un-Israelite practice.[338] The הֹזֶה will see nothing since the oracles will show "the deceit of the mind." (Jer 14:14; Zech 13:4) while the קֹסֵם will be "put to shame" and they "shall cover their lips," which was a sign of uncleanness (Lev 13:45) and the symbol of mourning and grief.[339] The consequence of false prophets' shameful acts and humiliation was the silence of God, as He will not answer their call for aid because He has withdrawn His protection.

2.3.4. Court Prophets

Prophets played an important role in the history of Israel. Throughout the history of Israel, prophets came from diverse walks of life and although they represented the same God, their own individual ministries were unique. Some played the role of a priest, some of a judge, some were advisers in the royal court, some historians and still some were solitary wanderers confronting kings and pronouncing judgements on the land. Each prophet was instrument in the hand of God as God changed the course of Israel's history be it the era of the judges, monarchy

334 Wolf, *Micah the Prophet*, 70.

335 Andersen & Freedman, "Micah," 364-365; Baker, "Micah-Zephaniah," 77; Sweeney, *Twelve Prophets*, 371.

336 Mays, *Micah*, 83.

337 Richard A. Horsley & John S. Hanson, *Bandits, Prophets and Messiahs* (San Francisco: Harper & Row Publishers, 1985), 142.

338 Anderson & Freedman, "Micah," 375.

339 Cf. Ezek 24: 17. Baker, " Micah- Zephaniah," 78.

or the exile. In this section, discussion will focus on two court prophets-Gad and Nathan.[340]

2.3.4.1. The Call of Gad and Nathan

There are no records as to the call of both the prophets-Gad and Nathan. Now this does not nullify their ministries and the role they played as prophets of Yahweh. Their very ministries itself validate their authenticity of their call and authority. David's acceptance, respect and adherence to these prophets show that they were acclaimed and accepted in the land. Both Gad and Nathan seemed like they were called by Yahweh to be personal and royal prophets to Yahweh's chosen kings. Gad was considered as the "king's seer." Nathan was with David till the king's death and even with Solomon, the one who became king after David.

2.3.4.2. The Role of Gad and Nathan

The ministries of both the prophets were mostly directed towards the king of Israel and his family. However, this does not rule out the possibility that they were prophets for the Israel community as a whole. During the reign of David, "the prophets appear as the king's political advisers and his privy-councillors directing all their efforts towards consolidating the newly-established monarchy."[341] They were court prophets conveying God's messages to the king and exercising their influence over the government of the State.

The name of Gad first appeared in I Samuel 22 and with the title "prophet." When David fled and lodged in the cave of Adullam—his family and many socially distressed persons joined him—having become the object of Saul's anger. Gad appeared as a counsellor to David advising him to leave the cave and settle in Judah and David complied with his counsel (I Sam 22:5). So we can see that Gad figures as a prophetic counsellor of David whilst a fugitive from Saul.[342] Again in II Samuel 24, Gad appeared when King David took a census of his increasingly numerously people, Gad offered David a selection of 1 from 3 punishments for the prideful act; David selected a pestilence in the land as a preferred punishment. While the pestilence raged, Gad instructed David to sacrifice on an altar to be erected on a chosen plot. David again followed the seer's instruction: He purchased the plot, erected the altar, and sacrificed; the pestilence ceased.[343] Here we see Gad more in a figure of a classical prophet confronting a king for his sinful act.

340 Gad, an Israelite חֹזֶה (I Chron 29:29) and נָבִיא (I Sam 22:5) was a contemporary of King David. Nathan was also a prophet (נָבִיא) contemporary of King David but his ministry extended up to Solomon's reign.

341 R. W. Corney, "Gad," *The Interpreter's Dictionary of the Bible: An Illustrated Encyclopedia* (vol. 2; ed. George Arthur Buttrick; Nashville, New York: Abingdon Press, 1962), 335.

342 Jerald J. Petter, "Gad," in *ABD* (Vol. 2; ed. David Noel Freedman; New York: Doubleday, 1992), 865.

343 Petter, "Gad," in *ABD,* 865.

II Samuel 7 (paralleled at I Chron7) records the first appearance of Nathan. His first words were delivered to David "in his own authority" that he should build a house for Yahweh which was later overruled by Yahweh himself. Nathan also delivered the promise of perpetual dynasty of David. It was that night Yahweh appeared to Nathan in a vision with his message about David's dynasty and his son in building Yahweh's house. Nathan then delivered this message via the classical formula (thus says YHWH) and David responded with the prayer of thanksgiving.

The greatest moment for Nathan as court prophet came when he had to confront King David for the two great sins the king had committed (II Sam 12): adultery with Bathsheba and murder of Uriah the Hittite. But, the prophet instead of flatly pointing out and denouncing the king's crime he subtly induced David to confess it. Nathan is portrayed as diplomatic and uncompromising but forth right courteous.[344] His stand against David's unacceptable behaviour ranks him as one who spoke with authority and boldness resembling the classical prophets of the eighth century BCE and later. Here, we see Nathan who is a subject under David and yet God's mouth piece and David's judge.

Nathan played a major role in the succession of Solomon. Nathan allied with Bathsheba to gain David's support for Solomon. Nathan instructed Bathsheba to visit the king and to remind him of his promise that Solomon would succeed him. In response, David authorized Solomon's installation as king (II Sam 12:28-37); consequently, Nathan and Zadok the priest anointed Solomon king, and Adonijah was displaced.

2.3.4.3. Summary

Both the prophets' ministries were similar in nature. Both of them held the office as king's court prophets and both belong to the same period of time. The written records as to the prophets' messages are not available as the documents (the Chronicles of Gad the seer and the Chronicles of Nathan the prophet) mentioned in I Chronicles 29:29 and II Chronicles 9:29. However, one can draw the elements of their messages from the historical narratives recorded in I and II Samuel and I Chronicles.

The messages of Gad and Nathan made a huge impact on David's life. Gad's message or advice was one of encouragement at the same time authoritative when David was a fugitive hiding in cave of Adullam from King Saul. Later, when King David took a census of his kingdom, Gad delivered a message of confrontation and of judgement towards the king's act of pride. The message of Nathan to David is almost the same where Nathan encouraged David to build Yahweh's house, though Yahweh himself rejected it. I Chronicles 17 records the words of Yahweh for King David which was delivered by Nathan. A message of God's greatness, of mercy and the exaltation of David and his household by God made

344 Howard Jr., "Nathan," 1029.

King David humble and made him offer a prayer of thanksgiving. Yet, in later time, one can see in II Samuel 12, Nathan confronting David's sinful act with the use of a fictional legal case and pronouncing judgement upon him and his family. Their messages were delivered at critical junctures of David's life. Thus, they functioned both as classical prophet at the same time advisers to the king in the court. As it has been considered, both Gad and Nathan were no less among the prophets of the Old Testament. They were called by Yahweh for a purpose and they remained faithful to their own prophetic ministry.

2.3.5. A Call Experience of the Prophets

The prophetic tradition of Israel has a rich and colourful history. In spite of the variety of prophetic phenomenon in space (north, south and exile), and in time (pre-monarchial, monarchial, exilic, and post-exilic), the prophets enjoyed the common bond with the past and the future acts of God: the new era of God's coming, the transformation of all things, the judgement of the wicked, and the vindication of the righteous. The prophetic life is based upon a prophetic call, and thus the prophetic career begins with a call.[345] Israel's prophets were not appointed by a king, or a priest, or elders, or by popular choice (except in case of court-prophets like Gad and Nathan). Nor did a prophet come into his or her office by reason of birth (no hereditary claim to the office). The call to be a prophet came by divine choice and was not prescribed by any human standards or regulations. Lindblom asserts that in Israel the certainty of being called by Yahweh was one of the most characteristic features of the prophetic consciousness.[346] The divine call made the individual conscious of being in the presence of God. The essential mark of a prophet is a consciousness of a divine call. Scott observes that the assurance of a divine call was a primary element in the prophetic consciousness.[347] We see this kind of experience in the lives of the prophets who had gone through personal encounter with God. Moses, one of the earliest of Israel's prophets, is one such example. He became aware of God's closeness through the burning bush (Exod 3-4). He was not left to his own resources to explain this phenomenon of a flame of fire or burning bush. Through a divine revelation, its significance was evident as God broke the silence and made Moses conscious of the presence of a holy God.[348]

345 Lindblom, *Prophecy in Ancient Israel*, 64. The call experience of the prophets in ancient Israel is on scholarship discussion since some prophets recorded their call and some do not.

346 Lindblom, *Prophecy in Ancient Israel*, 182.

347 R. B. Y. Scott, *The Relevance of the Prophets* (New York: The Macmillan Company, 1953), 88.

348 Edward J. Young, "Call of Moses," *WTJ* 30 (1967): 1-23. The fact that God was calling Moses was so explicitly clear that Moses never had any doubt about his divine encounter. Subsequently he spoke with certainty to Aaron, to the Israelites, and even to Pharaoh about the fact that God had called him his mission of delivering the Israelites from Egyptian bondage. During the course of his ministry the Israelites contested the divine call of Moses. Repeatedly God confirmed to Moses and to the Israelites that He had called him to his place of leadership

Likewise, God used various means of making a prophet conscious of His presence. Samuel became aware of God's presence as he heard a voice which he acknowledged as a divine call to be a prophet in Israel (I Sam 3:3). Jeremiah did not offer any detail account of his call, but he simply stated that God was speaking to him (Jer 1). Throughout his book he reaffirmed the fact that he was called by God to be a prophet.[349] Jeremiah recorded his feeling of inferiority when he was called to become a prophet. As he struggled, he said, "I do not know how to speak, for I am only a youth." But, he was told to rest himself in the eternal purpose of God, and to be girded with strength from God for his struggle with the kings, the prophets, the priests, and the people of the land. The mental distress out of which he gave himself to a heroic task was but the prelude to greater suffering. However, this initial act of faith gave him momentum and strength for other times of crises. Jeremiah often found himself in critical situation, but he always found God's faithfulness, and he found God's peace in continuing to do His will.

The prophets experienced Yahweh while they were fully conscious; they heard, they considered, and they answered. Isaiah may have been in the environs of the temple as he became keenly aware that a holy God was commissioning him to be His messenger. He heard the questioning voice: "Whom shall I send?" In free decision he responded: "Here am I! Send me!" (Isa 6:8). Because he understood that it was the voice of the divine Sovereign calling for a messenger and knew that the call was meant for him (Isa 6).[350] Isaiah was called to proclaim again and again the word of Yahweh. The more people rejected it the more their judgement was speeded up. Isaiah was destined to be a prophetic missionary whose mission was to bring the people to Yahweh. For Isaiah, the voice of Divine duty was more impelling than the voice of human pleasure, so his turmoil of soul was quenched by his choice to live heroically and speak prophetically.

Ezekiel seems to have had the most elaborate and extensive manifestation of God's presence (Ezek 13). Coming from a priestly family and possibly having been brought up in the environs of the temple of Jerusalem, Ezekiel may have needed such a vision to make him aware of God's presence in the midst of a pagan Babylonian environment. He was set as a watchman over Israel in order that he might warn them to turn from their wicked ways (Ezek 2:8). This divine encounter made Ezekiel aware of his mission among the Israelite exiles.[351] In the

---

and responsibility (Num 12:6-8; 16:28). His role as a prophet was not dependent upon any delegation or committee from the Israelite nation but was of divine appointment.

349 Lyn Mehl, "The Call to Prophetic Ministry: Reflections on Jeremiah 1:4-10," *Currents in Theology and Mission* 8 (1981): 151-155; Ronald F. Youngblood, "The Call of Jeremiah," *Criswell Theological Review* 5 (1990): 99-108.

350 Paul R. House, "Isaiah's Call and Its Context in Isaiah 1-6," *Criswell Theological Review* 6 (1993): 220-221; Julian P. Love, "Call of Isaiah: exposition of Isaiah 6," *Interpretation* 11 (1957): 291-294.

351 Robert R. Wilson, "Prophecy in Crisis: The Call of Ezekiel," *Interpretation* 38 (1984): 117-130.

case of Ezekiel, the call is concentrated with message. Ezekiel regarded the death of his wife as a message from God about the fate of Jerusalem. He was forbidden to mourn her death because of this greater tragedy which is to befall Judah. This awareness of God was an overwhelming force and the prophet knew he had no choice but to speak.

Amos did not give any details about his call but did definitely reflect the fact that God spoke to him, and subsequently he could not resist giving forth God's message (Amos 3:8; 7:15). Amos stated that how undesired it was to him: "The lion has roared; who will not fear? The Lord God has spoken; who can but prophesy?" (Amos 3:8). Myer expresses that Amos' whole argument with Amaziah, the priest at Bethel, reflected that his "call was from God."[352] These men were conscious of God's summoning and sustaining them as they sought to reveal His message to the people. The prophets had experienced the force and their message reflected the awareness of God's authority. Harold Knight notes that "this experience" of the soul's confrontation by the living God "is central and determinative" of all that is to follow.[353]

Many prophets do not record their calls, but the evidence for their divine commission is apparent in their ministry. They all saw an inescapable urgency confronting them.[354] It created entirely new circumstances in their lives. The consciousness of being in the presence of God and hearing an explicit commission from a God constitutes a divine call. Without this one could not be a prophet. The call, which is initiated by God, this divine encounter marked the beginning of a prophet's career. Victor H. Matthews affirms, "the call transforms the individual. This person, who may have been undistinguished to this point in his or her life, now becomes a dynamic spokesperson for God. The call invests the new prophet with special powers, a message, and a mission."[355] To answer the call to represent God's purposes in word and deed may be exercised within (Nathan, Isaiah) or outside of the power structures (Elijah, Jeremiah), but in either case it will involve risk and vulnerability. The prophets understood that their call focused, not on their own self-fulfilment or their own urgent analysis of their context, but on what God was doing in Israel and the wider world. The demand upon them was to become a part of God's project in the ongoing drama stretching from creation to redemption. The call was an impelling force in the lives of the prophets and at the same time, a source of confidence and fortitude.

We also see that leadership does not directly relate to what skills a person possesses, because ultimately it is not the power structures, the connectedness to the royal families, the oratory, the management expertise, the personal flair,

352 C. F. Myer, "The Prophet: A Heavenly Messenger," *Restoration Quarterly* 9 (1966): 292-293.

353 Harold Knight, *The Hebrew Prophetic Consciousness* (London: Lutterworth Press, 1947), 102.

354 Hans Walter Wolff, "Prophecy from the Eighth through the Fifth Century," in *Interpreting the Prophets* (eds. J. L. Mays and P. J. Achtemeier; Philade;phia: Fortress, 1985), 17.

355 Matthews, *Social World of the Hebrew Prophets*, 27.

or the intellect that makes the "not by might nor by power, but by my spirit [presence], says the Lord" (Zech 4:6). This is the basic idea that is expressed in all of these narratives. And that acknowledgement of the power and presence of Yahweh active in the world is enough to sustain the leader. This brief information also affirms that the call plays an important role in prophetic mission because all the prophets take their call as a compelling force throughout their ministry. If a prophet is called to proclaim the word of Yahweh he/she has no option, however distasteful it may be, he/she must proclaim it.

The prophets' response to their call is often one of disbelief, reluctance, and a feeling of inadequacy, which clearly shows how they take the word of Yahweh to embody through their lives. The prophets themselves believed that their calling confronted them with a range of tasks and duties. Like Moses, Yahweh's words cleared the nature of his mission as the deliverer of the Hebrew slaves. The nature of Jeremiah's mission isolated him from the community. He was denied an ordinary life. In the divine plan, Jeremiah's lamentation was intended as a form of prophetic proclamation. His mission was to announce the forthcoming judgement of Yahweh. The mission of Jeremiah and its lamentation dimension spoke for itself.

No missionary can avoid the negative role of the mission. He has to become a prophet of doom for those who try to destabilize and destroy the divine designs for the cosmos. To attack the evil structures of the society in its economic, political, social, cultural and cultic realm are the essential elements of the mission. This will naturally engender opposition and ostracism. Sometimes the missionary will be asked to become the living symbol of the coming judgement of Yahweh. In Jeremiah we see a truly human being who was crushed by the burden of his mission. Though he lamented and protested, he remained faithful to his call.

2.3.6. Prophetic Inspiration

H. Wheeler Robinson is right when he says that "many attempts have been made" to explain "how" God spoke to the prophets, since OT records do not reveal a definite formula for receiving a message from God.[356] Instead of finding a "set formula," it will be discovered that God spoke to the prophets in different ways. The things of everyday life, the context where they lived, of their own life, of the natural world around them served as points of contact whereby God revealed His will to the prophets. This can be seen clearly in the transcripts which the prophets gave of their call-experience (e.g. Amos).

The prophets did not speak of a resolution or purpose formed by themselves to devote themselves to the prophetic ministry. They described a moment in which they received a call from God. They were "conscious of a sudden intuition, impressing itself upon them with irresistible clearness and force, and, in certain

356 H. Wheeler Robinson, *Inspiration and Revelation in the Old Testament* (Oxford: Clarendon Press, 1946), 178.

instances, communicated to them in the form of a vision."[357] Robinson further explains that whenever the account of a prophet's call is given, it can naturally be expected to be a primary document for the understanding of the man and his message for this experience was the supreme moment in his life.[358] "The Lord Yahweh has spoken," says Amos, "who can but prophesy?" Isaiah writes, "Yahweh spoke thus to me with strength of hand." It was in this experience that the prophet's human personality encountered the divine in an especially intense contact, and an indelible imprint was left on his thinking.

The impartation of this message was divinely initiated and not precipitated by the prophet seeking revelational contact or achieving an ecstatic state or frenzy.[359] The initial message was usually imparted when the prophet was called to communicate a message for God to people.

The most keenly discussed question in connection with prophetic inspiration has been that of the significance of "ecstasy" for an understanding of the prophets.[360] Ecstasy, according to Wilson is "the *means* by which divine-human communication takes place" and "the *observable behavioral characteristics* exhibited by a person in communication with the divine world."[361] It has been held by many scholars that "ecstasy" was the distinguished characteristic of the Hebrew prophets and that it provided a criterion without which neither the prophet nor his audience would be satisfied.[362] Johannes Lindblom expresses that the use of the term "ecstasy" is to describe the culminating point of religious experience whereby perfect union with God is realized in direct though ineffable experience. He further remarks, when inspiration strongly intensified it turned to ecstasy.[363] According to Robert L. Alden, "ecstasy arises either from natural or humanly initiated efforts or it is a gift from above. The latter is Theo-tropic;

---

357 S. R. Driver, *Isaiah: His Life and Times and the Writings which Bears his Name* (New York: Fleming H. Revell Co., n.y.), 16. Cf. J. Philip Hyatt, *Prophetic Religion* (New York: Abingdon-Cokesbury Press, 1947), 13.

358 H. Wheeler Robinson, *The Religious Ideas of the Old Testament* (London: Duckworth & Co., 1956), 115.

359 For the view that the prophets of Israel were ecstatic seeking divine contacts even as the Canaanites did. Knight, *the Prophetic Consciousness*, 80-81; H. H. Rowley, *The Faith of Israel* (London: SMC Press, 1956), 37-39.

360 H. H. Rowley, "The Nature of Prophecy in the Light of Recent Study," *The Harvard Theological Review* 38 (1945): 1.

361 R. Wilson, "Prophecy and Ecstasy: A Reexamination," *JBL* 98 (1979): 321-37.

362 For Example, Jeremiah's oracle in 4:19 ("my anguish, my anguish, I writhe in pain") seems closely connected to ecstasy, and the fact that Jeremiah's speech could be described as that of a madman (Jer 29:26) suggests that at least some of the prophet's utterances were given while in ecstasy. Again ecstasy is indicated by Jeremiah (23:9), where the prophet describes himself as shaking and like a drunken man because of the words of Yahweh.

363 Lindblom, *Prophecy in Ancient Israel*, 4.

the former is anthropotropic."[364] Philo notes, a prophet possessed by God will suddenly appear and give prophetic oracles. Nothing of what he says will be his own, for he that is truly under the control of divine inspiration has no power of apprehension when he speaks, but *serves as the channel* for the insistent words of Another's prompting. For prophets are the interpreters of God, who makes full use of their organs to set forth what he wills.[365]

Theodore H. Robinson explains that the very name נָבִיא (prophet) implies ecstatic behaviour, and that it would not have been used if the prophets had not been ecstatic.[366] This is inconclusive, since the philology is more than doubtful and words have a history as well as a derivation. That there was a large element of abnormality in the canonical prophets is unquestionable. But this does not necessarily prove that every prophetic utterance was given either while in a condition of ecstasy or as a result of an ecstatic experience.

Ecstatic communication was practised among the Hittites, in Ugarit, in Hamath and the like.[367] The prophets fell into a trance and received revelation/ messages from their deity for the king. Prophecies usually contain a warning and a promise of divine protection. For instance, in one of the letters it is reported that a certain Akhatum went into a trance and spoke as follows:

> O Zimri-Lim, even though you for your part have spurned me, I for my part shall embrace you. I shall deliver your enemies into your hand, and the men of Sharrakiya I shall seize and gather them to the destruction of Belet-ekallim.[368]

However, it is also important to understand that the real test of a genuine oracle was not its being an ecstatic utterance but rather its content. The prophets were men and women of superior intellectual ability. But, let it be said that these prophets were not spokespersons of God just because they had superior intellects. Their oracles came to them as a result of something more than concentrated meditations. If they can be properly called "religious geniuses" or "religious experts," it is because God had chosen them and revealed to them knowledge of his character which they did not possess before. This knowledge of God, as a result of the divine initiative in an act of self-disclosure, qualified them to speak as his interpreters.

---

364 Robert L. Alden, "Ecstasy and the Prophets," *Bulletin of the Evangelical Theological Society* 9 (1966): 153.

365 Philo, *De Specialibus Legibus,* 65, cited by Heschel, *The Prophets,* 335-36.

366 Theodore H. Robinson, *Prophecy and the Prophets in Ancient Israel* (London: Duckworth and Co., 1953), 44-45; William Foxwell Albright, *From the Stone Age to Christianity* (Baltimore: The Johns Hopkins Press, 1957), 231.

367 Johannes, *Prophecy in Ancient Israel,* 31; Wilson, *prophecy and Society in Ancient Israel,*104.

368 William L. Moran, "Akkadian Letters," in *ANET,* 630.

The prophets hear from God in dreams and visions that have significance for individuals and for entire communities. Sometimes these dreams and visions are called such. Other times, the text simply says that the "word of the Lord came to" the prophet, and then what follows has a strong visual component (Jer 1:11-14; Ezek 4:1-7; Amos 7:4; Zech 5:5-9). Through visions and dreams, prophets see God's purposes: some times for Israel or Judah, sometimes for the whole earth-symbolized and enacted before their very eyes. The prophets predict the future and God's word inevitably comes to pass. It is apparent that the prophets' aim was to acquaint their audience with Yahweh himself and to assist the people in recognizing the divine attributes such as his justice (Amos 1:1-2:3), his dominion over all (Amos 4:13; 5:8-10; Mic 1:3-4), his majesty (Isa 2:10-11), his sovereignty (Amos 9:5-6), his holiness (Isa 6:3; 39:23; 57:15), his righteousness (Amos 7:7-9; Isa 28:17), and his love (Isa 45:23-25; Joel 2:13; Isa 1:18; Hos 11:1).

Unlike ecstasy or announcements by inspired messengers, the dream messages conform to a larger pattern of experience in the AWA world. Some of the dreams do differ substantially in detail from the common patterns. It is of special interest to note that the majority of the private persons received their message in a dream. The dream apparently was the primary means of communication for non-technical and non-cultic persons. The significance of dreams was a subject of written analysis in most of the AWA countries namely, Mesopotamia, Egypt and Hatti. Sometimes a dream contained a straightforward verbal communication from gods and needed no specially trained interpreter. Mari texts mentioned the god Dagan appears to the prophets in dreams and sends them to convey messages to the king.[369] The following Mari text reveals to us that prophets were called or considered as messengers of god (Dagan):

> In a dream of mine I was set on going in the company of another man… to Mari. *On my way* (*ina paniya*) I entered Terqa and right after entering I entered the temple of Dagan and prostrated myself. As I was prostrate, Dagan opened his mouth and spoke to me as follows: 'Did the kings of the Yaminites and their forces make peace with the forces of Zimri-Lim who moved up there?' I said, 'They did not make peace.' Just before I went out he spoke to me as follows: 'Why are the messengers of Zimri-Lim not in constant attendance upon me, and why does he not lay his full report before me? Had this been done, I would long ago have delivered the kings of the Yaminites into the power of Zimri-Lim. Now go, I send you. Thus shall you speak to Zimri-Lim saying: "Send me your messengers and lay your full report before me, and then I will have the kings of the Yaminites *cooked* on a fisherman's *spit*, and I will lay them before you."[370]

369 A. Malamat, "Prophetic Revelations in New Documents from Mari and the Bible," *SVT* 15 (1966): 207; W. L. Moran, "New Evidence from Mari on the History of Prophecy," *Biblica* 50 (1969): 26.

370 William L. Moran, "Akkadian Letters," in *ANET*, 623.

In the Neo-Assyrian period, the *sabru* (a professional dreamer/visionary) usually received messages through dreams. The messages are mostly related to the victory and prosperity for the king Asurbanipal especially when he is about to go for a battle. Here is one of *sabru's* dreams:

> During the night in which I appeared before her, a *sabru*-priest lay down and had a dream. He awoke with a start and then Ishtar caused him to see a nocturnal vision. He reported to me as follows: 'The goddess Ishtar who dwells in Arebla came in. Right and left quivers were suspended from her. She was holding a bow in her hand, and a sharp sword was drawn to do battle. You were standing in fornt of her and she spoke to you like a real mother. Ishtar called to you, she who is most exalted among the gods, giving you the following instructions: 'Wait with the attack; (for) wherever you intend to go, I am also ready to go.' You said to her, 'Wherever you go, I will go with you, O goddess of goddesses!' She repeated her command to you as follows: 'You shall stay here where you should be. Eat, drink wine, make merry, praise my divinity, while I go and accomplish that work to help you attain your desire. Your face will not be pale, nor your feet shaky, and need not wipe off your (cold) sweat in the height of battle.' She wrapped you in her lovely babysling, protecting your entire body-Her face shone like fire. Then [she went out in a frightening way] to defeat your enemies, against Teumman, king of Elam, with whom she was angry.[371]

Kings were warned by gods through the dreamers or visionaries. King Zimri-Lim was once warned not to set out on a campaign but to stay in Mari, if Zimri-Lim leaves Mari on a campaign, perhaps the city will fall. In the dream of Addu-duri (who was regarded as dreamer) "she says she saw the temple of Belet-ekallim abandoned by its god and images, and heard a voice crying: 'Come back, Dagan!'"[372] This dream clearly anticipated the fall of Mari at that time.

In summary, prophets were inspired persons, and the one compelled to speak, whether the message came from an obedient Isaiah or a rebellious Jeremiah, a magnanimous Hosea or a non-professional Amos, or any of the prophets, all of them recognized the source of their message as coming from Yahweh and whether it was one of woe or weal, it had to be preached.

2.3.7. Prophetic Functions/Roles

The Prophets played a significant role in both AWA and in Israel. In Israel, prophets were called spokespersons for God. They admonished, warned, directed, encouraged, interceded, and counselled the people. They brought the word of God to the people of God and called the people to respond. They can undertake a huge variety of roles. This is an expression of the creativity of God. They may

---

371 Robert D. Biggs, "Akkadian Didactic and Wisdom Literature," in *ANET*, 606.

372 Simon B. Parker, "Official Attitudes Towards Prophecy at Mari and in Israel," *VT* 43 (1993): 54.

act in every role occasionally, but mostly they will move in one or two of these roles. No two prophets should be the same, but each should be a reflection of God's creativity and calling. The following are some of the roles that most of the prophets undertake. This section will be divided into two: Implicit leadership roles and explicit leadership roles of the prophets.

2.3.7.1. Implicit Leadership Roles

2.3.7.1.1. Prophets as Representative of God and People

Prophets as leaders acted as representatives of God and people played twofold roles. On the one hand, they delivered God's word to people; on the other hand, they delivered the people's word to God.[373] In the one role, the prophet spoke (and acted) as God's representative, the men and women of God's commissioned to deliver God's word (not their own) to particular situations. W. A. Vangemere calls the prophets as the spoken-persons for God.[374] On behalf of God, the prophet spoke on several issues to people. The issues included religious, eschatological, spiritual, social and political matters. Many prophetic oracles begin with the formula (introducing their messages) "Thus says the Lord," or "Hear the word of the Lord," and proceed to speak in the first person as if God is directly addressing the people through the prophet as mouthpiece.

In their other role, the prophets spoke as the people's representative. Prophets articulated their response to God, whether in the form of praise or petition, thanksgiving or protest. On such occasions, the prophet assumed the role of "prayer," one praying the prayers of his people, on their behalf and for the purpose of securing their well-being. Thus, we find prayer was essential to the prophetic ministry. It came naturally to the prophets and was the life-blood of their ministry. Prayer was their principal means of communication with God and lay at the heart of their personal relationship with God. The prophets were successful as leaders because they lived a prayerful life.

Walter Brueggemann expresses that the prophets' call to represent God, in ancient Israel is usually a commitment to a consciousness alternative to the dominant cultural consciousness. He notes,

> *The task of prophetic ministry is to nurture, nourish, and evoke a consciousness and perception alternative to the consciousness and perception of the dominant culture around us.* . . . The alternative consciousness to be nurtured, on the one hand, serves to *criticize* in dismantling the dominant consciousness. ... On the other hand, that alternative consciousness to be nurtured serves

373 A. R. Johnson, *The Cultic Prophet in Ancient Israel* (Cardiff: University of Wales Press, 1962), 59.

374 W. A. Vangemere, *Interpreting the Prophetic Word* (Michigan: Zondervan, 1990), 42.

to *energize* persons and communities by its promise of another time and situation toward which the community of faith may move.[375]

In that case prophets were also called as mediators between God and the people. They provide oracles and represent the people before God through prayers. One of prophets' fundamental roles is that of mediator of the covenant between God and the people of Israel. In this regard Moses plays that role not only in the institution of the original covenant (Exod 19-24) but also in its renewal after it has been broken in the incident with the golden calf (Exod 32-34). The Prophet stood before people as a person who had been made to stand before God.

2.3.7.1.2. Prophets as Proclaimers and Predictors

Foretelling or predicting was one of the functions of the prophets as leaders. Robinson notes that prediction played an important part in prophetic utterance.[376] It was part of the prophetic ministry. David L. Petersen expresses that prophets were concerned with Israel's past, present and future.[377] Prophets were not central to the narrative. God's Word was the story. They came with a word from Him. At times, the message was eschatological in nature.

But, more often, prophets were preachers rather than predictors. They came with a genuine word from God and spoke on behalf of the great king, Yahweh, and did not look for the king's favour. Heschel asserts that "the task of the prophets is to convey the word of God."[378] The prophets were God's servants in time applying God's word during crises in the covenant relation between God and His people. They spoke a language their contemporaries could understand and in forms suited to their audience. Through their fellowship with the eternal God, prophets had access to the future.

Sometime they were called seers who had insight into God's purposes for history. However, whatever they saw for the future was always related to the present. They warned of future judgements so that people will change their behaviour in the present. They spoke of future blessing to give hope for the present. Prophet spoke to the present in light of the future that God has revealed to them. For example, Isaiah warned Hezekiah that he would die (II Kgs 20:1, 2; Isa 38:1). Prophets saw more than others the continuing influences that issue from the past and profoundly affect the present and the ultimate future. They saw the continuum, the unbroken span of past, present and future.

375 Brueggemann, *The Prophetic Imagination*, 3.

376 Robinson, *Prophecy and the Prophets in Ancient Israel*, 46.

377 David L. Petersen, *The Prophetic Literature: An Introduction* (Louisville, London: Westminster John Knox Press, 2002), 9.

378 Heschel, *The Prophets*, 26.

2.3.7.1.3. Prophets as Watchmen/Watchwomen and Shepherd

The prophets of ancient Israel were also called to play the role of watchmen and to lead their people in justice and righteousness. The word צֹפֶה the active participle of the same root meaning "to watch" is attested throughout the Hebrew Bible in its basic meaning "guard," or "watchmen" (e.g. II Sam 18:24-27). The idea of the watchmen is closely connected with that of an intercessor. J. Carl Laney mentions that "the prophets also functioned as watchmen over the people of Israel."[379] They stand on the walls of the city of God to see what God is doing. They look into the distance to see what is coming. They often see a long way ahead.

Several scriptures describe the role of the watchman. Hoses 9:8 pronounced "the prophet is the watchman over Ephraim." Ezekiel is one of the prophets who acted as a real watchman for his people, modelling the care and investment that the leader must make for the growth and nurture of the followers. In Ezekiel's day crisis followed crisis, not only in Israel but in the international scene as well. The times were out of joint. Old structures were passing away and new power-blocks were emerging. The chosen people seemed doomed to extinction, swallowed up by heathen nations in their quest for conquest. In this kind of situation, Ezekiel "stood as a watchman on the walls of Zion ready to trumpet a warning against religious apostasy. He warned the people against political and military alliances with foreign powers, the temptation to become involved in idolatry and Canaanite cultic worship, and the danger of placing excessive confidence in religious formalism and sacrificial ritual."[380] He confronted the false leaders in the community, who were using their power, not for the nurture of the community, but to draw people to themselves, to put themselves on a pedestal above the rules and values of the community.

The term "watchman" is also used as metaphor. In Ezekiel 3 and 33, the watchman metaphor reaches its peak. These two chapters elaborate on the watchman's task to warn his audience of the coming divine punishment. In both texts, the call to be a watchman stands in close proximity to Ezekiel's call to be a prophet.[381] The texts declare that "Ezekiel was appointed by the people as a watchman (*ṣôpeh*) with a twofold responsibility: blowing the trumpet to warn against attack from external enemies and delivering moral exhortation or more often combination directed at both the reprobate and the well-disposed within the community."[382] Ezekiel used terms "watchman or shepherd" to express his

---

379 J. Carl Laney, "The Role of the Prophets in God's Case Against Israel," *Bibliotheca Sacra* 138 (1981): 315.

380 Laney, "The Role of the Prophets in God's case Against Israel," 315 (Ezek 3:17).

381 Lena-sofia Tiemeyer, "The Watchman Metaphor in Isaiah LVI-LXVI," *VT* 55 (2005): 379, 381.

382 Joseph Blenkinsopp, "The Social Roles of Prophets in Early Achaemenid Judah," *JSOT* 93 (2001): 47.

conception of his office.[383] Both images of watchman and shepherd lay heavy responsibility upon the prophet. The shepherd was responsible to his master for the lives of his sheep and the watchman was responsible for the safety of the city. The watchmen in Ezekiel 3:17; 33:2, 6-7, however, are condemned because of their negligence to their task. They were greedy and addicted to strong drink.[384] Ezekiel says that the soul that dies without the prophets' warning will be laid to the charge of the prophet. Thus, it is punishable for any prophet who neglects their responsibilities as watchmen and shepherds.

2.3.7.1.4. Prophets as Miracle Workers

Prophets as leaders were expected to perform mighty acts by their followers. Throughout the history of prophetic ministry in Israel we find many miracles that were performed by the prophets. Miracles are seals of a divine mission and they are proof that they were messengers of God by the prophets. These miracles were inspired by God and performed by His power through these prophets. So, prophets were sometimes called miracle workers. They sometimes performed their miraculous acts by external means. For instance, Elijah's mantle, everything that belonged to him was, so to speak, charged with power. Even his clothes possessed power.[385] But, more frequently it is said that the prophet worked by means of his word. The prophetic word was thought of as charged with energy and power so it is effective and a creative word.[386] Most of the miraculous cures recorded in the biblical narratives were performed through the power or intercession of the

---

383 In an ancient city with its protective walls and gates there had always to be a watchman upon the wall to give warning of any approaching enemy from without or peril from within. The prophet's warning cry was therefore an expression of his care for Israel and the harshness of his words of judgement a sign not of unloving anger but rather of the urgency of his alarm. The prophet as shepherd guards the flock night and day against harm from enemies but he also guides them by day to the sources of food and water.

384 Blenkinsopp, "The Social Roles of Prophets in Early Achaemenid Judah," 45.

385 Among the external means we may include Elisha' staff, which Gehazi laid upon the face of the son of the Shunammite (II Kgs 4:20-37). Further, the living body of a prophet made a dead corpse living (II Kgs 4:34); an iron axe which had fallen into the water was made to float by means of a stick (II Kgs 6:16); and a handful of meal made noxious food sound (II Kgs 4:38-41). Such methods for carrying out extraordinary deeds are used in all quarters of the world and are well known to every student of primitive culture and religion. Elijah and Elisha struck the waters of the Jordan with the prophetic mantle and divided them so that the prophets could pass over (II Kgs 2:8, 14).

386 The son of the widow in Zarephath was restored to life in response to the prayer of Elijah (I kgs 17). On Mount Carmel the fire of Yahweh descended and consumed the burnt-offering of Elijah after the prophet had prayed fervently to his God (I kgs 18:20-38). Elisha prayed to Yahweh when he was about to recall the son of the Shunammite to life (II Kgs 4:8). Cf. Stuart Lasine, "Matters of Life and Death: The Story of Elijah and the Widow's Son in Comparative Perspective," *Biblical Interpretation* 12 (2004): 117-144; Neil Glover, "Elijah Verses the Narrative of Elijah: The Contest Between the Prophets and the Word," *JSOT* 30 (2006): 449-462; Nachman Levine, "Twice as Much of your Spirit: Pattern, Parallel and Paronomasia in

prophets. Prophets Elijah and Elisha healed the sick; it was to demonstrate God's power over life and death.

2.3.7.1.5. Prophets as the Guardian of the Divine Law

Prophets were the defenders or the protectors of the covenant of Yahweh. Throughout the history of Israel, the prophets kept the תּוֹרָה alive in the lives of the people. Whenever the people of Israel went astray from Yahweh, they reminded them and corrected them in the light of the teaching of תּוֹרָה. For instance, the story of David and Bathsheba is well known, as is the encounter between Nathan and David. The prophet appeared to David when he committed adultery with the wife of his warrior Uriah and arranged Uriah to be killed in the battle. Nathan spoke for the murdered Uriah who has no one to represent him. Nathan spoke for a philosophy of government in which the king or petty despot is bound by the same law as any other person in society. Unlike other nations, Israel's king could not stand above or outside the law. Thus, the prophet confronted the king in the name of Yahweh and His commandment: "You shall not murder," "You shall not commit adultery" (Exod 20:13, 14). Nathan challenged the king and promised punishment. Nathan as an advocate spoke for a form of kingship that will place the king under the rule of law. Matthews explains that when David had taken a military census in order to muster an army to protect Israel, Gad denounced David's action as treason and reminded him that only Yahweh, and not the king, protected Israel.[387]

During the ninth century BCE Israel, Elijah, the prophet appeared and challenged the crime of the one in authority viz., Ahab the king of Israel who had misused his royal influence to take possession of what belonged to a citizen by name Naboth (I Kgs 21) and stoned him to death with false accusation. The result of Ahab's deeds was elimination from the throne. Elijah proclaimed the Decalogue of Yahweh: "You shall not murder," and "You shall not covet your neighbour's house" (Exod 20:13, 17). Elijah also argued against Ahab and Jezebel (I Kgs 17) because of the worship of foreign deities in Israel. The prophet withstood the practice of worshipping idols in the name of the first commandment "You shall have no other gods before me" (Exod 20:3).

During the eighth century BCE, Israel's prophets namely, Amos, Isaiah, Hosea and Micah appeared and defended the law of Yahweh. They pointed to the anti-social activities of the greedy people. For instance, in Amos 4, the prophet singled out the women who indirectly oppressed the poor. And in Isaiah 5:8, the prophet targeted the group of people who were not satisfied with what they already have but bought more properties. According to the prophet, this practice violated the "old ordinance allocating the land by lot, and giving a share to every

---

the Miracles of Elijah and Elisha," *JSOT* 85 (1999): 25-46; Crottanelli, *Kings and Prophets: Monarchic Power, Inspired Leadership, and Sacred Text in Biblical Narrative*, 129-131.

387 Matthews, *Social World of the Hebrew Prophets*, 23.

member of God's people" (Lev 25).[388] For the prophets "the law of Yahweh" is for life long, to live and to stand for. Thus, the prophets are described as mediators of Yahweh's law. As stated in II Kings 17:13 where Yahweh warns the people: "keep my commandments and my statutes, in accordance with all the law that I commanded your ancestors and that I sent to you by my servants the prophets." It is explicitly mentioned in Deuteronomy 18:15-19. Here the prophets are portrayed as successors of Moses, mediator of the law *par excellence*.

2.3.7.1.6. Prophets as Religious Educators

The prophets of biblical Israel were undeniably teachers of their people. Claus Westermann notices that "the possibility of a man as *[sic]* being able to deliver the message of God to other men is something essentially different. Actually there is something about this that is absurd and impossible to the ancient world; a messenger of God can actually only be a god or a divine creature!"[389] According to Donal A. Leggett, biblical prophets have been referred to as "brilliant religious individualists" and commended for "their genius for religion."[390] Some see the exilic and post-exilic prophets as functioning more obviously in the role of educator than did those before the exile, because their messages were more specific regarding ethics and practical matters. Post-exilic prophets were more involved in institutionalized cultic activity and with what may be seen as institutionalized religion than had been of their pre-exilic predecessors. Their role and message centred on maintaining the law and those activities supportive of the temple. This role would be passed on to the scribe, who would preserve, interpret, and teach the law and the other traditions of God as people. Religious educators like ancient Israel's prophets can be agents of liberating their faith communities by teaching for liberation. They can also do so by influencing the shape of theology. More specifically, religious educators must be more proactive in dialogue with theology and assertive in forming the theologies of their respective faith communities.

The prophets were seen as moral teachers and interpreters of the תּוֹרָה. The term תּוֹרָה is generally denotes "instruction," "teachings," or "education," and thus comprises more than legal stipulations.[391] Basically, the Hebrew Bible uses the term תּוֹרָה in three different contexts. In Israelite wisdom tradition, תּוֹרָה designates the oral instruction of the teacher or father (Prov 4:1-2; 28:7) and the mother (Prov 1:8; 6:20; 31:26). In priestly circles, תּוֹרָה denotes the oral instruction of the priests in general (Deut 33:10; Ezek 7:26; Mic 2:8) or a single cultic regulation

388 Zimmerli, *The Law and the Prophets*, 67.

389 Claus Westermann, *Basic Forms of Prophetic Speech* (trans. Hugh Clayton White; Louisville: Westminster/John Knox Press. 1991), 115.

390 Donald A. Leggett, *Loving God and Disturbing Men Preaching from the Prophets* (Grand Rapids: Baker Book House, 1990), 8.

391 See Gunnar Östborn, *Torah in the Old Testament: A Semantic Study* (Lund: Hakan Ohlssons, 1945); E García López, "Torah," in *TDOT* 15, 609-39.

(Exod 12:39; Num 5:29-30; Lev 7:1). In Deuteronomy, תּוֹרָה most often refers to the written law (Deut 4:8,44; 27:26; 31:12). The portrait of prophets as teachers of תּוֹרָה strengthens their significance as true prophets. Prophets taught the law by applying it to particular situation. As religious educators, prophets were not only committed to the critical examination of the religion, but they also presented religion as offering a critique of social and personal values.

2.3.7.2. Explicit Leadership Roles

2.3.7.2.1. Prophets as Advisors

Prophets also played the role of advisors. Some prophets had the ear of kings and gave advice. Many, of course, were unpopular with Israel's political and religious leaders, but even they often had support among the people of the land. Heschel stresses that "the prophet's duty is to speak to the people, 'whether they hear or refuse to hear.'"[392] All of the prophets understood their proclamation of God's Word in the context of the traditions of covenant community. They appeared as advisors in many occasions. Cristiano Grottanelli remarks that "the priestly and 'prophetic' functions are given over to the respective specialized personnel linked to the king."[393] The prophet Nathan and the priest Zadok were included in bureaucrats, in the group of 'faithful,' the royal leaders of the nations, during the reign of David and Solomon.[394] Prophets had a powerful role in providing advice to kings and rulers. When God wanted to give guidance to a ruler, He often gave it through a prophet. David had the prophets Nathan and Gad in his palace. They advised him about a whole range of matters (II Sam 7:1-4, 17; I Sam 22:5). They also confronted the monarch when he did wrong. They appeared as advocates for an old order of morality and spoke out for leadership with integrity.

Among all the prophets, court prophets were directly advisers to and critique of the kings. Like Samuel, the court prophets were the guardians of the monarchy. They gave advice including political matters, rebuked, declared God's judgement when they went wrong, and kept record of the deeds of the kings.[395] Matthew states that "in the political realm, the prophets served as the conscience of the kings. It was their job to remind the monarch that he was not above the law and could be punished like any Israelite for an infraction of the covenant."[396]

Some of the prophetic stories also give the impression that prophets in Judah and Israel had easy access to the king, for instance, Nathan and David (I

392 Heschel, *The Prophets,* 19.

393 Cristiano Crottanelli, *Kings and Prophets: Monarchic Power, Inspired Leadership, and Sacred Text in Biblical Narrative* (New York, Oxford: Oxford University Press, 1999), 101-102.

394 Crottanelli, *Kings and Prophets: Monarchic Power, Inspired Leadership, and Sacred Text in Biblical Narrative,* 102.

395 In II Samuel 12, Prophet Nathan is seen as against David's adultery. He is depicted as a member of David's royal court. One might expect that, as such, he would be a loyalist advisor.

396 Matthews, *Social World of the Hebrew Prophets,* 35.

Kgs 1:23). The stories depict prophets as delivering their oracles in the presence of the king, although there is no clear evidence for prophets residing at the royal palace. The story clearly shows that Nathan as one of King David's staff played a part in matters connected with the cult at the palace. The prophet brought Yahweh's authority of rejection on the plans of David to build a temple. Lindblom explains that "in II Sam 7 it is expressly said that he played an outstanding part as David's counsellor when the king was planning to build a temple for the Yahweh cultic Jerusalem."[397] On the other hand, Nathan also promised David that Yahweh intended to build for him a house (i.e. dynasty).[398]

Then, in another occasion, Nathan brought the word of promise (the David covenant), and made sure that Solomon succeeded David as king (I Kgs 1:34). He also delivered God's message of judgement on David, who responded positively. Omer Sergi explains that in all these occasions prophet Nathan is portrayed as an advisor to the king who can influence David's deeds by means of support (II Sam 7) and criticism (II Sam 12) and by using sophisticated rhetoric (including promises [II Sam 7:11b]; parables [II Sam 12:1-4]; and manipulation [I Kgs 1:11-30]). His main role is to provide divine legitimacy for the Davidic dynasty and to guarantee its existence.[399] I Kings 18:19 mentions prophets that "eat at Jezebel's table." This reflects a position of high esteem with the queen, or in other cases the king, or simply refers to food rations provided by the royal court, rather than permanent residence at the royal court (cf. II Sam 19:29; I Kgs 2:7).

In the story of the war between Ben-hadad and King Ahab in I Kings 20, we are introduced to a prophet as a military advisor. Klaus Koch states that "an Israelite king never waged war without having a nabi beside him."[400] Prophet Isaiah in the eighth century BCE., is also seen as advisor to King Ahaz when he was threatened by King Razin of Aram and Pekah, King of Israel (Isa 7). In various stories concerning Isaiah, in II Kings 19:1-7, Hezekiah sends his officials to consult the prophet Isaiah; and in various occasion in Jeremiah, royal officials likewise appear as a mediating party between prophet and king (Jer 36-38). Further, Jeremiah advised King Zedekiah to surrender the city of Jerusalem to the Babylonians (Jer 21:1-10; 38:17-18).[401] The prophets also challenged the monarch: Elijah confronted the powers of state (king) and temple (priests) and predicted a three-year drought and famine throughout the land of Israel (I Kgs 17:1). These stories offer the understanding that prophets in Judah and Israel could function as advisors to the king. At least, since prophets were believed to

397 Lindblom, *Prophecy in Ancient Israel*, 76.

398 Walther Zimmerli, *The Law and the Prophets* (trans. R. E. Clements; New York: Harper & Row, 1967), 63.

399 Omer Sergi, "The Composition of Nathan's Oracle to David (II Sam 7:1-17) as a Reflection of Royal Judahite Ideology," *JBL* 12 (2010): 266.

400 Klaus, *The Prophets: The Assyrian Period*, 27.

401 Matthews, *Social World of the Hebrew Prophets*, 35.

be able to determine the divine will, their words could play a role in the political decision-making. It also shows that throughout the history of Israel prophets acted as advisers to the monarchs and to the royal leaders, although some rulers did not heed the ministry of the prophets, they never gave up their leadership to the ministry of the monarchs.

Similarly, prophets in AWA context also played important roles in various circumstances. They encouraged and advised monarchs in times of wars and treaty between countries. People believed that the gods conducted war affairs and helped them in battle fields and since prophets always had access to the will of the deity, they sought god's will to find out whether the battle will be a successful one.[402] Here the close association of kings and prophets is seen. In Mesopotamia, prophets, diviners, and magicians gave counsel to the king. They joined with the king on his military campaigns and all worked together to please him. The prophets mostly proclaimed victory and prosperity for the king. Zakir king of Lu'ash and Hamath, admitted himself that Ba'al-Shamayn stood by him and made him king. He said,

> And I lifted up my hands to Ba'al-Sha[may]n, and Ba'al-Shamay[n] answered me, and Ba'al-Shamayn [spo(12)ke] to me [by] means of seers and by means of messengers; and (13) Ba'al-Shamayn [said to me], 'Do not fear, for I have made [you ki]ng, [and (now) I (14) will st]and by you, and I will rescue you from all [these kings who] (15) have laid a siege against you.' And [Ba'al-Shamayn] said to [me, . . .] (16) all these kings who have laid [a siege against you.[403]

The above discussion shows that in both Israel and AWA contexts, prophets enabled the monarchs to understand their responsibilities as leaders of the nations when they failed to fulfill their duties. Prophets also appeared to the monarchs and reproved them in times of wrong decision and mismanagement in the administration and passing wrong judgement to the poor and weak in the society.

2.3.7.2.2. Prophets as Intercessors

The prophets' role as intercessors is bound up with their positions as mediators between God and human. They are identified with God as His appointed messenger, and with their people whose experiences they share. Prophets stand before people in obedience and faithfulness to God, and they are able to represent them before God.[404] Their intercessions arise from their positions of identification

402 Hans M. Barstad, "No Prophets? Recent Developments in Biblical Prophetic Research and Ancient Near Eastern Prophecy," *JSOT* 57 (1993): 53.

403 James F. Ross, "Prophecy in Hamath, Israel, Mari," *Harvard Theological Review* 63 (1970): 1.

404 Such a mediatorial role also belongs to the priest in the OT but the personal involvement of the priest is not emphasized in the OT as it is of the prophet. The prophet, unlike the priest, receives a direct divine call and continuing direct experience of the divine word, and

with God knowing His character and will at the same time knowing the people for whom they are deeply concerned.

Various passages in the Bible describe the prophets as one who "stands in the breach" to defend the people against the onslaught of God's punishing righteousness. For instance, Moses is regarded as the intercessor par excellence: for 40 years in the wilderness, he interceded before God to put aside wrath and spare, again and again, this sinful people. Moses stood between the people and God. Time after time, he stood in the gap on behalf of the nation before an angry God. Consequently, intercession played a vital part in Moses life. As a prophet Moses felt in his heart the burden of the message he brought to the people. He was deeply moved when Israel did not respond to the command of God. Recall, the intercession by Elijah (I Kgs 17:17-24); Amos (7:1-6); Isaiah (37:1-7); Jeremiah (18:20; 42:9); prophetic intercession often succeeded in its purpose and moved God to relent of punishment.

There is a tension inherent in the prophets' position because of their double identification, and their intercessions give evidence of this. On God's behalf they announce judgement, but as the people's representative they plead for mercy. As God's representative they bear the brunt of the people's opposition to God, and they suffer because of their sin. Their intercession is part of this suffering role as they pray to God on behalf of their enemies. Yet they pray for mercy because of their identification with God whose nature is to have mercy.

The prophets' positions show something about God himself. They take on their role by God's appointment: they do not take it upon themselves. Because of God's initiative alone they are there to speak God's word and intercede. In their whole life they interpose themselves between God and people and their intercessions are part of their total commitment. When they intercede they remind God of their own character and purpose—His justice, mercy, compassion, commitment to his the people.

As the prophets' intercessions reflect God's own nature and His purposes, they reveal a tension within the character of God: the struggle between His justice and His mercy. By God's appointment the prophet both announces judgement and pleads for mercy. For instance, in Numbers 21:7, Moses is described as praying or interceding for Israel with the purpose of asking God to desist from his judgement.[405] Again in I Samuel 7:5, the role of intercessor is attributed to Samuel, who instructs the house of Israel: "Assemble all Israel at Mizpah, and I will intercede with the Lord for you" (cf. I Sam 12:19, 23). As a matter of fact, from the eighth century BCE on conception of a "true prophet" was one who functioned "like Moses" (Deut 18:15), a conception suggesting that intercession

he/she acts in obedient response to the word as it comes directly to him/her. Cf. Petersen, *The Prophetic Literature*, 7; Klaus, *The Prophets: The Assyrian Period*, 26.

405 Cf. Num 11:2; Deut 9:20.

was one of the functions of the true prophet.[406] Jeremiah may have seen himself as an intercessor after the manner of Moses and Samuel.[407] The suffering involved for the prophet is a reflection of that involved for God himself who must act justly but desires to have mercy. This suffering is most strikingly seen in the Suffering Servant, spoken of almost as a divine figure who suffers judgement on behalf of transgressors, interceding or interposing himself for them, and secures God's mercy.

When the prophets respond to God's revelation in intercession, they do not speak in opposition to God's plans. On the contrary, but their relationship with God, they shares in God's attitudes and pray in harmony with God's own concerns. They remind God of His own character and urge the fulfilment of His purposes. In this way the prophets' intercessions serve to reveal God himself.

Prophets further played an important role in times of war as intercessors. Judges 6 shows a good example of prophets' participation in wars. Here we read how Yahweh sent a prophet to help the Israelites when they were in danger of losing the war against the Midianites. Similar story is found in I Samuel 15, where Samuel intervenes in the war against the Amalekites and in chapter 7, Samuel is described as both prophet and judge, acting as intercessor and mediator between Yahweh and the people before the battle with the Philistines. Intercession, then, appears to have been one of the responsibilities of the prophets. Thus, prophets would serve as intercessors for their people, a role for which they were peculiarly qualified due to their privileged position within the council of God (cf. Jer 23:18, 22).

2.3.7.2.3. Prophets as Cultic Leaders

The prophetic ministry can often play an important part in worship. Mowinckel defines the prophetic role in relation to Israel's worship. Based on the involvement of Moses and Samuel in Israel's worship (cult), he explains that the people consulted the priests for divine oracles and thus the prophetic institution was associated with cultic sites.[408] Petersen expresses that "prophets were truly boundary figures, standing between the world of the sacred and secular."[409] They represented people before Yahweh (Amos 7:2) as well as Yahweh to people (Amos 5:4).

Prophets act with Yahweh's power within the ordinary and everyday world (e.g., Elisha) or they envision the cosmic world (Amos 7:4; Zech 1:7-17). They participated in the divine council (Isa 6; I Kgs 22) as well as analyse the plans of

406 Wilson, *Prophecy and Society in Ancient Israel*, 165.

407 William L. Holladay, "The Background of Jeremiah's Self-Understanding-Moses, Samuel, and Psalm 22," *JBL* 83 (1964): 153-164; idem, "Jeremiah and Moses: Further Observations," *JBL* 85 (1966): 17-27; Wilson, *Prophecy and Society in Ancient Israel*, 240.

408 Sigmund Mowinckel, "Cult and Prophecy," in *Prophecy in Israel: Search for an Identity* (ed. David L. Petersen; Philadelphia: Fortress Press, 1987), 74-98.

409 Petersen, *The Prophetic Literature: An Introduction*, 7.

humans (Mic 3). Prophecy that speaks of the glory and wonder of God will inspire his people to worship. I Chronicles 24 lists a number of men who were set aside for the ministry of prophesying to the accompaniment of musical instruments as part of the temple worship. In small fellowships, it can be provided by the gift of prophecy. Large meetings for celebration will benefit from prophets who can bring a word from Yahweh to build the worship. Miriam, the prophetess led the Israelites in worship after they had crossed the red sea (Exod 15:19-21). In the temple, there were people whose role was to prophesy as part of the worship. They were professional worshippers and prophets, responsible for leading the worship in the house of Yahweh (I Chron 25:1, 6).

Similar role is played by AWA prophets. They were considered as cultic leaders who led in cultic/worship songs and performed dances during worship. Mari sources inform that the prophets involved in the ritual of Istar, which is one of the most essential religious festival for the people. Martti Nissinen explains that during this ceremony "the prophets, together with the musicians, turn out to play an important role in this royal ceremony involving a great number of cult functionaries."[410] They mostly delivered oracles in the hearing of the worshippers in the temple. They usually get into frenzy/ecstasy and prophesied the messages that received from their gods. For instance, an eleventh century BCE papyrus from Egypt relates the adventures of Wen-Amon, an Egyptian official sent to the Phoenician port-city of Byblos. The story tells that Wen-Amon was robbed on his way and was detained in the harbour. During his stay, a boy from the town of Dor was possessed by the god (seized with a prophetic frenzy).[411] Though no oracles were uttered, the action or the message of the boy was mean for Wen-Amon. Thus, prophecy usually comes to the attention of the official in one of two ways: either at the initiative of the prophet, who brings his divine message to the official or on a cultic occasion in the temple when the official is present. Prophecy in AWA context was recognized as a comprehensive phenomenon.

As cultic leaders, prophets dealt with cultic issues. In Israel's context, the most obvious issue in the prophetic indictment of the cult was idolatry because it is a fundamental violation of the covenantal demand for sole loyalty to the Lord. Worship of other gods, whether the Baal of the eighth century BCE or the lure of Babylonian religion during exile, was not only an abandonment of Israel's own covenant God but was regarded by the prophets as a folly since these were all false gods—not gods at all. (Hos 4:12; cf. Isa 44:9-20; Jer 10:1-10). The cultic indictment of the prophets included more than idolatry. It was concerned with the hypocrisy of pious practices in the absence of covenant obedience, especially as marked by a lack of knowledge of Yahweh and lack of justice and righteousness (Amos 5:21-24; Hos 4:1; 6:6; Isa 1:12-17; Jer 6:20).

---

410 Nissinen, *Prophecy and Prophecy in the Ancient Near Eastern*, 80.

411 John A. Wilson, "Egyptian Myths, Tales, and Mortuary Texts," in *ANET*, 25-26.

Attention to covenant integrity in the cult was the special responsibility of the priests, so the prophets often had harsh words for their failures to maintain covenant loyalty and obedience. Hosea proclaimed, "My people are destroyed for lack of knowledge; because you have rejected knowledge, I reject you from being a priest to me" (Hos 4:6; cf. Mic 3:11). Even the temple and the royal sanctuaries fall under indictment if their practices reflect service to royal power and the privileges of wealth (Jer 7; Mic 3:12). The life setting of Hosea 4:1 is "priestly" which is related to worship. Therefore, the phrase דַּעַת אֱלֹהִים (Knowledge of God) is related to sacrifices and offerings. According to Watts, "in both places where the full phrase is found, knowledge is listed beside righteousness and steadfast love as necessary counterparts of offerings and sacrifice in the ritual."[412] Hosea 2:22 and 5:4 indicate that "knowledge of God" is a ritual formula.

The corruption of Yahweh's covenant people was nationwide. They engaged themselves in idol worship and cult prostitution which were against the worship of Yahweh (Hos 4:12-14; 5:3, 4). Prophet Hosea laid the responsibility for this moral and spiritual corruption at the doorsteps of the irreverent, negligent and greedy priests. Smith claims that the priests "lived upon the vice of the day and possessed a vested interest in the crimes of their society."[413] Much of the blame have been placed upon the religious leaders whose duty was to discern the significance of the Covenant, understand its application and provide guidance and direction accordingly to the nation.[414] However, the priests misinterpreted or deliberately falsified the Law (Mic 3:11; Jer 8:8-10) for their personal benefit. The תּוֹרָה "law" signifies *instruction* or even *revelation* and "has a wider meaning than a national code of laws."[415] Hosea 4:7-8 portrays the character of the priests in the reign of Jeroboam II–the more they increased in numbers, the more they increased in wealth because they unscrupulously extracted wealth from the offerings brought by the people. They increased in both numbers and affluence, because it was a period of prosperity for Israel where there was a huge gap between the upper class and the lower class. The rich or upper class exploited the poor section of the society. Thus, instead of enhancing the religious institutions, and improving the teaching of the way and will of God, they deteriorated as leaders.

The question arises as to how the religious official who were to instruct and lead the people fulfil their duty when they themselves were guilty of their wrongdoing? From the time of Moses to the end of Judah the history of Israel was one long and sad story of a nation that was rebellious toward Yahweh and always inclined toward idolatry. Israel's lack of saving knowledge of Yahweh no doubt

412 John D. W. Watts, "The Knowledge of God in the Old Testament," *Review and Expositor* 55 (1958): 157.

413 George Adam Smith, "The Book of the Twelve Prophets," *The Expositor's Bible* (ed. W. Robertson Nicoli; Grand Rapids: Wm. B. Eerdmans Publishing Co., 1943), 506.

414 Jacob Myers, *Hosea to Jonah* (LBC, London: SCM Press Ltd, 1959), 23.

415 Myers, *Hosea to Jonah*, 23.

is largely due to a corrupt spiritual leadership. Therefore, prophets emphatically placed the responsibility for this lack of knowledge on Israel's priesthood.

2.3.7.2.4. Prophets' Participation in Political Affairs

Prophets were not only interested in the cultus, however, but also in political affairs, For as politics and religion were intimately related. When the nation was under the Philistine heel, the national religion was threatened and the national God dishonoured, and therefore the devotees of God and of the cultus through which He was worshipped were behind the national resurgence. It was Samuel, the seer, who encouraged Saul to take the lead, and the bands of frenzied prophets who kindled the ardour of the people. Later it was Ahijah who instigated Jeroboam to head the northern revolt (I Kgs 11:29-37), and Elisha who sent a member of one of the prophetic bands to promote the revolution of Jehu (II Kgs 9:1 -13). We also find the confrontations between royals and prophets. Those confrontations according to Matthews "were not simply personality conflicts but were instead part of a sociopolitical process that prevented the monarchs from becoming absolute."[416] Elisha was also heavily involved in politics, for example helping the king's forces attack Moab and defend Israel against Syrian attacks. Grottanelli remarks that both Elijah and Elisha opposed kings like Ahab, who had a wicked Phoenician wife, Jezebel, followed gods other than Yahweh, and did not respect the tribal rights of the people of Israel.[417]

The action of prophet Isaiah is another good example who participated in State political affairs. Isaiah ministered in the time of political crises: Isaiah played an important political role during Syro-Ephraimite crisis (Isa 7),[418] the Ashodod Affairs (Isaiah must appear naked before the rulers to announce political disaster Isa10-22), the anti-Assyrian rebellion and Jerusalem's siege (Isa 28-32; 36-37). In all these crises Isaiah took stand that Judah should not participate in any political alliance. Jeremiah was asked to wear an ox-yoke on the back (Jer 27:2-15) to announce political catastrophe. Thus, with the appearance of the prophets, that which has been announced begins to enter into the history of Israel.

2.3.7.2.5. Prophets as Encourager

Encouragement simply means giving hope in critical circumstances. Prophets in ancient Israel were seen as courageous individuals who were willing to stand against power on behalf of the weak and marginalized. In this, one raises questions such as: how does one begin to identify the prophets as encourager? In what way did the prophets encourage the people of Israel? One notices several prophets who used their voice of encouragement in different/various situations.

---

416 Matthews, *Social World of the Hebrew Prophets,* 22.

417 Grottanelli, *Kings and Prophets,* 130.

418 Joseph Blenkinsopp, *Isaiah 1-39: A New Translation with Introduction and Commentary* (AB; New York: Doubleday, 2000), 230.

Encouraging the people was one of the prophetic gifts in ancient Israel to lift them up and to revive them with a word from Yahweh. Sometimes it was like an instant healing. One sees the burdens fall to the ground as a great weight lifts off their sunken shoulders. The mission of the ancient Israel's prophets were to encourage life, by strengthening individuals spiritually, emotionally, physically, socially and economically, motivation and inspiration. In the Book of Judges, we have the fascinating story of Deborah and Barak. A general in the army, Barak, was commissioned to go to the front lines by God. However, he made a deal with the king's resident judge, Deborah. He said, "If you will go with me, I will go." Deborah agreed and God gave them a great victory. Deborah encouraged Barak to do the right thing and God's people were saved from an evil king.

One of the classic examples of such encouragements is seen in the life and ministry of Prophet Elisha. He served others till the day he died. When he was on his deathbed, Jehoash, the king of Israel, went to Elisha for advice and Elisha gave the king a strategy to defeat his enemies (II Kgs 13:14). Throughout history, people of Israel have endured the loss of many things but not hope. Hope is how they live for said the prophets to the people of Israel. In the Book of Hosea, one finds one of the more powerful expressions of encouragement offered by the prophet in the prophetic corpus. The final description of Israel's destruction is recorded in Hosea 11, judgement against a disobedient and unfaithful people, but hope for the faithful ones. Another such encouraging message is seen in Isaiah 11 which proclaims powerful words of promise. This is a passage which Watts affirms as a positive word of encouragement from prophet to people.[419]

In the context when war devastated the land, the words of Micah encouraged all who despair over humanity's inability to choose peace over war (Mic 4:3). In the passage Micah describes a time without fear, a day when Yahweh assembles the broken, even those broken by Yahweh's own judgement, to experience the reign of Yahweh forever. Jeremiah contributed extensively to the picture of prophets as encourager. In Jeremiah 18, the prophet, as a leader offered words of encouragement, hope and promise based on the character of Yahweh. In the account of the potter's house, Yahweh is the potter and He can reshape even spoiled vessel into one useable. Here Judah is giving another chance of hope that she can be useable if they are in the hands of the potter.

Ezekiel, leader of the Babylonian exile also added significantly to the image of the prophet as encourager though he proclaimed powerful words of condemnation and the certain judgement of Yahweh against the unfaithfulness ones. He also introduced encouragement in bold new ways. In Ezekiel 18:2, Ezekiel challenged old ideas with new understandings of Yahweh's interaction with Yahweh's people. The post-exilic prophet Zechariah is another classic example of a prophet through whom Yahweh spoke a tremendous word of encouragement (Zech 2:6-13). All

419 John D. W. Watts, *Isaiah 1-33* (WBC, vol. 24; Nashville: Thomas Nelson, 1985), 174.

throughout the history of Israel prophets were seen as encourager in different kinds of circumstances.

2.3.8. Appraisal

The understanding of the office of the prophet which we have found in prophets certainly is the result of a long historical development. There is no doubt that the offices of prophet, priest, and king did not exist together as harmoniously as is often assumed. Especially the origin, tradition, historical development, and theological implications of the office of the prophet and of the king necessitate competition. It is of fundamental importance to recognize that the concept of the kingship of Yahweh by no means has its presupposition in the earthly Davidic kingdom, but rather is linked with the prophet as his vizier.

During monarchic era, particularly in the reign of David, prophets were given more freedom to exercise their function even in the royal court. It is important to notice that throughout the history of Israel, prophets gained more and more freedom in their role as prophets; they played a "dialectical" role in most of the occasions, like that "performed by Nathan" in judging the sin of King David. Grottanelli has rightly points out that prophets defended the rights of the poor and the tradition of Yahwism, both of which were often betrayed in the corrupt atmosphere of the rapacious court, which inclined to the cultic practices of "foreign peoples." This dialectical role will enable them, under direct orders from Yahweh, actually to "make" new kings by opposing them to their predecessors, just as Samuel opposed David to Saul.[420]

All through the millennia of human history God has had His spokespersons who came and went with the years. The line begins in Genesis and runs through the historical books, the Psalms, and other prophetic writings. Its richest flowering, however, is found in the works of the four major and twelve Minor Prophets. These great men and women, who moved under the impulse of the divine Spirit, gave to the world, by inspiration of God, a body of literature in which people and nations have found hope and consolation, correction and reproof for their day. They dealt with the spiritual needs of the people and political, social, and religious conditions and affairs of the time.

The prophet represented a voice independent of that kingly power, a voice from God to the power structures primarily, but also to and for the people. They also proposed and advocated such remedial measures and counsels as would bring the nation and people back into a proper relationship with God. All of the prophets understood their proclamation of God's Word in the context of the traditions of covenant community. They were interpreters of the community faith traditions and sought their renewal in concern for love of God and neighbour. Prophets admonished, warned, directed, interceded, taught and counselled. Far more importantly they stood at the walls to see what Yahweh is doing that he may

420 Grottanelli, *Kings and Prophets,* 104.

call the body to respond. In short, the prophets model a pattern of leadership that finds its authority in God but its context in God's people.

Conclusion

This survey of the leadership in AWA and ancient Israel shows that they explicitly mention the idea of leadership several times and use it in different ways. The leadership structure, concept of leadership, and roles of leaders at every levels of AWA and Israel societies that have been explored in this chapter are essential to the people's daily lives as well as to their collective existence. AWA kingdoms had a well set up administration of class-based system consisting of kings, priest, and prophets. They had a hieratical system (structure) of leadership, where the king was the highest and overall in-charge in the administration and the development of the kingdom. For instance, the king in Mesopotamia was a mortal made to carry a superhuman charge. Thus, the study shows that royalty was not of human origin but added to society by the gods. No human can remove the king but only god could remove at any time to bestow upon another. Therefore, the royal leadership was supreme to all the leaderships that existed in AWA. The next prominent leadership that we find is priestly leadership. Priests served under the command of the kings in one way or the other. In Egypt the priests were the appointees of the king. In most of the AWA religious administrative context, the main duties of priests was to keep the shrine and sacred things in order, and also to perform religious duties.

In both societies, though prophets did not hold any set-up or permanent office, they played important role in the lives of the people in general and monarchs in particular. Their main task was to convey the message of god or Yahweh to the monarch and intervened in critical situation particularly on political crisis. Thus, the study shows that in AWA society, the three leadership offices maintained cooperation to each other for smooth functioning of the administration and to create a peaceful atmosphere in the kingdom. In Israelite society, we see a different scenario. Although, the king was an exalted figure among people and considered to have a special relationship to Yahweh, he is neither the son nor a representative of Yahweh. He is a ruler chosen by Yahweh who must reign according to the purpose of Yahweh which is characterized by righteousness and justice. According to the history of Israel, priestly office was very ancient and the most prominent. They were called into a high vocation, to be mediators between Yahweh and the people, and thus, they were supposed to contribute to the development of the religious and civil life of the nation.

In short, leaders are to exist for the well-being of those they lead, and they are not to exploit their positions for personal advantage or selfish gain. The lust for power, the lust for status and self-gratification, and the lust for wealth, remain paramount temptations in every age. In Israel, responsible headship was never about power or privilege; it was always about securing the well-being of those under one's charge. While a few leaders in the history modelled the ideals of the Torah's leadership (Josh 1:8-9, Josiah, in II kgs 22:18-19, and the like). However, most of the monarchs and the priests failed to performed their assigned duties or responsibilities. Thus, prophetic criticism was focused on them. The prophets spoke of what Yahweh will do, because of what he is. They confronted the leaders in the present with the God of Israel's past. Researcher will probe into the next two chapters which include exegetical study of the selected texts from the eighth century BCE prophetic literature and prophetic criticism on leadership.

Chapter 3

Leadership Challenges in the Eighth Century BCE Israel
A Historical Overview

Introduction

Eighth century BCE Israel posed many challenges to the leadership crises. Crisis is any event that is, or expected to lead to, an unstable and dangerous situation affecting an individual, group, community or whole society. Crises are considered to be negative changes in the political, economic, societal, and religious affairs. In the eighth century BCE Israel, the nation plunged into various crises because of the lack of proper leadership, and the unfaithfulness of leaders. Political leaders did not dwell on faith and trust in God but were confident on false security. The political situation of the nation affected its social, economic, and religious life. Thus, the purpose of this chapter is to study the leadership crises and issues of the century which demanded proper leadership.

3.1. Political Crisis in the Eighth Century BCE Israel

The eighth century BCE was a period of tense communal relations and political instability in both North and South Israel. After the reign of King Solomon, when the kingdom was divided into North and South, the North chose to adopt democratic government whereas South Israel chose to continue with Davidic leadership. Thus, in the history of South Israel there was no much problem or difficulty to enthrone the successive monarch. That could be the reason why South Israel experienced a more stable government than North Israel. On the other hand, political unrest and the struggle for power was the hallmark in the history of North Israel. Political unrest in North Israel disrupted the whole nation from free and peaceful living. In order to understand some of the major political issues faced by the eighth century BCE Israel, it is necessary to discuss the general context of the political condition of the century. Thus, the first part of this section deals with historical overview of political situation and its issues.

In the initial years of the eighth century BCE Israel and Judah with its influential kings Jeroboam II and Uzziah respectively enjoyed political constancy, in the absence of a super power. Assyria was its weakest and other kingdoms were not a threat to Israel.

There are different views about the marking of dates of the beginning of Assyrian conquest in Palestine.[421] The Assyrian conquest begins in the years 733-732 BCE in the north, in 712 BCE and 701 BCE in Philistia and Judah respectively.[422] However, since the ninth century BCE, Assyria had changed its policy of treaties with the conquered nations in which the treaties were signed with the whole nation instead of the king. During the time when Damascus' domination over the Aramean states like Syria, Phoenicia, Israel, Judah and Philistia was declining, Assyria rose to power and inaugurated the era of powerful empires.[423] In the first place, Adad-nirari III (811-783 BCE) gave way to the Assyrian imperialistic domination through two of his military campaigns (805-802 BCE) and these campaigns not only ended Damascus' claims over the Aramean states, but they gave Adad-nirari III a tribute of gratitude and viewed him as a saviour.[424] In a situation such as this, Israel and Judah were able to stand against Damascus, and Joash (801-786 BCE) defeated Ben-Hadad of Damascus three times and recovered the towns of Israel.[425] Joash also attacked Amaziah of Judah (800-783 BCE) who was trying "to control the trade route in the Edomite territory."[426] He broke the northern wall of Jerusalem, looted the temple and the royal court and brought some hostages in Samaria, thus, Judah became a vassal of Israel. Thereafter, politically, Judah under Uzziah (783-742 BCE) and Israel under Jeroboam II (786-746 BCE) enjoyed a period of peace, since Damascus had been weakened and Assyria was busy trying to control the Urartu (a region around Lake Van, north of Assyria).

However the situation changed as Tiglath-pileser III (745-727 BCE), possessing all the military power and administrative skills ascended the throne

421 Ephraim Stern, "Israel at the Close of the Period of the Monarchy: An Archaeological Survey," *The Biblical Archaeologist* 38 (1975): 27.

422 Stern, "Israel at the Close of the Period of the Monarchy...," 27.

423 Bright, *A History of Israel,* 256.

424 II Kgs 13:5. Bright, *A History of Israel,* 256.

425 II Kgs 13:25. G. W. Anderson, *The History and Religion of Israel* (Oxford: Oxford University Press, 1966), 98.

426 II Kgs 14:7. Anderson, *The History and Religion of Israel,* 98.

marking the rise of the Assyrian empire for the second time.[427] The prophets Amos, Hosea, Micah and Isaiah prophesied during this period. Nadav Na'aman remarks that according to the tradition of II Kings 15:27, "in the fifty-second year of Azariah king of Judah Pekah the son of Remaliah began to reign over Israel in Samaria, and reigned twenty years."[428] Pekah's second year marked the ascension of the throne of Uzziah's son Jotham (II Kgs 15:32) and in the seventeenth year of Pekah, Jotham's son Ahaz began to reign (II Kgs 16:1). In the twentieth year of Jotham, Hoshea killed Pekah (II Kgs 15:30). Therefore, according to Bright, during this period, assassinations continued in Israel and they resulted in the accession of Pekah (737-732 BCE) who teamed up with Razin of Damascus to attack Ahaz (735-715 BCE) of Judah in order to convince him to join their anti-Assyrian coalition.[429]

Ahaz called upon Assyria and introduced Judah under Assyrian vassalage which was against Isaiah's advice. During the reign of Pekah, the campaigns of Tiglath-pileser (733/34-732 BCE) against Damascus and Israel were conducted.[430] Tiglath-pileser undertook his second western military campaign in 734-732 BCE and Damascus fell in 732 BCE. Philip mentions that "the other Syro-Palestinian states, including Judah and Israel paid tribute to Assyria which extends its borders until the Wadi-el'-Arish."[431] King Hoshea (732-724 BCE) became an Assyrian vassal and portions of Israel's population was deported. However, Hoshea gave in to anti-Assyrian sentiments around him which was supported by Egypt and the angry Assyrian king Shalmanaser V (727-722 BCE) undertook a military campaign that ended in the vassalage of Egypt, and the destruction of Samaria in summer of 722 BCE by Sargon II (722-705 BCE).

Israel's populations were again deported (Isa 7:8b) and resettled in Halath (north-east of Nineveh), on the Harbor (the Khabour River), and in the highlands of Medes (north-west Iran) and the kingdom was divided into various provinces like Dor, Megiddo, Gilead, and Samaria was repopulated and rebuilt as capital province.[432] In Judah, Hezekiah (727-697 BCE) resisted to join the Ashdod revolt that Sargon II defeated in 712 BCE with the help of the Egyptians, Hezekiah rebelled against Sennacherib (705-681 BCE) who, weakened by his victory over

427 Bright, *A History of Israel,* 256.

428 Nadav Na'aman, "Historical and Chronological Notes on the Kingdoms of Israel and Judah in the Eight Century BC," *VT* 36 (1986): 74.

429 Bright, *A History of Israel,* 257.

430 Na'aman, "Historical and Chronological Notes on the Kingdoms of Israel and Judah in the Eight Century BC," 76.

431 Philip J. King, *Amos, Hosea, Micah: An Archaeological Commentary* (Philadelphia: Westminster Press, 1988), 88, 135.

432 King, *Amos, Hosea, Micah,* 137.

Egypt and Judean cities, could not sustain the siege of Jerusalem.[433] Though the city was miraculously spared, Judah paid a heavy tribute to Assyria until the fall of Nineveh in 612 BCE.

3.1.1. Political Power Struggle

Power struggle simply means violent competition for power. It is a situation where two people or groups try to become the more or the most powerful, each of whom is equally committed to winning. The power struggle in North Israel between the supreme leaders could lead to violence. Violence and political instability have increased across Israel since leaders attempted to gain power by violence. For instances, Jehu ascended himself on the throne in a violent manner.[434] He assassinated the entire royal family of Jehoram (a descendant of Omri) and founded a new dynasty of five kings who successively occupied the throne for almost a century, nearly half of the time of North Israel's existence. Despite a high level of national prosperity and increasing economic activity during Jehu's dynasty, Israel continued to be racked by internal social and political unrest.

After the death of Jeroboam II (one of Jehu's descendant), there was a sharp decline in the political power of Israel which was sapped from within by a rapid succession of palace revolutions and royal assassinations. The dynasty of Jehu and Jeroboam II came to an end when Zechariah son of Jeroboam II was assassinated by Shallum after a reign of six months.[435] However, after a month, Menahem was helped to strengthen his position on the throne by Tiglath-pileser III, but at the cost of paying heavy tribute to Assyrians.[436] Pekah an army captain murdered Menahem, the pro-Assyrian and ascended himself on the throne. He planned to organize an anti-Assyrian revolt along with Rezin of Damascus. However, his policy failed and ended up with paying a heavy price and also his wide areas were detached and incorporated into the Assyrian provinces. Now, the pro-Assyrian party led by Hoshea used this failure as excuse for murdering Pekah, to replace him with a king. But in 724 BCE Hoshea rebelled against Assyria with the support

---

433 Isa 36-37. Na'aman, "Historical and Chronological Noteson the Kingdoms of Israel and Judah in the Eight Century BC," 76.

434 The dates offered to the dynasty of Jehu differs from individual scholars: for instance, J. Maxwell Miller & John H. Hayes, 845-747 BCE. *A History of Ancient Israel and Judah* (2nd ed.; Louisville, London: Westminster John Knoz Press, 2006), 408; Samuel J. Schultz, 841-743 BCE., *The Old Testament Speaks (*5th ed.; San Francisco: Harper Collins Publishers, 2000), 193.

435 Albertz, *A History of Israelite Religion in the Old Testament Period,* 162; Schultz, *The Old Testament Speaks,* 198; Bruce K. Waltke, *An Old Testament Theology: An Exegetical, Canonical, and Thematic Approach* (Grand Rapids, Michigan: Zondervan, 2007), 695, 715-716, 731; Herbert Donner, "The Separate States of Israel and Judah," *Israelite and Judaean History* (ed. John H. Hayes and James Maxwell Miller; London: SCM Press, 1977), 423.

436 Donner, "The Separate States of Israel and Judah," *Israelite and Judaean History*, 423; Schultz, *The Old Testament Speaks,* 197.

of Egypt.[437] Then in 722 BCE Samaria was captured by Tiglath-pileser III and the kingdom of Israel was put to an end. The crisis here is the lack of proper leadership and the weakness of the nation's leaders that brought one nation to an end.

3.1.2. Misuse of Political Power or Authority

Another issue was the Israelite monarchs' misused political power for their personal gain. Abuse of authority is an arbitrary exercise of power by a military member, federal official, employee that injures, adversely affects the rights of a subordinate by autocratic, careless conduct, severe abusive language that result in personal gain or advantage to themselves. Misuse of authority includes a wide range of subjects such as improper use of title, position or rank. Further, the abuse of authority involves discrimination, creating a hostile work environment, being abusive, intentional or improper use of government resources. Political corruption is the abuse of political power relations for private or personal gains. Corruption exists where there is monopoly of discretionary power and lack of accountability for it. This ultimately boils down to the failure of the political market (i.e., government) and the economic market resulting from the polarization of political and economic power respectively.

Ancient Israel had a new political power structure developed during the peak of Solomon's reign. From the time of King Solomon the monarchs lived in palaces built in princely style by foreigners and the state administration was greatly enlarged. A new fiscal system was introduced and special royal officials of high rank were appointed. Then royal administration came into being which soon developed into an aristocracy.[438] The aristocrats controlled the central government or the administration. The burdens came in the form of taxes that hit the life of the peasants. Thus, political corruption began to creep in during the transition of monarchy and it continued throughout the history of Israel. In this context, Soggin comments that we no longer find isolated cases of corruption or suppressive on the contrary we must speak of a system so corrupt and repressive.[439]

Politics in the eighth century BCE Israel was also corrupted. The kings and the political leaders acquired every power and exercised them for their own personal benefit. One of the good examples of a failed leader among the eighth century BCE Israel's kings was Ahaz, king of Judah. He misused the political power when he was forced to face Syro-Ephramite crisis.[440] Ahaz was challenged whether

437 Albertz, A History of Israelite Religion in the Old Testament Period, 162; Schultz, *The Old Testament Speaks,* 199; Donner, "The Separate States of Israel and Judah," *Israelite and Judaean History*, 427, 432.

438 Edward Neufeld, "The Emergence of Royal-Urban Society in Ancient Israel," *HUCA* 31 (1960), 41.

439 J. Alberto Soggin, *Introduction to the Old Testament* (London: SCM Press, 1976), 231.

440 Pekah, king of Israel and Razin, king of Damascus in a coalition against Ahaz, since he refused to join anti-Assyria.

to hold on pro-Assyria stance or join anti-Assyria coalition. Yet, in the midst of the crisis Isaiah, the prophet, appeared and argued for one political principle or advice-to stay away from the alliance, neither with a foreign power nor with the Syro-Ephramite forces, and trust in Yahweh. Amidst Isaiah's warning, Ahaz decided to follow another policy. He invited the Assyrians for help by offering his own submission and paid a heavy tribute from the temple and palace treasuries in Jerusalem. Assyria, under Tiglath-Pileser III, attacked the Syro-Ephramite forces and brutally defeated and reduced them to Assyrian provinces. With the help of Tiglath-pileser III, Ahaz was free from the Syro-Epharmite invasion, yet, he sold out the freedom of Judah to Assyria by becoming a mere vassal state.

Ahaz then inculcated all the pagan practices of the Assyrians, reproducing the Damascas altar in the Temple at Jerusalem (II Kgs 16:15). Bright states that the kingship of Ahaz was "one of the worst periods of apostasy that Judah had ever known."[441] Schultz also remarks that Ahaz promoted the most obnoxious idolatrous practices, though Isaiah the prophet advised him on various issues.[442] Thus, it is apparent that king Ahaz misused his power to promote and propagate pagan religion which was an anathema to the religion of the people of Israel. The wrong decision of Ahaz ruined the political freedom and brought political instability in Judah. As a king, he was supposed to protect and provide security for all the citizens, but he failed when he choose trust in political power rather than to trust in Yahweh.

Misuse of political power is also seen in misusing justice. It means practising injustice by the elite group of the people and oppressing the peasants in the society. Oppressed people are obviously excluded from power and control; they are the victims of human injustice. The eighth century BCE prophets' preaching was, view from below and it offered a check point for human dignity *vis-a-vis* solutions to oppression. To what extent are those solutions respectful of human dignity? How comprehensive are the changes sought in relationship to the beneficiaries of those changes? The eighth century BCE prophets saw the religious apparatus, state politics, and financial elite of their time as the justice-denying social amalgam ultimately responsible for the fate of the oppressed. For Amos to have focused his attention on the contributions of the oppressed to their own fate would have meant to blame the victims. The danger with an individualistic concept of sin is the tendency to neglect the role that oppressive social structures play in people's well-being.

3.1.3. Lack of Vision in Leadership

Visions are simply the first step in the goal setting and planning process. Vision has always been considered an important component in leadership. True leaders see things differently. For leaders, vision is not a dream; it is a reality that is yet

441 Bright, *History of Israel*, 277.

442 Samuel J. Schultz, *The Old Testament Speaks* (New York: Harper & brothers, 1960), 209.

to come into existence. Vision is palpable to leaders; their confidence in and dedication to vision is so strong they can devote long hours of labor over many years to bring it into being.[443] For instance, "Isaiah spent his life trying to get Israel to become acquainted with God and His Word."[444] In this way, a vision acts as a force within, compelling a leader to action. Jon Byler remarks, "the force created by the vision not only energizes the leader, but also gives strength to followers. They see the vision and the energy of the leader, and are encouraged to get involved in making the vision become a reality."[445] It gives purpose to a leader, and the power of the vision and the leader's devotion to it work to inspire others. Leaders must maintain a balance between a clear understanding of the present and a clear focus on the future.

Unfortunately, however, many of the kings of the eighth century BCE Israel could not keep a clear vision of the present and the future. The supreme leaders of North Israel killed one another because of the love of power and position. Some kings contended with success, wealth, material prosperity and political achievement like Jeroboam II, who was deeply into pleasure.[446] Ahaz, king of Judah was concerned only about himself and his time of reign, that was why he shunned the advice of prophet Isaiah and appealed for alliance with Assyrian king.[447] Hezekiah blew off the chances of being a good king towards the end of his reign. He trusted the upcoming powerful kingdom, the Babylon and his king. He never had far-sightedness for the kingdom and its people.

Leaders are strategic thinkers who are willing to take risks. Their actions, together with the actions of those who follow them, determine what the future will be. Leaders do not create something out of nothing. They look at what they know to exist and search for relationships, the way things are meant to fit together. Once they find the connections, they share them with other people and work with them to bring about desired changes. However, the eighth century BCE Israel's kings failed to build relationship with people who supported them in building a peaceful kingdom, especially, the prophets, who were always longing to create a good relationship with them, in good times and bad times.

---

443 John C. Maxwell, *Developing the Leader Within You* (New Delhi: Satyam Enterprises, n.y), 146.

444 M. Chandra Kumar, *Leadership Insights from Heroes of the Bible* (Secunderabad: Authentic Books, 2008), 254.

445 Jon Byler, *Th Art of Christian Leadership* (Secunderabad: Authentic Books, 2008), 77.

446 Walter C. Kaiser, *A History of Israel from the Bronze Age through the Jewish War* (Nashville: Boardman and Holman Publishers, 1998), 351; H. Donner, "The Separation State of Israel and Judah," in *Israelite and Judean History* (ed. J. H. Hayes and J. M. Miller; Philadelphia: Westminster, 1977), 400.

447 J. Alberto Soggin, *An Introduction to the History of Israel and Judah* (Valley Forge: Trinity Press International, 1993), 249; Donald H. Mason, *Thus Saith the Lord: An Introduction to the Prophets of Israel* (Madras: Christian Literature Society, 1962), 69.

3.2. Social and Economic Crises in the Eighth Century BCE Israel

In the eighth century BCE Israel, during the reign of Jeroboam II[448] and Uzziah,[449] both North and South Israel experienced exceptional economic growth that caused tremendous social and economic changes in Israelite society. There was territorial expansion which brought immense material wealth to both the kingdoms. Scholars argue that during the second half of Jeroboam II Israel enjoyed a period of national restoration and expansion.[450] The writer of Kings (II Kgs 14:23-29) mentions that the military victories of Jeroboam II which resulted in vast territorial expansion. This has been recorded as from Lebo-Hamath as far as the sea of Arabah, although the identity of these places is debatable. This territorial expansion was set against a background of bitter hostility between Israel and the Aramean kingdom of Damascus. In fact, this expansion gave Jeroboam II complete control of Damascus and Hamath, which was the territory realized under David and Solomon.[451] Thus the statement Jeroboam "restored the boundaries of Israel from Lebo-hamath to the Sea of Arabah," (11 Kgs 14: 25), the ideal borders of the Promised Land and the farthest limits of the United Monarchy, reflects an ideology which saw the Israelite king as achieving the glories of David and Solomon.

---

448 The chronologies given in Kings and Chronicles contain internal discrepancies; the dates offered by scholars for individual reign are usually only approximate. Indeed, scholars have different proposals about the period of the reign of Jeroboam II. For example, Cogan and Tadmor, 789-748; Albright, John Bright, MacLean, Philip J. King, 786-746; Miller-Hayes, 787-747. All these proposals are very close to each other. He ruled for 41 years including the ten-year co-regency with his father Joash. Cf. S. J. De Vries, "Chronology of the OT," in *IDB*, vol. 1, 587.

449 Ca. 792-740 BCE (II Chron. 26). John D.W. Watts, *Isaiah 1-33* (WBC, Waco/Texas: Word Books Publisher, 1985), 7.

450 Philip J. King, *Amos, Hosea, Micah--An Archaeological Commentary* (Philadelphia: The Westminster Press, 1988), 30; Bright, *A History of Israel,* 258; Miller and Hayes, *A History of Ancient Israel and Judah*, 291-296; Anderson and Freedman, *Amos*, 19. The southern border is described as the Sea of Arabah (II Kgs 14:25). According to Josh. 3:16 and 12:3 the Sea of Arabah is glossed the Salt Sea i.e., the Dead Sea. In Amos 6:14, however, the designation of the southern border of Israel is the brook valley of Arabah. Most scholars (Hobbs, Miller, Hayes, Cogan, Kaiser and others) conclusively identify the Sea of Arabah as the Dead Sea. However, there is no consensus among the scholars about the specific location. According to Yohanan Aharoni Lebo-Hamath is to be identified with Lebweh situated on one of the sources of the Orontes north of Baalbek. Yohanan Aharoni, *The Archaeology of the Land of Israel from the Prehistoric Beginning to the End of the First Temple Period* (Philadelphia: The Westminster Press, 1982), 72. This region was forested and only sparsely settled in antiquity; it served in all periods a natural boundary in the middle of the Beqa. T. R. Hobbs also asserts, the city name, Lebo-Hamath appears in the other documents from the AWA in various forms, from the city lists of Thutmoses III to the records of Tiglath Pilesar III. T. R. Hobbs, *2 Kings* (WBC, vol. 13; ed. David A. Hubbard, *et* al; Waco/Texas: Word Books, 1985), 183.

451 Walter C. Kaiser, *A History of Israel from the Bronze Age through the Jewish War* (Nashville: Boardman and Holman Publishers, 1998), 351.

In the South, Uzziah took the initiative of mending the walls and fortifications of Jerusalem and the army was also reorganized.[452] He conquered Edom came under his control and developments such as opening up of industries and port facilities of Ezion-geber were taken up (II Kgs 14:22) where the Red Sea trade was perhaps revitalized. Some of the states like Negev and the north and east parts of the Philistine Plain were amalgamated with Judah. The international trade was "a source of substantial wealth" and of competition between Israel and Phoenicia on one hand and Judah and Philistia on the other against Damascus.[453] Goods were transported from the Phoenician ports to Israel and Judah by the merchants. There were also trade routes passing through Transjordan to northern Arabia which were under the control of Israel and Judah.[454] As production increased consumerism, individualism, greed and overconfidence grew as well.

Uzziah also rebuilt Elath, restored it to Judah, and made remarkable victories against the old enemies, both East and West (II Kgs 14:22; II Chron 26:2) as well as took control of the Negeb and the southern desert. He subdued the Edomites and the Philistines put the ammonites under subjection. He encouraged agriculture and the domestic acts of peace and raised a large powerful army (II Chron 26:1-5).[455] Agriculture flourished though occasional crop failures occurred. International trade was a source of substantial wealth and competition between the Israelites and the Phoenicians as the major international trade routes were controlled by Jeroboam II. It must be stated that the economic circumstances were relatively favourable for both nations.

However, the prosperity and economic growth brought unwanted socio-economic changes. In the socio-economic scene, the ruling aristocrats (leaders) started controlling more than half of the total goods and services, therefore, the economic growth, military victories and the territorial expansion had a negative impact upon the general society. Both North and South Israel were faced with several social and economic issues and some of the issues will be discussed in the following.

3.2.1. Issue of Class System

Peace and prosperity prevailed during the first part of the eighth century in Israel and Judah under the reign of Jeroboam II and Uzziah, however, during this period Solomon's stratification of society reached its peak.[456] The society was then divided

---

452 II Chron 26:9, 11-15. Pfeiffer, *Old Testament History*, 322.

453 Bright, *A History of Israel*, 245.

454 Pfeiffer, *Old Testament History*, 322-323; Premnath, *Eight Century Prophets*, 72.

455 Bright, *A History of Israel*, 258 (II Chron 26:9-15); Theodore H. Robinson, *A History of Israel* (vol.1; Oxford: Oxford University Press, 1948), 359; Giuseppe Ricciotti, *The History of* Israel (vol. I; Milwaukee: The Bruce Pub. Company, 1955), 348; Keith W. Whitelam, "Jeroboam II," in *ABD* (vol. 3; ed. David Noel Freedman, et al; New York: Doubleday, 1992), 745.

456 Bright, *A History of Israel*, 243.

into two distinct groups: upper class (aristocracy or rich) and lower class (peasantry or poor) where there was a wide gap between the two. Israel was transformed from being traditionally an agrarian and pastoral society to becoming a commercial and industrial superpower. Originally Israel's society had an egalitarian set up without class distinctions. As a community they enjoyed equal rights and shared equal responsibilities. However, with the development of the monarchy, the system of society changed and the class system appeared. Meanwhile with the boom in trade and industry especially during Jeroboam II and Uzziah, there was the emergence of a wealthy class of people, and Israel was no longer merely a nation of small farmers. The old conservative and rural lifestyle developed into a new urban life. The status of the underprivileged class was pathetic under the new economic structures.

The socio-economic scenario was marked by a growing inequality between the rich and the poor which resulted in class distinction. Robinson calls the new emerged group merchant princes (aristocrats).[457] Aristocrats were as those in an agrarian economy, who without themselves engaging in agricultural labour live off the land by controlling the peasants so as to be able to take from them a part of their product. Gottwald states that "social classes may be said to exist whenever one social group is able to appropriate a part of the surplus labour product of the other groups."[458] This means that class is seen to exist when society is divided into categories and some people living by the production of others. Richard J. Coggins remarks that the economic prosperity of the Israelites "had led to various changes in the make-up of the community, with greater prosperity for a few and unjust oppression for many others."[459]

The rich developed a town or city-culture by separating themselves from the poor and the peasant. This gave birth to two different and distinct cultures within the same society. The members of the elite did not recognize the peasant or the urban poor as fellow human beings. E. W. Davies adds that there developed "a society where the rich led lives of luxury and rivalry, where many were arrogant and over-confident, and where there was little concern for the plight of the poor and underprivileged."[460] Bright notes that "the upper class was a minority made of the king, the royal family and the aristocratic nobility-governors and maintainers of royal estates; and the lower class was made of artisans, labourers, herdsmen

457 Theodore H. Robinson, *A History of Israel* (vol.1; Oxford: Oxford University Press, 1948), 361.

458 Norman K. Gottwald, "Social Class as an Analytic and Hermeneutical Category in Biblical Studies," *JBL* 112 (1993): 4.

459 Richard J. Coggins, "The Old Testament and the Poor," *The Expository Times* 99 (1987): 13.

460 Robert B. Coote, *Amos Among the Prophets: Composition and Theology* (Philadelphia: Fortress press, 1981), 25; E.W. Davies, *Prophecy and Ethical tradition of Israel* (Sheffield: JSOT Press, 1981), 38.

such as the prophet Amos who formed the majority."[461] The upper class were the beneficiaries and were accumulating much wealth and various means were used to extract heavy amounts of economic surplus from the lower class which led to the deterioration of the plight of peasantry who constituted the majority of the population.[462] Thus, Israel's social structure had gone through a radical change of character.

Aristocrats were educated, merchant elite living in the cities. Their functions were military, tax collection and the corn trade. They also built palaces, temples and used the peasants for the same. The accumulation of wealth was mainly through holding more cultivated land area. Money lenders were part of this class in order to "help" the poor. The peasants were in the majority. For Bernhard Lang, "a peasant is not a farmer or an agricultural entrepreneur but rather one who maintains a household. Instead of earning a profit he wants to feed his family which is the basic economic unit."[463] He did not produce for the market but for himself and his family. Peasants did weaving, carpentry, pottery, and the like. Peasants were rural cultivators and small agricultural producers whose surpluses were transferred to a dominant group of rulers. It was observed that the privileged upper-class accumulated wealth by extracting it from the incomes or earnings of the poor. The agricultural products of the underprivileged were taxed in order to maintain a comfortable and luxurious life for the elite.[464]

In the meantime, they also used their wealth to secure personal enjoyment and luxury, especially food and drink, clothing and furniture, weapons and armour. A vast change was introduced in the lifestyle of the people of the elite. Consumption was no longer a means to stay alive but it itself became the way of life, a status symbol to show off one's wealth. Expensive feasts, entertainment, costly presents, and elaborate attire became the paraphernalia for displaying one's economic strength. Abstention from hard labour had become an expression of superior economic achievement, respectability and a requisite of decency. From the sophisticated lifestyle of the elite group, one can conclude that the class system of the eighth century BCE was a big issue protested by the prophets.

3.2.2. Economic Issue (Market based economy): from need based to market based

The national prosperity and restoration brought about economic transition from a closed economy to a commercial economy. In a subsistence economy the major concern of the peasant is to provide for the members of the family by cultivating the land. This exhibits a physical or corporeal-sense of property. In an economy

---

461 Bright, *A History of Israel,* 244.

462 Premnath, *Eight Century Prophets,* 43.

463 Bernhard Lang, "The Social Organization of Peasant Poverty in Biblical Israel," *JSOT* 24 (1987): 48.

464 Albertz, *A History of Israelite Religion in the Old Testament Period,* 160; D. N. Premnath, *Eighth Century Prophets: A Social Analysis* (St. Louis: Chalice Press, 2003), 21, 27.

where the market begins to play a vital role, an intangible sense of property emerges related to the access to the market. But, in the market set-up, service is turned into a profession and labour into a commodity, an abstract quantity to be offered for sale in the market. This might have led the eighth century BCE Israel underprivileged, the poor people to feel exploited as they were treated poorly by the privileged class who controlled the market economy. Things were sold to the poor people at a high price. The rich people had provision for stockpiling grain and could have complete control of the economy in times of agricultural failure.[465] The business changed from a need based to a market based economy.

With the expansion of the market network, trade developed in the area of both export and import. Production came to be controlled not by the needs of the people but by the market demands. Cash crops served as effective media of exchange because they were worth more than subsistence crops. The upper class owner of the land forced the peasants to grow cash crops rather than food crops. So, the peasants had to buy the staples, which they once produced themselves, to survive with the meager resources at their disposal. The need to buy staples forced them into an unfamiliar market system where the merchants would cheat them with false measures and rigged scales. The competitive mentality of a capitalistic society was clearly manifested in corrupt business practices (Amos 8:5, 6; Hos 12:7). The elite oppressed the underprivileged class by promoting a corrupt market economy and manipulating the economy of the society.[466] Thus, we see that cheating and exploitation in the market were common during the time of the eighth century BCE Israel. James Luther Mays observes that while selling grain to the poor, those cunning merchants used a small "peck" to measure what they gave, whereas a heavy weight was used to determine what they bought.[467] This shows that there was economic exploitation and it practised in different ways:

(i) Reduced the quality of grain, while buying and selling the elite shrink the *ephah*.[468] This was practised by reducing the measure of the corn or

465 James Luther Mays, *Amos, A Commentary* (London: SCM Press, 1969), 143 (Amos 8:5).

466 Coote, *Amos Among the Prophets,* 33.

467 Mays, *Amos*, 144. Such practice was prohibited in Israelite society for this would be a violation of the commandment against stealing (Lev19:35, 36; Deut 25:13-16). Archaeologists found two sets of weights, dating to the eighth century BCE, while making excavations at Tirzah shops, assuming that one set might have been used for buying and other for selling.

468 The *ephah* was the basket in which the grain was measured out to the customer. The use and misuse of weights and measures are common themes even in AWA. In Egypt, the instruction of Amen-em-opet, the king declared himself that "I have neither increased or diminished the grain-measure. I have not had diminished the *aroura.* I have not falsified a half-*aroura* of the land. I have not added to the weight of the balance. I have not *weakened* the plummet of the scales." John A. Wilson, "Egyptian, Myths, Tales, and Mortuary Texts," in *ANET*, 34. The *ephah* was approximately equivalent to forty liters. Wolff, *Joel and Amos,* 327. There was substitution of a small *ephah* for the a large *ephah,* Deuteronomy 25:14 forbids various *ephah* baskets used to exploit the buyer. According to RusselFuller, the various norms of capacity

selling the short measure of grain. As a result the poor buyer will receive less than the actual weight. During this time the poor struggled to keep both ends meet. Mays remarks that "at root the practice was a breach of the commandment against stealing (Exod 20:15)."[469] In this context, reducing the quality by cheating through less measurement was adding fuel to their poverty.

(ii) Economic exploitation was also done through increasing the (price) *shekel*.[470] It is the weight to employ the purchase price, weighing gold, silver or bronze, which was used before the usage of coins. When the greedy merchants increase the weight the purchase price will go up accordingly. The customer pays more than what he should for the goods he bought. After reducing the quality of grain, increasing of money becomes double exploitation in the market.

(iii) Another economic exploitation was done through tampering the balance/scale by bending one of the bowls or the cross beam or shifting the fulcrum from the middle of the beam. The milder way to explain this situation may be the collapse of the entire ethical and moral system of values in the society.

(iv) The fourth kind of economic exploitation was in the form of selling the chaff of wheat. Anderson and Freedman remark that the merchants not only reduced the quantity and increased the price but the product itself

---

may explain laws against the unscrupulous who exploit the customers by selling them a small *ephah* for the price of a large *ephah*. Russel Fuller, "אֵיפָה," in *NIDOTTE* (vol. 1; ed. Willem A. VanGemeren, et al; Cumbria: Paternoster Press, 1996), 38. Amos 8:5 condemned the practice of making the *ephah* smaller to defraud the buyer. If its full capacity is reduced by changing its form, the buyer receives too little. Wolff, *Joel and Amos*, 327.

469 Mays, *Amos*, 144.

470 The *shekel* was the unit of weight used on the scales. It commonly means to weight something in the balance to measure its amount i.e., weighing silver or gold as payment for something. Monetary transactions were made by weighting pieces of silver or bronze using the shekel weights. Yigal Ronen, "The Enigma of the Shekel Weights of the Judean Kingdom," *BA* 59 (1996): 122. The word שקל and its derivations are common even in AWA literatures. The meaning is the same as in Hebrew, however, the weights are varied according to time and places. For Hermann J. Austral, שקל was a common unit of weight throughout Canaan and Mesopotamia. "שקל," in *TWOT* (vol. 2; ed. R. Laird Harris; Chicago: Moody Press, 1980), 953. For R. B. Y. Scott, there are three standards of Shekel in Palestine. "Weights and Measures," *Biblical Archaeologist* 22 (1959): 32-39. The *shekel* was a weight employed in weighing the purchasing price. If the weights are enlarged, we cannot call it just weight but deceitful weight. Therefore, using weight like this will increase the purchase price. In this context the issue of boosting the price (make the great *shekel*) refers to the practice in the Israelite society of using a larger one than ordinary shekel weight to cheat the customers out of the proper value of their merchandise. Jerry E. Shepherd, "שקל," in *NIDOTTE* (vol. 4; ed. Willem A. VanGemeren, et al; Cumbria: Paternoster Press, 1996), 238. Wolff remarks that "when weights and measures are falsified the result is the complete perversion of the economic and social order." Wolff, *Joel and Amos*, 327.

> was too inferior.[471] The chaff that falls when grain is processed is actually useless for food. It may be mixed with the food of animals. However, here, it was re-mixed with the clean grain and sold to the poor.[472] The rich merchants even refused to give up the selling of the wheat mixed with chaff. When greed takes over, there is no principle or morality is left. All these resulted in a conflicting economic differentiation, producing many debtors, impoverished farmers, and unemployed people.

The use of false balances and deceitful practices were prohibited in the Israelite law (Deut 25:13-15). In a true sense, the monarchy and the religious leaders were generally responsible for maintaining such standards (Deut 17:8-20; II Sam 12:1-25; I Kgs 3:16-28). Instead of being the protectors of the poor from injustice, they become the promoters of economic exploitation. When weights and measures are falsified, the result is the complete perversion of the economic and social order. According to Wolff, these procedures gave unfair advantage and profit to the seller.[473] The honesty issue in the market place directly affected the economy of the poor. This kind of practice was done when one group monopolised the market. Hayes declares that for Amos, mercantile deceit and economic exploitation were exceptionally costly because they will lead the poor to the debt and ultimately to slavery.[474] All these portray the attempt to abuse the poor economically.

3.2.3. The New Urban Life-Style: Issue of Elimination of Peasants from the Land

Israel was an agrarian society where the majority of the population were peasant cultivators. Gottwald states that ancient Israel distinguished as a communitarian mode of production is "composed of a majority of cultivators of the soil and also practised animal husbandry."[475] They had a strong family and village based mode of life. Land was a major component of an Israelites' family household. It is the core foundation of the Israelite society. It reflects their identity as a community so that to lose their land meant to lose their identity as a community. It also relates to the religious festivals such as the Sabbath, sabbatical year, jubilee, which protect the rights of the poor: the widow, the orphan and the alien. The basic concept was that the land belonged to God.[476] Therefore, the land could not be sold

471 Anderson and Freedman, *Amos,* 808.

472 Mays, *Amos,* 145.

473 Wolff, *Joel and Amos,* 327.

474 Hayes, *Amos,* 209.

475 Norman K. Gottwald, "Sociology," in *ABD* (vol. 6; ed. David Noel Freedman, et al; New York: Doubleday, 1992), 83.

476 Deut 15:1-11; 14:28-30; Lev 23:3; 25.

permanently as it reflected the identity of the community (I Kgs 21:3). However, by the eighth century BCE few elite classes in Israel developed a monopoly on productive land.[477] Thus, accumulation of land by a small minority at the expense of the common peasant became the heart of the issue in the eighth century BCE Israel.

One of the reasons was that the bad climate conditions made the economy of the small farmers very pathetic. In order to save themselves and the land, they had to go to the money lenders, and failure in paying back the debt resulted in taking over the land by money lenders. Later on, when the debt increased, they sold themselves as slaves for their lifetime.[478] Moreover, when the cities became the centres of political and economic life, prices went up causing the further alienation of the poor from the land. Here, the widening social distinction between the merchant class and the consumer class is clearly shown. This is evident from the use of the terms in Amos 8:4 "trample" and "destroy." This was equivalent to finishing off the poor from the land. The intention was to monopolise the market, to take over the land of the poor and to make them bankrupt. As a result the poor were virtually exterminated from the land.

3.2.4. Exploitation and Oppression of the Poor

In any society when justice is denied to people, there is oppression. During the eighth century BCE Israel, Justice was denied to the poor and lower classes of the society. The corrupt economic practices were common in the Israelite cities. Since the wealthy privileged people controlled the whole society, they become the leaders over the poor and they led the peasants from their independent situation to helplessness. The poor were being exploited in various ways. For example, at the time of the planting of the crops, the small farmers often had to borrow money from the rich at a high rate of interest.[479] Most often, loans were obtained on the value and security of the next harvest. When crop production failed to meet the requirement due to bad weather, the peasants went deeper into debt because they could not pay back the loans. Moreover, they would borrow again for survival in the next year. Failure in paying back the debt resulted in the loss of land at the hand of the money lenders. If the debt increased further, they sold themselves as slaves for a lifetime.[480] Shalom M. Paul states that these unscrupulous traders in

477 P. P. Thomas, *Jeroboam II the King and Amos the Prophet: A Social-Scientific Study on the Israelite Society During the 8th Century BCE* (Delhi: ISPCK, 2003), 182; Carol J. Dempsey "Economic Injustice in Micah," *BT* (1994): 272 76.

478 Robinson, *A History of Israel*, 359 (Amos 2:6).

479 J. Philip Hyatt, "The Book of Amos," *Interpretation* 3 (1949): 342; Premnath, *Eighth Century Prophets*, 95. It is said that the Assyrian empire of the eighth century BCE had the interest rate of 20 percent or higher and in Palestine the rate of interest would have been 25 percent or more. The interest rate in Israel during the eighth century BCE is not clearly mentioned.

480 Theodore H. Robinson, *History of Israel* (vol.1.; Oxford: Oxford University Press,1948), 359. The poor could be sold into slavery for a paltry indebtedness. Selling the poor man for a pair of

grain are traders in human slavery too.[481] It is to buy or purchase rather than to sell the poor in Amos 2:6b. For Jorg Jeremias, the poor are those who were ruined through deceptive commerce and economic exploitation.[482]

The people mentioned here are not just grain merchants or the slave traders but the wealthy elite. They gave loans to the poor; they have cheated them in the business especially of cereals, so that they will not be able to pay back the loans. The immediate way before the poor was to sell their farming lands, then their own houses and become just the labourers in the fields of the elite. This will naturally end up in debt slavery. Rainer Albertz notes that in this way the poor became permanently impoverished and became debtor-slaves.[483] Thus, we see that the worst part during eighth century BCE Israelite society was buying the poor for a meagre amount without any ethical standards. Even if the poor owned a small amount, they were sold off to slavery.

The slave-traders gave loans knowing that the poor will not be able to repay, so that ultimately they would become slaves to the traders. All kinds of social influence of the elite and the merchants were used for their economic advantage over the poor and needy. It was at this juncture that the prophetic indictment was proclaimed. Another exploitation of the poor farmer by the merchants is explained by Premnath. He observes that "the peasants were forced to sell their crops at the time of harvest when the price was always the lowest…the peasants were often shortchanged through false weights and measures."[484] The alienation from the land and thereby the exploitation of the poor became a reality in the society.

There was crisis even in the law-court. The peasants were denied justice from the law-court. Those who were deprived of their land or property could appeal to judges in grievance procedures against their oppressors. But, the oppressors bribed the judges. J. Philip Hyatt notes that "the wealthy bought 'justice' in the law courts; there was one law for the poor, and another law for the rich."[485] This type of action shows that justice had been commercialized. Judges abhorred justice and stood in opposition to all that was right. They were corrupt and hated just judgement. Those who were responsible for the administration of justice became only concerned with seeking their own advantage by taking bribes. Page H. Kelly

---

sandals may be an idiom for a transfer of land (Amos 2:6). Mays inform us that "in the ancient Near East footgear was used as a probative instrument in the transfer of real property. Men were sold either for money or land."James Luther Mays, *Amos: A Commentary* (London: SCM Press Ltd, 1969), 45; cf. Albertz, A *History of Israelite Religion in the Old Testament Period*, 160.

481 Shalom M. Paul, *A Commentary on the Book of Amos* (Minnepolis: Fortress Press, 1991), 259.

482 Jorg Jeremias, *The Book of Amos: A Commentary* (Louisville: John Knox Press, 1998), 148.

483 Albertz, *A History of Israelite Religion in the Old Testament Period*, 159-60.

484 D. N. Premnath, *Eighth Century Prophets: A Social Analysis* (St. Louis: Chalice Press, 2003), 96.

485 J. Philip Hyatt, "The Book of Amos,"*Interpretation* 3 (1949): 142. Amos points an accusing finger at them as well (Amos 5:12).

observes that "the love of money had become the overriding concern of their lives and had blinded their eyes to the injustices perpetrated against the innocent."[486] At this point, judges had become the companion of thieves and confirmed the materialistic concept of service. Partiality or favouritism played an important role in the courtroom. Peitro Bovate remarks having favourites, keeping a favourable eye on certain categories of people or learning toward one of the disputants in a trail is intrinsically to negate the very act of judging.[487] Those who had no money were refused a hearing but instead given false testimony and denied a right judgement in the law-courts, whereas the rich were given preferential treatment. The unnatural judicial verdicts of the law-courts signify an act of inhuman oppression against the poor. In the administration of justice, the poor were discriminated and falsely accused by the corrupt judges. Thus, the decay of ordinary justice can be seen through the abuses of power by corrupt law-court. In this way, administrators and judges lost their honesty and failed to perform their responsibility to safeguard the rights of the poor.

Exploitation and oppression of the poor is clearly seen in the proclamation of Amos. He used various words and phrases for "poor" to denote the depth of their exploitation.[488] The various types of enjoyments of the elite group in the society were at the expense of the poor. All the means such as power, rituals, legal system and balances were used to accumulate wealth. This group enjoyed an unshakable political and social self-confidence.[489] The trading community became the community of oppressors. The rich merchants were greedy in their transactions. The craze in accumulating wealth and the indulgence in luxury were at the expense of the poor.

The elite group denied human rights of the poor. Moses P. Manohar defines "human rights" as "the recognition of the inherent dignity of human rights."[490] Every individual is born to this world with the right to life, freedom and equality. Every society has to guarantee such fundamental rights to its members, so that everyone will be able to develop their personality fully. In the OT the concept of human rights is not clearly mentioned. However, the system of value that constitutes "human rights" is present in the Israelite worldwide.

The Biblical understanding of human rights is based on the Hebrew understanding of human being created in the image of God. This kind of idea teaches that all people are equal and no one can claim superiority over another. At

486 Page H. Kelley, "Micah, Nahum, Habakkuk, Zephaniah, Haggai, Zechariah, Malachi," *LBBC* (vol. 14; Nashville: Broadman Press, 1994), 194.

487 Pietro Bovate, *Re-Establishing Justice: Legal Terms, Concepts and Procedures in Hebrew Bible* (Sheffield: JSOT Press, 1994), 191.

488 Amos uses the vocabularies, אֶבְיוֹן, דַּל and עֲנָוִים.

489 Amos 4:1; 6:1-6, 13; 8:5.

490 Moses P. Manohar, *Poverty and Human Rights: A Theological Perspective* (Delhi: ISPCK, 1997), 3.

this point, the focus is of maintaining justice and it is the basic principle of human rights. In the light of this understanding, the Israelite respected the rights of their fellow beings. In such situation, Israelite's law code stood for elimination of all kinds of oppression and injustice. However, in eighth century BCE Israel, the basic human rights were denied to the poor of the community. They were those who were victimised by the unjust structures of the society. The human rights violations were that the poor were bartered for money, sold into slavery, trampled to dust, snatching away the fundamental rights and forcing the poor to sell out their dignity and values by the powerful group of people. As they institutionalised violence, the poor were always the target of violence and cruelty. The authoritarian oppressive against the innocent and powerless is done to increase one's wealth in the form of trampling the poor which implies a deliberate and forcible action.

3.3. Religious Crisis in the Eighth Century BCE Israel

The temple of Jerusalem in Judah and the sanctuary of Bethel in Israel were prominent religious centres, places for sacrifices and other offerings during the reigns of Jeroboam II and Uzziah and these sanctuaries were furnished by some accumulated wealth, such as gold and ivory.[491] For the prophets, nevertheless, justice was more important than cultic sacrifices. Indeed, Yahweh cannot be made happy by bringing offerings and sacrifices.

Under Assyrian vassalage, the Assyrian policy toward local religious cults was ambiguous, local cults were destroyed and restored, as mentioned in II Kgs 17:24-28 and the Assyrian campaign "yoke of Ashur" were signed in the name of *Ashur*, the "lord of all lands." For Israel, however, the fall of Samaria was not only a human disaster, but also a theological challenge. Since war between human nations involved war between their respective deities, the question may arise – could Yahweh be defeated by *Ashur*? also, the loss of the land questioned "the relevance of the covenant with Yahweh."[492]

The material prosperity developed into an era of moral and religious decay in Israel. It is noted that the cult is a true act of worship, by which a human being accepts and proclaims the Lordship of Yahweh, accompanied by real concern for unity of humanity.[493] Truly, Israel was a community of Yahweh clothed with the ideology of oneness, which was the outcome of the community recognizing Yahweh as Lord of all creation. In this way, social justice and cult were closely related. In the course of time, the Israelite community fell into religious hypocrisy. The true worship of Yahweh was no longer maintained since social justice was neglected and oneness of community living was undermined.

491 Joseph Blenkinsopp, *A History of Prophecy in Israel: From the Settlement in the Land to the Hellenistic Period* (Philadelphia: The Westminster Press, 1983), 83.

492 Blenkinsopp, *A History of Prophecy in Israel*, 83.

493 K. J. Scaria, "Social Injustice in the Old Testament," *BB* 4 (1978): 163-192.

The Israelites disregarded the ethical demand of Yahweh which was contained in the religious practices and the system of worship became mere externalism. Religious leaders were greedy for money and as corrupt as the judiciary. Instead of teaching the people a true nature of Yahweh and learning together to live according to the will of Yahweh, the prophets and priests enriched themselves by charging extra for their services and misleading the people. They converted religion into a business by commercializing the name of Yahweh in order to make maximum profits, motivated by love of money. In this way, they led people stray and demolished pure Yahweh worship. Thus, because of the misleading of religious leaders, there was religious crisis and therefore, religious issues arose within religious community.

3.3.1. Idolatry and Immorality

In the eighth century BCE, the religious life of the entire Israelite society has underwent a tremendous change. The Israelites lived among the Canaanites who had a strong belief in their own religion. It is evident that there was a tension between the traditional Israelite faith and the Canaanite religion, which later developed to syncretism. It was easy for a deity like Baal to come to be worshipped under the name of Yahweh. The people felt that they were genuinely worshipping Yahweh but the worship of Yahweh was no more than a revival of the old Baal cult.[494] Soggin observes that gradually "gratitude to Yahweh for benefits was replaced by a mysticism connected with fertility of the soil."[495] Israel's religion had adopted many of the Canaanite elements of worship. Thus, in the course of time, Canaanite Baal worship had replaced pure Yahweh religion in Israel.

Idolatry was rampant among the Israelites. Astonishingly the leaders led the citizens into idol worship.[496] Religious centres were thronged with sacrifices and burning incense dedicated to the idols. The prominent religious centres, namely, Bethel, Gilgal, and Beersheba were religious centres of idolatry and religious syncretism (Amos 4:4; 5:4-5). They offered freewill and thanksgiving offerings and tithes regularly. But, those offerings were only outward expressions, and without inner conviction. It is true as B. E. Willoughby points out that "by all criteria, the Israelites assumed that they were performing the cultic and ritual requirements necessary to appease Yahweh."[497] The spirit of self-sufficiency and self-satisfaction thrived on material prosperity. The wealth, such as gold and ivory that the privileged class accumulated was drawn upon to furnish these sanctuaries.

494 Theodore H. Robinson, *A History of Israel* (vol.1; Oxford: Oxford University Press, 1948), 369; J. Alberto Soggin, *Introduction to the Old Testament* (London: SCM Press, 1976), 224.

495 Soggin, *Introduction to the Old Testament*, 224.

496 II Chron 28:2-4; II Kgs 16:10-16.

497 B. E. Willoughby, "Book of Amos," in *ABD* (vol. 1; ed. D. N. freedman, et al; New York: Doubleday, 1992), 206. Their wealth and security served as evidence that Yahweh was pleased with them.

Hyatt comments that "many of the wealthy were probably very prominent in the temples. Most Israelites thought that religion consisted largely of formal observances paying tithes, attending religious festivals, making sacrifices, and the like."[498] On the other hand, they neglected the important requirements of righteousness and social justice.

Religious functionalists were corrupted and religious practices were dishonourable. The problem was that the failure in living up to ethical standards had been covered over by their material prosperity and temporal peaceful atmosphere. Along with idolatry, immorality also appeared in the religious practices of the people. Injustice and oppression flourished in the worship. The wealthy elite appeared to be religious minded, but their reality of lust for gain and power reflected their immorality.[499] Hans Walter Wolff remarks that people seek self-gratification through pilgrimages instead of submitting to the law of God; they seek to subordinate God to their own wills through pious acts.[500] This brought religious decay and affected the purity in Israelites' religion of Yahweh worship, providing external evidence that the people had departed from their wholehearted devotion and love of Yahweh.

3.3.2. Outward Cultic Observances

As far as the practice of cult life is concerned, Israelites in the eighth century BCE did all the right things. Religious ceremonies and rituals were well observed but without real value, which was a hindrance to true religion. They were especially thorough about making the proper offerings in their temples. Prophets considered that the over emphasis on religious practices without righteousness was in fact a spirit of rebellion against Yahweh. According to prophet Amos, their religious practices against the background of their oppression of the poor became a mockery of God.[501]

In certain cases, the act of worship itself proved to be an act of oppression. Robert B. Coote notes that "the festival gatherings at Bethel were provided in large measure by the tithe. The tithe was a 10 percent tax on produce, probably conceived of as a land tax on Yahweh's land, administered by the religious elite."[502] The primary idea of the tithe was to make Israelites realize their dependence on

---

498 Hyatt, "The Book of Amos," 142.

499 John Eaton, *Mysterious Messengers: A Course on Hebrew Prophecy from Amos Onwards* (London: SCM Press, 1997), 59-60.

500 Hans Walter Wolff, "Prophecy from the Eighth Through the Fifth Century," *Interpreting the Prophets* (ed. James Luther Mays and Paul J. Achetemeier; Philadelphia: Fortress Press, 1987),17-30.

501 Nolam P. Howington, "Towards an Ethical Understanding of Amos," *Review and Expositor* 63 (1966): 409-10 (Amos 4:4; 5:4; Isa 1:14-17).

502 Robert B. Coote, *Amos Among the Prophets: Composition and Theology* (Philadelphia: Fortress Press, 1981), 107.

Yahweh and the commandment was this tithe had to be distributed to the poor of the land every third year (Deut 14:28-30).

The cult, which was primarily aimed at the internal transformation of the people of God, provided a religious foundation for arrogance. The religious leaders and elite observed every religious practice, such as offerings, sacrifices, and rituals, without justice. However, according to prophets, their noisy religious festivals, offering and sacrifices were all provocations of Yahweh. Gerhard von Rad comments that "sacrifices offered by people who scorned his will as expressed in law could have no value in Yahweh's sight."[503] Therefore, outwardly, they appeared to be deeply religious with solemn assemblies and those costly sacrifices, but this was only a false sense of religion which in fact was unreal, formal and barren, a false sense of religiosity. Yahweh hates Israel's feast and festivals. Therefore, a cult without a religious and moral life is an offence against Yahweh.

3.3.3. Ethical and Moral Issues

The Israelite came to believe in a cult devoid of ethics and indulged in hollow religious practices. Morality was at low ebb in the society. Religion had no social morality. Religion was divorced from justice, piety from kindness, and sacrifices from mercy.[504] Injustice and piety were practised together in Israel. The selling of an honest debtor, enslaving the poor man for an insignificant sum, trampling the rights of the poor, seeking their ruin and sexual abuse of the weak and humble were practised along with their religion (Amos 2:6-7). Drunkenness was common among religious leaders (Isa 28:7; Mic 3:11). Money was spent for intoxicating drink at the expense of the fines or taxes extracted from the poor people. Thus, the greed or lust led to acts of adultery, violence, deceit, injustice, oppression and self-indulgent living.[505]

Temple prostitution was also common and becoming a characteristic of Israelite religion.[506] Sexual immorality was evident from the remarks of Amos that "father and son use the same girl" (Amos 2:7a). Even though this has no direct religious connotation of temple prostitution, the phrase which followed, "profane my holy name" (Amos 2:7b), had something to do with worship.[507] The tragedy exemplified through the life of Hosea and his indictment on illicit sexual activity in Hosea 4:14 strengthen this argument. It was a religious system which had no personal ethics, exploiting others for their own gain. It was in clear contradiction to Mosaic covenant (Deut 12:1-9). Religious functionalists were corrupted and religious practices were unethical. Hence, the heterodox worship at Bethel, Gilgal

503 von Rad, *The Message of the Prophets*, 106.

504 Stephen Winward, *A Guide to Prophets* (Atlanta: John Knox Press, 1976), 37.

505 Hos 2:13; Amos 5:24; 6:1-6; Mic 6:12-16.

506 Bull, *The Rise of the Prophet*, 80; Donald H. Mason, *Thus Saith the Lord: An Introduction to the Prophets of Israel* (Madras: Christian Literature Society, 1962), 57.

507 Robinson, *A History of Israel*, 368.

and Beersheba were categorically condemned. The Israelites failed to live up to the ethical standards and violated the covenantal codes.

3.3.4. Misuse of Religious Authority

The religious leaders especially the priests in ancient Israel were considered as "perfect beings" without any sin, because they performed all the religious rites and taught Torah to the Israelites. They were prominent religious leaders who are supposed to live an exemplary life to the rest of the Israelites. They not only took care of the spiritual matters but even the physical development and maintenance of the Temple, for instance, performing construction, looking after the furnishings, transporting the tabernacle, performing religious rites, other services, and singing Psalms in the Temple. They were physically and spiritually attached to the sanctuary. Their concern should be for the benefit of the Israelite's society. However, we understand from the action of Amaziah, the priest of Bethel that the priests gave more attention for the welfare of the king, his reputation, and the kingdom. Amaziah exercised religious power or authority with the notion that he was authorized by the royal authority. Since his assignment as a priest might have come from the royal appointment, he manipulated the religious office in favour of priestly leadership and royal office. This shows that the religious leaders manipulate the whole system of worship and misused the religious and the temple treasury.

The religious leaders controlled the cultic practices and manipulated tithes, offerings and sacrifices. Instead of teaching the people the true nature of Yahweh, they enriched themselves by charging extra for their services and misleading the people. Thereby, they made the cultic places more important than worshipping Yahweh.[508] The cult became a mockery of God for they replaced God of justice with a cultic God for the personal gain of the rich and the religious leaders. The cult became a profession of the priests, and a source of huge income for the Temple staff and a rite for infallibly procuring blessings from God. They replaced an ethical God by a cultic God. The cult, which was primarily aimed at the internal transformation of the people of God, provided a religious foundation for their arrogance. Thus, prophetic criticism was concentrated on cultic places such as Gilgal, Bethel, and Jerusalem. Amos, Micah, and Isaiah condemned sacrificial feasts and the practices associated with them. For Amos, God's action has a decisive connection with these particular places.[509] He proclaimed that Bethel cannot stand as a symbol of national security and a centre for celebration; it will come down because worshipping Yahweh there is a creation of the human imagination. Yahweh will not be mocked nor manipulated. Without ethics and

---

508 Hans Walter Wolff, "Prophecy from the Eight through the Fifth Century," in *Interpreting the Prophets* (ed. James Luther Mays & Paul J. Achtemeier; Philadelphia: Fortress Press, 1987), 17-30.

509 Klaus Koch, *The Prophets: The Assyrian Period* (vol. 1; London: SCM Press Ltd, 1982), 53-54.

virtues, there can be no acceptable worship or a viable social life. Thus, prophets announced Yahweh's dislike of Israel's religious feasts, and his total rejection of their offerings and songs.[510]

3.3.5. Misuse of Religion for Business Motive

The people of Israel used the festival of the new moon and the weekly Sabbath observance to add profit to their own account by inappropriate means. This also shows that profiteers are impatient in Sabbath because it causes delay in corrupt business practices and in getting unfair profit. The reason is that they were unable to conduct their business during that time.

It brings out in more detail the commercial side of the oppression.[511] According to Wolff, the verb פָּתַח in Amos 8:5 (literally "to open") assumes to open the sack which contains the grain for sale.[512] For Jan De Waard and William A. Smalley, it may mean opening the storehouse where the wheat is kept for sale.[513] The impatient merchants were guilty even at the very foundational level of their religious commitment. Religion is merely a mask so they were not capable of sharing the joy of these festivals because those days limit their greed. The merchants were grudgingly waiting for the holidays to pass in order to return to their business.[514]

The spirit of commercialism had rooted itself too deeply into the life of the people. Here the priests and the profiteers were collaborators like the merchants and the magistrates as it is mentioned in Amos 5:10-12. Thus, the spiritual rottenness is evident at the heart of the commercial prosperity. The practise of corruption business ethics in the cult is vividly seen in their religious activities. Religious leaders were greedy and as corrupt as the judiciary. Instead of teaching the people a true nature of Yahweh and learning together to live according to the will of Yahweh, the prophets and priests enriched themselves by charging extra for their services and misleading the people. They converted religion into a business by commercializing the name of Yahweh in order to make maximum profits, motivated by love of money. In this way, they commercialised their God and led the citizen astray from true and pure worship.

510 Amos 5:21-23; Isa 1:14-15; 5:11-12; Mic 3:12.

511 Anderson and Freedman, *Amos*, 802.

512 Wolff, *Joel and Amos*, 327.

513 Jan De Waard and William A. Smalley, *A Translators Handbook on the Book of Amos* (Stuttgart: United Bible Societies, 1979), 163.

514 Hayes, *Amos*, 208.

Conclusion

From the above discussion, we see that the eighth century BCE witnessed tremendous changes in different spheres of the Israelite society. The adverse effect of the achievement of political stability resulted in the accumulation of wealth of the elite, exploitation of the poor and using the religion for economic gain. Israel was down with multiple crises: political, social, economic and religious crises that brought political instability, social unrest, and religious nominalism.

Politicians, the top leaders of the nation entered into power struggle. That led into political instability in South and North Israel caused a downfall of the kingdoms. They misused political power for their personal benefit. They failed to create a "just" and "peaceful" society, where every citizen can exercise their rights freely. Most of the issues created in this century (as discussed above) are the result of the weakness of the leaders. Thus, the nations experienced unavoidable circumstances.

Socially, the society has lost its moral and ethical values. Thus, at all levels corruption, greed, oppression and exploitation crippled the just society. The social sins, however, dispense justice, which had left bitterness behind and affected their relationship with Yahweh.

Religiously, the sacred cord of right relationship with Yahweh was broken. Israelites failed to live up to the ethical standards and violated the covenantal codes. All these happened because of the lack of proper leadership and thus, the situation demanded leaders who can lead the people of Israel through the crises. The eighth century BCE Israel prophets demonstrated a model leader that the people of Israel needed. The next chapter will discuss the leadership that demonstrated by the eighth century BCE prophets, namely, Amos, Hosea, Isaiah of Jerusalem and Micah.

Chapter 4

Prophetic Leadership in the Eighth Century BCE Israel

Introduction

In response to the crises that were discussed in the previous chapter,[515] in the eighth century BCE prophets, namely, Amos, Hosea, Isaiah and Micah emerged with different characteristics to the earlier prophets.[516] For example, they were less politically influential, although Isaiah did have access to the royal court. It seems that a professional class of court prophets was established by this time, but that these were yes-men or, to quote Bright, "timeservers" who had capitulated completely to the existing order.[517] Although, the eighth century BCE prophets certainly had spiritual experiences, they did not prophesy in a state of ecstasy and neither were they miracle-workers. They relied more on argument, reasoning

515 A historical overview (political, social, economic, and religious) of the eighth century BCE Israel shows that the situation demanded a leader who can lead people through the crises.

516 Before the emergence of classical prophets, the prophets were preaching and prophetic activity was centred around the temple and royal court. From eighth century BCE onwards, prophecy became an independent institution and took the role of criticism on various socio-economic-political and religious issues. It took a spoken form and later a literary form, and adapted forms from other contexts and institutional settings like the covenant law. While the recipients of the pre-classical prophets were kings or leaders of the people, the writing prophets addressed the people as a whole. The common threads in the message of all these were ethics, justice, unjust economic practices and the shallowness of religion. Anthony Ceresko, *The Old Testament: A Liberative Perspective* (Mumbai: St. Pauls, 1992), 23.

517 Bright, *A History of Israel,* 261.

and preaching. They have a genuine concern for social justice, who aspired for a peaceful society. Their appearance created a great impact in the history of Israel.

The prophets of the eighth century BCE Israel were raised up by Yahweh from the society and sustained a prominent relationship with society as political advisers, religious leaders, proclaimers and reminders of the Law, predictors of future judgement, watchmen over the spiritual life of the nation, intercessors for the people, and prosecutors against covenant breakers. They were public men, concerned with political, social, and religious questions of the day. They were concerned with relationships, particularly with regard to the covenant, with the manner in which the people of God had failed to continue in a covenant relationship with God, rather resorting to oppression of the poor. As they came bringing a message from Yahweh to his people, they were themselves products of the society in which they lived. They were also concerned with international events and the future. At the same time, they were practical in dealing with the concerns of their own localities and generation. They had a definite concern for social justice as well as religious orthodoxy. They rebuked unequal and unkind practised in the administration. They warned their religious apostasy. Thus, the purpose of this chapter is to critically analyse their responses to the crises and the leadership role that they undertook in times of crises, which serves as a great model for the leaders.

4.1. AMOS

Amos was the earliest of the canonical prophets of the OT whose prophetic inspiration derived from a direct call from God while he was a shepherd. The main theme of his message was that the increasing affluence among the leaders of Israelite society had produced an unjust social order in which the poor were exploited, and that in consequence, God would put an end to Israel's special status by causing the nation's downfall. Amos' personal life and messages taught the Israelites especially the leaders a good example to follow, although the leaders misunderstood his purpose of ministry.

4.1.1. The Call of Amos

Amos began his prophetic career by a definite call. He declared that he prophesied not out of personal choice, but because "God took him from following the flock" and inducted him into the prophetic ministry (Amos 7:14-15). He entered the prophetic ministry because of the constraint of Yahweh's will. Motyer remarks, Amos "denies that his authority is in any way whatsoever self-generated. He was neither by nature nor self-appointment *a prophet,* nor had he ambitions or plans such as would have made him enter the probationary stage by becoming *a prophet's son*, a member of a school or guild presided over by a senior prophet."[518] Amos' statement in Amos 7:15 evidently declares his call to be a prophet applies

518 J. A. Motyer, *The Day of the Lion: The Message of Amos* (London: InterVarsity, 1974), 172.

primarily if not exclusively to the northern kingdom. Amos call to be a prophet is confirmed by the phrase לֵךְ הִנָּבֵא "go prophesy." Amaziah in fact understood Amos coming to Northern country and prophesying in Bethel of his own choice that he earned his living as a prophet.[519] Thus, Amos is expected to prophesy in Judah but not in Israel, for Amaziah thought Amos is creating problem. Amaziah sarcastically denounces Amos as a "seer" implying that a "seer" is a lowly person (Amos 7:10-13). Amos answered that he does not earn his living as a prophet, but he is fulfilling his specific mission to Israel as per his commission or call.[520] In the intimate experience of his own life, Amos knew that Yahweh was the Lord of faith. He spoke about his own experience in terms of the expressed authority of Yahweh. Yahweh was real to Amos in the spoken word. Thus, he could not listen to Amaziah, his opinion. Klaus Koch remarks that "the call made him practise the prophetic way of listening to the 'inner' voice, as well as visionary withdrawal and inwardness."[521] The distinctive point of the prophetic understanding of God lay in the combination of God's infinite might and its expression in his speech to humankind. Amos puts it in the words: "The Lord Yahweh has spoken; who can but prophesy?" (Amos 3:8b). The calling of Amos was not inherited. Yahweh chose him for a specific task and that ministry was with the king and priest in Northern Israel. He did not use any authority other than the phrase, "Thus says Yahweh." He claimed to speak the words which Yahweh gave him and yet he was not simply God's tape-recorder. He was great and had a strong personality.

The experiences of Amos as a man of Tekoa, his call, and the message that he received (those materials) still remain to be illustrated in each generation. One can agree with Harper who remarks that "the language of Amos is rich in figurative speech drawn from many sides of life, nothing is more apparent than the influence exerted on his utterance by the life and occupation which he followed."[522] This understanding of the prophet captured the interest of the scholars in academic studies.

4.1.2. Amos and Cult/Religion

The religion preached by Amos became an important issue in scholarly discussions. Amos is the realist among prophets, the man of the people who into politics brings facts, into religion vision. He is like a modern socialist reformer, who protests against wrongs in the religion. Smith remarks that "the Book of Amos opens one of the greatest stages in the religious development of mankind (sic)."[523] Amos is well understood in Cornill's words as "one of the most wonderful appearances

---

519 Zevit, "Misunderstanding at Bethel," 784.

520 Zevit, "A Misunderstanding at Bethel: Bethel," 784; Mays, *Amos*, 138-39.

521 Koch, *The Prophets: The Assyrian Period*, 38.

522 Harper, *Amos and Hosea*, cv.

523 Smith, *Book of the Twelve prophets*, 71.

in the history of the human spirit."[524] Amos did not condemn the society and religious activities but action of the Israelites who pushed religion with an almost unrelieved abruptness. This shows that Amos exposed the inner religious action or behaviour of the people of Israel that finding her guilty of self-confidence and self-righteousness.

Amos protested against religious practices. Sell comments that "the boldest action a man (sic) can take" is nothing else but the "denunciation of the licentious, immoral and evil character and customs of an outwardly flourishing and prosperous community."[525] Such is the person of Amos. In his preaching, Amos emphasizes moral law. Driver notes that "disregard of the moral law is the first charge which he brings against Israel itself."[526] In an ongoing scholarly discussion, Robinson brought out an issue which Amos uncovered as "moral unsoundness" in the land such as victimizing the poor, confiscating their garments for debt, unbridled licentiousness even under the cloak of religion, hypocritical tithing, and hollow Sabbath-observance, even pilgrimages to far distant shrines.[527]

The most important thing in the proclamation of Amos is that all his preaching is based on the legal demands of Israel's God. The problem for Amos was not a failure of law. What was happening was permitted and ordered under the customary laws that applied. It was legal in the sense of what was appropriate to their culture. The prophet understood that the law was embedded in the reality of the covenant and of the gracious election of God. Thus, true religion according to Amos begins in recognition of the holiness of God. In other words, real religion embodying an ethical course of conduct was to become a reality in one's life.

4.1.3. Amos' Ministry in North Israel

The ministry of Amos took place in the days of Uzziah, king of Judah, and in the days of Jeroboam, son of Joash, king of Israel (Amos 1:1). The overlapping years of rule of Uzziah of Judah and Jeroboam II of Israel are 767-753 BCE.[528] The general period was marked by an earthquake, which was remembered more than two centuries later (Zech 14:5). Mays observes that the title in Amos "specifies a precise year for Amos, 'two years before the earthquake.' The earthquake may have occurred about 760 BCE and if the suggested date is correct, Amos is to be placed in the last years of the fourth decade of the eighth century."[529] Basing on

524 Cornil (1894) in Smith, *Book of the Twelve prophets*, 71.

525 Canon Sell, *The Minor Prophets* (Madras: Diocesan Press, 1922), 11.

526 S. R. Drivers, *Introduction to the Literature of the Old Testament* (Edinburgh: T&T Clark, 1907), 317.

527 George L. Robinson, *The Twelve Minor Prophets* (New York: Harper & Brothers Publishers, 1926), 52, 53.

528 Roland K. Harrison, *Introduction to the Old Testament* (Grand Rapids: Eerdmans, 1969), 884.

529 Mays, *Amos*, 2; cf. William A. VanGemeren, *Interpreting the Prophetic Word* (Grand Rapids: Zondervan Pub. House, 1990), 127; Hubbard, *Joel and Amos*, 90. Argument for 750 BCE date

this statement Harrison remarks that the ministry of Amos should perhaps be placed about 750 BCE.[530] Concerning the span of Amos' ministry in the North, there are few views among scholars. For Rosenbaum, Amos made only one speech that lasted only twenty to thirty minutes, during a single appearance at Bethel.[531] According to Hayes "Amos' preaching at Bethel probably lasted only a single day at least and a few days at most."[532] Wolff makes a point that short, self-contained oracular units are clearly distinguishable but still the superscription of the book two years before the earthquake might indicate the date of his ministry and this assumes a period less than a year.[533]

4.1.3.1. Amos' Social Struggle

The concern for social justice was the genuine subject of Amos' prophetic message. He denounced injustice at all levels of Israelite society. Amos' prophetic social criticism is direct, vivid, and hard-hitting. While addressing the targeted groups about their responsibility in matters of injustice and corruption, Amos also highlights the drastic consequences of their policies and practices for the underprivileged class of the society. Amos points out the privileged elite's failure to recognize that the effect of their conduct led to the ruin of Joseph (Amos 6:6). In fact, corruption was so rampant that anyone who dared to act with integrity and dispense justice incurred the wrath and scorn of their colleagues (Amos 5:10). The concern in this section is perhaps, to analyse the reasons of Amos' criticism of Israelite society.

4.1.3.1.1. Amos' Critique on Israel's Social Life

The prophetic social critique by Amos can be seen in his message to the people.[534] According to Amos, Israel's guilt lies within the domain of the everyday oppressive behaviour of its citizens toward one another. Hence, Amos addresses the existing exploitation, oppression and injustice: Israel oppressed and exploited its citizens by extracting taxes (Amos 5:11), selling the righteous and the poor into feudal slavery (Amos 2:6-8). Sweeney argues that the situation during the time of Amos is worse because the referable to a pair of sandals suggest that people were put

---

is also found in J. H. Hayes, *Amos, the Eighth-Century Prophet: His Time and His Preaching* (Nashville: Abingdon, 1988), 16-27, 45-7.

530 Harrison, *Introduction to the Old Testament*, 884. Cf. Simon Cohen, "The Political Background of the Word of Amos," *HUCA* 36 (1965): 153.

531 Stanley N. Rosenbaum, *Amos of Israel: A New Interpretation* (Macon: Mercer University Press, 1990), 76, 100.

532 Hayes, *Amos, His Time and His Preaching*, 40.

533 Wolf, *Amos and Joel*, 90.

534 Amos 2:6-8; 3:9-15; 4:1-3, 4-5; 5:4-7, 10-13; 21-27; 6:1-8, 11-12; 8:4-7. J. Carl Laney, "The Prophets and Social Concern," *Bibliotheca Sacra* 147 (1990): 35.

into debt slavery for relatively small obligations.[535] The poor and needy were sold as slaves even when they owed only a pair of sandals. It shows how the poor were sold for ridiculously low prices. The value of human beings has diminished to the price of sandals before the wealthy elite.

The prophet Amos uses striking terminology to describe the lack of compassion exhibited toward the poor: they are bought and sold as commodities because of their debts (Amos 2:6; 8:6); their heads are trampled in the dust (Amos 2:7); they are crushed (Amos 4:1); and they are treated upon and despised (Amos 5:10-11). Those in power accumulate violence like so much stock in a store (Amos 3:10). As part of the exploitation flagrant injustice is done when אֶבְיוֹן is bought for a pair of sandals and the דַּל for silver. According to Fabry Amos 8:6 refers to the buying of debtors, and therefore to the purchase price, whose trifling nature betrays a culpable lack of respect for human worth. In Amos 2:6 people owe little; in Amos 8:6 they cost little. In addition to the unjustified enslavement for debt, he further notes that "Amos exposes this whole system, the evil that the 'poor, weak, lowly, and innocent' were made the object of mercantile calculations of the 'early capitalistic' upper class."[536] There was a lack of respect for humanity. The prophets cried out against taking advantage over in the courts and the way in which the poor suffered from the economically elite.

Amos' critique of Israel's society emphasizes the interrelation of his concepts, namely, *Justice* and *righteousness*. Amos used *justice* and *righteousness* consistently as terms for the qualities which ought to be present in the social order of a covenant society (Amos 5:7, 24; 6:12). *Justice* was associated with the judicial process by which right order is maintained in social relations, especially the protection of the weak and the poor. *Righteousness* is the rightness belonging to those who fulfil the responsibilities which may be expected from them in their relationship to others.[537] *Justice* and *righteousness* are now at the centre of what Israel disregards and abuses, rather than allowing the legal system to flourish as a constructive benefit so that all receive their due. J. Carl Laney remarks that "Amos appealed for people to let these two qualities characterize their dealings with God and other individuals. Only then would society function according to divine norms."[538] Because according to Amos the nation and its leaders pervert it and change it into a bitter herb; they toss it to the ground as something of little importance, as something to take advantage of and trample on even as they trample upon the needy. Amos 5:7, 6:12 reveals that the pursuit and maintenance of justice is

535 Marwin A. Sweeney, *The Twelve Prophets* (vol. 1; ed. David W. Cotter; Minnesota: The Liturgical Press, 2000), 264.

536 Fabry, "דַּל," in *TDOT*, 223.

537 Mays, *Amos*, 108; J. Du Preez, "Social justice, a Motive for the Mission of the Church," Journal *of Theology for Southern Africa* 53 (1985): 36-37; Max E. Polley, *Amos & the Davidic Empire: A Socio-Historical Approach* (New York, Oxford: Oxford University Press, 1989), 133-135.

538 Laney, "The Prophets and Social Concern," 36.

not simply an abstract ideal. Justice requires a certain attitude, an active inner interest in fairness and lawfulness. Unfortunately, the Israelites failed to act out both justice and righteousness in their day to day living. The elite faithfully participated in and were actively involved in religious practices, but inwardly they denied justice and righteousness to all. Yahweh did not want their outward observance of religious practices and ceremonies because they were worthless and valueless without true godliness.

4.1.3.1.2. Amos' Critique on Economic Issues

Economic cheating and striving for unreasonable profit (Amos 8:5-6) were obvious in Israelite society. Amos could notice the internal violence of oppression in the market place. The violence resulted from the lack of justice. The peasants who were unable to produce enough grain or food for their own needs were forced to buy it in the corrupted market of the towns. Amos pointed out that the merchants diminished the אֵיפָה and added to the שֶׁקֶל (Amos 8:5). They also cheated the buyer even with "just balances" by tampering with the scale, bending out the shape of the crossbeam of the balances. Thus, "just balances" become false balances.[539]

4.1.3.1.3. Amos' Critique on Judicial System

Amos' social criticism also points towards corrupt court systems (Amos 5:7, 10). Even the governmental and judicial officials, who were responsible for preserving justice, were contributing to what the prophet considered to be an ungodly social imbalance. The role of judicial courts had the function of maintaining justice based on the principle of entitlement. But, the courts had become the very instruments of undermining justice (Amos 5:12). Hence Amos singled out the judicial officials who "turn justice to wormwood" (Amos 5:7). He denounced the corruption of the judges who acquit the guilty because of a bribe.

4.1.3.1.4. Amos' Critique on Ethical Issues

Jeroboam II's success in military campaigns and economic stability increased abundance and a luxurious life-style among the elite Israelites. With this life-style came moral decline (immoral sexual behaviour) and religious indifference which the prophet Amos boldly challenged. In other words, it was a day of moral and religious decay. The father and the son are accused of committing the same crime

539 Wolff, *Joel and Amos*, 327. Balances were used to measure weights. They consisted of two pans suspended by cords from a beam which was suspended by a cord in its centre. The weighing was done by placing an already measured weight- a stone on the one pan and the object to be weighed on the other. The word מאזני occurs fifteen times in the OT. It was usually describing a symbolism like punishment (Jer 32:10; Ezek 5:1-4). In the literal sense, the demand of Yahweh is to use honest scales (Lev 19:36; Ezek 45:10). Honest scales are from Yahweh but deceitful scales are an abomination to Yahweh (Hos 12-7: Mic 6:11).

(*man and his father go in to the same maiden,* Amos 2:7). Though they failed to live up to the ethical standards and violated the covenantal codes, they attributed their prosperity to Yahweh's special favour and as a reward for their solemn cult at the sanctuaries. They believed in a cult devoid of ethics and indulged in hollow religious practices. The Israelites thought that with splendid rituals and with multiplicity of sacrifices they could win the favour of Yahweh. Amos condemned such empty religious practices and cult.

4.1.3.1.5. Amos' Critique on Life-Style

Amos noticed the elites misusing wealth (Amos 3:10, 15; 6:4), and the enjoyment of a life of luxury (Amos 4:1; 6:4-7) at the expense of the underprivileged poor. It is generally understood that Amos condemned wealth in principle and supported an egalitarian society; however, H. B. Huffmon supplements that "an important aspect of the potential role of Amos' message is that he does not condemn wealth in principle. Instead, the issues are how one acquires wealth and how one uses it."[540] Here Amos' concern is the excessive use of wealth for enjoyment and satisfaction. The women of Samaria are also targeted agents of oppression, for they make their husbands the instruments of their wicked desires and rule Israel from behind the scenes. Amos' critique of the Israelites' life-style was not only confined to the overt act of oppression or self-indulgence, but it was equally involved in the disposition of the will. This foundational quality of Israelites' unrighteousness is described in Amos 4:6-12.

According to Amos the splendid residences of the wealthy upper class of Samaria are also destined for demolition. Those who enjoy the present life of pomp, pleasure, and prosperity will soon witness the demise of their self-indulgent life style.[541] Hans Walter Wolff points out that the verb הִכֵּיתִי (נָכָה) "I will smite" in Amos 3:15 means the destructive wrecking of buildings, which leaves nothing but broken pieces.[542]

He pinpoints the life-style of the rich, who are enjoying life at the cost of the poor in society, even having two separate houses. Owning summer and winter houses demonstrate the luxurious living standard of people belonging to the upper classes. The question arises: are the summer house and the winter house different buildings in different places, or are they two dwellings within the same structure in one place? Wolff presents examples of two-storey houses, with a heatable lower storey and a cooler upper story; a room within the larger building; and summer house and winter house side by side. However, he argues

---

540 H. B. Huffmon, "The Social Role of Amos' Message," *The Quest for the Kingdom of God: Studies in Honor of G. E. Mendenhall* (eds. H.B. Huffmon *et* al; Indiana: Eisenbrauns, 1983), 114; cf. Mays, *Amos,* 11.

541 Shalom M. Paul, *Amos: A Commentary on the Book of Amos* (Minneapolis: Fortress Press, 1991). 125.

542 Wolff, *Joel and Amos,* 201 (Amos 3: 15; 6:11).

that "designations 'winter house' and 'summer house' meant houses differently situated, erected for appropriate seasonal use."[543] According to Shalom M. Paul, the winter and summer mansions refer to the two separate pleasure estates, which the wealthy residents of Samaria built for themselves in accordance with the climatic conditions of their country, and between which the wealthy residents divided their time.[544] For a king, in an agrarian setting, to have two separate palaces was a sign of some opulence. Nonetheless, from Amos' criticism we can argue that besides the king, newly rich members of the civil service, as well as the upper class in general, also availed themselves of the luxury of two dwellings. Having winter and summer houses is the prosperity of the rich which had allowed them to satisfy their pride by constructing residences like those which earlier only kings could build.[545] Amos critiqued that the wealth that the nation acquired should be shared with every Israelite in society and every Israelite citizen had right to enjoy the national prosperity.

Another accusation made by the prophet Amos concerns the House of ivory בָּתֵּי הַשֵּׁן (Amos 3:15) which refers to l uxurious manor houses whose walls and furniture were adorned and decorated with ivory. According to Philip J. Kings, house of ivory is not to be understood literally; the epithet refers to domiciles adorned with sumptuous ivory panelling and furniture decorated with elaborate ivory inlays. He states,

> The carvers' marks on the fragmentary remains of the Samaria ivories make it clear that Amos is referring to ivory inlays and insets. To the prophets, especially Amos, such luxury was possible for the wealthy class only by exploiting the poor of the land. Here was a flagrant example of the social injustice against which they railed.[546]

Thus, Amos condemned the rich privileged people and those who should have been taking care of the national prosperity and wealth for the entire population of the nation.

4.1.3.2. Amos 7:10-17 (Amos' Religious Struggle)

During Amos' time people were religious. Pilgrimages to Bethel, Gilgal, and Beersheba and many other sacred precincts were part of their piety (Amos 4:4; 5:5). However, all these worship centres became centres of idolatry and religious syncretism. Freewill, thanksgiving offerings, tithes, religious festivals, and religious assemblies were held regularly (Amos 5:21-23). The failure in living up

543 Wolff, *Joel and Amos*, 201.

544 Paul, *Amos*, 126. I kings 21:1 informs us that in the ninth century BCE, Ahab owned one palace in the warmer Jezreel plain and verse 18 says another on Mount Samaria, to catch the summer breeze.

545 Wolff, *Joel and Amos*, 202; Mays, *Amos; A Commentary*, 70.

546 King, *Amos, Hosea, Micah—An Archaeological Commentary*, 139.

to ethical standards had been overruled by their temporal prosperity. The cult became a mockery of God for they replaced the God of justice with a cultic God, for the personal gain of the rich and the temple officials. The cult became a profession of the priests, a source of income for the temple officials (that is the reason Amaziah, the priest did not allow Amos to preach in the temple) and a rite for infallibly procuring blessing from God. It was a human made God. They replaced an ethical God by a cultic God. The cult, which was primarily aimed at the internal transformation of the people of God, provided a religious foundation for their arrogance.

4.1.3.2.1. Translation

7:10. *Then Amaziah (the) priest of Bethel sent to Jeroboam king of Israel, saying, Amos has conspired against you in the midst of the house of Israel, the land is not able to bear all his words.*

7:11. *For thus Amos has said, Jeroboam shall die by the sword, and Israel must go into exile away from his land.*

7:12. *And Amaziah said to Amos O seer, go flee away to your land Judah and eat there bread and there prophesy.*

7:13. *But never prophesy again at Bethel, for it is king's sanctuary, and it is a house of the kingdom.*

7:14. *The Amos answered to Amaziah, no prophet I and no a son of a prophet I for a herdsman,*[547] *and a dresser of sycamore trees.*

7:15. *And Yahweh took me from following the flock and Yahweh said to me, Go prophesy to my people Israel.*

7:16. *And now hear the word of Yahweh, you say, don not prophesy against Israel, and do not speak against the house of Isaac.*

7:17. *Therefore thus says Yahweh: your wife shall be a harlot in the city, and your sons and your daughters shall fall by the sword, and your land shall be divided by the line: you shall die in an unclean land and Israel shall surely go into exile from its land.*

4.1.3.2.2. Form/Setting/Structure

The section 7:10-17 is a part of a unit (Amos 7:1-8:3) that contain five distinguishable subunits. The only section of pure narrative in Amos, the story of the prophet's meeting with the priest of Bethel is told in the third person. Much of the telling is taken up with Amos' oracle to Amaziah (Amos 7:16-17). This leads some to call the section an *apophthegma* claiming that the "historical episode is presented solely for the purpose of making intelligible a pointed

547 בּוֹקֵר "herdsman," it is the collective noun for a herd of cattle. The earliest Septuagint texts have the verb αιπολοζ "a goatherd," perhaps it reads as נוֹקֵד "shepherd" (cf. 1:1).

prophetic oracle."[548] This narrative is not really a narrative, but a saying with a long introduction.

Wolff contends that this section belongs to the "old school of Amos" which describes material receives from a circle of Amos' disciples or from Amos himself. They added to Amos' words and to the cycles of international judgement and reports of visions. The following passages are included: the mention of the earthquake (Amos 1:1), and of Beer-sheba (Amos 5:5a); the third-person account of Amos' conflict with Amaziah (Amos 7:10-17) and the preceding oracle (Amos 7:9) which uses "Isaac" for Israel; Amos 5:13-15; 16:2; 8:4-7, 9-10, 13-14; 9:9-10. Wolff's proposes that these materials functioned for two or three decades after Amos' ministry.[549] According to Douglas Stuart, however, the setting of Amos 7:10-17 is hard to determine, how near to or far from the events that composition took place cannot be known.[550] Some of the scholars agree that the author of this section (Amos 7:10-17) must have been a contemporary of Amos, may be a disciple, someone who is personally acquainted with the proclamation of the prophet as well as with all his ministerial experiences.[551]

This is a biographical narrative consisting mainly of a short dialogue in which Amaziah, the priest of Bethel, addresses a few disgraceful words to Amos. The pericope can be divided into three parts: (1) Amaziah's report to Jeroboam about Amos' alleged conspiracy (Amos 7:10-11); (2) Amaziah's order for Amos to leave Bethel (Amos 7:12-13); and (3) Amos' response to Amaziah (Amos 7:14-17).

4.1.3.2.3. Comments

The text Amos 7:10-17 is about the controversy between the prophet and the priest. The central characters in this conflict are identified immediately. On the one side is Amos, prophet from the southern kingdom, and Yahweh, the God of Israel, who has sent Amos; on the other side is Amaziah, priest at the national shrine at Bethel, and the king Jeroboam II, to whom he reports. The conflict can be presented in the following ways:

Amaziah's perspective (Amos 7:10-13) versus Amos' perspective (Amos 14-17)

Jeroboam is King	The Lord is king
"Thus Amos has said" (v.11)	"Thus says the Lord" (v.17)
"Jeroboam shall die by the sword" (v.11)	"I (the Lord) will rise against the house of Jeroboam with the sword" (v.9)

548 Hans Walter Wolff, *Joel and Amos* (ed. S.D. McBride Jr.; trans.W. Janzen, S. D. McBride and C. A. Muenchow; Hermeneia. Philadelphia: Fortress, 1977), 308.

549 Wolff, *Joel and Amos,* 106, 107, 308.

550 Douglas Stuart, *Hosea-Jonah*, 37.

551 Wolff, *Joel and Amos,* 308; Douglas Stuart, *Hosea-Jonah*, 377.

"Amos has conspired against you" (v.10)	the *Lord* took me ...and *the Lord* said to me, 'Go, prophesy' (v. 15)
"house of Israel" (v.10)	"my people" (v.15)
Amaziah claims authority over Amos	"The Lord took me ... and the Lord said to me, 'Go prophesy ...'" (v. 15)
Amos should prophesy in *Judah* (v.12)	"Go prophesy to my people Israel" (v.15)
Bethel is the king's sanctuary and a temple of the kingdom (v.13)	Bethel is the Lord's sanctuary (implicit)
Amaziah threatens Amos (flee) (v. 12)	Amos announces judgement on Amaziah (vv.16-17)
Amaziah said to Amos, 'Go' (v.12)	The Lord said to me, 'Go'(v.15)

When Amos declares Yahweh's third vision, announcing the fall of the dynasty of Jehu and of North Israel, the rich, powerful, prestigious priest of Bethel, Amaziah, criticizes and rejects Amos' message.

Amos 7:10-11. In this pericope, Amaziah, the priest sent a report to Jeroboam II, the king of Israel, to inform him of Amos' conspiration (he accused Amos the prophet to be a conspirator). There can be no doubt about the target of Amos' words and their intent. According to Amaziah's quote, Amos' prophecy is aimed explicitly at the king and the kingdom of Israel and announces its coming demise (Amos predicted that Jeroboam II will die by the sword, and Israel will go into exile).[552] The text does not inform us where the confrontation took place, however the designation of Amaziah as כֹּהֵן בֵּית־אֵל "priest of Bethel" suggests the temple there as the location.[553] Amaziah designated the Bethel temple as "the king's sanctuary, a royal temple" and thus both stressing its national importance and unconsciously its purpose.[554] As its כֹּהֵן "priest"[555] Amaziah held an important position in Israel and communicated directly with the king. Thus he sent a report

552 Hans Walter Wolff, "The Irresistible Word (Amos)," *Currents in Theology and Mission* 10 (1983): 5.

553 Andersen and freedman, *Amos,* 764.

554 Andersen and Freedman note that the title "priest of Bethel" is unique and "it points to a head of a specific shrine. No other Israelite is so named, not for any temple or city. Andresen and Freedman, *Amos,* 766. Bethel was especially significant place, not only as one of two royal temples in the Northern Kingdom, but as the site of many patriarchal stories particularly of Jacob's vision (Gen 28:19). Israel's problems were made worse by the temple at Bethel, which gave Israel the name of the Lord and the veneer of religion, but failed to address the people's injustice and immorality.

555 Singular presumably not because this important sanctuary had only one priest, but because Amaziah is the chief.

to king regarding Amos' ministry in North Israel. But Amaziah misunderstood Amos' oracles. While reporting to Jeroboam II, Amaziah omitted reference to Yahweh that He will destroy the dynasty of Jehu. Amaziah rejected that Amos was the messenger and the spoken words were from Yahweh.[556] Charles L. Feinberg and William Rainey Harper state that the priest failed to mention the reasons for the judgement (viz. Israel's sins) and prophet's intercession for the people on at least two occasions (Amos 7:1-6; 5:4, 6) and that he had held out hope if there would be repentance.[557] In this conversation we find two characters: a prophet and a priest, a third character, the king, is involved off-stage. The text does not mention the reason why the third character, the king, is off-stage. Gene M. Tucker observes that Amaziah represents the king and that the reply of the king is complicatedly silent.[558] However, Wolff argues that at the time of recording Jeroboam II had already died a natural death (II Kgs 14:29).[559]

There is no record of Amaziah's response to Amos' prophesy until this time when the prophesy against Jeroboam II, the king, had been pronounced. Amaziah wanted to silence Amos, thus, he referred to Amos' activity as a conspiracy against the king. The inaccuracy of this statement was no conspiracy of any kind.[560] Amos was simply reporting to the people of Israel the content of the visions that God had given him, visions that warned of Israel's destruction by a God that was holding them responsible for their sin. If there was any threat involved here, it was a perceived threat to Amaziah as this prophet was speaking a message that was contrary to the position of the priest, thus undermining his authority, and exposing him as a fraud to all the people. Consequently, Amaziah was acting in the harshest way possible.

In Amos 7:12-13, Amaziah turned his attention to Amos. The text does not state whether or not the king responded or authorized Amaziah to intervene directly. Wolff notes that Amaziah took action on Amos before the arrival of a royal decree, most probably on his independent initiative.[561] Harper also has the same view and says that Amaziah in his own authority took action on Amos: either because the king's reply was unsatisfactory or to avoid the king's wrath

556 Thomas J. Finley, *Joel, Amos, Obadiah* (Chicago: The Moody Bible Institute, 1990), 291; Andersen and Freedman, *Amos,* 768.

557 Charles L. Feinberg, *The Minor Prophets* (Chicago: Moody press, 1976), 114; William Rainey Harper, *Critical and Exegetical Commentary on Amos and Hosea* (Edinburgh: T&T Clark, 1905), 169.

558 Gene M. Tucker, "Prophetic Authenticity: A Form Critical Study of Amos 7:10-17," *Interpretation* 27 (1973): 427.

559 Wolff, *Joel and Amos,* 310.

560 A conspiracy is an event where people get together to collectively execute a controversial plan.

561 Wolff, *Joel and Amos,* 310.

to prophet.[562] We can assume that Amaziah had the authority to act and that considering the gravity of Amos' words; he was, in any event, acting with the tacit approval of the king. Mays remarks that Amaziah could command Amos to prophesy no more at Bethel because he had official authority based on royal appointment.[563] However, Klaus Koch argues that though Amaziah has authority to command Amos to leave Bethel he was also "nervous of the charismatic" leadership performed by the prophet, which is not in him.[564]

The reason of Amaziah confronting Amos and commanding him to leave North Israel and never enter into this land again or preach there, is because Bethel is "the king's sanctuary, and it is a temple of the kingdom." Amaziah tried to safeguard the sanctuary and the king. In the Hebrew text, the word בֵּית־אֵל "Bethel" (Amos 7:13) appears first at the head of the sentence, in clear contrast to Judah in Amos 7:12. This establishes once more that the real issue is not the status of Amos as a prophet or whether his wages should come from Judah, but rather where Amos should and should not prophesy.

Moreover, the phrase לֵךְ בְּרַח־לְךָ "go flee away" in Amos 7:12 is important to notice that Amaziah did not suggest Amos should stop prophesying altogether. His restraining order is very explicit. The priest told Amos to go to the "land of Judah." Therefore, what seems to be at stake here is not so much Amos' status but the setting of his ministry.[565] This geographical emphasis is particularly well highlighted by a little-noticed structural construction.

The author emphasizes location by the emphatic use of the adverb of place שָׁם "there" at the end of Amos 7:12; not only does the adverb appear twice but the perfect chiasm created by the inversion of verb and adverb in the second stanza brings the matter of location clearly to the fore: וֶאֱכָל־שָׁם לֶחֶם וְשָׁם תִּנָּבֵא "and eat there bread and there prophesy." J. A. Motyer asserts that "Amaziah takes it for granted, or pretends to take it for granted, that Amos is in the job for the money and that therefore he will be interested in knowing that in Judah stipends are better and are paid with a regularity which guarantees where the next meal is coming from.[566] Soggin suggests that Amos might have "eaten at the table and had

---

562 William Rainey Harper, *Critical and Exegetical Commentary on Amos and Hosea* (Edinburgh: T&T Clark, 1905), 170.

563 James Luther Mays, *Amos: A Commentary* (Philadelphia: The Westminster press, 1969), 136.

564 Klaus Koch, *The Prophet: The Assyrian Period* (London: SCM Press, 1978), 36.

565 Mays, *Amos,*137. The close repetition of the adverb of location שָׁם "there," in Amos 7:12, strongly indicates that Amaziah is primarily concerned with the setting or the location of Amos' prophetic ministry and not with the definition of his prophetic status. Mays suggest that the issue here jurisdictional, because there is nothing in Amaziah's statement to suggest that the priest is explicitly questioning the fundamental calling of Amos as a prophet. Rather, that which is at stake is Amos' authority to prophesy in Israel: Amaziah is clearly telling Amos that he is no longer authorized to function as a prophet in Israel; he must leave Israel and prophesy in Judah.

566 Motyer, *The Day of the Lion: The Message of Amos,* 171.

been expelled by the priest hence the sarcastic invitation."[567] Harper explains that in the earlier Israelites' society, there were soothsayers (and later called prophets) who were famous for their predictions about future and receive rewards or gifts from charity.[568] Thus, Amaziah assumed Amos was one of them a חֹזֶה "seer" who gave message for a certain fee, and so this may be the reason for the reference about eating bread.

In Amos 7:16-17, Amos proclaimed Yahweh's message to Amaziah in two parts: (i) Amos quoted Amaziah's previous message: Amos, Do not prophesy against Israel (Amos 7:16). (ii) Amos responds to Amaziah's command was personal: Mays remarks that "the desecration of his wife, the end of his house, the loss of his inheritance in Israel, and his contamination-all, in effect, constitute a fearful divesting of office. His priesthood will be brought to a terrible and final end."[569] The land owned by Amaziah will be parcelled out by land among the invading Assyrians, and Israel will surely go into exile to Assyria (Amos 7:17). Lastly, he would further suffer the humiliation that would come upon exiled leaders, a further insult to his identification as the priest of Israel.

Amos' oracle to Amaziah must have shocked the priest. He might have tried to save Amos' life, or at least his freedom and employment, but is told בָּעִיר תִּזְנֶה אִשְׁתְּךָ "Your wife shall be a harlot in the city." Soggin suggests two interpretations for this phrase: "she will be raped by the conquerors to outrage her noble husband, and the second that she will have to follow her husband into exile, there earning her livelihood in a precarious way."[570] One thing that noticed here is the events Amos describes fall without discrimination. Amaziah's wife is not involved in their conflict, yet she suffers worse than her husband. The phrase תְּחֻלָּק "The land shall be divided by line" refers to the measuring line, the distribution of land to colonists in accordance with the Assyrian policy after the time of Tiglath-pileser III.[571] Amos pronounced that Amaziah will die in טְמֵאָה "unclean" land. According to Stuart "unclean land" may refer to exile "where Amaziah would die."[572] Israel also considered any land in which Yahweh was not present was unclean.

4.1.3.2.4. Prophetic Leadership of Amos

The above discussion shows two types of leadership: bureaucratic and persistent leadership. Amaziah represents bureaucratic leadership, an authoritarian leader, who high-handedly holds the office and manipulate the office of the priesthood. Motyer comments that "Amaziah cloths himself with all his ecclesiastical pride of

567 Sogin, *Amos*, 127.

568 Harper, *Amos,* 170-71.

569 Mays, *Amos*, 140.

570 Soggin, *Amos,* 129.

571 Harper, *Amos,* 173.

572 Stuart, *Hosea-Jonah,* 378.

position."[573] As the priest of the state temple, he had a specific hand in all activities of worship. He might have served as a powerful official of the king and exerted his economic status and gain political power as well. Andersen and Freedman note that "Amaziah presumably belongs to a line of orthodox priests, attending to the legitimate interests of the most important cult installation of the northern kingdom."[574] Since he was the chief priest, he controlled the cultic practices and manipulated tithes, offerings and sacrifices. He was the leading official in charge of the cult at the Bethel sanctuary who stepped forward to oppose the prophet Amos from Judah. Being influential with the king, Amaziah attempted to silence the prophet by civil power. According to his own admission, Amaziah's highest overlord was the king of Israel. As the responsible official in charge, he banished Amos from the country. We find from the story of Amos' occupation or profession and calling in Amos 7:14-15 which is primarily to contrast with Amaziah's role as professional priest of the king and the kingdom. Amaziah rejected Amos' leadership because he thought Amos is interfering with his position as a leader.

On the other hand Amos represent persistent leader. True leadership exacts a heavy charge on the whole person and the more effective the leadership, the higher is the price to be paid. Perhaps in Amos' case, God's will did not allow the ministry to be successful without opposition and difficulties. Amos portrays a leader "faithful to the commission of the prophet to speak for Yahweh and not for his messenger, to confront the hearer in Israel with the word of God rather than to play up the story of his spokesman."[575] Amos was motivated to proclaim social justice in Israelite society by the faith that he had in God, who is just and righteous. For Amos, justice and righteousness are the characteristics of God and thus must come from God. With this, Amos challenged both the priest Amaziah and king to possess God's character and act it out in their day to day living (Amos 5:24). God's justice is obstructed when God's people cease to seek God and seek instead their own interests, be these political or religious, moral or economic. One is unable to measure adequately one's sense of justice from a position of power and control. It is necessary to take the perspective of the oppressed. Amos could do that because of his persistent quality in his leadership.

4.1.4. Summary

The perspectives of the two leaders are different from each other. They have differences in their mission objectives: Amaziah's concern is to safeguard the king and the state whereas Amos' concern is towards the covenant people. Amos speaks of and to a covenant people whose ruler is understood to be in fact Yahweh. Amaziah's words present a view of the northern kingdom totally as a nation state whose ruler is the king. Koch remarks, "Amaziah wants to prevent

---

573 Motyer, *The Day of the Lion,* 171.

574 Andresen and Freedman, *Amos,* 766.

575 Wolff, *Joel and Amos,* 308.

his king from dying by the sword, and Israel from being torn from its homeland, in which case the priest's own children too would be drawn into the orbit of the destructive sword, and Amaziah himself would lose his land forever."[576] Although, Amaziah is chief priest at the principal place where Yahweh was worshipped in Israel his total concern is not for the will and worship of Yahweh but for the safety and preservation of the king and the state. He thus perceives Amos' oracles condemning the national life and announcing judgement on king and people as a threat to the welfare of king and state rather than words from Yahweh. He sees Amos not as a messenger of Yahweh but as a conspirator against the king. Thus, we find that Amos and Amaziah's leadership perspectives are different from one another although both were religious leaders of their days.

One of the ethical implications for individuals can be seen by noting the responsibility of civil and religious leaders, represented by Jeroboam II and Amaziah, for their communities. The leaders' decisions can cause the people to suffer. The individual may not be able to choose a different civil leader, but the individual can choose a different religious leader and can choose whether to follow the state religion. The individual has a responsibility to discern true leaders from false, true correction from false assurances of safety. Amos 7 does not tell us how to discern true ministers from false, but it reminds us that we should.

4.2. ISAIAH

Isaiah of Jerusalem is considered one of the greatest prophets of the OT. He witnessed one of the greatest tragedies in Israel's history when Israel was decimated by the Assyrians but continued to preach courageously. He showed a remarkable consistency throughout his long ministry in rejecting the idea that Israel could gain security for itself by a politics of military preparedness and defensive alliances with the major powers of the era, whether Assyria or Egypt. Thus, the purpose of this section is to explore the life and personal qualities of Isaiah the man as a leader, and his contribution into the history of the prophetic literature.

Little is known of the personal life of Isaiah. He was the son of *Amoz* (or אָמוֹץ *'amotz*). According to Jewish tradition *Amoz* was the brother of King Amaziah, and both were sons of King Joash, thus Isaiah would be a grandson of King Joash, and cousin of King Uzziah.[577] However, Williamson argues that since *Amoz* is referred to as Isaiah's father only one time, that does not prove enough evidence that he was the "brother of king Amaziah."[578] To all appearances, his prophetic work was done in Jerusalem of Judah in the eighth century BCE.[579]

576 Koch, *The Prophets*, 38.

577 Hans Wildberger, *Isaiah 1-12: A Continental Commentary* (trans. Thomas H. Trapp; Minneapolis: Fortress Press, 1991), 4.

578 H. G. M. Williamson, *Isaiah 1-5* (ICC, New York: T&T Clark, 2006), 20.

579 Marvin A Sweeney, *Isaiah 1–39: With an Introduction to Prophetic Literature* (FOTL 16.; Grand Rapids, MI: Eerdmans, 1996), 51.

Almost all the scholars agree that Isaiah was a native of Jerusalem and perhaps born and educated in Jerusalem, with high social standing, and easy access to the court and the King, especially during the reign of Ahaz and Hezekiah.[580] Joseph Jensen remarks that Isaiah's access to Ahaz (Isa 7:3) and Hezekiah (Isa 37:1-7) indicates that he may have been from the aristocratic class, while his knowledge of wisdom traditions points to his being an educated person.[581] The book records that Isaiah was married to a "prophetess," and had two sons, Shear-jashub (Isa 7:3) and Maher-shalal-hash-baz (Isa 8:1, 3). How long the prophet survived is uncertain. However, according to tradition, he was martyred in the days of Manasseh (II Kgs 21:16).

4.2.1. The Call of Isaiah

Isaiah had a distinct prophetic call, emphasizing the holiness of God (Isa 6). Isaiah's call is dated from the year of King Uzziah's death (ca. 739 BCE).[582] The Jerusalem Temple provided the setting.[583] The account demonstrates significant similarities with the vision of the heavenly court of Yahweh in I Kings 22:19-23. The Bible witness that Isaiah received his call in the holiness setting of the heavenly assembly. He heard the proclamation of holiness of Seraphs.[584] This phenomenon was intended to make the prophet aware of his mission to proclaim the glorious and holy presence of Yahweh into the whole earth. Isaiah was called

---

580 To mention few C. R. North, "Isaiah," in *IDB* (ed. George A. Buttrick, et al; 4 vols; Nashville, New York: Abingdon Press, 1962), 732 (Henceforth, this reference shall be referred to as "Isaiah," IDB); R. E. Clements, *Isaiah 1-39: The New Century Bible Commentary* (ed. R. E. Clements; Grand Rapids: Wm. B. Eerdmans, 1980), 12; John N. Oswalt, *The Book of Isaiah 1-39* (Grand Rapids, Michigan: William B. Eerdmans Publishing Company, 1986), 82.

581 Joseph Jensen, *Isaiah 1–39* (OTM 8; Wilmington/DE: Michael Glazier, 1984), 20.

582 Many scholars argue that Uzziah's death greatly affected Isaiah. For example, George Adam Smith thinks this king, who had led Israel so effectively, was probably the young prophet's hero. *The Book of Isaiah, chapters 1-39* (rev. ed.; New York: Harper & Brothers Publisher, 1927), 58. John N. Oswalt notes that Uzziah was the only king Isaiah had known. Thus, his death, and the mounting Assyrian threat brought on by Tiglath-Pileser III's ascendancy, helped Isaiah realize that Israel was at a crossroads. *The Book of Isaiah 1-39* (Grand Rapids/Michigan: William B. Eerdmans Publishing Company, 1986), 177. Ultimate spiritual and political decisions would soon be made. Smith's theory is interesting but has no support in the text. Oswalt's comments are probably accurate. Early readers of Isaiah would definitely recognize the transitional nature of this time. Of course the call could have come before Uzziah's death, in the same year. Cf. George Buchanan Gray, *The Book of Isaiah 1-27* (Edinburgh: T&T Clark, 1975), 102.

583 John Bright, *History of Israel* (3rd ed.; London: SCM Press, 1981), 254; R. Knierim, "The Vocation of Isaiah," *VT* 18 (1968): 47-68; Julian Price Love, "The Call of Isaiah: An Exposition of Isaiah 6," *Interpretation* 11 (1957): 282-296; Paul R. House, "Isaiah's Call and its Context in Isaiah 1-6," *Criswell Theological Review* 6 (1993): 217; Jacob Milgrom, "Did Isaiah Prophesy During the Reign of Uzziah?" *VT* 14 (1964): 164-182.

584 Their voice brought a response from the cosmos. The very foundations of the thresholds shook, and the sanctuary was filled with smoke (Isa 6:3-4).

to preach the transcendence and immanence of God. Isaiah received the call with a specific task, a mission associated to Ahaz (Isa 7-8) and to his son Hezekiah (Isa 37-39). In this, he is compared to Micaiah in I Kings 22.[585] Isaiah's commission is extremely difficult. He can expect few positive results. He can expect restoration to come at a high national cost. Still, he can depend on the power, holiness, and mercy of God. The holy of God must destroy sin, yet will do so to create a holy people.

4.2.2. Isaiah's Ministry

Isaiah's ministry may be divided into four periods. They are as follows:

- The Period of Social Criticism (745-740 BCE)
- Isaiah and Political Crisis (ca. 734-732 BCE)
- The Anti-Assyrian Rebellion: the Ashodod Affairs (Isa 10-22. 715-711 BCE)
- The Anti Assyrian Rebellion and Jerusalem's Siege (Isa 28 32; 36 37. 705-701 BCE)

4.2.2.1. The Period of Social Criticism (745-740 BCE)

4.2.2.1.1. Isaiah's Critique on Social Life

Though Judah was a vassal state of Assyria, it did not experience economic decline. Bright states that the national economy was not affected much due to the strong foundation laid by Uzziah (783-742 BCE).[586] Finkelstein and Silberman also share similar view of economic stability of that time, through archaeological evidences, that Judah witnessed a rise in economic development in the latter part of the eighth century BCE.[587] In spite of the economic prosperity, Bright observes that the same factors that led to the decline of Israel were visible in Judah as well.[588] That the social condition of Judah, in spite of its economic stability, was unfavourable to Yahweh can be seen from the prophecies of Isaiah of Jerusalem (Isa 1-5). Like the other eighth century BCE prophets (Amos, Hosea and Micah), Isaiah too spoke out against "social corruption and oppression of the poor."[589] Charles F. Pfeiffer also points out that the prophet Isaiah was not swayed by the

---

585 Hans Wild Berger, *Isaiah 1-12* (Minneapolis: Fortress Press, 1999), 246-278; Martin O'Kane, "Isaiah: A Prophet in the Footsteps of Moses," *JSOT* 69 (1996): 42; R. Knierim, "The Vocation of Isaiah," *VT* 18 (1968): 47-68.

586 Bright, *History of Israel*, 278.

587 Israel Finkelstein and Neil Asher Silberman, "Temple and Dynasty: Hezekiah, the Remaking of Judah and the Rise of the Pan-Israelite Ideology," *JSOT* 30 (2006): 264.

588 Bright, *History of Israel*, 278. He points to "paganism" as the major factor as it was a violation of "Yahweh's covenant," threatening the very basis of Israelite society.

589 G. W. Anderson, *The History and Religion of Israel* (London: Oxford University Press, 1966), 120. Some of the social evils such as land-grabbing, perversion of justice, etc, come under the condemnation of Isaiah (Isa 3:16-4:1, 5:8-23).

affluence of the people.[590] In spite of the extravagant offerings in the Temple, Isaiah was not deceived by the insincerity of such offerings (Isa 1:11-15).

Isaiah's critique of the society is evident in the passage usually known as the "Song of the Vineyard" (Isa 5:1-7). Victor H. Matthews suggests that the background of this passage is the "harvest festival" where Isaiah announces judgement.[591] The vines, recognized as Israel and Judah, had become corrupted due to injustice and bloodshed (Isa 5:7). Matthews lists the "injustices" as (i) the encroaching of the land of the poor by the rich to expand their property (Isa 5:8), (ii) drunkenness and self-indulgent living (Isa 5:11-12), (iii) dishonesty by the leaders of the community (Isa 5:18-21), and (iv) bribery (Isa 5:23).[592]

Accumulation of land by the rich people was one of the major issues in Isaiah's time. The prophet Isaiah explains this issue in Isaiah 5:8 by using the phrase "joining/touching house to house" בַּיִת בְּבַיִת and "field to filed" שָׂדֶה בְּשָׂדֶה. Here the meaning of the word בַּיִת is not only restricted to "house." W. Moran has studied extensively the use of the Akkadian *bitu* in Ugaritic documents from the second millennium dealing with the transfer of immovable property. On the basis of his analysis, he concludes that property in these texts was referred to either בַּיִת "house" or as שָׂדֶה "field" or as "house and field/land" or even just "land."[593] Thus, the term *bitu* was used in a variety of ways to refer to house, and to land. It is significant that the Ugaritic formula linking houses and fields occurs in this condemnation of land accumulation. According to Motyer, the phrase "adding house to house" causes "house to touch house to house" that "means acquiring a house and adding to it to create a 'big house' in a huge estate from which all the others have been evicted so that the new 'squire' lives *alone in the middle of the land*."[594] The same condemnation is found in Micah 2:2 and also in Amos 3:15. Wolff notes that it "recalls the amassing of real estate and land holdings in the hands of a small upper class, a phenomenon which thus dissolved the ancient Israelite system of property laws."[595] It is these members of the ruling class who owned large estates, and in Isaiah 5:8, 9 the verbal and nominal forms of יָשַׁב "dwell/live" should be seen in the context of the process of land accumulation.

The semantic field/form of יָשַׁב includes the ownership of land. Gottwald has concluded that.

590 Charles F. Pfeiffer, *Old Testament History* (Washington, D.C.: Canon Press, 1973), 358.

591 Victor H. Matthews, *Social World of the Hebrew Prophets* (Massachusetts: Hendrickson Publishers, 2001), 83-84.

592 Matthews, *Social World of the Hebrew Prophets,* 87.

593 W. Moran, "The Conclusion of the Decalogue (Exod 20:17= Deut 5:21)," *CBQ* 29 (1967): 549.

594 Motyer, *The Prophecy of Isaiah*, 70.

595 Hans Walter Wolff, *Joel and Amos* (trans. Waldemar Janzen, et al; ed. S. Dean McBride; Philadelphia: Fortress Press, 1977), 202.

> *yoshev/yoshevim* are leaders in the imperial-feudal statist system of social organization, with primary reference to every kings but embracing other functionaries in the statist system. As Israel developed statist sociopolitical organization of its own, the term was increasingly applied to Israelite functionaries in the state apparatus and, on occasion, referred to persons of power in the upper socioeconomic strata irrespective of their holding political office.[596]

The accusation in Isaiah 5:8 is followed by judgement in Isaiah 5:9 and 5:10. The prophet foretells that there will be no one to possess land (there will be no landowners). The rich landowners will be bereft of their large landholdings. According to Isaiah, the crime of the rich landowners of accumulating large estates by joining the small plots of land which were the inheritance of the peasants was a violation of the sacred ordinance, the principle of distribution of land under Yahweh's ultimate ownership. Thus, the judgement is definite upon the rich landowners.

Isaiah also condemned "official judges" in Jerusalem, the king's appointees. Hans Wildberger remarks that "they (judges) are supposed to be those to whom one could turn when making appeal in official proceedings. In carrying out this function, the judge would have to distinguish themselves as possessing a high degree of integrity. But, they let themselves to influenced by pay-offs."[597] Even the governmental and judicial officials, who were responsible for preserving justice, were contributing to what the prophets considered to be an ungodly social imbalance.

The role of judicial courts, in fact, had the function of maintaining justice based on the principle of entitlement, to safeguard the misinterpretation of justice, to judge justly between right and wrong, to declare the innocent and to help one gain justice, to protect the rights of the innocent in legal disputes over life and property and to maintain pure justice in setting disputes.[598] But, the courts had become the very instruments of undermining justice (Isa 3:11; 5:23; cf. Amos 5:7, 12; Mic 3:11). Hence, the prophets singled out the judicial officials who "turn justice to wormwood." They denounced the corruption of the judges who acquit the guilty because of a bribe. In ancient Israel's law, bribery is strictly forbidden.[599] However, it appears that justice had been commercialized. The administrators performed their duty just for personal profit and according to

---

596 Gottwald, *The Tribes of Yahweh*, 532.

597 Wildberger, *Isaiah 1-12: A Commentary*, 211; Pietro Bovati, *Re-Establishng Justice: Legal Terms, Concepts and Procedures in Hebrew Bible* (Sheffield: JSOT Press), 194; Richard Schultz, "Justice משפט," in *NIDOTTE* (vol. 4; ed. A. VanGemeren, et al; Carlislie: Paternoster Press, 1997), 837-846.

598 Deut 16:18; II Chron.19:6-7; Schultz, "Justice משפט," 837-846.

599 "You shall take no bribe, for a bribe blinds the officials and subverts the cause of those who are in the right." Exod 22:8; cf. Deut 16:19; 27:25.

the size of the bribe. Thus, even though there was apparently economic stability and to some extent, prosperity during the reign of Ahaz, the social condition of the people was affected by the evils of corruption practised by those in power.

4.2.2.1.2. Isaiah's Critique on Religious Life

The "society" to which Isaiah speaks is the covenant people of Yahweh. The prophet admits that there is no lack of devoutness and religious activity. Indeed, there is so much activity at the temple that he can picture it as the "trampling of Yahweh's courts" (Isa 1:12) and a "multitude of sacrifices" (Isa 1:11). According to Isaiah, activity at the various shrines and national affluence are no accurate measurement of the spiritual condition of the community.

Isaiah 1:11-17 refers to the human senses that Yahweh uses in responding to the people's offerings: in Isaiah 1:11, it is the sense of taste when Yahweh declares that he is sated with the animal sacrifices; his sense of sight is mentioned in Isaiah 1:12, 15, 16, and his sense of hearing is suggested in Isaiah 1:15. Isaiah 1:13 becomes clearer of Isaiah's challenges to religious people. Oswalt remarks that Isaiah opposes the offerings because they are vain, not because they are cultic activity.[600] The last phrase of Isaiah 1:13 is crucial "I cannot endure solemn assemblies with iniquity." That is referring to "religious sin" which is very serious matter in Israelite society.

In Isaiah 1:11 the rhetorical question is posed ("What are your many sacrifices to me?") that demonstrates Yahweh's frustration with the people. Elsewhere in the OT, Yahweh states that he does not appreciate the most important outward signs of the Temple cult.[601] Following the question in Isaiah 1:11b, Yahweh begins to list the offerings he abhors: whole-burnt offerings, rams, fatlings, and the blood of bulls, lambs and goats. As Brueggemann remarks that all were heretofore accepted, legitimated offerings; all are now flatly rejected.[602] Jensen also points out the order and progression of what is being rejected, "for the listing goes from the external rites (sacrifices, food offerings, incense Isa 1:11-13a) to the less tangible matters of feasts and assemblies (Isa 1:13b-14) to prayer itself (Isa 1:15)."[603]

600 Oswalt, *The Book of Isaiah 1-39*, 97.

601 Amos 5:21 "I hate, I reject your feasts, nor will I even take delight in your solemn assemblies;" Jer 6:20 "Of what use to me incense that comes from Sheba, or sweet cane from far-off lands? Your whole-burnt offerings find no favour with me, your sacrifices please me not;" Ps 50:8 "Not for your sacrifices do I rebuke you, nor for your whole-burnt offerings, set before me daily"; and Mal 1:10 "Oh, that one among you would shut the temple gates to keep you from kindling fire on my altar in vain! I have no pleasure in you, says Yahweh of hosts; neither will I accept any sacrifice from your hands."

602 Walter Brueggemann, *Isaiah 1–39* (WBC; Louisville: Westminster John Knox, 1998), 17.

603 Jensen, *Isaiah 1–39*, 45.

In Isaiah's time, sacrifices were offered in the Temple in Jerusalem. The system of sacrifices was established and in good working order.[604] Clearly, people would have thought Yahweh could not but be pleased with their coming to the Temple to worship. Nonetheless, the accusations continue into the next verse (Isa 1:16), for the sacrifices are not the only things that Yahweh views as abhorrent. Yahweh has become fatigued with the people who bring offerings since they are not coming with the proper attitude that he expects.

But, Yahweh states, שָׂבַעְתִּי "I am satisfied" (Isa 1:11), and לֹא חָפָצְתִּי, "I am not pleased" (Isa 1:11); his displeasure increases in Isaiah 1:13 to לֹא־אוּכַל, "I cannot endure," and concludes in Isaiah 1:14 with, שָׂנְאָה נַפְשִׁי "I hate to my soul." All these statements show that Yahweh finds no pleasure in the surplus of animals brought into the Temple as sacrifice. The problem of displeasing Yahweh is because of the failure to accompany sacrificial and festal worship with a lifestyle of justice and righteousness. Yahweh's נֶפֶשׁ (soul) hates the religious activities, meaningless festivals of the people. According to Hans Wildberger the word "שָׂנֵא (hate) is the harshest of the expressions which the prophet uses to describe the reaction of God to the cultic activities in Jerusalem."[605] Yahweh rejected sacrificial worship of the people because it is characterized as something the people have chosen rather than responded to as the genuine call of God. Yahweh requires more than outward sacrificial worship.

The people are not at one with their God; he considers their insincerity an outrage. The incense they offer through the priests is rejected; their celebration of the feasts has been performed with the wrong attitude. Childs speaks of the mass of worshippers who crowd into the temple to fulfil their sacrificial obligations as well as the various appointed sacral feasts. He says they are merging obligations and feasts, riding roughshod over careful priestly protocol, so that Isaiah rejects them all as scandalous in the eyes of the very God whom they believed had called for these forms of worship.[606]

Isaiah challenges the worshippers and their activities, and explains how the people's cultic actions affect Yahweh. Thus he attacks sacrifices and prayers, two of the main parts of the religion of his time (Isa 1:11, 12), and he declares that Yahweh wants social welfare; He does not want religious ceremonies. He makes it clear that because of the insincerity of the leaders in worship, there appeared unresolved social issues.

---

604 Joseph Blenkinsopp, *Isaiah 1–39: A New Translation with Introduction and Commentary* (AB 19; New York: Doubleday, 2000), 184.

605 John D. W. Watts, *Isaiah 1-33* (WBC; vol.24.; ed. David A. Hubbard, *et al*; Texas: Word Books Publisher, 1973), 20; Hans Wildberger, *Isaiah 1-12: A Commentary* (trans. Thomas H. Trapp; Minneapolis: Fortress Press, 1991), 46; Watts, *Isaiah 1-33*, 21.

606 Brevard S. Childs, *Isaiah* (OTL; Louisville: Westminster John Knox, 2001), 19.

4.2.2.2. Isaiah and Political Crisis

4.2.2.2.1. The Syro-Ephraimite Crisis (ca. 734-732 BCE)

The Syro-Ephraimite Crisis that occurred in the eighth century BCE is one of the important events in the history of Israel. Several biblical writers mentioned it as a dark event (II Kgs 16:1-20, II Chron 28:1-27 and Isa 7:1-17). Thus, the purpose of this section is to briefly summarize the biblical occurrences of Syro-Ephraimite Crisis and the response of different leaders groups in Judah.

4.2.2.2.1.1. Background of the Syro-Ephraimite Crisis

The main parties involved in Syro-Ephraimite crisis were Pekah of Israel (Ephraim) and Rezin of Damascus (Aram) in an alliance against Jotham and his son Ahaz (II Kgs 15:37;16:5). Almost incidental to the well-known title of this war is the largest player on the world scene at this time, Tiglath-pileser III of Assyria (744-727 BCE). The fact that Assyria is not referred to in the title is ironic because when one begins to discuss the reasons for the war, it does not take long before he/she becomes a definite player in the ensuing conflict. The threat of the Assyrian Empire provides the impetus for the parties involved to engage in their clash. It is assumed that the war was an international plan. However, some scholars argue that one of the causes of Syro-Ephraimite war was local rather than international affair.[607]

During this time, king of Israel, Pekah, joined in a conspiracy with Rezin, king of Syria, in an attempt to break through from the existing Assyrian domination. They wanted Ahaz, king of Judah to join. Ahaz appears initially to have been unwilling, but now the coalition has a plan to replace him by force with a puppet-ruler of their own choosing, "the son of Tabeel," and Ahaz is possibly wavering. Failing to induce Ahaz of Judah to join in their plans, they attempted to conquer Judah. Syria and Israel's reaction to Judah's refusal to join their coalition resulted in the Syro-Ephraimite War. The downfall of these three countries stemmed from decisions made during this war. Therefore, acknowledgement of this war is crucial to understanding the scattering and gathering of Israel.

4.2.2.2.1.2. Analysis of the Biblical Texts

The major biblical information about the Syro-Ephraimite crisis under Ahaz and the Assyrian crisis under Hezekiah comes from the books of Kings, Chronicles and Isaiah. In the unfolding of these political events, Isaiah's interactions with the Judean kings play a significant role. Isaiah ministered in Jerusalem during the time of political crises. Three major events in the political life of Judah are critical for pinning down the message of Isaiah. The first is "Syro-Ephraimite crisis."

607 Roger Tomes, "The Reason For The Syro-Ephraimite War," *JSOT* 59 (1993): 70; Bustenay Oded, "The Historical Background of the Syro-Ephraimite War Reconsidered," *CBQ* 32 (1972): 153-154.

There are several texts in the Bible that directly and indirectly connects to the Syro-Ephraimitic crisis;[608] however, for the purpose of this study, the discussion will be limited to only three texts (II Kgs 16:1-20, II Chron 28:1-27 and Isa 7:1-17), which have direct references to this event.

4.2.2.2.1.2.1. II Kings 16:1-20

The theological motif of the Deuteronomistic writer is highlighted in II kings 16:2b *and he did not do right in the eyes of Yahweh his God.* According to deuteronomistic writer, Ahaz followed the ways of the kings of Israel.[609] Volkmar Fritz notes that Ahaz committed two different cult practices: "child sacrifice and sacrifice outside the temple of Jerusalem."[610] Although, child sacrifice was forbidden in Israel (Deut 18:10), Ahaz sacrificed his son in the fire, imitating other neighbouring nations.[611] He also offered sacrifices in every possible place as other nations do. These charges are typically Deuteronomistic because they are forbidden in Deuteronomy 12:2 and 18:10.[612] The text does not inform why king Ahaz continued to engage in all kinds of cultic worship. The answer to this question is crucial in understanding the Syro-Ephraimitic crisis. It is highly possible that he followed AWA kings who sought power, strength and security through cultic practices. At this time king Ahaz was desperately seeking some kind of divine favour that would guarantee his security. He was surrounded by strong nations who were a constant threat to his kingdom and his life. This might be the possible reason why he was so readily and actively willing to turn to any pagan gods or powerful kings, who can rescue him and his nation from any kind of threats. II Kings 16:7 declares that after King Ahaz got frustrated with his search for divine favour, he turns to Tiglath-pileser III, the king of Assyria, surrendering himself and saying עַבְדְּךָ וּבִנְךָ אָנִי "I am your servant and your son." Then Ahaz offered tribute from the temple and the royal treasury to Assyria in return for protection from Israel and Syria. Vann D. Rolfson, remarks,

> Assyria gladly accepted the gift and turned his attention toward Syria. In the short term, Judah was freed from war with Syria and Israel. In the long term, by willingly becoming a tributary state to Assyria, Ahaz placed Judah into a difficult position from that time forward in being required to give

---

608 Robert I. Vasholz, "Isaiah and Ahaz: A Brief History of Crisis in Isaiah 7 and 8," *Presbyterion* 13 (1987). 79-84. II Kgs 15:37; 16:5-9; Isa 7:1-9; II Chron 27:1-9; 28:1-27.

609 Jehoram (II Kgs 8:18) and Ahaziah (II Kgs 8:27) were also accused of same sins.

610 Volkmar Fritz, *1 & 2 kings: A Continental Commentary* (trans. Anselm Hagedorn; Minneapolis: Fortress Press, 2003), 340.

611 As mentioned in II Kings 17:17, this sin among other sins provoked Yahweh to destroy Israel (II Kgs 21:6; 23:10, and Jer 32:35). Volkmar Fritz, *1 & 2 kings*, 340.

612 Stuart A. Irvine, *Isaiah, Ahaz and the Syro-Ephraimitic Crisis* (Atlanta: Scholars Press, 1990), 78.

tribute to Assyria. If Ahaz had not paid tribute to Assyria, there may not have been a pretext for the later Assyrian conquest of Judah.[613]

In this text, the plan of the story remains focused on Ahaz's search for divine power apart from Yahweh. We also see his religious sins continue even after the Syro-Ephraimitic War (II Kgs 16:10-18). After the victory of Tiglath-pileser III over Israel and Syria, Ahaz on his way to greet and show his submission to him, saw an altar in Damascus, then he sent a word to Uriah, the priest, to build an altar "according to the specifications of the foreign model."[614] Scholars debate on the ethnic identity of the newly found altar (Assyrian, Phoenician, and Aramaean) used for cultic reformation.[615] According to II Chronicles 28:22-23, Ahaz imitated the Syrian religion, but according to II Kings 16:18, the practice is in deference/respect to the king of Assyria. Since he was not committed to monotheistic worship of Yahweh, he might have practised two different cults at the same time.

4.2.2.2.1.2.2. II Chronicles 28:1-27

Chronicler tells the story of the Syro-Ephraimitic crisis in different details and perspectives. II Chronicles 28:5 declares that the Syro-Ephraimitic crisis was a divine punishment to king Ahaz. Unlike II Kings 16, here the emphasis is not on the continuity of the religious sins of king Ahaz only, but on the stubbornness of his unfaithfulness. As we find in II Chronicles 28:22 "in his time of trouble king Ahaz became even more unfaithful to the Lord." The troubles in this text are:

Aramean attack: Many people were taken as prisoners to Damascus (II Chron 28:5).

Israelite attack: Killed Maaseiah the king's son, Azrikam the in charge of the Palace and Elkanah, second to the king (II Chron 28:7).

Taken as prisoners: two hundred thousand wives, sons, and daughters. Great plunder taken to Samaria (II Chron 28:8).

Edomite attack: attacked and took prisoners (II Chron 28:18).

Philistine attack: Land taken Beth Shemesh, Aijalon, Gederoth, and Soco with its villages, Timnah with its villages and Gimzo with its villages (II Chron 28:18).

---

613 Vann D. Rolfson, "The Syro-Ephraimite War: Context, Conflict, and Consequences," *Studia Antiqua* 2 (2002): 97.

614 Mordechai Cogan and Hayim Tadmor, *II Kings: A New Translation with Introduction and Commentary* (AB; NY: Doubleday & Company, Inc, 1988), 192-193; John Gray, *I & II Kings: A Commentary* (OTL; Philadelphia: The Westminster Press, 1970), 635. The action of Uriah, the priest is on scholarship discussion. Why the priest did not object to build an alter of foreign god in Judah? Uriah and the prophet Isaiah seems to have a good relation (8:2) "he was cited as a witness by the prophet before the final fall of Damascus in 732." John Gray, *I & II Kings: A Commentary* (OTL; Philadelphia: The Westminster Press, 1970), 635.

615 Cogan and Tadmor, *II Kings: A New Translation with Introduction and Commentary*, 192.

The chronology of these events in the text highlights the growing insecurity of King Ahaz. It also explains why he sent a desperate appeal to Tiglath-pileser III, king of Assyria for help. The detailed description of the ministry of the prophet Oded[616] to Israel in II Chronicles 28:9-13 sheds a new light on this event (not found in II Kgs 16 and Isa 7). His ministry is significantly important because it explains why the leaders of Israel protested (II Chron 28:12) against their own army and why the prisoners were treated well and the plunders were returned (II Chron 28:14). It is also noticed that Chronicler has different interpretation of Assyrian king's assistance to Ahaz. II Chronicles 28:20 reads וַיָּצַר לוֹ וְלֹא חֲזָקוֹ "but he gave him trouble instead of help." With his tribute, Ahaz indentured Judah to Assyrian vassalage. Tiglath-Pileser III led his armies west to deal with the countries that had refused to pay tribute, regardless of Ahaz's request for assistance.

The writer closes the section with a rehash of his further sins against Yahweh (II Chron 28:22-27). The point of the Chronicler is to highlight the specific theological emphasis of sin and God's judgement. Thus, we can summarize the purpose of the Chronicler's narrative of Syro-Ephramiate Crisis in the following: (1) The religious sins of Ahaz made him the most disobedient and worst king in Judean history, he failed to live up to the Israelite ideal of king,[617] (2) Yahweh punished the faithlessness of the king by giving him into the hands of his enemies, and (3) In the time of his distress, Ahaz did not repent. Thus, he received full and just retribution.

4.2.2.2.1.2.3. Isaiah 7:1-17

The theological motif of Isaiah in this text is clearly different from that of II Kings 16 and II Chronicles 28. Nevertheless, the account of Isaiah supplements valuable information in understanding some of the details on the event. There is break between Isaiah 7:1 and 7:2. After stating that "the king Rezin of Aram and Pekah son of Remaliah king of Israel marched up to fight against Jerusalem, but they could not overpower it," and second verse begins afresh "Now the house of David was told, 'Aram has allied itself with Ephraim,' so the hearts of Ahaz and his people were shaken." This construction highlights the severity of the new situation and explains why king Ahaz and his people were now in terror. First, the break affirms the circumstances of king Ahaz emphasized in II Chronicles 28:16. Second, the failure of their first individual invasion gives a logical reason for the formation of their alliance. Third, since king Ahaz and his people had already experienced the terror of their first attack, their united attack must have appeared to them unconquerable. Fourth, the alliances were so sure of their victory that

616 Apart from this incident "nothing more is known of the prophet Oded." Raymond B. Dillard, *2 Chronicles* (WBC, vol. 15; Waco, Texas: Word Books, publisher, 1987), 222; Jacob M. Myers, *II Chronicles: Introduction, Translation, and Notes* (AB; NY: Dubleday & Company, Inc, 1965), 162.

617 Dillard, *2 Chronicles*, 224.

they had designated their puppet king Tabeel to replace Ahaz (Isa 7:6), and thus it was a serious situation for Judah.

The passage Isaiah 7:1-17 consists of two aspects: Isaiah 7:1-9 and 7:10-17, each of which has at its core an oracle addressed to Ahaz. The original word is an oracle of encouragement for Ahaz. The prophet encourages the king who is in a threatening situation, which can be inferred from the oracle itself.[618] Furthermore, the threat is described in Isaiah 7:2-3 an early note on the historical setting of the oracle. According to Isaiah 7:2, the army of Aram is camping in the country of Ephraim to invade Judah (Isa 7:6).[619] This launches the wider political scene of the day.

Assyria was a growing force in the east. Syria and Ephraim had formed an alliance in the hope of being able to defend themselves against Assyria. Ahaz, though, had refused to be part of the Syria-Ephraim alliance, and that is most likely the reason for the attack. Syria and Ephraim wanted to get rid of Ahaz and put another king in his place who would cooperate with them in defending themselves against Assyria. Ahaz's strategy was to try to be Assyria's friend. If they are too powerful to withstand, then run to them for help (II Kgs 16:17). Thus Ahaz submitted himself to Assyria's power. The house of David is referred to in the singular (contrary to Isa 7:13). Furthermore, the name of Isaiah's son, Shear-jashub (Isa 7:3a), is likely to represent an early tradition. It forms a clear analogy with the "sons" with symbolic names in Isaiah 7:14 and 8:3.[620] The name Shear-jashub can be interpreted as suggesting the destruction of Judah's enemies Ephraim and Aram.[621] A further addition consisted of Isaiah 7:8b, "within sixty-five years Ephraim will be shattered, no longer be a people," which interrupts the coherence of Isaiah 7:8a and 9a and does not make sense within the scope of the oracle.

The most significant addition to the oracle is Isaiah 7:9b: "If you do not stand firm in faith, you shall not stand at all." It is unlikely that 7:9b belonged to the original oracle. First, it addresses a plural subject, in contrast to the oracle, which is addressed to Ahaz in the singular (Isa 7:4, 5 suffix). Second, the conditional threat expressed in Isaiah 7:9b contrasts with Isaiah 7:4-9a as an oracle of encouragement. The oracle exhorts Ahaz to persist in his policy of neutrality and not to give in to the pressure of the anti-Assyrian coalition.[622] Isaiah 7:9b on the other hand introduces a condition of faith addressed to a plural

618 John D. W. Watts, *Isaiah 1-33* (WBC; Waco, Texas: Word Books publisher, 1985), 92.

619 Watts, *Isaiah 1-33,* 88.

620 Watts, *Isaiah 1-33,* 90.

621 Motyer, *The Prophecy of Isaiah*, 81. The oracle has been expanded in various ways. Some minor additions were made in Isaiah 7:4 and 7:5 to explicitly identify the offenders as Rezin and Pekah. Isaiah 7:4b explicitly mentions Rezin and Pekah as the referents of "these two smouldering stumps of firebrands."

622 Watts, *Isaiah 1-33,* 97.

subject. In II Samuel 7:16, Yahweh says, "Your house and your kingdom shall be made sure forever before me; your throne shall be established forever." Isaiah 7:9b reformulates the Davidic covenant by changing the promise into a negative condition. In this way, it gives a new interpretation to the oracle to Ahaz.

The second aspect of Isaiah 7:10-17, can be equally explained from the suggestion of the original oracle of salvation. The oracle of birth of Immanuel is a straightforward announcement of salvation.[623] Its immediate context however consists of threatening words that announce judgement over the house of David. The original oracle consisted of Isaiah 7:14b, 16 is the announcement of a sign, which takes the form of a birth oracle. It consists of the following elements: 1) statement or announcement of pregnancy, 2) announcement of the birth of a son, 3) order for name-giving, 4) explanation of the significant meaning of the name. Ahaz is the recipient of the birth oracle. Since within birth oracles the order of the name-giving is always directed to the addressee of the oracle, the subject of the ambivalent/uncertain form וְקָרָאת in Isaiah 7:14b must be Ahaz.[624] Immanuel was disconnected from Ahaz as name-giver in order to make the announcement valid for later times. Whereas in the original oracle, Yahweh's benevolence implied by the name Immanuel applies to Ahaz, the alternative reading "she will name him" creates the possibility of interpreting Yahweh's benevolence as referring to a circle different from the king and the sinful people.

The two oracles of encouragement, Isaiah 7:4-9a and 7:14b, 16, are closely related. Both address Ahaz and are intended to support him in an urgent situation. The name Immanuel refers to the imminent rescue from the aggressor and reinforces the exhortation to resist the anti-Assyrian coalition and the promise of salvation by Yahweh. The birth oracle of Isaiah 7:14b, 16 is an announcement of salvation for Ahaz. However, Isaiah 7:14a seems to introduce a word of judgement in reaction to Ahaz's disbelief. Within the composition, Isaiah 7:13 functions as an accusation against Ahaz, which is followed by an announcement of judgement. In this way, the birth oracle is incorporated in a literary context that gives the oracle a new interpretation. Isaiah's critical encounter with Ahaz in Isaiah 7:10-13 is followed by an announcement of judgement in Isaiah 7:14-17. The house of David, addressed in plural, is accused of stubbornness. The Davidic dynasty, represented by Ahaz, is accused of the kind of behaviour mentioned in Isaiah 6:9. The plural forms imply that the criticism applies not only to Ahaz, but also to the Davidic dynasty as a whole.[625]

623 Otto Kaiser, *Isaiah 1-12: A Commentary* (2nd ed.; Philadephia: The Westermann Press, 1983), 161.

624 The reading of a third person feminine singular is to be rejected on form-critical grounds. Besides, it requires a change of the consonant text to וְקָרָאה. The reading of a third person feminine singular corresponds with the birth oracle.

625 Motyer, *The Prophecy of Isaiah*, 84; Watts, *Isaiah 1-33, WBC*, 97.

The composition reflects the view that the kings of Judah, represented by Ahaz, by their continuous disobedience and lack of trust have exhausted the patience of Yahweh and his prophets, represented by Isaiah. Isaiah 7:13-14a is connected with Isaiah 7:9b. Both passages are in the plural and display a dynastic-critical tendency. So, both aspects, Isaiah 7:1-9 and 7:10-17, contain an oracle of salvation for Ahaz that is enclosed in a literary framework characterised by threat and criticism. Whereas the oracles address Ahaz, the plural passages address the Davidic dynasty as a whole. Isaiah's opposition to the Davidic dynasty in Isaiah 7:1-17 parallels his opposition to the people in Isaiah 6:9-10 and 8:6, 11-12. To some extent, the people are included in the compositional perspective of Isaiah 7:1-17 as well. The lack of faith, exemplified by Ahaz, will cause disaster both for the dynasty and for the people (Isa 7:17).[626]

The criticism in Isaiah 7:1-17 is not directed at Ahaz's foreign policy in particular, but to the policy of the Davidic dynasty in general, which ultimately resulted in disaster. The passage Isaiah 7:1-17 concludes with an announcement of judgement (Isa 7:17). The phrase "Ephraim's removal from Judah," refers to the division of the Davidic Kingdom (cf. I Kgs 12).[627] Something worse is declared here: the destruction of Judah and the end of the Davidic dynasty (Isa 7:17). Isaiah 7:1-17 uses the example of the disobedient Ahaz, who represents the Davidic dynasty as a whole, to explain the disaster that overcame both dynasty and people.

In the midst of this God's word comes to Isaiah that king Ahaz must stand firm in his faith (Isa 7:9). But, faith requires looking beyond human reason and experience. Ahaz had doubts and thus he was advised to ask for a sign from the Lord, but he refused (Isa 7:12). It is not clear why a king who was trying all kinds of religious practices to seek the divine favour, as reported in II Kings 16 and II Chronicles 28, would refuse to seek a sign from Yahweh.

4.2.2.2.1.3. Summary

One needs to take into consideration the urgency of king Ahaz's political situation here. We have seen that Tiglath-pileser III's westward campaigns played a role in the circumstances that led up to the Syro-Ephraimite Crisis. From a practical standpoint, the political machinations that occurred seem understandable in comparison to the great power of Assyria. Yet in a theological sense, the Syro-

626 7:9b alludes to the motif of the disobedient people. The condition of trust means trust in Yahweh. The accusation of lacking trust in Yahweh occurs especially with regard to the people of Israel in the wilderness (Num 14:11; Deut 1:32; 9:23; II Kgs 17:14; Ps 78:22, 32, 37; 106:24). Despite the signs Yahweh showed them the people did not believe (Num 14:11). In Isa 7:1-17, the lack of trust is indirectly connected with the 'sign' given by Yahweh. Cf. John H. Walton, "Isa 7:14: What's in a Name," *JETS* 30 (1987): 29; Kaiser, *Isaiah 1-12: A Commentary,* 163.

627 Watts argues that Isaiah 7:17 announces judgement not only for Aram and Ephraim but also for Judah's king and people. Watts, *Isaiah 1-33,* 90, 106.

Ephraimite Crisis is another indicator that God will not be mocked as it relates to sin. Vann D. Rolfson concludes that "the Syro-Ephraimite War was a key factor in leading to the fall of Syria, Israel, and the scourging of the Judean countryside and cities a generation later. These were the critical elements of the scattering of Israel."[628]

4.2.2.2.1.4. Responses of the Leaders to Syro-Ephrimaite Crisis

The campaigns of Syria and Ephraim devastated Judah. Samuel J. Schultz notes that Ahaz's time in power was weighed down with troubles.[629] When Judah was assaulted from all sides, Ahaz was confused to take firm decision. There were political parties who suggested a different opinion to Ahaz during this political crisis: to stay as pro-Assyria and to join Syro-Ephraimitic alliance. The situation was crucial: if Judah refused the Syro-Ephraimitic alliance, the two nations will attack and if Judah decided to join with the struggle for freedom for the two nations, consequences will be punishment from Assyria.

As the events unfolded, Isaiah personally (accompanied by his son Shear-Jashub) confronted the monarch of Judah to encourage him to stand firm against this threat. Joseph Blenkinsopp remarks that Isaiah attempted to intervene in the Judean crisis by appealing to Ahaz to remain faithful to Yahweh.[630] Here Isaiah emphasizes faith and trust in Yahweh because it was the demand from Him. Thus, Scott declares that "what Isaiah says concerning faith is one of the most significant of his contributions to religion."[631] When he offers Ahaz a sign from God to reinforce his belief in the reality of divine protection, however, Ahaz palters, whereupon Isaiah declares that God himself will give him a sign. Not only does Isaiah appeal to Ahaz to not fear, there also is the essential challenge of faith. In Isaiah 7:9, prophet Isaiah challenges Ahaz by saying "if you do not stand firm in your faith, you will not stand at all." What Isaiah intended to say here is that the threatening alliance of Syria and Ephraim would be crushed by God if Ahaz believed, and Ahaz had no need to turn to any other nations for rescue. The prophet regards Ahaz's action as indicating a lack of faith in divine support, and he also believes that such an attack will not materialize. For Isaiah faith is as a firmness of soul, a resolve to commit oneself without reserve to the object of faith. Whereas for Ahaz trembling at an enemy's threat, he declares that courage

628 Vann D. Rolfson, "The Syro-Ephraimite War: Context, Conflict, and Consequences," *Studia Antiqua* 2 (2002): 100.

629 Schultz, *The Old Testament Speaks,* 208. Especially the Syro-Ephraimite alliance put Ahaz under dire stress, who lost "battles and hostages" (II Chron 28:5-15), in Iain Provan, Philips Long, and Tremper Longman, *A Biblical History of Israel* (Louisville: Westminster John Knox Press, 2003), 279.

630 Blenkinsopp, *Isaiah 1–39*, 100.

631 R.B.Y. Scott, "Biblical Research and the Work of the Pastor: Recent Study in Isaiah 1-39," *Interpretation* 11 (1957): 268.

is the fruit of confidence, a confidence that can maintain itself with patience and resolution while God is working out his purpose.[632] Clearly this is precisely what happened with Ahaz. He did not stand firm in faith to Yahweh and was soon oppressed by Assyria. Blenkinsopp states that "Ahaz appealed to Assyria against the Syrian-Samarian axis with the result that Judah became an Assyrian vassal and the allies were defeated and eventually incorporated into the Assyrian Empire."[633]

Ahaz could have continued to hold a neutral course, not involving Judah in any foreign alliances, either against Assyria or with Assyria. But, despite Isaiah's repeated use of the phrase "fear not" and "we rely on Yahweh" his message brought little support to Judah's leaders. Finally Ahaz decided to appeal to Tiglath-pileser III, king of Assyria for help (II Kgs 16:5). Since Ahaz did not join the anti-Assyrian coalition, Judah got away from the fate that came upon Israel.[634] Rainer Albertz illustrates, Isaiah's thoughts on Ahaz's wrong plans and concludes that "instead of safeguarding his own power by submitting to the Assyrians, with all the economic, political and cultural uncertainties that would involve for the country, in Isaiah's view Ahaz would have done better to wait in trust until Yahweh clarified the threatening situation and gave him a new opportunity."[635] Hence, Ahaz totally shunned Yahweh's offer. Isaiah pronounced the punishment or Judgement against both Israel and Judah. The general consensus that Isaiah prophesied against both Pekah of Israel and Ahaz of Judah is for his effort to overthrow the Davidic dynasty and Ahaz for not trusting God.

In response to the disappointing political move, Isaiah received another revelation from God in Isaiah 8:11-15. God warned Isaiah and his supporters not to call everything treason which this people called treason, nor to fear what they feared, nor to be terrified by what terrified them. Rather they were to sanctify Yahweh of Hosts and make him their object of fear and their object of terror. The presence of Assyria as a serious threat to Israel and Judah was a constant background for the messages of the eighth century BCE prophets. Isaiah and Micah prophesy that Yahweh is going to use Assyria as a punitive means to correct the problems within Israel and Judah.[636]

632 Scott, "Biblical Research and the Work of the Pastor: Recent Study in Isaiah 1-39," 268.

633 Blenkinsopp, *Isaiah 1–39,* 230.

634 It was during this time that Israel fell in 722/721 BCE under the leadership of Hoshea, who withheld tributes from Assyria and approached Egypt for help. This proved to be disastrous for Israel, and consequently Israel as a nation came to an end (II Kgs 17:1-6).

635 Rainer Albertz, *A History of Israelite Religion in the Old Testament Period: From the Beginnings to the End of the Monarchy* (Louisville, Kentucky: Westminster/John Knox Press, 1994), 167.

636 Isa 11:16; 27:12; Mic 5:4-5; 7:12.

4.2.2.2.2. The Anti-Assyrian Rebellion: the Ashodod Affairs (Isa 10-22. 715-711 BCE)

The Philistine revolt against Assyria was led by Azuri, the Philistine king of Ashdod sometime around 716/715 BCE. He sent letters to the surrounding nations to form anti-Assyrian coalition. The Assyrians got word of the planned revolt (perhaps from a loyal vassal like Ahaz) and an Assyrian army appeared on the Egyptian-Philistine border and removed Azuri from his throne, replacing him with his brother Ahimeti and later overthrown by Yamani or Yadna.[637] In the meantime Ahaz, king of Judah died, and was replaced by Hezekiah, his son, in 715 BCE. Yamani wrote to Hezekiah and to the other national states in the area, again encouraging them to join Ashdod in a revolt against Assyria. Philistia seems to be rejoicing over Ahaz's death, because they considered Ahaz, the faithful Assyrian stooge, their enemy, and perhaps because they felt the more nationalistic Hezekiah would be more apt to join their rebellion (Isa 14:28-32).

Isaiah, however, responds that Hezekiah would be an even more fearsome opponent of Philistia than Ahaz had been. He bitterly opposed the anti-Assyrian alliance and calling Hezekiah to respond negatively to the Ethiopian ambassadors. At this time, Isaiah "symbolically illustrating the folly of trusting in Egypt by walking about Jerusalem barefoot and clad only in a loincloth."[638] At the same time he also appeared naked before the foreign ambassadors assembled at Jerusalem to show them their potential future as deportees and thus to discourage them from taking part in the anti-Assyrian rebellion (Isa 20). From Assyrian's action over the anti-Assyrian coalition shows that Isaiah was successful in persuading Hezekiah not to join the Ashdod coalition. When Assyria crushed the Ashdod revolt, Judah was spared, most probably because Hezekiah did not join the revolt.

4.2.2.2.3. The Anti-Assyrian Rebellion and Jerusalem's Siege (Isa 28-32; 36-37. 705-701 BCE)

Another political event that Judah faced during Isaiah's time was the invasion of the Assyrians under Sennacherib (704-701 BCE). Hezekiah begins his kingship by giving greater emphasis and attention to the centrality and worship of Yahweh. His pro-Assyrian policy helped him to concentrate on stable government. However, taking the advantage of the momentary leadership crisis, which was caused by the death of Sargon II, the Assyrian king, Hezekiah seized the opportunity for revolt by Syro-Palestinian states against Assyrian suzerainty.[639] Isaiah was fully opposed to Hezekiah's policy (Isa 30:1-5). Thus, Isaiah's message was trust in

637 J. Maxwell Miller and John H. Hayes, *A History of Ancient Israel and Judah* (2nd ed.; Louisville, London: Westminster John Knox Press, 2006), 406-407; Bright, *History of Israel,* 281.

638 Bright, *History of Israel,* 281. Cf. Victor H. Matthews, *Social World of the Hebrew Prophets* (Peabody: Hendrickson Publishers, 2001), 92-93.

639 Motyer, *The Prophecy of Isaiah*, 20.

Yahweh, instead of trusting in foreign alliances and political conspiracies. Isaiah uses the same imagery here of a sanctuary as in Isaiah 8:14, and the security is to be found by trusting in God's promises to Jerusalem (Isa 7), the city he founded (Isa 14:32), and in the light of those promises, behaving with justice and righteousness, the measuring lines by which one can know that one remains on Yahweh's solid foundation.

Hezekiah, however, believed in power politics (political power) and assumed to be free from Assyrian dominance. In Isaiah's view "Hezekiah's trust in weapons and the military power of Egypt was diametrically opposed to trust in Yahweh; Hezekiah's policy of military alliances was apostasy from God."[640] Thus, in Isaiah 31:1-4, he attacks Judah's leader for going down to Egypt for help and for trusting in the large number of chariots and horses that Egypt could supply. Motyer remarks that Judah's trust in Egypt was because horses and chariots were a well known Egyptian strength and pride for the ages.[641]

Thus, the judgement was that Yahweh used Assyria as a punishment to Hezekiah. Sennachrib immediately subdued Syro-Palestinian alliance and captured the second largest city in Judah (Lachish) then he moved to Jerusalem.[642] Hezekiah was forced to pay a huge tribute in order to save his kingdom.[643] At this time Yahweh intervened because of Assyrian field (military officer) commander blaspheming Yahweh. Then Hezekiah realized his wrong policy, and finally he chose to trust in Yahweh that resulting, the deliverance of the city (II Kgs 19:36-37; Isa 37:37-38). Then Isaiah promised healing to Jerusalem and Hezekiah's sickness and Yahweh once again blessed him (Isa 38:5). However, not very soon Hezekiah sinks into wealth, politics and military power.[644] Hezekiah could have trusted Yahweh, instead of depending upon the accumulated wealth of Judah

640 Albertz, *A History of Israelite Religion in the Old Testament Period*, 168.

641 Motyer, *The Prophecy of Isaiah*, 254-245. Cf. Oswalt, *The Book of Isaiah 1-39*, 543. He makes fun of the tribute they send to a useless ally (Isa 30:6-7), and he characterizes Judah's leadership as rebellious children who are unwilling to hear the instruction of Yahweh (Isa 30:8-9) and who demand that the prophets and seers, who apparently opposed their policy, keep silence (Isa 30:10-11).

642 Bright, *History of Israel*, 304; Oswalt, *The Book of Isaiah 1-3*, 11. Philip J. King remarks that "in Hezekiah's time Lachish was a city of strategic importance, second only to Jerusalem." "The Eighth, the Greatest of Centuries," *JBL* 108 (1989): 5.

643 This is found in the account of Sennacherib's invasion (II Kgs) "as to Hezekiah, the Jew, he did not submit to my yoke, I laid siege to 46 of his strong cities, walled fronts and to the countless small villages in their vicinity, and conquered (them)"... Himself I made a prisoner in Jerusalem, his royal residence, like a bird in a cage... Hezekiah himself, whom the terror-inspiring splendour of my lordship had overwhelmed...send me...30 talents of gold, 800 talents of silver, precious stones, antimony, large cuts of red stone, couches (inlaid) with ivory...all kinds of valuable treasures." A. Leo Oppenheim, "Babylonian and Assyrian Historical Texts," in *ANET*, 288; Matthews, Social World of the Hebrew Prophets, 94; Oswalt, *The Book of Isaiah 1*-39, 12.

644 Isaiah 39 and II kings 20 report the weaknesses of Hezekiah towards the end of his reign.

and trusting the nations, as represented by Babylon. The prophet criticized the anxious political and military strategy which was designed to manipulate the situation (Isa 39).

4.2.2.2.4. Isaiah 39:1-8 (Isaiah and Hezekiah)

4.2.2.2.4.1. Translation

39.1. *At that time Merodach-baladan the son of Baladan, king of Babylon, sent documents/letters*[645] *and ambassadors and a gift to Hezekiah, for he heard*[646] *that he had been sick and had recovered.*[647]

39.2. *And Hezekiah welcomed/rejoice upon them; and he showed them his treasure house,*[648] *the silver, the gold, the spices, the precious oil, and all his house article, and all*[649] *that was found in his storehouses. There was nothing in his house and in all his realm that Hezekiah did not show them.*

39.3. *Then Isaiah the prophet came to King Hezekiah, and said to him, "what did these men say? And where did they come to you?" Hezekiah said, "they have come to me from a distance land, from Babylon."*

39.4. *And he said, "what have they seen in your house?" Hezekiah answered, "they have seen all that is in my house; there is nothing in my storehouses that I did not show them."*

39.5. *Then Isaiah said to Hezekiah, "Hear the word of Yahweh tsebaoth:"*

---

645 MT reads סְפָרִים וּמִנְחָה as "documents/letters and a gift." BHS proposes to read with Septuagint επιστολαν και πρεσβεις και δωρα "letters and ambassadors and gifts." It is necessary to emend MT because it perceives the need to list the emissaries since the rest of the story speaks of them, not of the letters or the gifts.
Some MSS read as סופרים/סִפרים "scribes," a position which included representation/account of the monarch in Isaiah 36:3 and 37:2. Some perhaps refers Akkadian *sapiru* "envoy" or "eunuchs." Blenkinsopp, *Isaiah 1-39,* 487; Oswalt, *The Book of Isaiah 1-39*, 694. According to A. D. Crown, the story presumes that letters and gifts must be delivered by messengers. A.D. Crown. "Messenger and Scribes," *VT* 24 (1974): 368. Oswalt assumes that "letters stresses Merodach-baladan's personal involvement, while the sending of such letters implies the necessity of envoys to carry them. Oswalt, *The Book of Isaiah 1-39*, 694.

646 MT reads וַיִּשְׁמַע "and/for he heard." BHS proposes to read with II kings 20:12, it reads שָׁמַע כִּי "because he had heard," a variation or differences in the syntax or grammar and that is somewhat more specific. It may be a careless scribble error. Therefore, read with BHS.

647 Following the reading of the MT וַיֶּחֱזָק, "recovered" almost same with DSS[Isa] ויחיה "but had lived/survived." Suggestion matches the wording of Isaiah's oracle in 38:1. Whereas II Kings 20:12 reads חִזְקִיָּהוּ "Hezekiah." Hezekiah says nothing of his recovery and implies that the visit is one to the sickbed.

648 The word כָּל is missing in MT, and is supplied from DSS[Isa], some MSS, and II Kings 20:13.

649 The second כָּל "all/everything" is missing from II kings 20:13.

39.6. *Behold the days are coming when all that is in your house, and that which your ancestors have stored up until this day, shall be carried to Babylon; nothing shall be left, says Yahweh.*

39.7. *And from out of your sons, who are born to you, shall be taken away from you;*[650] *and they shall be eunuchs in the palace of the king of Babylon.*
39.8. *Then Hezekiah said to Isaiah, the word of Yahweh which you have said*[651] *is good. For he thought, there will be peace and security in my days.*

4.2.2.2.4.2. Form/Setting/Structure

The form and setting of Isaiah 39 discusses with Isaiah 34-39. Childs agrees with P. R. Ackroyd that Isaiah 36-39 (the prophet's ministry in the court of Hezekiah) have been deliberately inserted between First and Second Isaiah: he argues that "they are edited in such a way as to anticipate the Babylonian exile."[652] Marvin A. Sweeney remarks that chapters 36-39 form a bridge or transition between chapters 2-35 and 40-66. Chapters 2-35 look forward to a judgement of Judah by means of Assyria and her subsequent restoration. Isaiah 40-66 presuppose that the judgement has already taken place and restoration is imminent. Isaiah 36-39 explain the delay in the judgement and the change of agent from Assyria to Babylon as due to the piety of King Hezekiah.[653]

The date of Merodach-Baladan's emissaries' visit to King Hezekiah has a chronological problem. Watts notes that despite the chronological problems in relating it to Hezekiah's illness after the 701 BCE siege, the expression in Isaiah 39: 1 *for he heard that he had been sick and had recovered* relates it to a time shortly after his illness.[654] Clements notes that Isaiah 39 is pre-exilic. The fact is that nothing is said about the removal of the kingship or Davidic dynasty from Jerusalem and the destruction of the temple.[655]

The content and arrangement of the book of Isaiah is difficult to determine. Hence, over against the scholarly consensus that divides the book of Isaiah as

---

650 Following the reading of the MT מִמְּךָ "from you." DSS[Isa] reads ממעיכה "from your belly/lions." *BDB,* 588.

651 וַיֹּאמֶר- בְּיָמָי- "and he said...." II Kings 20:19 reads וַיֹּאמֶר הֲלוֹא אִם-שָׁלוֹם "and he said is it not (so), if there shall be peace." For MT's כִּי "if" and transposes יִהְיֶה "there be" to a position after "security," which hardly changes the sense. Septuagint δη "indeed, doubtless" reads כִּי as an assertive. Hezekiah said that there would be peace and security in my days. This might be perhaps addition.

652 Childs, *Introduction to the Old Testament as Scripture*, 332-333.

653 Marvin A. Sweeney, *Isaiah 1-4 and the Post-Exilic Understanding of the Isaianic Tradition* (BZAW 171; Berlin: de Gruyter, 1998), 111, 426; Craig A. Evans, "On the Unity and Parallel Structure of Isaiah," *VT* 38 (1988): 129-147.

654 Watts, *Isaiah 34-66*, 64.

655 R. E. Clements, *Isaiah 1-39* (NCB; London: Marshall, Morgan & Scott; Grand Rapids: Eerdmans, 1980), 294-296. It is focus on Jehoiachin and the Davidic dynasty rather than on the destruction of the temple in 587 BCE.

1-35(39), 40-66, C. R. Seitz has proposed that in the final presentation of the book the division is Isaiah 1-33 and 34-66. In this way Isaiah 36-39 is a concrete example of God's care at one moment in Zion's history framed by 34-35 affirming Zion's final triumph and Isaiah 40-66 with the same line of interest.[656] This matches the structure of Isaiah 1-33, with general word of judgement on Judah and Jerusalem, followed by a concrete example of the reason for judgement, and then further general development of the theme. Exilic and post-exilic redaction of Isaiah is much easier to discern.

Interest has begun among scholars concerning on the literary and theological relationship of Isaiah 36-39 to the rest of the book of Isaiah. Important studies providing an impetus have been those of Ackroyd,[657] Clements,[658] Conrad,[659] Sweeney,[660] and the work of Seitz.[661] Groves turns to the theological significance in his work on "actualization,"[662] while Williamson, as part of his investigation of material used by Second Isaiah, reviews the changing attitudes to the relationships of Isaiah 36-39 to the rest of the book.[663] Isaiah 38-39, on the other hand, look toward Babylon and the Babylonian captivity, the major subject of the second half of the book. Isaiah 38-39 should precede chronologically the events of Isaiah 36-37, since Merodach Baladan had fled Babylon in 702/701 BCE. Thus his ambassadors to Judah must have been sent in 703 BCE.[664] Smelik suggests that Isaiah 36-39 were written in the Persian period. The chronological relationship of the events in Isaiah 36-39 is difficult to understand, however, it is assumed that all these events happened at about the same time, probably within a year or two. During this period Hezekiah trusted God twice and failed to trust God once.

656 C. R. Seitz, *Zion's Final Destiny: The Development of the Book of Isaiah: A Reassessment of Isaiah 36-39* (Minneapolis: Fortress, 1991), 34-51.

657 P. R. Ackroyd, "An Interpretation of the Babylonian Exile: A Study of II Kings 20, Isaiah 38-39," *SJT 21* (1974): 329-52.

658 R. E. Clements, *Isaiah and the Deliverance of Jerusalem: A Study of the Interpretation of Prophecy in the Old Testament* (JSOTS 13; Sheffield: JSOT, 1980); idem, *Isaiah 1-39* (NCB; London: Marshall, Morgan & Scott; Grand Rapids: Eerdmans, 1980); idem, "Unity of the book of Isaiah," *Interpretation* 36 (1982): 117-29.

659 E. W. Conrad, "The Royal Narratives and the Structure of the Book of Isaiah," *JSOT* 41 (1988): 67-81; and idem, *Reading Isaiah: Overtures in Biblical Theology* (Minneapolis: Fortress, 1991), 34-51.

660 Sweeney, *Isaiah 1-4 and the Post-Exilic Understanding of the Isaianic Tradition* (BZAW 171; Berlin: de Gruyter, 1988); and *Isaiah 1 39, With An Introduction to Prophetic Literature* (Grand Rapids: Eerdmans, 1996), 454-511.

661 Seitz, *Zion's Final Destiny.*

662 J. W. Groves, *Actualization and Interpretation in the Old Testament* (SBLDS 86; Atlanta: Scholars, 1987), 191-201.

663 H. G. M. Williamson, *The Book Called Isaiah: Deutero-Isaiah's Role in Composition and Redaction* (Oxford: Clarendon, 1994).

664 Hayes and Irving place Isaiah 36-39 in 712-711 BCE. Hayes and Irving, *Isaiah*, 13-14.

The structure of Isaiah 39 can be considered as follows: The arrival of the Babylonian ambassadors with letter, a gift from Merodach-Baladan (Isa 39:1); Hezekiah's joy (Isa 39:2); Prophet Isaiah's questions (Isa 39:3-4); followed by Isaiah's oracles for Yahweh (Isa 39:5-7); and Acceptance of judgement by Hezekiah (Isa 39:8).

4.2.2.2.4.3. Comments

Isaiah 39:1. Scholars rearrange its sense in terms of II Kings 20:12. The two texts present different accounts of the same event. II Kings 20:12 portrays the Babylonian king as sending a diplomatic mission to Hezekiah because he heard Hezekiah was ill. Isaiah 39:1 states that the Babylonian king sent a mission to Hezekiah and then heard that he had been ill and had recovered.[665] The consecutive action in the grammatical form of the verb וַיִּשְׁמַע "and he heard" cannot allow it to suggest that the Babylonian king sent envoys to Jerusalem because he heard that Hezekiah was ill. Furthermore, the verb וַיֶּחֱזָק "and he had recovered" at the end of Isaiah 39:1 describes Merodach son of Baladan's reaction, that he proceeded to prepare. Instead of showing/describing Hezekiah's recovery, the verb וַיֶּחֱזָק suggests the Babylonian imperial agenda. The royal plan here is that Hezekiah's treasure will soon go off into the hands of Babylonians.[666] The version of the story preserved in II Kings 20 states that "Hezekiah heard concerning them," that is, the Babylonian envoys. According to Blenkinsopp, this kind of expression is used exclusively by Deuteronomic writers and in the context of treaty-making (Josh 9:6) or of foreigners' coming to view the disasters inflicted on Judah (Deut 29:21; I Kgs 8:41).[667]

The phrase בָּעֵת הַהִוא "at that time," the timing is uncertain. Some would place this before Sennacherib's invasion, on the grounds that Merodach-baladan would have been seeking an alliance against Assyria. Sennacherib claims to have driven him out of Babylon before the invasion of Judah. But Merodach-baladan's embassy was one of many that followed the Assyrian defeat (II Chron 32:22-23).[668] However, Motyer argues that the phrase does not refer to a particular date but here it refers to "an occasion charged with some special significance."[669] The word מִנְחָה "gift" is a significance of closeness or fellowship. In ancient Israel whenever

665 Otto Kaiser, *Isaiah 13-39: A Commentary* (Philadelphia: The Westminster Press, 1974), 410. "for the exchange of embassies on the occasion of illnesses.

666 Blenkinsopp, *Isaiah 1-39*, 487; Kaiser, *Isaiah 13-39*, 410.

667 Blenkinsopp, *Isaiah 1-39*, 489.

668 Kaiser, *Isaiah 13-39*, 409. He suggests the visit of Merodach-baladan might happened between 713-711 BCE during the revolt of Philistine, or in 703 BCE when a coalition was formed against Assyria (anti-Assyrian) in the west under the leadership of Hezekiah. See also Oswalt, *The Book of Isaiah 1-39*, 693-94.

669 Motyer, *The prophecy of Isaiah*, 295.

an official visit take place from one monarch to another it always includes gifts as a mark or symbol of friendship between the two nations.[670]

Isaiah 39:2. Regardless of the relative age of one version over another, that the account in Isaiah portrays the king as rejoicing- concerning the envoys is significant for constructing an image of the king as it relates to wealth and power. That Hezekiah rejoices concerning the Babylonian emissaries. The phrase חִזְקִיָּהוּ וַיִּשְׂמַח עֲלֵיהֶם "and Hezekiah was glad/rejoice of them" means, he found pleasure in them. They were the object of his joy. It is not hard to understand why, since it would be very flattering to receive an embassy from such a far distance (II Chron 32:27-29). John N. Oswalt notes that Hezekiah portrays human heart and mind. He was a generally good and godly king, but it is to point out that he was, in fact, not infallible.[671]

In Isaiah 39:3, Isaiah appeared in Hezekiah's court and confronted him with critical questions of Babylonian envoys visit to Judah: "What did these men say? And from where did they come to you?" (Isa 39:3). Isaiah is curious about their motives. Here several options can be drawn: Were they proposing an alliance? Were they offering congratulations on the victory over Sennacherib, or on Hezekiah's recovery? The former is not possible because there is no indication that they were interested in such an alliance. The answer is defective in two ways:

First, Hezekiah only answers the second part of the question. Far from taking advantage of their opening speech to glorify Yahweh, he passes by it entirely. He is not looking for ways to exalt Yahweh. Perhaps Hezekiah is ashamed of how he mishandled the visitors' greetings, and thus skips over Isaiah's first question.

Second, note in particular how he picks up Isaiah's אֵלֶיךָ "to you." He emphasizes, בָּאוּ אֵלַי "they have come to me." He sees himself as the centre of their interest, even though the "wonder" about which they came to inquire was done by Yahweh. The wonder really "belonged to Yahweh," as the writer of I Kings 10:1 says of the fame of Solomon. They would have been prepared to hear an explanation in spiritual terms. Yet Hezekiah deflects their interest to himself. Watts concludes that Hezekiah's failure to assess carefully the situation compromised his throne, his palace, the Temple, all his possessions, his capital city, and even the future generation of his own family. All these he surrendered for the impossible dream of freedom and independence. It was fantasy because it was not based on God's strategy and God's leading.[672]

Isaiah 39:6 is about the judgement upon the nation. A very clear and explicit link between Isaiah's preaching and the event of the fall of Jerusalem to the Babylonians is made in the narrative of the sending of emissaries from Merodach-baladan to Hezekiah, in which Isaiah plays a role (II Kgs 22:12-

670 A. S. Herbert, *The Book of the Prophet Isaiah 1-39* (Cambridge: University Press, 1973), 214.

671 Oswalt, *The Book of Isaiah 1-39*, 694-696.

672 John D. W. Watts, *Isaiah 34-66* (WBC, vol. 25; Waco/Texas: Word Books, Publisher, 1987), 67.

19).[673] Joseph Blenkinsopp asserts that Isaiah's prediction was fulfilled with when Nebuchadnezzar, king of Babylonian first assault/attack Jerusalem in 597 BCE resulting in the deportation of Jehoiachin together with his *sarisim* 'officials/ scribes,' and the confiscation of his treasures.[674]

Isaiah 39:8. Hezekiah's thought that there will be שָׁלוֹם וֶאֱמֶת "peace and security" in his days. Morally obtuse Hezekiah is not able to comprehend what אֱמֶת "security" and שָׁלוֹם "peace" truly mean. According to Watts, "security" here is translated as "firm, true, and which has integrity."[675] The book of Isaiah presents a characterization of Hezekiah that holds the king to the same culpability of moral blindness and deafness that marks the entire nation. Otto Kaiser notes that Hezekiah's thought of "peace and security" is of "partly apotropaic in intention, and partly the expressions of a degree of submission to God and at the same time certain egotism."[676] Others think that Hezekiah is exhibiting insensitive indifference to the oracle of judgement that he has just heard. For Ackroyd, Hezekiah's statement that there will be שָׁלוֹם "peace" and אֱמֶת "security" in his time is an understandable sigh of relief. He sets out his positive slant on Hezekiah's comment about peace and security as a rejoinder to scholars who might take Hezekiah's comments as smug.[677]

4.2.2.2.4.4. Prophetic Leadership of Isaiah

Most of the scholars view Hezekiah as well-disciplined and religious king. The Book of Kings also assessed Hezekiah's reign positively, concentrating on the achievement of Hezekiah's cultic and military role.[678] These were his main royal duties. There is possibility that because of all his good deeds, the Book of Kings seeks to contrast Hezekiah with Ahaz.[679] However, reading the narrative of Isaiah 39:1-8 in terms of the ethical demands of the Book of Isaiah as a whole produces a negative judgement of Hezekiah's character and his leadership. The critique of Isaiah is that Hezekiah lost his trust in Yahweh and sought help from Babylonian king. It is simple because of the pride of royal accomplishment.

673 Peter R. Ackroyd, "An Interpretation of the Babylonian Exile. A Study of 2 Kings 20, Isaiah 38-39," *SJT* 27 (1974): 329-52.

674 Blenkinsopp, *Isaiah 1-39*, 488. Cf. Kaiser, *Isaiah 13-39: A Commentary*, 410.

675 Watts, "Isaiah 34-66," 66.

676 Kaiser, *Isaiah 13-39: A Commentary*, 410.

677 Ackroyd, "An Interpretation of the Babylonian Exile: A Study of II Kings 20 and Isaiah 38-39," 329-52.

678 Diana Edelman, "Hezekiah's Alleged Cultic Centralization," *JSOT* 32 (2008): 396 (II Kgs 18:4-5, 8, 22).

679 For instance, Hezekiah was forced to submitted to the Assyrian king and paid tribute (II Kgs 18:13-16), in-order to save the nation from further punishment from the powerful Assyrian king, whereas Ahaz did it voluntarily (II Kgs 16:7-9). The author of Kings further illustrates that Hezekiah listened to Isaiah (II Kgs 19) while Ahaz order policy to Uriah the priest (II Kgs 16:10-16).

According to prophet Isaiah, the reasons for God's judgement were that the leaders, rulers, and prophets had led the innocent people astray. He also argues that the possibility of divine judgement was the failure of the leaders to put their trust on God, who had shown His faithfulness to them, by side-lining him and having a confidence in the horses and chariots. Thus Isaiah proclaimed prophetic protest against a wrong political action. He called the king and the people of Judah to just and righteous action since it alone would be consonant with their status as the covenant people of Yahweh. This may help us to understand why the prophet calls first for trust and only secondarily for reform. Trust is the necessary pioneer to any legislative or other reform measures. Thus, according to Isaiah, trust is the only measure that will see Judah to safety.

The above discussion shows different kinds of leadership portrayed by the prophet from that of Judah's royal leadership. In contrast to his political opponents, Isaiah maintained a consistent view throughout his long ministry. Peace, security, and well-being could not be obtained by the politics of fear, by ruthless and oppressive military preparations, or by cunning and dishonest military alliances. The political leaders' search for security in violence and cunning, in a treaty with powerful neighbouring nations, is like seeking shelter in a fortress whose walls are not vertically aligned on a solid foundation but bulge dangerously outward with spreading cracks. In fact, true security lays in making God one's primary object of fear and then trusting God to keep his promises. It also lies in living out that trust by the righteous and just treatment of one's fellow citizens. Isaiah's view is, when one has made Yahweh one's object of fear, one can remain calm in the face of other fears and thus live out God's demands to give relief to the poor and needy, to live by God's standard of justice and righteousness.[680]

4.2.3. Summary

Ahaz, Hezekiah and the royal officials had failed to see any crisis in the absence of justice in their society. Indeed, they profited from it, perhaps they even brought it into being. For those bureaucrats, the crisis was the threat that national political institutions would not survive. For the prophet, the government's attitude toward social ethics was the indicator of whether it was headed for Yahweh's judgement or vindication. Preserving national institutions had become a fetish and a blank check for wrongdoing. Thereby, according to Isaiah, the community, through its corrupt leadership, had betrayed its very purpose for existence.

4.3. HOSEA

Hosea was one of the significant prophets that lived in the eighth century BCE. We find that he stands as a man of great insight and importance, whose destiny

---

680 As Isaiah 32:17-18 puts it, "The effect of righteousness will be peace, and the result of righteousness, quietness and trust forever. My people will abide in a peaceful habitation, in secure dwellings, and in quiet resting places" (NRSV).

was to have been called upon to proclaim God's message at a time of crisis and uncertainty. Tragically he saw his message fall on deaf ears, his forewarnings of disaster realized, and his hopes frustrated. The picture we are left with is of a man standing amid the ruins of a nation that he loved, who was to witness sufferings he had hoped to prevent. He saw his nation falling headlong towards a devastation which all his preaching insisted was not inevitable. Yet out of his experience of such frustration and suffering, there emerged a proclamation of hope which was to have very great importance for the future history of Israel. That Hosea is seen as a visionary leader who could lead his people in the midst of crises, and thus the purpose of this section is an attempt to discuss of Hosea's leadership achievements.

4.3.1. The Call of Hosea

Nothing is known of Hosea the man, apart from the matter of his marriage to Gomer,[681] the daughter of one Diblaim (Hos 1:3) and his father, Beeri.[682] James Luther Mays however, observes that Hosea was apparently a young man, of marriageable age, when he became a prophet.[683] The metaphors in Hosea 7:4-8 hardly prove that he was a baker. However, according to Harrison from the various agricultural allusions in the book it could be maintained with equal seriousness that Hosea was a farmer.[684] Abraham J. Heschel offers an analysis of the numerous suppositions about Hosea:

> From his use of certain striking figures of speech it has been suggested that he was a baker, lived as a farmer on the land, was associated with the priesthood and the sanctuaries, had a strongly developed sex instinct which he vigorously repressed. With the same right we could suggest that he was a lover of the desert and an expert on lions, panthers, and bears.[685]

Wolff makes the important observation that Hosea's numerous similes, "the thing being compared more often precedes the image of comparison than follows it."[686] From the places mentioned in his sayings namely, city of Samaria (Hos 7:1; 8:5; 10:5, 7; 14:1) and the cultic centres at Bethel (Hos 4:15; 5:8; 10:5; 12:5) and

---

681 Gomer probably must be one of the sacred prostitutes of the fertility cult. R. K. Harrison, *Introduction to the Old Testament* (Grand Rapids: Eerdmans, 1969), 862.

682 But there is no evidence that this is the Beerah, a Reubenite prince, who is mentioned in 1 Chron 5:6. Hans Walter Wolff, *Hosea* (trans. Gary Stansell; ed. Paul D. Hanson; Philadelphia: Fortress Press, 1974), xxii; J. Andrew Dearman, *The Book of Hosea* (NICOT; Grand Rapids, Michigan: Wm. B. Eerdmans Publishing Co., 2010), 3; John Mauchline and Harold Cooke Phillips, "The Book of Hosea," *The Interpreter's Bible* (vol. 6; ed. George A. Buttrick; New York: Abingdon Press, 1956), 553, 567.

683 James Luther Mays, *Hosea,* Old Testament Library (Philadelphia: Westminster Press, 1969), 2.

684 R. K. Harrison, *Introduction to the Old Testament* (Grand Rapids: Eerdmans, 1969), 859.

685 Abraham J. Heschel, *The Prophets* (New York: Harper & Row, 1962), 39.

686 Wolff, *Hosea,* 1974, 83.

Gilgal a prophet to his own land/people.[687] Perhaps those were the places where most of his oracles were spoken (Hos 4:15; 9:15; 12:12). Hosea is known by his message (emphasis on love). Theodore H. Robinson expresses that Hosea "was a man possessed and dominated by his love."[688] Hosea 1:1 informs, however, about his times of ministry. The only northern king mentioned is Jeroboam II. The last southern king listed is Hezekiah and that shows that Hosea spent his last years in Judah. Thus, most probably Hosea's ministry spanned till the last king of Israel (Hoshea) and might witnessed its fall to Assyria in 722/721 BCE.

4.3.2. Hosea 4:1-10

Hosea 4:1-10 is chosen in order to evaluate the character of the leaders and the critique of Hosea.

4.3.2.1. Translation

4:1. *Hear the word of Yahweh, O sons of Israel; for (the) Yahweh has a controversy/ dispute with the inhabitants/dwellers of the land. That there is no faithfulness and there is no kindness, and there is no knowledge of God in the land.*

4:2. *Swearing, and lying, and killing, and stealing, and committing adultery; they broke out*[689] *and blood touches blood.*

4:3. *Therefore the land mourns, and all who dwell in it languish,*[690] *with the beasts of the field,*[691] *and the birds of the heavens (air); and also the fish of the sea are taken away.*

4:4. *Surely let no man contend, and let no man reprove, and your people contend, O priest.*[692]

---

687 Mays, *Hosea*, 2; Harrison, *Introduction to the Old Testament,* 859.

688 Theodore H. Robinson, *Prophecy and the Prophets in Ancient Israel* (London: Gerald Duckworth & Co. Ltd, 1960), 77.

689 Reading with the MT פָּרָצוּ qal perfect 3rd person common plural "they broke out/to break through." BHS proposes to read with LXX κεχυται επι της γης, equal to פרצו בָּאָרֶץ– "they break through in the land." Probably וּפָרִין "and break through." Perhaps suggests to read as פֶּרֶץ פָּרָצוּ– "bursting forth they break through."

690 Following the MT reading וְאֻמְלַל – Conj. perfect 3rd person masculine singular, אמל– "waste away/to be feeble/languish." It is absent in LXX (συν πασι), perhaps the editor suggests to read as (כָל) בְּ– "in (all)" or (כָּל) עִם- – "with all."

691 MT reads הַשָּׂדֶה -article + noun common masculine singular absolute, שָׂדֶה -"the field." LXX adds και συν τοις ερπετοις τωης γης, equal to וּבְרֶמֶשׂ הָאֲדָמָה -"and with the creeping things of the ground." Compare Hos 2:20, perhaps insert on account of the metre; others delete aγb. Read with the MT based on the strength of witness.

692 וְעַמְּךָ כִּמְרִיבֵי כֹהֵן "and your people contend, O priest." Corrupt; perhaps the editor suggests to read as וְעִמְּךָ אֲנִי רָב (הַ) כֹּהֵן -"for your people I am the defender of the priest." Or וְעִמְּךָ רִיבִי (הַ) כֹּהֵן -"for your people are my dispute of the priest." Read with the MT because there is no support from other manuscripts.

4:5. *And you shall stumble by day,*[693] [694]*and the prophet also shall stumble with you by night;*[695]*and I will destroy*[696] *your mother.*

4:6. *My people are to be destroyed*[697] *for lack of knowledge; because you have rejected knowledge, I will reject you*[698] *from being a priest to me. And you have forgotten the law of your God, I also will forget your sons.*

4:7. *Thus the more they increased, the more they sinned against me; I will change their glory*[699] *into dishonor.*[700]

4:8. *They feed on the sin [sin offering] of my people; and they carry the punishment for his (their) soul.*[701]

4:9. *And*[702] *it shall be like people, like priest; I will punish him for his ways, and I will bring back him for his deeds.*

---

693 MT reads הַיּוֹם- article + noun common masculine singular absolute – “the day.” LXX reads ημερας. However BHS proposes to read בְּיוֹם -“in day” or יוֹמָם -“by day/in the day time.” Suggestion can be accepted.

694 וְכָשַׁל גַּם־נָבִיא עִמְּךָ לָיְלָה -“and the prophet also shall stumble/fall with you (in) the night.” Deleted gloss? Read with the MT based on the strength of witness.

695 וְדָמִיתִי אִמֶּךָ-“and I will destroy your mother.” BHS proposes to read as ודמית אֶת־אִמֶּךָ -“you will destroy your mother.” Read with the MT because there is no support from other manuscripts.

696 Reading with the MT וְדָמִיתִי - qal perfect 1st person common singular, דָּמָה -“and I will destroy.” Perhaps BHS suggests to read as וְדִמִּיתָ - piel perfect 2nd person masculine singular, דָּמָה -“and you will destroy.” Compare Vulgate.

697 MT reads נִדְמוּ-niphal perfect 3rd person common plural of דָּמָה -“they are destroyed.” The editor proposes to read as נדמָה -Qal imperfect 1st person common plural (cohortative), דמם -“let us perish/destroy.” Read with the MT because there is no support from other manuscripts.

698 Following the reading of the MT וְאֶמְאָסְאךָ-conj. + qal imperfect 1st person common singular suffix 2nd person masculine singular, מָאַס -“and I reject you.” ואמאסך “א” is missing in many Hebrew manuscripts; corrupt out of/from ואמאסך אֲנִי “and I reject you I am.”

699 כְּבוֹדָם-noun common masculine singular construct suffix 3rd person masculine plural, כָּבוֹד -“their glory.” Tiqqun sopherim has כבודִי -noun common masculine singular construct suffix 1cs – “my glory.” Read with the MT based on the strength of witness.

700 Following the reading of the MT אָמִיר- hiphil imperfect 1st person common singular, מור “I will change.” BHS proposes to read (Targum and Syriac) הֵמִירוּ, hiphil perfect 3rd common plural – “they changed,”

701 MT reads נַפְשׁוֹ- noun common singular construct suffix 3rd person masculine singular, נפש -“his soul.” However, BHS proposes to read plural form נפשָׁם, noun common singular + suffix 3mpl, נפש “their soul.” Plural form fits the context better. Therefore MT needs to be emended.

702 The editor suggests that the whole verse is added. Read with the MT because there is no support from other manuscripts.

4:10. *And they shall eat, but they will not be satisfied; they shall commit the harlot,*[703] *but not multiply;*[704] *because they have forsaken Yahweh*[705] *to keep harlotry.*

4.3.2.2. Form/Setting/Structure

The book of Hosea has two major divisions. Hosea 1-3 are concerned with Hosea's marriage and are seen as the first unit. Hosea 4-14 are the second major unit in the book. This section contains a series of oracles which often seem to have little systematic arrangement beyond catchwords or similar ideas.[706] Hosea 4 clearly indicates the societal structure of the eighth century Israel in general and Israel during Hosea's time in particular. The oracle is set in the context of a society where "syncretism" seems to be the order of the day and which led people indulged in immoral activities. In Hosea 4 God addressed the Israelite society as a whole but identified sins of their priests in particular.

Few indications can be brought out to understand the *sitz im leben* of this passage. The first three chapters of Hosea seem to have been written in the reign of Jeroboam II, so the setting of Hosea 4 belongs to the period of anarchy which followed the death of Jeroboam II. However, Stuart supposes that this passage is written during the time of the reign of Jeroboam II asserting that there was stability in the political situation and that prosperity was the order of the day for the group of priests who enjoy the decadence provided for in the cult (Hos 4:7, 8, 11). The increase in the number and influence of the priests points to the prosperity under Jeroboam II. He also states that the times appear to manifest a conspicuous sort of complacent self-indulgence of the kind associated with the days prior to 745 BC.[707]

Scholars today doubt that [the bulk of] the book comes from the messages of Hosea himself, but many attribute the actual commitment of his words to writing not to the prophet but to a group of disciples (mentioning prophet in

703 Reading with the MT הִזְנוּ hiphil perfect 3rd person common plural, זָנָה. However BHS proposes with 2 Hebrew manuscripts and read וְהִזְנוּ -"and they committed harlotry." Others read יזנו -Qal imperfect 3rd person masculine plural, זָנָה - "they will commit harlotry."

704 כִּי־אֶת־יְהוָה עָזְבוּ לִשְׁמֹר-"because they have left Yahweh to guard." The editor suggests that it is probably added.

705 אֶת־יְהוָה-"Yahweh." The editor suggests that perhaps it should be read as אִתִּי -Accusative with 1st person common singulars -"with me." Read with the MT because there is no support from other manuscripts.

706 Artur Weiser, *The Old Testament: Its Formation and Development* (trans. Dorothea M. Barton; New York: Association Press, 1961), 236. Weiser feels that this lack of any systematic arrangement proves that the oracles were not placed in their present positions by the prophet himself. Cf. G. W. Anderson, *A Critical Introduction to the Old Testament* (London: Gerald Duckworth, 1959), 42. However, Samuel R. Driver says the oracles were "arranged probably by the prophet himself at the close of his ministry." *An Introduction to the Literature of the Old Testament* (Edinburgh: T&T Clark, 1907), 303.

707 Stuart, *Hosea-Jonah*, 73.

the third person Hos 1:2,3).[708] This outlook on the writing of the prophetic books is not founded on solid evidence, however. A number of scholars contend that the book has a fair number of redactional interpolations. One opinion is that the references to Judah are from two Judaic redactions of the book; the first was a "pro-Judah" redaction designed to distance Judah from the condemnation pronounced against Israel (e.g., Hos 1:7; 3:5). The second was a redaction that took the condemnatory oracles originally delivered against Israel and redirected them toward Judah (e.g., Hos 5:5; 6:11).[709] A few scholars maintain that the "optimistic" oracles do not stem from Hosea, but this tendency to regard the prophets as incapable of complex attitudes regarding the place of Israel before God is rightly fallen out of favour. In Hosea's case, the sayings of condemnation and the sayings of salvation are so thoroughly intertwined, and the style is so evidently uniform, that any effort to treat the positive statements as secondary should be abandoned. The multitude of metaphors and similes found in Hosea has elicited comment from many scholars.[710]

The question of the authorship of Hosea 4:1-3 is one of the most difficult problems that must be confronted. While the material in Hosea 4:1-3 is in the third person and is attributed to God, Hosea 4:4-10 are in the first person. This change of person indicates that the text is a collection of oracles. This raises the possibility that some of the materials of Hosea 4 may have been added by the editor who arranged them. For instance Hosea 4:1 is assuming to be the same redactor of the superscription in Hosea 1:1 and the following verses (Hos 1:2-3), the judgement speech belong to the early part of Hosea's prophetic ministry.[711] Harper includes Hosea 4:1-3 in a list of oracles attributable to Hosea.[712] Hosea 4:4-10 does not belong to a rhetorical unit, it points to the result of punishment especially to the priests.

The historical setting of the book falls for the most part between 747 BCE and 722 BCE in the Northern Kingdom of Israel.[713] According to Hosea 1:1, we know that an editor of the book placed the beginning of Hosea's prophetic

---

708 Wolff, *Hosea*, xxix; Andersen and Freedman, *Hosea*, 53; Francis S. North, "Hosea's Introduction to His Book," *VT* 8 (1958): 429-432.

709 Wolff, *Hosea*, xxxi-xxxii, and W. H. Schmidt, *Introduction to the Old Testament* (London: SCM, 1979), 204.

710 Wolff, *Hosea*, xxiv, xxvii-xxviii; James Luther Mays, *Hosea* (OTL; Philadelphia: Westminster Press, 1969), 9-10; G. I. Davies, *Hosea* (NCBC; Grand Rapids: Wm. B. Eerdmans for Marshall Pickering, 1992), 34; Gottwald, *The Hebrew-Bible*, 359-60; P. A. Kruger, "Prophetic Imagery: On Metaphors and Similes in the Book Hosea," *Journal of Northwest Semitic Languages* 14 (1988): 143.

711 Wolff, *Hosea*, 66.

712 William Rainey Harper, *A Critical and Exegetical Commentary on Amos and Hosea* (Edinburgh: T&T Clark, 1905), clx. But he offers no discussion of his reasons for this decision.

713 For this discussion see James M. Ward, "The Message of the Prophet Hosea," *Interpretation* 23 (1969): 387-407. A similar discussion will also be found in Mays, *Hosea*, 3-5.

ministry before the death of Jeroboam II of Israel (746 BCE) and ending after Hezekiah of Judah began his reign (715 BCE). There is possible suggestion to the Syro-Ephramite invasion of Judah (735-733 BCE) in Hosea 5:8-15. The political instability of Israel's last years is alluded to in Hosea 7:3-7 and 8:4-10.[714] According to Ward, the final editing of the book occurred for the benefit of a Judean audience between the time of Judah's survival of the Assyrian siege in 701 BCE and her destruction in 587 BCE.[715] If it can be shown that Hosea 4:1-3 is a part of the oral material originating with Hosea, then one may conclude that the oracle originated sometime before the fall of the Northern Kingdom in 722/721 BCE.

The dating of individual units in some particular part of Hosea's ministry is difficult, although the section Hosea 4:1-10 may reflect the last years of the reign of Jeroboam II.[716] The final concern of the literary criticism of Hosea 4:1-3 is the intention of the unit. This question is also tied to the form of the passage. However, some tentative answers may be given in isolation from the form critical analysis. Some imply that Hosea 4:1-3 was composed by an editor as a general introduction to the following oracles.[717]

The structure of Hosea 4:1-10 is a text of special importance. Formally, it is a judgement scene: God calls first the people (Hos 4:1-3) and then the religious leaders to account (Hos 4:4-10). The second section is divided into two: Hosea 4:4-6 a threat to the priests (Israel's religious leaders are singled out and pronounced punishment or judgement because of their unfaithfulness and misleading the fallow Israelites), and Hosea 4:7-10 announcement of the judicial sentence.[718]

4.3.2.3. Comments

4.3.2.3.1. Hosea 4:1-4 (Hosea and the Leaders)

Hosea 4 unloaded enormous burdens which the prophet carries for the nation. Hosea's first attention was to the inhabitants (people) of the land. Because of their violation of the law of Yahweh, the whole of God's creation is wounded and

714 Mays, *Hosea*, 3-5. However, Douglas Stuart suggests that Hosea 3 belongs to the peaceful and prosperous time of Jeroboam II, since there is no indication of political instability. *Hosea-Jonah* (WBC; Nashville: Thomas Nelson Publishers, 1987), 74.

715 Ward, "The Message of the Prophet Hosea," 388.

716 Mays, *Hosea,* 16.

717 See instance for Andersen and Freedman, Hosea 4:1-3 is the introduction to Hosea 4-7. *Hosea,* 331; for D. A. Hubbard, it introduces Hosea 4-11. *With Bands of Love: Lessons from the Book of Hosea* (Grand Rapids: Eerdman's press, 1968), 95-96; for Mays these verses introduces Hosea 4-14. *Hosea* 61; Wolff, *Hosea,* xxix-xxx. However, it is possible that the compiler may have done nothing other than collect and arrange individual units of oral tradition.

718 Michael Deroche, "Structure, Rhetoric, and Meaning in Hosea," *VT* 33 (1983): 185-198; Stuart, *Hosea-Jonah*, 73.

victimized. Then Yahweh's lawsuit is followed by the accusation by mentioning the lack of three key covenantal qualities: אֱמֶת "faithfulness," חֶסֶד "love/kindness," and דַּעַת "knowledge" these are guiding starts of prophetic thought.[719] These qualities can be interpreted either morally or religiously. The prophet declares:

(i) There is no אֱמֶת. This term is related to the concept of truth and carries the notions of constancy, reliability, and integrity in word and deed. Yahweh himself is the standard by which this faithfulness is measured (Hos 2:20).[720] אֱמֶת is a synonym of אֱמוּנָה "faithfulness," which God shows in the time of salvation. The word אֱמֶת occur in this verse alone.[721] According to Wolff, this term "denotes an unconditional reliability in which one has confidence in the other," in terms of word and service.[722]

(ii) Secondly, no חֶסֶד "loving concern/kindness/steadfast love." It denotes the attitude and activity which founds and maintains a relation (bond of loyalty). In Hosea the sphere of חֶסֶד is the covenant with Yahweh and his "faithful relationship with his people."[723] Harrison remarks that חֶסֶד "embodies the concept of true love in the light of some specific relationship, and is marked by a profound emotional and spiritual content."[724] Here a reciprocal relationship is presupposed, and this bond is to be made manifest in actions. In the context of the prophets, this relationship is the covenant: Yahweh has committed himself to a particular people, and they are called to reflect this חֶסֶד concretely with one another in the community.[725]

(iii) The third accusation is no דַּעַת "knowledge." One of the major charges against the people was that there was וְאֵין־דַּעַת אֱלֹהִים בָּאָרֶץ "no knowledge of God in the land." The term "knowledge of God" according to

719 Andersen and Freedman, *Hosea,* 336.

720 See A. Jepsen, "אָמַן," in *TDOT* (vol.1; ed. G. Johannes Botterweck and Helmer Ringgren; trans. John T. Willis; Grand Rapids: Eerdmans, 1974), 292-323; W. C. Kaiser, *Toward Old Testament Ethics* (Grand Rapids: Zondervan, 1983), 222-34.

721 Wolff, *Hosea*, 67.

722 Wolff, *Hosea,* 67 (Exod 18:21; Josh 2:12; 24:14; I Kgs 10:6; 22:16; I Sam 12:24).

723 Wolff, *Hosea,* 67. The book of Hosea contains one of the most impressive examples of the covenantal love of Yahweh for Israel. In ancient times, a covenant conveyed the idea of a treaty in which there were two parties that were bound by it. If one of these parties failed to fulfil its obligations, the other party would be excused from fulfilling the contract. However, Hosea portrays how the divine חֶסֶד -the unfailing love of Yahweh-goes beyond the norm and, in a way, contrary to the legal expectations.

724 Harrison, *Introduction to the Old Testament,* 872.

725 H. J. Zobel, "חֶסֶד," in *TDOT* (vol. 5; Grand Rapids: Eerdmans, 1986), 44-64; Davies, *Hosea* (Grand Rapids: Eerdmans, 1992), 94-97; B. C. Birch, *Let Justice Roll Down: The Old Testament, Ethics, and Christian Life* (Louisville: Westminster John Knox, 1991), 151-53; D. A. Hubbard, *With Bands of Love: Lessons from the Book of Hosea* (Grand Rapids: Eerdmans Press, 1968), 186. For Hosea, the essential fact was that Israel was bound to Yahweh by חֶסֶד.

James M. Ward involves not only knowing what God expects but also accepting these demands as valid and binding.[726] James L. Mays contains that the term also means the whole response of Israel to the acts and words of Yahweh.[727] This relationship between Yahweh and his people is to be a close personal relationship, much as that between a man and his wife (Hos 2:19, 20).

Hosea expands his meaning of knowledge of Yahweh to include the revelation of Yahweh as their only Yahweh at the Exodus (Hos 13:4), and that Yahweh gives them the good things of the land (Hos 2:8). In the context of the book of Hosea, this knowledge certainly does refer to a certain theological content, such as the traditions of the Patriarchs (Hos 12:3-4, 12), of the Exodus (Hos 2:14-15; 11:1-4; 12:9, 13; 13:4) and of the Wilderness (Hos 9:10; 13:5) and the teachings of the *Torah* (Hos 4:6; 8:1, 12). But, the term includes as well an understanding of Yahweh's covenantal demands which is to be reflected in obedience and moral conduct.

The list of five charges that follow in Hosea 4:2a offer an application of the three sins of omission in Hosea 4:1 within human relationships. Some commentators hold that the term, "knowledge," summarizes and is the basis of the preceding two.[728] Although the knowledge of God is a more general concept, the lack of אֱמֶת "faithfulness" probably could be taken as fleshed out in swearing and lying, and the absence of חֶסֶד "loving concern/kindness/steadfast love" in killing, stealing, and adultery. Each of these five corresponds to one of the Ten Commandments.[729] The last line of Hosea 4:2 is very problematic,[730] but it is possible that the reference is to two acts of cruel violence, making a total of seven

726 James M. Ward, *Hosea* (New York: Harper and Row, 1966), 85. Some have tried to draw a distinction between "knowledge of God" and "knowledge of Yahweh." John L. McKenzie, "Knowledge of God in Hosea," *JBL* 74 (1955), 22-27, feels that "knowledge of Yahweh" referred to knowledge of religion in general, whereas "knowledge of God" was a more specific reference to Hebrew morality. Ward, *Hosea*, 85; James L. Mays, *Hosea* (Philadelphia Westminster Press, 1969), 63, and Sydney Lawrence Brown, *The Book of Hosea* (London Methuen and Co, 1932), 39, however, see no distinction between the terms "knowledge of God" and "knowledge of Yahweh" in this context.

727 Mays, *Hosea,* 52; Stuart, *Hosea-Jonah,* 75.

728 Stuart, *Hosea-Jonah,* 75; C. E. Keil, *The Minor Prophets* (Grand Rapids: Eerdmans, 1977), X: 74; William Rainey Harper, *Amos and Hosea* (Edinburgh: T&T Clark, 1979), 250.

729 Waler Brueggemann, *Tradition for Crisis: A Study in Hosea* (Richmond, Virginia: John Knox Press, 1968), 38-43; Hubbard, *Hosea*, 97; Walter C. Kaiser, *Toward Old Testament Ethics* (Grand Rapids, Michigan: Academie Books,1983), 17.

730 The three primary options concerning the difficult פָּרָצוּ are to consider it as: (1) the finite verb for the preceding five infinitive absolutes. Wolff, *Hosea*, 68; Mays, *Hosea*, 65; Stuart, *Hosea-Jonah*, 72; Davies, *Hosea*, 116. (2) Connected with the following clause describing the bloodshed. Andersen and Freedman, *Hosea*, 338; Hubbard, *Hosea*, 98. (3) A separate item with its own meaning. T. McComiskey, *The Minor Prophets: An Exegetical & Expositional Commentary, I: Hosea, Joel, and Amos* (Grand Rapids: Baker, 1992), 57; Keil, *The Minor*

violations.[731] Thus, the indictment is poetically emphasized, as the sins of Israel add up to a perfect number; their wickedness is complete.[732] These seven sins will be evident in cultic deviation and in the degrading activities of the people's worship (Hos 4:4-5:7), and then both in the refusal to trust him in national political affairs and in the struggles for power and influence (Hos 5:8-7:16). The result is that the whole of Yahweh's creation is wounded and victimized by this touches blood. It is suggested that the mention of וְדָמִים בְּדָמִים נָגָעוּ "blood touches blood" in Hosea 4:2 may be a reference to the internal political intrigues of 746-745 BCE, which resulted in the assassination of two successive kings, Zechariah and Shallum.[733] Although this conclusion is far from certain, the situation described in Hosea 4:2 could also fit other periods in Hosea's ministry. It could also mean power struggles (leadership crisis) that result in hate-rates (violence) between individuals, which led to the broken relationship with fellow Israelites. The emphasis thus seems to be on internal difficulties rather than international strife. This description best fits the period prior to the death of Jeroboam II.

From the point of view of the interpretation of the passage, this conclusion helps the exegete see the focus of Hosea's prophecy in Hosea 4:1-3 as centring more on the problems of internal societal decay than on external threats. Some translate this phrase more literately, for instance Macintosh remarks, "they multiply bloodshed to the extent that the blood of one victim touches the blood of the next."[734] Hosea 4:1 is a call to the בְּנֵי יִשְׂרָאֵל "sons of Israel" and to the יוֹשְׁבֵי הָאָרֶץ "inhabitants of the land" and Hosea 4:3a announces punishment on כָּל־יוֹשֵׁב בָּהּ "all who dwell in it." This thematic inclusion in this introductory pericope helps to emphasize that the whole population including animals stands guilty before Yahweh (Gen 9:5, beasts and humans are included in the law about murder). The crimes of God's people affect beasts, birds, and fish as well as the land itself. The transgressors are not limited to certain groups; all in one way or another are involved in the conduct condemned by the prophet.

Thus Hosea 4:1-3 introduces the primary concerns of Yahweh and declares His judgement on the whole Israelites. The transgressions mentioned in Hosea 4:2 have to do with the individual's relationship to his or her neighbour. Thus,

Prophets, 75; Harper, *A Critical and Exegetical Commentary on Amos and Hosea*, 250. The last option can be taken into consideration in this context.

731 This follows פָּרָצוּ, "they break out," rather than the conjectured infinitive וּפָרֹץ, which would add another crime, that of violence to the list. If דָּמִים is taken as bloodshed, then stealing with murderous assault would fit, then human being can be the object of פרץ. However, according to Andersen and Freedman comment, "*Prṣ* describes a violent action by God, people, or animals. God can break out of his holy confines in angry destruction." Andersen and Freedman, *Hosea*, 337.

732 J. Limburg, *Hosea-Micah* (Atlanta: John Knox, 1988), 17.

733 Mays, *Hosea,* 4.

734 Macintosh, *A Critical and Exegetical Commentary on Hosea*, 130.

the emphasis seems to be on internal difficulties rather than international strife.[735] One can see the emphasis of Hosea's prophecy in Hosea 4:1-3 as centring more on the problems of "internal societal decay" than on external threats.

4.3.2.3.2. Hosea 4:4-6 (Hosea's Struggles with the Priests and the Prophets)

The next pericope of Hosea 4 (Hos 4:4-6) shifts the contention from the people in general to the priests.[736] The theme of God's controversy is repeated in Hosea 4:4 and serves as a link from the previous pericope as does the repetition of דַּעַת "knowledge" in Hosea 4:6. Mays suggests that this may be a continuation of Hosea 4:1-3, after the protest of a priest about the harshness of Hosea 4:1-3.[737] Hosea 4:4 explains the failure of the priest: No one should try to reprove or correct the prophet, and especially not the priest, because God's contention is specifically against the priests.[738] However, the priests will be brought down because of their sins and the false prophets will be brought down with them.

Hosea 4:5 points punishment against some unnamed individuals: priest or prophet. Wolff suggests unnamed individual כֹּהֵן "priest" probably meant a high official of an important sanctuary.[739] The phrase "Stumble by day and by night;" it does not specify the exact times each will stumble.[740] However, both priest and prophet will stumble all the time.[741] The phrase וְדָמִיתִי אִמֶּךָ "I will destroy your mother" seems problematic. The reason for bringing up the priest's mother is unknown. Andersen and Freedman note that the writer mentioning priest's mother here is because "she (priest's mother) exerted an important and baleful influence on the life and career of her son."[742] Mays supports MT's rendering of "your mother" since "mother is the symbolic role played by the nation…people

---

735 R. Michael Casto, "Conversing with the Text: Application of Conversational Exegesis to Hosea 4:1-3," *Duke Divinity School Review* 40 (1975): 25.

736 Andersen and Freedman, *Hosea,* 344. The address here may focus to the family of a chief priest, his mother, sons and daughters are mentioned.

737 Mays, *Hosea*, 66.

738 The end of verse 4 presents problems in the MT. As it stands now, it reads וְעַמְּךָ כִּמְרִיבֵי כֹהֵן "and your people contend, O priest" which does not seem to fit the context. Here one might agree with the scholar who says that "the Hebrew text of Hosea is probably more corrupt than any other Old Testament book," thus, at times a clear decision on textual problems is not possible. Harrison, *Introduction to the Old Testament*, 872.

739 Wolff, *Hosea*, 77.

740 Here Mauchlme suggests reading "You stumble continually" as referring to their continual failure to lead the people correctly. John Mauchlme, "Introduction to Hosea," *Interpreter's Bible* (vol.6; New York: Abingdon Press, 1956), 605.

741 Jack R. Lundbom argues that the verb כָשַׁלְתָּ "you shall stumble" addressed to the king of Israel whoever he may have been instead of priest and prophet. "Contentious Priest and Contentious People in Hosea 4:1-10," *VT* 36 (1986): 52-70.

742 Andersen and Freedman, *Hosea*, 351.

are involved in the consequences of the priests' failure."[743] In any case, the priest's family will share in his destiny (cf. Amos 7:10-17). It may, however, be referring to the nation of Israel as it does in Hosea 2:2-8.[744] This connects well with Hosea 4:6, where the people are destroyed because the priests have failed in their duty of teaching the people.

The priests will be rejected because they have rejected the "knowledge of God."[745] Since the priests have forgotten the law of God and failed to carry out their duties, God will reject both the priests who held the office and their children who would inherit it.[746] The verb מָאַס means "to reject," it is a concrete object. This verb is usually used in fulfilment action, for example, the "same verb is used in I Samuel 15:23,26 to describe Saul's rejection from office for rejecting Yahweh's word."[747] The priest will be rejected by God.[748] The passive verb in Hosea 4:6a indicates that the people have been ruined by the priest who rejected the knowledge, not that the priest has been corrupted by the people.[749] Hosea's portrayal of the priest is similar to the Chronicler's description of the teaching of Levites in II Chronicles 15:3;17:7-9; 19:8-10; 35:3; Nehemiah 8:5-8.

4.3.2.3.3. Hosea 4:7-10 (Hosea's Struggle with the Priests)

In Hosea 4:7-10 one finds a change from the previous verses. The priests are still addressed but now indirectly in the third person plural form. The shift from singular priest to plural shows the increase in the number and influence of the priests and thus it assumed to the time of Jeroboam II who led to the prosperity of the nation in both religious and secular.[750] The increase and development of the priesthood was good, but the more the number of priest increased, the amount of sin increased. Moreover the priests have become secularized, and instead of leading

743 Mays, *Hosea,* 68.

744 Brown, *The Book of Hosea,* 41; Mauchlme, "Introduction to Hosea," 605. However, William Rainey Harper argues that it may not mean the nation; instead it refers to the priest, the caste or clan of priests. *A Critical and Exegetical Commentary on Amos and Hosea* (Edinburgh: T&T Clark, 1905), 254.

745 The Word דַּעַת "Knowledge" Corresponds to the דַּעַת אֱלֹהִים "the Knowledge of God" in Hosea 4:1. Wolff, *Hosea,* 79.

746 Mays, *Hosea,* 69. Here the priest is clearly named as the one responsible for the people's inexcusable state. They lack knowledge because he has rejected knowledge and forgotten also the *torah* of his God.

747 Andersen and Freedman, *Hosea,* 353.

748 Wolff, *Hosea,* 77. The word מִכַּהֵן (piel inf constr of כהן) literally "to act as priest for/to me" the using singular priest, most probably Hosea, here is speaking of a high priest or chief priest at a central shrine, like Amaziah of Bethel in Amos 7:10.

749 Harper, *Critical and Exegetical Commentary on Amos and Hosea,* 258.

750 Mauchlme, "Introduction to Hosea," 606; Harper, *Critical and Exegetical Commentary on Amos and Hosea,* 257. Wolff, *Hosea,* 68. It seems unlikely that the priesthood would grow in the troubled and chaotic times after the death of Jeroboam II.

people towards God, they go along with the crowd and eventually in leading the crowd from knowledge of God to the knowledge of the Baals.[751] Thus, God charges that He will change their honour which is the respect of the true priest of Yahweh into shame.[752] The glory of the priests according to Wolff, "should have consisted in their cultivation of the דַּעַת אֱלֹהִים knowledge of God."[753] But, they have rejected the knowledge of God and exchanged their glory for dishonour. The plural pronounces of Hosea 4:7 (כְּרֻבָּם, חָטְאוּ.) originally may well have referred to the children/sons of the priest of Hosea 4:6.

Hosea 4:8 shows the extent of the corruption of the priests. Instead of taking care over the cult as a means of serving God, the priests have turned it into a way of making a living for themselves. This verse is in line with Hosea 5:6; 8:11; 8:13. The people offer many sacrifices to God, but it is not acceptable to God. The priests receive a portion of this sacrifice. The truth here is the priests take advantage on the command/law in Leviticus 7:28-38 where "the priest who officiated at a sacrifice had the right to a portion of the sacrificed animal."[754] Mays comments that the profit they made out of the sin-offerings of the people "has become the true goal of their vocation, and they have turned the institution of worship into a service to the clergy."[755] So, even though God does not accept the sacrifices, the priests encourage them because they are benefited.[756] The phrase חַטַּאת עַמִּי יֹאכֵלוּ "they feed on the sin of my people" is a very clear indication about thc sin of thc pricsts. Harper notes that the word חַטַּאת does not mean "sin-offering" here, rather it talks about the sin that the priests committed everyday because of their yearning greediness for their own benefit. This kind of behaviour encourages "the people in a false conception of Yahweh."[757] However, Wolff argues that the word חַטַּאת remain unclear whether it refers to "sin-offering," because it describes sin in general terms.[758]

---

751 Mays, *Hosea,* 70; H. D. Beeby, *Hosea,* 54. This is just the opposite of what should have happened and shows the decay of the priesthood. The linking of growth and prosperity with the increase of sin is a recurring theme in Hosea. Cf. Hos 8:11; 10:1.

752 Here both the MT and Septuagint read "I will change." The Syriac and the Targums, however, read "they will change" and this is possible. See Harper, *Amos and Hosea,* 257; P. R. Ackroyd, "Hosea," *Peake's Commentary on the Bible* (ed. Matthew Black and H. H. Rowley; London Thomas Nelson & Sons, 1962), 608, suggests that the reading "I will change" could represent a scribal change for theological reasons.

753 Wolff, *Hosea*, 81.

754 Stuart, *Hosea-Jonah*, 79.

755 Mays, *Hosea*, 70.

756 Harper suggests the singular suffix of נַפְשׁוֹ should change to the plural נפשָׁם in order to fit the context. He further explain the word נפש with its original meaning "throat, gullet" so it can translate as "yearning greediness." Harper. *Hosea and Amos*. 258.

757 Harper. *A Critical and Exegetical Commentary on Hosea and Amos*, 257-258.

758 Wolff, *Hosea*, 81.

Hosea 4:9 opens with the somewhat proverbial saying וְהָיָה כָעָם כַּכֹּהֵן "and it shall be like people like priest."[759] This, in the context of the condemnation of the priests, would seem to imply that there are no special privileges for the priests even though they should be closer to God. The priests will share the same punishment as the people, because they become like one of them.[760] By their sin they have become as corrupt as the people and disregard and even encourage sin (Hos 4:7). Because of this sin, they will share in the judgement pronounced on the people in Hosea 4:1-3.[761] Andersen and freedman contend that Hosea 4:9a argues a basic equality between priest and people-both in terms of their guilt and of what their punishment will be.[762] They propose three things: firstly the people dependent on the priest become like him (one would expect the priest to be better than the people); secondly the priest, conforming to the low standards of the people, has become as bad as they are, instead of maintaining a superior level of holiness; finally priest and people are indistinguishably guilty of the crimes listed.[763]

Harper further takes Hosea 4:9 to refer to the fall of the priest to the level of the people. His main argument is that the whole passage deals with the degeneration of the priests.[764] The remainder of Hosea 4:9 spells out the punishment of the priests in a strict, and hard justice. God will punish דְּרָכָיו "his ways" and מַעֲלָלָיו "his deeds" upon them and return his deeds to them. The evil which the priests have practised will now be turned back upon them in judgement.[765] The punishment of the priests is continued in Hosea 4:10. The priests will continue their immoral ways. The plural verbs in this verse correspond to those in Hosea 4:7-8, they will eat their sacrifices (Hos 4:8), but they will not be satisfied. Here the eating may refer to ritual feasts. They will take part in the immoral practices of temple prostitution but will not multiply by having children, or they will fail to bring about the fertility which was the aim of such ritual intercourse.[766] The verb translated "multiply" literally means פרץ "break out" and apparently refers to giving birth. The priests or the people thought cultic feasts and sex would bring crops and children, and that is the reason why they force "every woman

---

759 Here the use of singular for כֹּהֵן "priest" assume that it refers to the clergy, but not the people. Stuart, *Hosea- Jonah*, 80.

760 Ackroyd, "Hosea," 608; Mays, *Hosea*, 71.

761 Brown, *The Book of Hosea*, 43, cf. Harper, *A Critical and Exegetical Commentary on Amos and Hosea*, 258. This is held instead of the view that this verse refers once again to the people being led away by the priests. Here, rather, it is a continuation of the judgement upon the priests (curse type, the use of פקד "repay/punish" שוב "return/bring back" in Deut 5:9; Lev 26:16).

762 Andersen and Freedman, *Hosea*, 360-61.

763 Andersen and Freedman, *Hosea*, 360.

764 Harper, *A Critical and Exegetical Commentary on Amos and Hosea*, 258.

765 Mays, *Hosea*, 71.

766 Mauchlme, "Introduction to Hosea," 608; Mays, *Hosea*, 70; Harper, *A Critical and Exegetical Commentary on* Amos *and Hosea*, 258.

was required to prostitute herself once in the temple with a priest."[767] But, Hosea prophesied barrenness.

The phrase כִּי־אֶת־יְהוָה עָזְבוּ לִשְׁמֹר "they have forsaken Yahweh to keep harlotry" is the climax of the judgement against the priests. The phrase is introduced by the powerful כִּי "surely/because," "suggesting that this is the real point of the oracle."[768] The verb עָזְבוּ "they have forsaken" is third person common plural being perfect form, it describes some accomplished sin, and the following verse provides the reason and the basis for the judgement pronounced in Hosea 4:10a and this word has a connection with זנה (cf. Deut 31:16).[769] G. I. Davies remarks that since the verb הִזְנוּ "commit the harlot" is the causative stem of זנה, it may mean the men subject their daughters to cultic prostitution or it may mean the men practice fornication.[770] Wolff argues that "since the verse speaks of the priests, this is to be thought of chiefly as a reference to their official sexual relations with the sacral prostitutes in the performance of the 'sacral marriage.'"[771] The end of Hosea 4:10 closes the pericope by giving the real cause for the downfall of the priests of Yahweh. They have completely given up Yahweh and turned to harlotry.[772] The harlotry of the priests may be both literal and figurative here, as they participate in the cultic prostitution and lead the people away from true worship of God.

4.3.2.4. Prophetic Leadership of Hosea

Different groups of leadership mentioned in Hosea 4 are priestly, prophetic, and royal leadership. Though the third group of leadership is not particularly spelled out, they are implicated with the term "rulers" of the land. The priests were the preservers of the traditions of Israel. They were the guardians of the Torah, in which was enshrined the knowledge of God. This fact Hosea emphasizes in Hosea 4:6d, where תּוֹרָה is paralleled with "knowledge" in Hosea 4:6b.[773] Their spiritual adultery was caused by a lack of knowledge of God. Mays notes that "the knowledge of God is the peculiar responsibility of the priest, whose duty it was to pass on the instruction (תּוֹרָה) whose content is the acts and will of Yahweh."[774] However, religious ignorance of that day, according to Hosea, was first the fault

767 Harper, *A Critical and Exegetical Commentary on* Amos *and Hosea,* 258.

768 Brueggemann, *Tradition for Crisis: A Study in Hosea,* 53.

769 Andersen and Freedman, *Hosea,* 363.

770 G. I. Davies, *Hosea* (NCBC; Grand Rapids: Wm. B. Eerdmans for Marshall Pickering, 1992), 212.

771 Wolff, *Hosea,* 82. Cf. to Hos 4:2 and Exod 1:12.

772 Here the first word זְנוּת of Hos 4:11 is joined to the end of verse 10 to complete the rhythmic form of the second part of the verse. See Mays, *Hosea,* 66; Mauchlme, "Introduction to Hosea," 608.

773 H. D. Beeby, *Hosea: International Theological Commentary* (Grand Rapids: Wm.B. Eerdmans Publishing Co., 1989), 54-55.

774 Mays, *Hosea,* 63.

of the priests and teachers. They had utterly neglected their duty as teachers of Yahweh's word.

The second responsibility for the religious ignorance rested upon the people themselves. Spiritual ignorance among the people and corrupt priests led Israel to spiritual ruin. Israel worshipped false gods and looked to them for leadership in life. The kind of leadership that the priest, prophets and royalty portrayed was to bring destruction to the people of Israel. Thus, Hosea pronounced God's judgement upon the leaders. In fact, the way God had treated Israel; requiring justice and showing loyal love, was the model for how Israel was to exist as a community of the covenant. But, the leaders failed miserably thus far. They could not fulfil the requirement of Yahweh. In Yahweh's view, Israel has deliberately turned its back on him and enjoyed its sin. Thus, these verses paint a dark picture of the heart of the people.

The order of God's good creation has turned to near chaos as human beings irrupt into lawlessness and violence. Much of the responsibility for this situation fell upon the leadership (priests, prophets, and kings) because the priestly and political (Hos 4:4-5:7; 5:8-8:14) leadership bore the primary responsibility for Yahweh's rejection of Israel. The people themselves chose to follow this idolatrous leadership. Thus, Hosea shifted attention from the people to their religious leaders. Priests and prophets are called by God to be responsible for the whole of God's creation. They were responsible to maintain "faithfulness," "loving kindness" and "knowledge of God" in the land. However, priests and prophets actively rejected "knowledge of God" in favour of an easy religious teaching and practice that assure their own prosperity and place in the society.[775]

The priests knew that people like doing wrong. But they "feed on the sins" (Hos 4:8) of covenant people instead of inviting them to repentance. Priests are masters of the art of making the religious rituals and practices necessary. They had ignored their calling to lead the people into the knowledge of God (Hos 4:4-5; 5:1). They emphasised the traditional ceremonial forms of worship that took the focus away from the weightier matters of the law (cf. Hos 6:6).[776] The

775 The knowledge of God is a central motif in the book of Hosea, and everywhere it is Israel's lack of knowledge of her God which leads to her harlotry (Hos 4:6 cf.14; 5:4; 6:6; 7:11, 6,14; 13:6). For Hosea "knowledge of God" refers to the loving relationship with God that result from commitment of one's entire being to His revelation. Cf. C. L. Seow, "Hosea, Book of," in *ABD* (vol. 3; ed. David Noel Freedman; NY/London: Doubleday, 1992), 296, James D .Smart, "Hosea: Man and Book," *IDB* (vol. 2; ed. George Arthur Buttnck, et al; New York: Abingdon Press, 1962), 652. Israel's "heart" (i.e. mind) is false (10:2); she does not know her divine husband. For Hosea, this is the basic description of what is wrong with Israel. Brueggemann, *Tradition for Crisis: A Study in Hosea*, 53.

776 Issues of liturgical reform may lie behind the contrast between sacrifices and steadfast love. The Israelite religious establishment surely thought that ceremonial practices were a sufficient step in the right direction. James Limburg identifies here what *ultimately* can become "two fundamentally different notions of religion." *Hosea-Micah* (Atlanta: John Knox, 1988), 29, but in the eighth century BCE., context it is likely that Hosea believed that חֶסֶד "steadfast love" had

prophet is condemned along with the priest for stumbling, causing the people to be destroyed for lack of knowledge (Hos 4:5-6).[777] Having devoted themselves to fornication, priests and prophets permit a spirit of promiscuity to infect the people (Hos 4:10-12, 18-19). Thus, both priests and prophets fall under God's judgement. Most of the scholars believe that the prophetic judgements of Hosea 4:5-6 were a direct response to the invasion of Tiglath-Pilesar III in about 733/732 BCE which brought an end to the Syro-Ephramite war.[778] Hosea thus portrayed Yahweh as the metaphorical lion of judgement who, through the actions of Assyrian military power, has brought destruction to Israel and can now return to his den (Hos 5:13-15).

The problem with Israel's leaders is that they did not depend on God, rather they depended on their own strength and power, the nations, to supply the necessities and comforts of life. They did not "know" that it was Yahweh who provided the cash crops that secured their imported goods and silver and gold which they made into Baal.[779] They failed to be faithful leaders because they did not understand that the Knowledge is not mere intellectual comprehension; it is tied in with a right relationship with Yahweh.

When the nation's rulers failed to provide a true leadership, Hosea portrayed shepherding model of leadership. It is the pre-dominate leadership model in Bible. The message he conveyed was Yahweh's unconditional love, a fundamental quality of soul which serves as a spring and motive for all right action in personal relationships. Some would argue that Amos' message was one of harsh justice while Hosea preached love. G. Farr, however, argues that Hosea is not different from Amos; rather Hosea went beyond Amos.[780] In Amos, the people sinned by violating Yahweh's law. In Hosea, they sinned by violating Yahweh's love. Thus, Hosea emphasized much on חֶסֶד (Hos 2:19; 4:1; 6:4,6; 10:12; 12:6). Hosea's leadership was unique in that his whole life was symbolic, an object lesson of his message.

4.3.3. Summary

Hosea witnessed the most tragic incident in the history of Israel. He began his prophetic ministry towards the end of Jeroboam II's reign when the era was marked with military successes and economic prosperity, yet moral and religious decay

---

priority over the external observances. See Stuart, *Hosea-Jonah,* 110. Nevertheless, at the core of its being, Israel knew its place was with God because it was their God who thoroughly knew them in all their sinfulness and frailty/weakness.

777 As Andersen and Freedman, point out, the lack of "knowledge" is not simply ignorance, but the result of "rejecting" knowledge, and just as "forgetting" is a sin, not just a mental lapse. Andersen and Freedman, *Hosea,* 242.

778 II Kgs 15:29-31. For the historical issues see Stuart, *Hosea-Jonah,* 101-102; Wolff, *Hosea,* 110-112.

779 According to Harper, the silver and gold came from the sale of the grain, wine, and oil. Harper, *A Critical and Exegetical Commentary on Amos and Hosea,* 229-30.

780 G. Farr, "The Concept of Grace in the Book of Hosea," *ZAW* 70 (1958): 98-107.

overruled throughout the land. Hosea lived, loved, and anguished throughout his life. Yet, at its deepest level, what Hosea asserted was the truth, for it insisted that the love חֶסֶד of Yahweh does triumph, and must triumph, over wrath and judgement. The question of how soon this hope will take effect is quite secondary to the recognition that this hope exists because it is rooted in the eternal love of Yahweh. Hosea can therefore, be seen as a prophet whose message brought out, with remarkable poignancy, knowledge of the strength and pathos of the love of Yahweh. Such a knowledge came to the prophet as he witnessed a tragic fate overtake his people, and as he felt his own inner tensions between love for his people and anger against their sin. Although, Hosea does not explicitly refer to the poor like Micah, he takes a stand on oppression. Hosea also attacks the urban elite and the leading classes of society: the kings elected contrary to the will of Yahweh, the ignorant and greedy priests and the idolatrous bureaucracy of the urban establishment (Hos 4:1-11a; 5:1; 6:5; 13:10-11).

4.4. MICAH

Micah was known for his concern for the poor. His leadership character was different from that of his contemporary leaders, namely, priests, prophets and royal leadership. His prophetic critique was directed towards the ruling class and wealthy elite of the eighth century BCE Judean who denied the rights of the poor for their practice of injustice in the society. It was also directed to the religious leaders who were corrupt and even willing to shed blood if it was for their own advantage. This section aims to discuss the different leadership portrayed in the book of Micah and the prophetic critique on leaders.

4.4.1. The Call of Micah

Not much is known about Micah. His name is the shortened form of the older *Micāyāhû* (מִכָיָהוּ) "Who is like Yahweh?"[781] Scholars identify "Moreshtite" as Micah's home with Moresheth-gath in Micah 1:14, a rural locality bordering the Philistine territory.[782] Moresheth-gath was also one of the important administrative centres often visited by military and court officials from Jerusalem. From the socio-historical background, Wolff mentions two interesting things: Micah of Moresheth lived within a few miles of five of the fortress towns earlier established by Rehoboam (II Chron 11:7-9), and Micah would have been quite familiar with the Jerusalem officials coming and going in that area. He further argues that Micah

781 James Luther Mays, *Micah: A Commentary* (OTL; Philadelphia: Westminster Press, 1976), 1.

782 Harrison, *Introduction to the Old Testament*, 919; Bruce V. Malchow, "The Rural Prophet: Micah," *Currents in Theology and Mission* 7 (1980): 48; Eric A. Mitchell, "Micah-The Man and His Times," *SJT* 46 (2003): 57; Smith, Ward, and Bewer, eds., in *International Critical Commentary: Micah, Zephaniah, Nahum, Habakkuk, Obadiah and Joel*, 17; Juan I. Alfaro, *A Commentary on the Book of Micah* (Grand Rapids: WW.B. Eerdmans Publishing Co., 1938), 3. Moresheth is identified with the modern village of Tell-el-Judeideh, about twenty-five miles south-west of Jerusalem.

sharply distinguished between the powerful officials of Jerusalem (who were self-serving and exploitative) and his own "compatriots."[783] Micah, like Amos, may not have been part of the official prophets' guild. His trips to Jerusalem as a "country" prophet no doubt confirmed what he had heard from a distance. He shared with Isaiah, however, an unswerving commitment to the covenant of Yahweh and an abhorrence of the sin so prevalent in his day.

The call narrative of Micah is not directly mentioned in anywhere, but the passages such as Micah 3:8; 7:7 rightly affirm of his credentials that he was being moved by the Spirit of Yahweh. In Micah 3:8, Micah contrasts himself with the prophets. Unlike the prophets, Micah is filled with three things: "But as for me, I am filled with power, with the Spirit of the LORD, and with justice and might, to declare to Jacob his transgression and to Israel his sin."

(i) He is מָלֵא "filled" with כֹּחַ "power." Wolff tries to explain the meaning of the term that the word מָלֵא points to the impossibility of holding in or suppressing words that fill a person to overflowing.[784] This suggests that the prophets he spoke against were not filled with power. There is an apparent thought that the words of a prophet do not just predict disaster or peace, but can actually bring it about (cf. Amos 7:10). The fact that Micah views himself as an authentic spokesperson for God may be where the idea of being filled with power comes from. The words of the prophets will not stand, but Micah's words will because they are filled with the power of Yahweh. Here Micah contrasts his own "fullness" with the "emptiness" of those prophets who no longer receive an "answer from God." The word כֹּחַ power/strength refers to physical and psychic strength to stand up against opposition and discouragement. In Micah's view, "filling with power/strength" is ultimately to a prophetic call account, it is a report of a brief commission or a "complete summary of the basis and intention of his mission."[785]

(ii) He is also filled with the spirit of Yahweh. In the form of the text, the idea behind being filled with the spirit of Yahweh is parallel to being filled with power.

---

783 Moresheth was a small village 21 miles south west of Jerusalem, 9 miles East of Gathand 18 miles West of Tekoa. It lay within 6 miles of Rehoboam's fortress towns. Hans Walter Wolff, *Micah the Prophet* (Philadelphia: Fortress, 1981); idem, "Micah the Moreshrth-The Prophet and his background," in *Israelite Wisdom: Theological and Literary Studies in Honor of Samuel Terrien* (ed. Samuel L. Terrien and John G. Gammie; Missoula, MX: Scholars Press, 1978), 77-84.

784 Hans Walter Wolff, *Micah: A Commentary* (trans. Gary Stansell; Minneapolis: Augsburg, 1990), 105.

785 Wolff, *Micah: A Commentary*, 105; Mays, *Micah: A Commentary,* 84; W. Rudolph, *Micah, Nahum, Habakkuk, Zephaniah* (KAT; Gutersloh, 1975), 73. In Isaiah the term refers as the strength of God (Isa 40:26, 29, 31).

(iii) Micah is also filled with justice מִשְׁפָּט.[786] This is the same word used in 3:1. Justice is an overarching theme in Micah 3. What contrast if Micah did not view himself as a נָבִיא. Those in the land who had the specific duty to oversee justice in the land were failing, and Micah, not an official, is the lonely voice of justice in the land. He understands his prophetic office which is different or contrasts from the other prophets and his leadership pattern is different from the leaders (heads, rulers, judges) in the land. Micah states his purpose in Micah 3:8 which was to make the rebellious acts of the people known. Moreover, Micah's use of the statement, "thus says Yahweh" (Mic 2:3; 3:5), indicates that he speaks as Yahweh's messenger. Perhaps, like Isaiah (Isa 1; 2; 6), Micah's message came to him in visions (Mic 1:1), and the term חָזָה "saw" may indicate a "general reception of revelation."[787] Nothing more is stated as to Micah's location when he received the word of Yahweh, but the time frame of his prophetic ministry is revealed in 1:1.[788]

4.4.2. Micah's Profession

Since there is nothing mentioned about Micah's personal life as well as his family, most scholars have assumed that Micah arose from humble origins, and for that reason nothing is told of his or his family. Juan I. Alfaro asserts that "the contents, language, and style of the prophecy suggested that he was a small farmer" who wanted to protect his own interests along those of his equals.[789] He was also viewed as a person of substance who somehow had stumbled on the poor as victims of injustice. Alec Gilmore remarks that Micah identified himself with the oppressed group of people and thus became fearless defender of the human rights.[790] However, Delbert R. Hillers believes that Micah was a "Prophet of a New Age," belonging to some kind of an organized group, a member or a leader, striving to construct a more

786 Carroll, "Night Without Vision: Micah and the Prophets," 78; Mays, *Micah,* 85.

787 Wolff, *Micah: A Commentary,* 37.

788 According to 1:1 Micah prophesied in the days of the kings of Judah: Jotham (742-735 BCE), Ahaz (735-715 BCE), and Hezekiah (715-687/6 BCE). Micah's ministry, then, corresponded closely to that of his contemporary Isaiah (742-681 BCE) and spanned from 742-686 BCE. Isaiah's ministry began in the year Uzziah died (Isa 6:1) and extends at least until 681 BCE., since he reports the death of Sennacherib in that year (Isa 37:28). However, it must be noted that many would take this reference as a later editorial insertion. Micah's ministry lasted from the beginning of Jotham's rule to sometime after Sennacherib's invasion, but perhaps as late as 686 BCE. Bright, *A History of Israel,* 471; Mays, *Micah,* 15; Willem A. VanGemeren, *Interpreting the Prophetic Word: An Introduction to the Prophetic Literature of the Old Testament* (Grand Rapids/Michigan: Zondervan, 1990), 150.

789 Alfaro, *A Commentary on the Book of Micah,* 4.

790 Alec Gilmore, "Voice of the Voiceless," *The Expository Times* 105 (1993): 304-305. Any one of these views would have been enough to earn him the title of a Liberation theologian.

satisfying social order and cultural environment.[791] Wolff suggests that possibly Micah might have been one of the elder of Judah, who was really troubled by the injustice being inflicted on his poor fellow citizens.[792] Wolff's suggestion is probably accurate that Micah is distinguished not by the name of his father but by the name of his home town perhaps as an elder would have been distinguished when gathered among other elders.

In ancient Israel, the "elders of the land" gather together for several purposes. First, elders sat in judgement within their city at the city gate (Deut 19:12; 21:1-9, 18-21; Ruth 4:1-12). In the previous century, king Jehoshaphat had set up judges in all the towns of Judah (II Chron 19:5). Micah uses the term מִשְׁפָּט "judgement," or "justice," when talking of his commission (Mic 3:8) but the heads and rulers of the people do not know מִשְׁפָּט (Mic 3:1). Second, elders are shown gathering regionally to affirm a military leader (Jephthah at Tob/Gilead, Judg 11:1-11). Third, they could establish and confirm a king (Rehoboam at Shechem, I Kgs 12:1-15). Fourth, they were involved in the renewal of the covenant with Yahweh when king Josiah called the elders to Jerusalem for this purpose (II Kgs 23: 1-3).[793]

4.4.3. Micah 3:1-12

4.4.3.1. Translation

3:1. *And I said,*[794] *Hear now, you heads of Jacob and rulers of the house of Israel! Is it not for you to know justice?*

791 Delbert R. Hillers, *Micah* (Hermeneia; Philadelphia: Fortress Press, London: SCM, 1984), 807.

792 Wolff, *Micah the Prophet*, 18; idem, "Micah the Moreshrth-The Prophet and his Background," 77-84. Cf. Jer 26:17-18.

793 Wolff, "Micah the Moreshite: The Prophet and his Background," 78; Mays, *Micah,* 15; Eric A. Mitchell, "Micah: the Man and his Time," *South Western Journal of Theology* 46 (2006): 68.

794 Reading with the MT וָאֹמַר "and I said" *qal perf. 1cs.* However, BHS proposes to read with Septuagint και ερει "and he will says," and Pesh. *w'mr*, Vg (*dixi*) and Tg (*w'mryt*).
It is curious that while the MT has a first person perfect verb, and the Septuagint has a third person singular verb in the future tense "and he will say," which is quite different from וָאֹמַר "and I said." It is not altogether clear why there is a difference between the MT and the Septuagint. One possibility is that the consonantal Hebrew text was mistranslated into Greek as a third person. This is highly possible given the fact that it appears that the Greek and Syriac versions are the only ones that renders אָמַר as a third person verb, according to the apparatus of BHS. The weight this evidence tends toward the reading of the MT rather than the Septuagint. Hillers assumes וָאֹמַר as the original Hebrew text. Rudolph notes that the vocalization of ואמר assumed by Septuagint and Pesh. is erroneous. Some critics assume the word ואמר "and I said" as a remnant of a narrative omitted from an original version. Van der Woude sees it as proof of his disputation theory that Micah is now replying to the false prophets. Mays argues it as a simple report form in the first person in which Micah states the kind of response he makes to the opposition. James L. Mays emends this first section (Mic 3:1-4) by putting the latter half of Micah 3:2 at the end of Micah 3:3. His reasoning is that the pronouns in Micah 3:2 have no antecedent previous to it. It seems obvious that the antecedent

3:2. *You who hate good and love evil, who tear*[795] *the skin from off my people, and their flesh from off their bones;*

3:3. *And who*[796] *eat the flesh of my people, and flay their skin from off them*[797] *and break their bones in pieces, and chop them up like the meat*[798] *in a kettle, and like flesh in a caldron.*

3:4. *Then they will cry to Yahweh, but he will not answer them; he will hide his face from them at that time,*[799] *because they have made their deeds evil.*

3:5. *Thus says Yahweh concerning the prophets who lead my people*[800] *astray, who cry "Peace"*[801] *when they have something to eat, but declare war against him who puts nothing into their mouths.*

3:6. *Therefore it shall be night to you, without vision, and darkness*[802] *to you, without divination. And the sun shall go down upon the prophets, and the day shall be black over them;*

3:7. *The seers shall be disgraced, and the diviners put to shame; they shall all cover their lips, for there is no answer from God.*

---

is עַמִּי "my people" in Micah 3:3, so he puts the phrases with the pronouns in Micah 3:2 after that. However, these oracles were originally oral instead of written, so it is acceptable to accept the current arrangement of the text. Bruce K. Waltke, *Micah* (Grand Rapids; Michigan: William B. Eerdmans Publishing Company, 2007), 144; Hans Walter Wolff, *Micah* (trans. Gary Stansell; Minneapolis: Augsburg Fortress, 1990), 90; R. D. Hillers, *A Commentary on the Book of the Prophet Micah* (Hermeneia; Philadelphia, 1984), 41; W. Rudolph, *Micah, Nahum, Habakkuk, Zephaniah* (KAT; Gutersloh, 1975), 67; A.S. Van der Woude, "Micah in Dispute with the Pseudoprophets," *VT* 19 (1969): 244-60; Cf. James A. sanders, "Hermeneutics in True and False Prophecy," in *Canon and Authority: Essays in Old Testament Theology* (ed. George W. Coats and Burke O. Long; Philadelphia: Fortress Press, 1977), 21-41; Mays, *Micah: A Commentary* (OTL; Philadelphia: Westminster Press, 1976), 76-77; David Gerald Hagstrom, *The Coherence of the Book of Micah: A Literary Analysis* (Atlanta: Scholars Press, 1988), 30.

795 Following the MT גֹּזְלֵי qal part. m/p constr. גזל "to tear away," this verb has dropped out or it has transpose to Micah 3:3 and suggested it to read יִגְזְלוּ qal imperf. 3mp "they will tear away."

796 The word וַאֲשֶׁר (relative pronounce who, which) probably may be deleted.

797 הִפְשִׁיטוּ this word might be redactors' addition.

798 Reading with the MT כַּאֲשֶׁר, Septuagint has ων σαρκαν, it may read as כִּשְׁאֵר, which is probably the original reading. Wolff, *Micah*, 91.

799 The phrase בָּעֵת הַהִיא "at that time" could be editorial addition.

800 The phrase אֶת־עַמִּי "my people" is proposed to read as יהוָה את עם. "people of Yahweh." Read with the MT.

801 Reading with the MT. However, Septuagint and Targum proposes to add επ αντον "in him" after the term שָׁלוֹם thus read as "peace in him."

802 MT vocalizes the word as the more usual verb from חָשְׁכָה "to be dark," instead of as a noun. Septuagint and Vg και σκοτια reads in parallel to לילה as the noun וַחֲשֵׁכָה. Wolff, *Micah*, 91.

3:8. *But as for me, I am filled with power, with the Spirit of the Yahweh,*[803] *and with justice and might, to declare to Jacob his transgression and to Israel his sin.*

3:9. *Hear this now, you heads of the house of Jacob and rulers of the house of Israel, who abhor justice and pervert all equity.*

3:10. *Who build*[804] *Zion with blood and Jerusalem with wrong.*

3:11. *Heads give judgement for a bribe, and priests teach for hire, and prophets divine for money/silver; yet they lean upon Yahweh and say, "Is not Yahweh in the midst of us? No evil shall come upon us."*

3:12. *Therefore because of you Zion shall be plowed as a field; Jerusalem shall become a heap of ruins,*[805] *and mountain of the house will become high place*[806] *of a forest.*

4.4.3.2. Form/Setting/Structure

The form of Micah 3 is prophetic judgement speech. It contains three parts. The first part is directed at the political leaders in a rhetorical question reminding the authorities about their officials' responsibilities (Mic 3:1-4); the second is directed at the priests and prophets, expressing a contrast between him and other prophets whom he accuses (Mic 3:5-8); the third form-critical element address is directed at Israel's leaders (Mic 3:9-12). The pattern of Micah here, is to use incomplete synonymous parallelism (A: B: C:: B': C') with a tendency to develop lists.[807] Micah also uses participles to describe the perpetrators, for instance: "hating," "loving," and "tearing." They are used as titles.

The date of this particular oracle is difficult to ascertain. Some commentators have assigned it to the time of Hezekiah, particularly to either 722 or 701 BCE.[808]

---

803 The phrase אֶת־רוּחַ יְהוָה "the spirit of Yahweh" is assumes to be a later commentary on the verse.

804 The word בֹּנֶה "builder" is singular in MT, whereas Septuagint (οι οικοδομουντεν), Syraic (*banin*), Targum (דמנן) have plural form בְּנֵי בני, but all in line with MT בנה. Rudolph, *Micah, Nahum, Habakkuk, Zephaniah*, 68; Wolff, *Micah*, 92.

805 Few versions read as עיים (noun common m.p absolute) "heap of ruins." It has an Aramaic *nun* and the normal Hebrew form that reads עִיִּין, and appears at Jer 26:18. William McKane, *Micah: Introduction and Commentary* (Edinburgh: T&T Cark, 1998), 113.

806 MT reads as plural form לְבָמוֹת "into the high places" However, other versions proposes singular form במת "high place." The meaning probably suggests that the word is used in a physical rather than a cultic sense. It is because הַר is singular, so scholars tended to emend במות to במת. It is necessary to emend the MT based on the context of the text. McKane, *Micah*, 114.

807 Carol J. Dempsey, "Micah 2-3: Literary Artistry, Ethical Message, and Some Considerations about the Image of Yahweh and Micah," *JSOT* 85 (1999): 124; Francis I Andersen & David Noel Freedman, *Micah: A New Translation with Introduction and Commentary* (AB; New York: Doubleday, 2000), 344. The terms "'heads,' 'priests,' 'prophets' are three successive colons and the terms 'skin,' 'flesh,' 'bones,' 'meat,' are used in a complex pattern of repetition." Cf. Wolff, *Micah*, 92-94.

808 Mays, *Micah*, 14, 92; Hillers, *Micah*, 8-9; L. C. Allen, *The Book of Joel, Obadiah, Jonah, and Micah* (NICOT; Grand Rapids: Eerdmans, 1976), 243.

Others suggest the possibility that it might be around 728-725 BCE during the Syro-Ephraimite siege of Jerusalem.[809] Andersen and Freedman are of the opinion that Micah 3 contains standard eighth century BCE poetic prophecy and it makes it reasonable to date the writing of the oracle to this period of time.[810] Some believe Micah 1-3 to be authentic words of Micah.[811] For instance, Micah 3 begins with the verb וָאֹמַר "and I said" which seems to connect it to the previous section, but at the same time begins a new sub-section. Though it seems to be a new sub-section, it clearly has a thematic link to Micah 2.

Micah 3 expounds on Micah 2:1-11. The preservation of these oracles obviously served as a reminder and explanation of the reasons why Israel suffered at the hands of the nations around them. If there was an original narrative context to these oracles, the editors did not preserve the specific details. This gave these oracles a more timeless quality for the community of faith, Israel. The applications of Micah 3 for future generations would have been obvious. Those who were responsible for justice were to be impartial and upright in upholding justice. Those who were responsible for instruction in Yahweh's word were to carry out that role faithfully. Wolff suggests that the oracles content in Micah 3 were proclaimed in Jerusalem. He says,

> The ancient prophecies in this chapter were sayings proclaimed in Jerusalem itself. This is sufficiently clear from vv. 10 and 12...We may suppose that the locality was the outer court of the temple...If Micah had been a member of the elders of Judah, it is certainly intelligible that precisely in this place he would have stood to proclaim his message...The audience whom he faced and addressed as he indicted the political leaders and the prophets...may in particular have been circles of elders from the land who gathered in the forecourt of the temple.[812]

The text mentions internal social crisis caused by the defective leadership of Micah's time. It clearly illustrates/demonstrates the structure of monarchic society, as shaped by the "heads/rulers" (royals) and its priest and prophets, whose leadership pattern was quite different from Yahweh's prophet, who was full of Spirit.[813]

Micah 3 is made up of three sections (Mic 1-4; 5-8; 9-12). The first and third sections are marked by a summons to "hear" or "listen" שִׁמְעוּ. In Micah 4:1 with the modifier an (translated as 'now') denotes the urgency of the message. God's

---

809 Charles S. Shaw, *The Speeches of Micah: A Rhetorical-Historical Analysis* (Sheffield/ England: Sheffield Academic Press, 1993), 125.

810 Andersen & Freedman, *Micah*, 344; Cf. Wolff, *Micah,* 81.

811 Delbert R. Hillers, *Micah: A Commentary on the Book of the Prophet Micah* (Hermeneia; Philadelphia: Fortress Press, 1984), 807.

812 Wolff, *Micah,* 96-97; idem, *Micah the Prophet* (trans. Ralph D. Gehrke; Philadelphia: Fortress Press, 1981), 17-25.

813 Ehud Ben Zvi, *Micah* (Grand Rapids: Eerdmans, 2000), 81.

requirements of social justice and mercy cannot be neglected forever without causing detriment to the wellbeing of the community. So, the call is to stand up to the challenges of injustice and apathy and move the people toward proactive empathy. The second section is marked by a prophetic formula כֹּה אָמַר יְהוָה "Thus says Yahweh." Each of the three sections is parallel to each other in form and function. The basic purpose is a denunciation/criticism/accusation to one of the groups of officials in Israel (Priests, prophets, King, Judges and the like). Each section has the same basic layout.[814]

In Micah 3:1-12, Micah as an advocate for the cause of the invisible sections of the society, uses rhetoric persuasion, firstly, to expose the failure of his audience to keep Yahweh's requirements of justice and mercy, and secondly, to present Yahweh himself as one condescending to defend the oppressed against their oppressors by arguing their case. This aspect of advocacy is weaved into every layer of this prophetic passage and it serves as the unifying factor on the whole and also being expounded in the parts.

4.4.3.3. Comments

4.4.3.3.1. Micah 3:1-4 (Micah and the Nation Leaders)

Micah 3:1-4: Micah accused the rules of the false leadership. He strongly accused and condemned the misconduct of Israel's leadership as the cause of national punishment. The judgement speech, then, begins with a summons to hear addressing/speaking to a group designated by the parallel expressions רָאשֵׁי יַעֲקֹב "heads of Jacob" and וּקְצִינֵי בֵּית יִשְׂרָאֵל "leaders of the house of Israel." Hence, the charged are named by title and their roles. Here the term ראש is used in connection with קָצִין, designates those who have responsibility for justice. The word ראש "head" is a general term for leaders or heads or chiefs.[815] However, it is used a number of times with the meaning of a "chief" or "leader" (Judg 10:18; Deut 1:15; II Chron 20:27; Mic 2:13). Semantically, ראש is used to designate "head," or "leader" of a family or tribe. More specifically, in Exodus 18, Deuteronomy 1:9-15 and II Chronicles 19:4-11, the title is used of the able men chosen to function as judges who were responsible to administer justice.[816] According to

814 Ben Zvi, *Micah*, 70-71; Mingnon R. Jacobs, *The Conceptual Coherence of the Book of Micah* (ed. David J. A. Clines and Philip R. Davies; JSOTSup. 322; Sheffield: Sheffield Academic Press, 2001), 71-72.

815 David L. Petersen, *The Roles of Israel's Prophets* (JSOTSup, 17; Sheffield: JSOT Press, 1981), 14-15; Marvin A. Sweeney, *The Twelve prophets* (Collegeville: The Liturgical Press, 2000), 368, Joyce Rilett Wood, "Speech and Action in Micah's Prophecy," *CBQ* 62 (2000): 657; Shaw, *The Speeches of Micah: A Rhetorical-Historical Analysis*, 110; J. R. Bartlett, "The Use of the Word ראש as a Title in the OT," *VT* 19 (1969): 1-10.

816 Barlett, "The Use of the Word var as a Title in the Old Testament," 1-10; E. Hammershaimb, *Some Aspects of Old Testament Prophecy from Isaiah to Malachi* (Copenhagen: Rosenkilde & Bagger, 1966), 31; De Vaux, *Ancient Israel*, 152-55; Mays, *Micah*,78 (Exod 18:25). Here רָאשִׁים is used synonymously with שֹׁפְטִים and שָׂרִים as titles, and שׁפט used to describe the responsibility.

Waltke, the vocative רָאשֵׁי in Micah's context "refers principally to the appointed judges of the nation."[817] Furthermore J. R. Bartlett also remarks that ראשׁ is an office which has to be correlated with tribal character of ancient Israelite society in pre-monarchic times.[818]

The other title קָצִין, here used as a synonym of ראשׁ, is generally used to designate "chief," or "ruler" (Judg 11:6; Isa 3:6). Andersen and Freedman explain that the term is an old word for a tribal military leader that may have been elected and it is used in a military sense to refer to "head of an army" (Josh 10:24).[819] Willian McKane assumes that the term קְצִינֵי is directed to a responsible person for the well-being of the extended family (clan officer/leader). On the basis of its Arabic cognate, it has been suggested that קָצִין has the connotation of "judge." McKane further notes that the Arabic word *gdy* has been called into service to define the office of קָצִין as that of "judge" and to establish that the קָצִין discharged a narrow juridical role.[820] In Isaiah 1:10 it has the general sense of political leader. In Micah 3:la the paired titles designate in the most general sense, "leaders," and their responsibility is to administer justice as indicated by the accusation in Micah 3: lb-3. Thus, the two titles (ראשׁ and קְצִינֵי) are difficult to explain because they are used synonymously in eighth century BCE for the "rulers" or "leaders."

Here the argument of the prophet is not the titles or office but the abuse of the power by the "leaders" especially while making legal decisions by those who sit on the chair, which destroys a society rather than exercising care for its well-being. One will agree with Rudolph who says that the leaders abuse the society which they should nurture and they impose a selfish and a cruel tyranny instead of respecting constitutional rule and customary law.[821]

It is difficult to know whether Israel and Jacob were meant to refer to the Northern kingdom or to the people in general. The references to Judah, Jacob, and Israel are somewhat ambiguous due to the redactional history of the text. Claus Westermann asserts that judgement oracles of the eighth and the seventh centuries BCE were directed to Israel and here in Micah's language "Israel" refers to "all Israel" both northern and southern kingdoms.[822] Ehud Ben Zvi notes that it is difficult to understand because the lack of specific reference to the monarch is

817 Waltke, *Micah*, 146. Cf. Wolff, *Micah*, 97.

818 Bartlett, "The Use of the Word ראשׁ as a Title in the OT," 1-10. Cf. Wolff, *Micah*, 98.

819 Andersen & Freedman, *Micah*, 349. The words ראשׁי and קציני are use in synonymous parallelism and that they are alternative titles of the same office rather than names for two separate offices in Mic 3:1, 9.

820 William McKane, *Micah: Introduction and Commentary* (Edinburgh: T&T Cark, 1998), 99.

821 Rudolph, *Micah, Nahum, Habakkuk, Zephaniah*, 69.

822 Claus Westermann, *Basic Forms of Prophetic Speech* (Philadelphia: Westminster, reprint 1991), 169.

common in prophetic literature.[823] What is interesting here is that the king is not specifically mentioned, though he may be implicated by the parallel references to "rulers" and "heads."

In ancient Israel the king is the highest level of justice in the land. He is the ultimate court of appeal. It is possible that the judicial situation in Micah 3 is a reflection of the judicial reforms that Jehoshaphat initiated during his reign (I Chron 19:4-11). This reform shows that the judiciary in the land became more centralized, and that there was more control over the system by the priests and Levites.[824] Therefore, the condemnation includes all of the rulers and priests. Since the king is the highest court of justice in the land, he would be implicated in these condemnations.

Another possible suggestion is that if these oracles were spoken during the time of Hezekiah's reign, then the reason the king is not mentioned is because he initiated a reform and is believed to have a good character.[825] But, this does not seem likely because the amount of injustice this chapter seems to portray would still implicate the king since he has ultimate responsibility over the land. It would be best to see this as an extensive condemnation of all rulers in the land who were responsible for justice, including the king.

According to Micah, the "heads" and "rulers" are שֹׂנְאֵי טוֹב וְאֹהֲבֵי רָעָה "haters of right/good" and "lovers of wrong/evil." We could understand these participles as titles. There are similar ideas in other eighth century BCE prophetic literature, though the wording is not identical (for instance Amos 5:15; Isa 5:20). The condemnation begins with, הֲלוֹא לָכֶם לָדַעַת אֶת־הַמִּשְׁפָּט "Is it not for you to know justice?" The word מִשְׁפָּט "justice" is used in each of the three sections in this chapter. Justice is an overarching theme in these oracles. Indeed, justice is an overall theme in the entire book. In Micah's view, justice should be the primary concern of the leaders, but they failed in maintaining justice in their administration. Wolff writes, "Justice according to Micah means rescue for those who are endangered, help for those who have been hurt and surcease for those who suffered violence."[826] However, the rulers and leaders failed to protect the rights of the poor, instead they denied their rights by mean of violence and oppression. Thus, by mentioning שְׁאֵר "flesh" and עֶצֶם "bone" Micah further develops the accusation by portraying the leaders as cannibals.[827] The words for שְׁאֵר "flesh" and עֶצֶם "bone" are used repeatedly to heighten the violence of their injustice.

The immediate context gives no indication as to the specific nature of their faults. However, in the larger context, social injustice seems to be the root of the

823 Ben Zvi, *Micah*, 86. The monarch is not specifically mentioned, for example, Zeph 3:3-4; Isa 1:21-26; 5:8-11; Amos 5:7, 11-13.

824 Andersen & Freedman. *Micah,* 350.

825 Ben Zvi, *Micah*, 87; Andersen and Freedman, *Micah*, 371.

826 Wolff, *Micah: A Commentary*, 67.

827 Jennifer K. Berenson Maclean, "Micah 3: 5-12," *Interpretation* 56 (2002): 413-16.

problem. In this section (Mic 3:1-11), it is curious that the oracle moves from addressing the recipients from the second person (Mic 3:1) to (Mic 3:2, 3) third person. It seems unlikely that this is making reference to a different group of people since there is no new accusation in the text. Thus, Andersen and Freedman suggest that it is better to think of the condemnation as being pronounced "on" the leaders instead of "to" them.[828]

The prophet uses irony to portray the resulting justice that will come as a result of the injustice. Micah's biggest argument in this context is the new system or structure of society, which replaced the old tribal system of society, has a great impact on common people. Mckane clearly notes that the "new economic forces had created pressures which the old social structures could not withstand and under the weight of which they collapsed."[829] The third person plural יִזְעֲקוּ "they will cry out" in Micah 3:4 refers to the heads and rulers again. This is a judicial term. The reason for their cry is not specified in the text, yet the reason is because of their brutal action towards the poor in the land and covetousness. This seems to indicate that the heads and rulers of Israel will cry out for justice in the future, that Yahweh will not respond to their outcry. The presence and the favour of Yahweh will be no more with them.[830] Since they, who were responsible for justice, did not hear those suffering injustice, the time will come when Yahweh will not hear them either.

Micah pronounced that the judgement of God would occur. The cause of punishment/judgement was because the leaders failed to maintain justice in their administration. The behaviour of these leaders was different from what Yahweh desired. The words אָז and בָּעֵת הַהִיא in Micah 3:4 points to the time of Yahweh's judgement as the outcome of the total failure of the rulers to maintain justice. Micah delivered a prediction of punishment of the rulers who closed their ears to God's demand for justice for the helpless.[831] Yahweh not only will be silent, but also will withdraw from before them by hiding His face. The verse closes with the vital reason of Yahweh's silent nature and the hiding of His face because of their evil deeds. The rulers ruthlessly oppressed the poor and their self-interest that had brought the nation to disaster.

828 Andersen & Freedman. *Micah,* 348.

829 McKane, *Micah: Introduction and Commentary*, 102.

830 Daniel L. Simundson, *The Book of Micah: Introduction, Commentary and Reflections* (NIB, vol. 7; Nashville: Abingdon Press, 1996), 557; Wolff, *Micah: A Commentary*, 101; Mays, *Micah,* 80; John Merlin Powis Smith, William Hayes Ward, and Julius A. Bewer, eds., in *International Critical Commentary: Micah, Zephaniah, Nahum, Habakkuk, Obadiah and Joel* (Edinburgh: T&T Clark, 1965), 73-74.

831 Wolff, *Micah the Prophet,* 69.

4.4.3.3.2. Micah 3:5-7 (Micah and the Prophets)

In the second section of Micah 3, the oracles against the prophets are in the form of a judgement oracle. As in the first section, the text alternates between second and third person. However, the order is different in the second section. The address begins in the third person, (Mic 3:5b and v.6 continue in indirect speech), then moves to the second person in Micah 3:6, and then back to the third person in Micah 3:7. The text preserves both perspectives (second and third persons) side by side. It also preserves the prophets as characters in the distant past, but part of the message to them as a direct address in the second person. The effect of this makes the message of Micah 3:6 timeless for future generations. There is a possibility that Micah saw himself as a true prophet, while he viewed the other prophets to be false prophets.[832]

Another possible explanation for these alternations could lie in the fact that the text contains the perspective of telling about the prophets and the words of Micah spoken to the false prophets. Though they (prophets) received divine communication; they did not faithfully transmit the message which they have received. Berenson Maclean states that Micah accuses the state prophets of false prophecy.[833] Rudolph also terms them "false prophets" because they had a legitimate institutional function, but their action is falsehood.[834] On the other hand, there is also a possibility that Micah does not view himself as a נָבִיא "prophet" at all. The plural form נְבִיאִים "prophets" (Mic 3:6) likely arose during the monarchy as a person in an official capacity who was to advise the king on the will of God.[835] Micah condemns the נְבִיאִים "prophets" without exception and without identifying himself as a "true" נָבִיא "prophet." In this sense, Micah may be like Amos who claimed not to be a prophet nor the son of a prophet (Amos 7:14). Carroll builds his case that Micah was not a prophet even though he prophesied by the רוּחַ "spirit/wind" of God. The issue here is not whether a person is a true prophet or a false prophet. The truth is one group's "true" prophet may be another

832 Andersen & Freedman. *Micah,* 359-371. Hence the apparent disputes in the book of Micah are between *prophets* and *pseudo-prophets.* By identifying many of the salvation oracles with the work of the pseudo-prophets Van Der Voude is able to explain the work of the Micah in rational terms as a dispute between the true prophet and the pseudo-prophet. Van Der Woude, "Micah in Dispute with the Pseudo Prophets," *VT* 19 (1969): 244.

833 Maclean, "Micah 3: 5-12," 414.

834 Rudolph, *Micah, Nahum, Habakkuk, Zephaniah,* 71; Cf. R. D. Hillers, *A Commentary on the Book of the Prophet Micah* (Hermeneia; Philadelphia, 1984), 44. Rudolph assumes that שָׁלוֹם הַמַּתְעִים is an exegesis of עַל הַנְּבִיאִים "upon the prophets" and that verse 6a resumes כֹּה אָמַר יְהוָה Yahweh is the speaker here. Expressions of confidence in Micah 1-3, then, are not from Micah, but quotations from these false prophets whom Micah opposes.

835 R. P. Carroll, "Night Without Vision: Micah and the Prophets," In *The Scripture and the Scrolls: Studies in Honor of A. S. Van Der Woude on the Occasion of his 65th Birthday* (ed. Garcia Martinez, A. Hilhorst and C. J. Laubuschagne; New York: E. J. Brill, 1992), 74-84; Simundson, *The Book of Micah*, 558.

group's "false" prophet.[836] Thus, it is better not think in terms of true or false prophets, but in terms of true or false prophecies.

During Micah's time, there were prophets who were prophesying for personal gain and abusing their role, which led to the conflict between Micah and those prophets. It may be because of the connotation that may have arisen behind נָבִיא, those such as Micah and Amos may have wanted to distance themselves from it. However, the text makes it clear that Micah communicated the word of Yahweh (Mic 1:1). Therefore, this may be nothing more than a case of nomenclature, not description of function. Micah uses three different terms for the prophets in these verses. They are: נְבִיאִים prophets, קֹסְמִים diviners and חֹזִים seers. It is not clear whether these refer to the same people, or a "type" of people. נְבִיאִים (prophets) and חֹזִים (seers) are apparently interchangeable terms with the latter being an earlier one (I Sam 9:9). קֶסֶם "divination" appears to be something like prophecy (Num 22:7), but it is typically used of the activities of foreign prophets (cults) with a clearly negative connotation (I Sam 6:2; II Kgs 17:17; II Chron 33:6).[837] It is clearly a prohibited activity in Israel (Lev 19:26).

In the accusation against the prophets, Micah denounces them for abusing their prophetic abilities for nothing more than personal gain. Wolff clearly emphasizes that "Micah is not at all concerned about the methods they use to attain knowledge of God. But, he has sharply focused on the misuse of the authority of their office."[838] The messages of the prophets are based on nothing more than the amount people paid them for their services. Robert Wilson argues that charges of witchcraft or false prophecy are indicative of desperation and that such accusations are designed to destabilize society.[839] They prophesied שָׁלוֹם "peace" who gave them nothing. Literally, the text says that they קִדֵּשׁ "sanctified/ consecrated" war. As a result, they were leading Yahweh's people astray. According to Wolff תָּעָה "to lead astray" means "to cause someone to wonder about lost or to be so drunk as to be incapable of going to the desired direction."[840] Micah's sharp criticism of the prophets was leading people into false religiosity and proclaimed the wrong message.

In Micah 3:6-7, Micah ironically echoed the punishment against the false prophets. The irony of the situation is that darkness will rule the false prophets. Micah used these words in the metaphorical sense, such as "night," "darkness," "sun

836 Carroll, "Night Without Vision: Micah and the Prophets," 81. I Kgs 13 illustrates the shifting qualities of "true" and "false" when applied to prophets. Thomas B. Dozeman, "The Way of the Man of God from Judah: True and False Prophecy in the Pre-Deuteronomic Legend of 1 Kings 13," *CBQ* 44 (1982): 379-393; D.W. Van Winke, "1 Kings 13: True and False Prophecy," *VT* 29 (1989): 31-43. Cf. Carroll, "Night Without Vision: Micah and the Prophets," 79.

837 Mays, *Micah*, 84.

838 Wolff, *Micah: A Commentary*, 103.

839 Robert Wilson, *Prophecy and Society in Ancient Israel* (Philadelphia: Fortress, 1980), 21-86.

840 Wolff, *Micah the Prophet*, 70.

going down," and "the day shall be black," to express the silent nature of Yahweh. This metaphorical language pointed to the dark days of the silent of Yahweh.[841] Yahweh will remain silent as the consequence of the failure of the prophets to maintain covenantal justice and trust in the society. Thus, the judgement against the prophets would involve a loss of the ability to be able to prophesy. Micah describes it poetically as night without vision, a doubly dark time. The emphasis here is that they will not only loss of every means or sources of prophetic insight and sealed up but also the judgement ahead of them. It is curious that he parallels vision with divination. Is it possible that the prophets were prophesying by something other than or in addition to the power of Yahweh? If that were not the case, then Micah is using this negative term to highlight that they are no better than pagan prophets. Micah prophesies that there will be two results from the loss of vision. The first is בּוֹשׁ "shame," and the second is a עָטוּ עַל־שָׂפָם "covering of the mouth." This is a gesture of mourning, which suggests that the prophets will not only lose their prophetic ability, but their source of income that came from it. It could also be an anticipation of the judgement in Micah 3:12.

4.4.3.3.3. Micah 3:9-12 (Micah and the Administrators)

The third and final section of this chapter begins in nearly identical words as the beginning of the chapter. It is interesting to note that the condemnation of the "heads" and "rulers" seem to be more extreme than the condemnation against the prophets. Whatever the specific violations were, the "heads" and "rulers" of the land seemed to bear more responsibility than did the prophets. Here Micah directed his accusation towards the magistrates, and the judicial leaders together with them the priests and the prophets, the religious leaders of the nation (Mic 3:11). Leslie C. Allen notes that these groups of people were specified even by Isaiah because they were men of influence (Isa 3:2):[842] As in Micah 3:1, the Septuagint renders "rulers" as "remnant" in Micah 3:9. The accusation is more acute in this second round against the "heads" and "rulers." Instead of merely not knowing justice, Micah now accuses them of abhorring justice and twisting everything that is straight. Those who should have been upholding and loving justice actually detested justice.

The accusation begins to increase here. The text switches from second person in Micah 3:9 to a third person singular participle בֹּנֶה (*qal part. m.s. absolute*) "builder/one who builds" in Micah 3:10. In Micah's view, some individual is building Zion with bloodshed/violence. This should not be understood as sacrificial, but as oppression or even murder because "violent injustice" is parallel

---

841 Richard A. Horsley and John S. Hanson, *Bandits, Prophets and Messiahs* (San Francisco: Harper and Row Publication, 1985), 142.

842 Leslie C. Allen, *The Books of Joel, Obadiah, Jonah, and Micah* (NICOT; Grand Rapids: Eerdmans, 1976), 317. They are "hero and warrior, judge and prophet, soothsayer and elder, captain of fifty and man of rank, counsellor, skilled craftsman and clever enchanter."

to bloodshed. It may have some connection to Micah 6:7 which seems to indicate that human sacrifices were not ruled out during this time period. It is possible that Micah 3:10 could have been directed to the king.[843] Other scholars take the participle בֹּנֶה in the sense of "building up" the city of Jerusalem through forced labour and economic exploitation.[844] Others refer to the "magistrates" who mishandle justice or abuse of "justice" by taking bribes and made the innocent victims.[845] In fact, Micah tried to reflect back to the violent deeds of seizing the poor's property. Bruce Vawter points out the cause of bloodshed and violence in building Jerusalem city when he says, "they have squeezed the slender resources of their victims by nothing short of bloodshed to provide the brick and mortar for their flamboyant municipal works."[846]

Micah 3:11 develops the accusation against the heads even further. Their brand of so-called justice came with a price. Judges pronounced justice for a bribe which is a direct violation of covenant code (Exod 23:8; Deut 16:19-20). Priests who were to instruct the people on the rules of community life did so only when induced by money. They manipulate the oracle with the interest of the rich and powerful high class and for their personal enrichment. Thus, the same type of accusation extends to the priests and prophets who only exercised their role for profit.[847] In a single verse, Micah paints all those who should have been preserving justice and instructing the people in the way of Yahweh as being nothing more than greedy, evil people who were interested in nothing more than personal gain. Micah mockingly quotes the leaders in Micah 3:11. Shaw sums up Micah's accusation of the leaders in two points: firstly, they accepted שֹׁחַד "bribe," which prevented them from faithful executing their responsibilities. Second, they adhered to a false hope that Yahweh will protest Jerusalem in spite of their deeds.[848]

Micah shows them in Micah 3:12 that their confidence in Yahweh was nothing more than false security. He directly states that it is because of the leaders'

843 MaKane, *Micah*, 112; Shaw, *The Speeches of Micah: A Rhetorical Analysis*, 112; Andersen & Freedman, *Micah*, 379. Here "violence," is not the directly oppression of the poor and weak, but references to those who did not abide by Ahaz's decision not to align with Pekah and Rezin. They wanted to align with them and to do so would have meant building Jerusalem by bloodshed and war.

844 Wagner, "*banah*," in *TDOT* (vol. 2; ed. G. Johannes Botterweck and Helmer Ringgren; trans. John T. Willis; Grand Rapids, Michigan: William B. Eerdmans Publishing Company, 1975), 174; Mays, *Micah*, 88.

845 Waltke, *Micah*, 179.

846 Bruce Vawter, *Amos, Hosea, Micah: With an Introduction to Classical Prophecy* (vol. 7; ed. Stuhlmueller, et al; Wilmington: Michael Glazier, 1981), 147.

847 Smith, Ward, and Bewer, eds., in *International Critical Commentary: Micah, Zephaniah, Nahum, Habakkuk, Obadiah and Joel*, 80. Alfaro, *A Commentary on the Book of Micah*, 39; Wolff, *Micah: A Commentary*, 107 (Exod 22:9; Deut 17:8-13; Jer. 18:18; Ezek 7:26; Hag 2:11-14).

848 Shaw, *Speeches of Micah*, 114.

injustices that the symbols of Yahweh's presence, namely, the city of Jerusalem (Mic 3:12a) and the temple (Mic 3:12b), will be utterly destroyed. Micah apparently describes the destruction in terms of typical international treaty curses on vassals.[849]

Micah also spelled out the dread consequences of the fall of Jerusalem. First, Zion will turn into a field to be ploughed for cultivation; second, Jerusalem and its beautiful buildings will be reduced into piles of rubble; third, the mountain of the house will turn into a wilderness, covered only with scrub bush and other wild growth. Allen argues that the prediction is ironic as their own injustice would be the lever to set destructive forces in motion.[850] All these suggest that the leaders in the society failed in their responsibilities and caused the destruction of Jerusalem. The land had broken covenant with Yahweh by the way they were treating their fellow Israelites (their violent acts against the poor).

4.4.3.4. Prophetic Leadership of Micah

The text (Mic 3:1-12) presents the corruption created by the Judean rulers, priests, prophets and thus Judah and Jerusalem will face Yahweh's judgement or destruction (Mic 3:12). The first four verses of Micah 3 paint a vivid portrait of the dehumanizing and brutal treatment of the poor by the leaders of Judean society (Mic 3:2b-3). Micah opens this section reproaching Jerusalem for its failed leadership. Israel's political leaders not only failed to rule with justice as is required of them, but "hated good and loved evil." Their merciless and oppressive behaviour was like that of cannibals or hunters in search of a prey. Ordinary citizens were treated more like mere animals than human beings. In fact the responsible of the leaders were to declare justice to the one who have no legal standing (widows, orphans, poor and sick). Micah 3:5-12 focuses on the prophet's condemnation of his competitors. The prophets claim to preach a pleasant but all misleading message. They claim "peace" (Mic 3:5) and "security" of Yahweh so that no harm shall come upon them (Mic 3:11). But there was a gap between their message and their actions. Thus Micah proclaims divine judgement upon not just the perpetrators of these injustices but also the prophets who legitimatise this behaviour. Corrupted prophetic insight demands the coming of darkness (Mic 3:6), and those formerly respected will suffer public shame and disgrace (Mic 3:7).

---

849 Shaw, *The Speeches of Micah: A Rhetorical-Historical Analysis*, 112; Hillers, *Micah*, 9; MaKane, *Micah*, 115; Alfaro, *A Commentary on the Book of Micah*, 40. The book of Jeremiah quotes the oracle in Micah 3:12 (Jer 26:18-19) over a century later. The context in Jeremiah seems to indicate a previous narrative context for this oracle because it includes details concerning Hezekiah and his repentance. As a result of Hezekiah's repentance and reform, this prediction did not come to pass. What is interesting is that the book of Jeremiah sees the oracle as conditional. The text of Micah gives no indication that it is conditional.

850 Allen, *The Books of Obadiah-Micah*, 319-329. Cf. Sweeney, *Twelve Prophets*, 375.

Micah's address is direct and honest. He speaks to the leaders of Israel, those with responsibility for its common life (Mic 3:9a), and portrays them as corrupt, failing in their obligations for just dealings in public (Mic 3:9b), and maltreating those labouring on public and/or private building projects with a harshness that is careless of life (Mic 3:10).[851] McKane comments that Micah does not have in mind building operations which were careless of the human cost and treated fatal accidents to workers lightly. Rather it is the megalomania of those who build or acquire property ruthlessly without regard to the social damage which they inflict and the trail of human suffering which they leave in their wake.[852] The leadership in its various forms: both "secular" (rulers) and "spiritual" (priests, prophets) is venal; the justice and guidance that should enable healthy communal life have become commodities, to be had only for a price (Mic 3:11a). Yet apparently these leaders do not see their conduct as incompatible with strong religious claims; they acknowledge their dependence upon Yahweh. They claim Yahweh's presence "in our midst," which is clearly a reference to the Jerusalem temple as the focal point of Yahweh's presence with Judah; and they regard Yahweh's presence in the temple as a guarantee of security from their enemies. The leaders were complacent with their little kingdoms but apathetic to Yahweh's kingdom.

Micah 3 presents a survey of Micah's time of leadership and denounces it as corrupt, whether rulers, (false) prophets, or priests. If the leadership of the nation is corrupt, the nation itself will certainly be corrupt. Micah brusquely draws out the implications of the mismatch between the leaders' practice and their religious claims, and connects fault with fate. The text also functions as a recapitulation of the actual violent crimes for which the Israelite political and religious leaders were responsible.

With respect to the prophetic tradition, readers of the text hear: (1) the importance of the presence of empowered prophetic speakers and persons, especially in times of political and religious disintegration; (2) the critical need to remain faithful to the prophetic mission on account of the social responsibility that it entails; and (3) the significance of the fact that God is the one who empowers the prophet. The text also realizes that the divine and prophetic word does come to pass. What will happen to the people is not specified; though insofar as the site of city and temple returns to the wild, the implication is that its inhabitants will not be there to rebuild, and so will either be dead or deported into exile. Finally, the text makes clear to its readers that the most trusted representatives of the Israelite community are liable to sin and its consequences.

---

851 Interestingly, Micah does not specify or single out the king, yet Jeremiah 26:19 depicts King Hezekiah as a responsive recipient of Micah's message. Shaw, *The Speeches of Micah: A Rhetorical-Historical Analysis*, 123. Cf. Wolff, *Micah: A Commentary*, 97-98.

852 McKane, *Micah*, 112. On what grounds within the text McKane considers it possible to make this distinction and this judgement it would be interesting to know.

Micah encountered with the priests and the false prophets, and he grouped them along with political leaders, judges and merchants, who were the culprits of bringing injustice in the land. He targeted his attack with these groups of people for its failed leadership. Israel's political leaders not only failed to rule with justice as is required of them, but "hated good and loved evil." They turned a deaf ear to the pleas of orphans and widows so Micah preached that Yahweh would likewise turn a deaf ear to their pleas and cries when their judgement from a foreign oppressor. Micah then switched his attention to the failures of Israel's religious leaders who served not out of obedience and faithfulness to Yahweh but out of greed, vested interests and personal gain. They would modify their messages according the money they received, perverting truth and encouraging dishonest gain and favouritism, promising false security and half-truths of Yahweh's grace and mercy. As punishment, Yahweh would withhold prophetic revelations to them and cause them to suffer humiliation and embarrassment. Because of the privilege and power invested in society's leaders and the wider magnitude of their influence, Yahweh holds leaders on a higher level of accountability. Leadership failure that arises out of selfishness and self-centredness will be severely punished by Yahweh.

Micah turned early in his ministry to Samaria, which to that point had managed to survive the military ambitions of Assyria. Micah saw clearly that the capital of the Northern Kingdom could not withstand serious attacks by the Assyrians and in his utterances, he sought to awaken the kingdom by urging the inhabitants to take warning from the catastrophe that was to take Samaria. Micah had at heart the interests of the lonely peasant in the Judean country side. Micah's view was towards the fertile plains and beyond the Great Sea. Micah lived in a district rich in agriculture and among good, sturdy independent yeoman. Here there was food sufficient for people and beast but many suffered and longed for love, justice, and righteousness. In his disputes with the false leaders of Israel and Judah, Micah led the poor and humble to trust in Yahweh and to seek the righteous order of his kingdom.

Micah lived in a time of international fear and uncertainty. He was one of the fearless defender of Yahweh's rights over his people. He had Amos' passion for justice and Hosea's heart of love; knowing his fellow country people intimately and sympathizing profoundly with their sufferings and wrongs, his spirit burned with indignation as he beheld the injustice and oppression of their rich oppressors.[853] Micah was not carried away by the splendour of royalty or the lavish display of surplus wealth by the aristocratic circles. He was rather able to see the invisible side—the poverty and the oppression of the majority. Micah stands outside of the political and religious circles of his day (Mic 3:8), but he is not afraid to

853 Harrison, *Introduction to the Old Testament*, 920; John Merlin Smith Micah, Hayes Ward, and Julius A. Bewer, in *International Critical Commentary: Micah* (vol. 28; Edinburgh: T&T Clark, 1965), 18.

address the circles. He charged and condemned the false authority of those who had departed from the true standards of government, whether royals, prophets, or priests.

Conclusion

The forgoing study of "Prophetic Leadership in the Eighth Century BCE Israel" revealed that the prophets portrayed different kind of leadership from that of royal and priestly leadership. They displayed a good model of leadership through their life and ministry. Their concern was different from other leaders. They were the main critiques of the monarchs, royal officials, religious leaders and society in general. Thus one can conclude that without prophetic ministry, the executive or administrative role tends to revert to the kingly, the fallacy in which a human being or human structure becomes totalitarian and thus idolatrous. Institutions and structures are necessary if ministry is to take place, but institutions and structures and their executives or administrators are "skins" and not the "wine." Without prophetic ministry, structures become idols and executives become gods. Prophets in the eighth century BCE Israel are not seen exclusively over against the kings, but it is there that their rise and major impingement is chiefly seen. The king represented a heavy concentration of power, with far-reaching implications for all under that power. The prophet represented a voice independent of that kingly power, a voice from God to the power structures primarily, but also to and for the people. So, it is with prophetic ministry today. It is not indifferent to private morals or to so-called non-victim deviations, but its primary responsibility is to speak to issues and challenge power structures which are above individual competence.

Chapter 5

Patterns of Prophetic Leadership

Introduction

As discussed in the previous chapters, each of the Israel's prophets led their people in times of crises. They were leaders who contributed uniquely, in their qualities, abilities, and techniques, to the maturing and progress of religion, and from whose example important lessons may be learned. They were versatile and distinguished leaders who were distinguished in several fields. They were visionaries, advisers, preachers, missionaries and evangelists. Virtually all of prophets' services were rendered against the backdrop of some crises. Also the study of the eighth century BCE prophets individually, and the prophets in general enable us to understand that they were religious innovators who tried to maintain monotheism in a polytheist society. While trying to keep up the ancestral faith, they encountered religious leaders whom they condemned because of their unfaithfulness to their responsibilities as leaders and the injustice that they practised. It also enables one to see the following leadership characteristics that one can adopt as a model.

5.1. Servant Leadership

The image of the prophets as Yahweh's servants occurs in various passages.[854] As "servants of Yahweh" the prophets are presented as belonging to a past stage of the history of Israel and Judah, until the end of Judah as a state. The passages referring to the prophets as Yahweh's servants have different accents.

---

854 II Kgs 9:7; 17:13, 23; 21:10; 24:2; Jer 44:4 Ezra 9:11; Ezek 38:17; Dan 9:6, 10; Amos 3:7-8; Zech 1:6.

First, within the book of Jeremiah, we find the following picture of the prophets as Yahweh's servants: Yahweh has continuously, i.e. from Moses till the end, in the sixth century, sent his servants the prophets to the people, in order to urge them to turn from their evil ways, but the people refused to listen.[855]

Second, II Kings presents the prophets as predicting the harsh punishment Yahweh is going to bring over Israel and Judah.[856] In this respect, the prophets are part of the narrative framework: the end of the states of Israel and Judah is narrated by means of the pattern prediction and fulfilment.

A biblical image that is the most common and dominant for leaders is that of a servant. Most of the biblical prophets, especially prophets of the eighth century BCE Israel called or referred to themselves as servants.[857] Servant leaders display at least four characteristics: humility, service, focus on other, and love. Servant leaders lead with humility. They are characterized as humble or selfless leaders. Thus a critical element of leadership is how the leader serves. It is all about humility, not ego. As discussed in the previous chapter, prophets of the eighth century BCE Israel had demonstrated that kind of attitude from their lifestyle. For instance; Amos and Micah were servants of their master, Yahweh, who called them to be the messengers to His people. They were not the servants or employees of the kings or royal officers because they did not serve in the king's palace, but they were Yahweh's messengers. They lived and acted as servants of their master. This kind of servant attitude is clearly seem in Amos when he replied to Amaziah "Yahweh took me from following the flock," and "the lion has roared; who will not fear? The Lord God has spoken; who can but prophesy?" (Amos 7:15; 3:8). God sent him to preach his message to Israel, and until his work was done, and until God released him from it, he could not turn aside.

Servant leaders are primarily motivated by a desire to serve and to see life as a mission, not as a career. Prophets had passion for their work, seeing it as a kind of calling. They understood and accepted that they had a responsibility for their own people, and they saw their gifts and endeavours as contributing to a larger whole, much greater than themselves. As noted in preceding chapter, prophet Hosea has demonstrated that servant leaders should have passion for a greater ministry. Prophets were attentive to the needs and concerns of their people. They were responsible to take care of and nurture them. Prophets were servant leaders who were seen by people as a servant first and later acknowledged as a legitimate leader.

---

855 Jer 7:25; 25:4; 26:5; 29:19; 35:15.

856 II Kgs 17:23; 21:10-14; 24:2; cf. Ezek 38:17.

857 Kevin G. O'Connell, S.J., "Those Lively Prophets Hosea–A Prophet of Passion," *Currents in Theology and Mission* 4 (1977): 104-108; Paul S. Fideles, "The Cross of Hosea Revisited: The Meaning of Suffering in the Book of Hosea," *Review and Expositor* 90 (1993): 175-190; William Henry Cobb, "The servant of Jahveh," *JBL* 14 (1895): 95-113; R. Rick Marrs, "Micah and the Task of Ministry," *Restoration Quarterly* 30 (1988): 1-16.

One of the elements that is integral to servant leadership is love. The love of leaders for their followers is the reason servant leaders serve; it is their motivation. Servant leaders are proactive risk takers. They are not found merely standing around, waiting for orders. The reason is that the Master has already issued those orders. This kind of expression is explained from the call of Amos (Amos 1:2; 7: 14-15) and Isaiah (Isa 6). The posture of servant acknowledges immediately that leaders serve something or someone greater than themselves. The prophets first served the God they followed, then the mission that brings them and their followers into relationship, and finally the followers whose work achieves the mission. Leadership serves the God that the leader follows. It serves the mission that creates the organizational relationship of leader and follower. But also leadership serves the people who choose to follow. This is how leaders become servants and debtors. Debt is paid by providing the resources, space, delegation, encouragement, and accountability that people need to succeed. Servant leadership is about humbly serving others, not oneself.

Servant leadership begins with the natural feeling that one wants to serve, to serve first, and the care taken by the servant leader is to make sure that other people's needs are being served. Servant leaders are to place others' needs before their own and to serve those over whom they assume leadership. Surely these characteristics of the servant leader bring to mind the prophetic leadership model. Servant leaders do not seek rewards or commendation for the leadership they offer. They do not seek status or power therefore, confuse these with authentic leadership. The servant leader understands what he or she is expected to lead. Accepting the role of leader of the society, the leader recognizes the difference between position and task. The title of "prophet" does not make a person a prophet. People who rely on the position they hold or the title bestowed upon that position to get people to do what they want them to do will accomplish very little.

Servant leaders also endured sufferings for greater cost. In other words suffering with a preventive purpose. Prophet Amos taught that suffering was designed to prevent further tragedy, and such a teaching was very appropriate in his day. The prophets themselves suffered mentally and often physically because the Israelites had not suffered enough to force them to heed the prophetic message. The view that one might be strengthened through suffering probably grew out of the experience of the prophets. As servant leaders, the prophets suffered sacrificially, not the necessity of pain as a part of the doomed of the people of Israel, but by their choice to do all in their power to save the Israelites.[858] They were very lonely men because no one understood them except God Himself (Amos 7; Mic 7:4-7; Jer 12:5-7; 20:12-18). Thus, they entered in a measure into the redemptive love of Yahweh and in that measure their suffering became redemptive in its quality. They demonstrated in principle the sacrificial suffering.

858 Jimmie L. Nelson, "His Servants, the Prophets," *SJT* 24 (1981): 87-102.

The great leader is seen as servant first, and that simple fact is the key to his/her greatness. Prophets were actually the leader all of the time, but they were servant first because that was what they were, deep down inside. Servant leaders look for ways to challenge the status quo and capture the imagination of others regarding mission and purpose. The bureaucratic leader tries to get people to merely follow the rules that have been set regardless of whether they have anything to do with mission or not. As discussed in the fourth chapter, Amos challenged the status quo of Amaziah the priest of Bethel and showed him the purpose of the mission. The caretaker leader simply sees that what has been done continues to be done primarily maintaining the status quo with no new goals or new vision. The laissez-faire leader does not do anything to motivate people. They simply want people to be happy and be able to do whatever they want to do. Like the prophets of the eighth century BCE Israel, Christian leaders are servants with credibility and capabilities, who are able to influence people in a particular context to pursue their God-given direction.

5.2. Shepherd Leadership

As the human culture of the AWA moved from a hunting and gathering society to a more stable nomadic and then largely agrarian one, the domestication of animals played a major role. OT ancestors counted much of their wealth in "flocks and herds."[859] The imagery relating to sheep and the daily life of shepherds developed across the AWA.[860] Thus the survival of Israel was impacted by the way they cared for their sheep. Isaiah says, "We all like sheep have gone astray" (Isa 53:6). What God desires is for his prophets and a shepherd is to care for his sheep with the same intensity and determination that was characteristic of God's care.

The general impression of shepherd leaders is as gentle people. The shepherd image offers a fuller picture of the life of a leader than many others. The leaders of Israel were considered shepherds of the land. They were like shepherds who would provide security and prosperity (spiritual) for the people of Israel.[861] Like prophets, leaders become shepherds when they awaken to the reality that their actions and decisions can improve the quality of their followers' lives forever.

Shepherd leadership is whole-person leadership. It's about relationship with people. Scott Cormode remarks that "the Shepherd leader emphasizes relationships rather than roles, people rather than positions....Shepherds see the organization

859 The Hebrew word צאן, most commonly translated as "sheep" or "flock," but also referring less frequently to small cattle or goats and metaphorically to a "multitude," occurs more than 260 times in the OT. For examples of the various uses, see Francis Brown, S. R. Driver, and Charles A. Briggs, eds., *A Hebrew and English Lexicon of the OT* (Oxford: Clarendon, 1972), 838. For instance: Genesis alone the references to "flock and herds" in 13:5; 32:8; 33:13; 45:10; 47:1; 50:8.

860 Jack W. Vancil, "Sheep, Shepherd," in *ABD* (vol. 5; ed. David Noel Freedman; New York: Doubleday, 1992), 1187-90.

861 Gluck, "Nagid-Shepherd," 144-150.

not as a structure built of roles but as a community defined by its relationships."[862] It's not just a matter of thinking in a certain way or doing things in a certain way. It is fully integrated life, a matter of head, hand and heart. Shepherd leadership is a way of thinking, doing and being. The shepherd's first job in the field is to think and to think ahead. Although humans have this capacity, we know that not everybody uses it. For the poor people of the eighth century BCE Israel, the concerns of day-to-day survival often override any effort to plan for the future despite good intentions on the contrary. This is where prophets as shepherd leadership enter the picture.

Shepherd leaders are characterized by mental agility. They have the ability to shift gears from deep reflection to quick thinking and decision making in a matter of moments. The mind of a shepherd leader must always be out ahead, envisioning the next destination and the best way to get there. As noted in the previous chapter, Isaiah demonstrated shepherd leader when he ministered Ahaz and Hezekiah, kings of Judah in times of crisis, giving them advice about the next destination. In same way Alfaro also remarks that "Micah suffered deeply when he saw how the poor were despoiled. He dreamt often of a future shepherd, since he had a clear vision of what the leader of the people was supposed to be."[863] Royal leaders were filled with wealth, fame, and power. However, as a shepherd leader Micah was filled with spirit of the LORD, might and justice.

Shepherd leadership is a way of being. In particular, it is a way of "being with" the follower or with the people. By "being with" we mean going beyond doing things for the people or thinking about the people. When the leaders of the nation failed to provide a shepherd leadership to the people of Israel, Hosea provided it by shepherding with loving kindness, caring, and being with them. He leades me beside still waters.

5.3. Transformational Leadership

Transformational leaders take strategic decisions and give shape to changes, thereby ensuring that their society stay alert. Transformational leaders aim to transform people for good. The notion of mission-driven leadership is at the heart to transformational leadership. Transformational leadership is a far more complex process, the realization of which requires visionary and inspiring figures. Transformational leadership according to Peter G. Northouse, is to "involves an exceptional form of influence that moves followers to accomplish more than what is usually expected of them. It is a process that often incorporates charismatic and visionary leadership."[864]

862 Scott Cormode, "Multi-Layered Leadership: The Christian Leader as Builder, Shepherd, and Gardener," *Journal of Religious Leadership* 1 (2002): 79, 80.

863 Alfaro, *Micah*, 4.

864 Peter G. Northouse, *Leadership: Theory and Practice* (4th ed.; New Delhi: SAGE Publications India Pvt Ltd, 2007), 175-176.

The goal of a transformational leader is to transform people and change minds and hearts; enlarge vision, insight, and understanding; clarify purposes; make behaviour congruent with beliefs, principles, and values; and bring about changes that are permanent, self-perpetuating, and momentum building.[865] As discussed in the previous chapter, prophet Amos tried to correct the wrong attitude of Amaziah, the priest, who controlled the temple as his own. When he took a stand for the truth, he was personally attacked and accused of being someone he was not. The preaching of Amos might have troubled Amaziah that was the reason why he informed the king and asked Amos to leave the place. As a transformational leader Amos might have tried to abolish the principles of inequality based on class system. However, the nation leaders refused the policy of change.

Transformational leaders have a strong set of values and ideas, that influence the followers, and whose role becomes models for the followers.[866] John C. Maxwell explains that "true leadership cannot be awarded, appointed, or assigned. It comes only from influence, and that can't be mandated."[867] Robert K. Martin also remarks that "leaders act to change or influence persons, whether directly or indirectly."[868] The prophets of the eighth century BCE Israel were leaders with idealized influence, and thus they are honoured, appreciated, and trusted. People admire them, identify with them, and try to imitate them.

The prophets never used their positions and abilities to achieve personal interests, but they directed them to use the potential of others to achieve shared goals. The prophets gave themselves to the task of social reform only after they had experienced a moral transformation within their own lives. Thus, transformational Leadership begins with awareness: awareness of one's own thoughts and feelings, and how these affect ones actions, and the states of others. As one's awareness grows, one begin to see one's own inner motivating force, what drives one's passions and values, and how these affect one's thoughts, feelings and actions, and that of others. As transformational leaders, the task of the prophets with people, the priests, the false prophets, the royals, and the kings was to call that genuine and vital and transforming faith in God which worked its way into every area of personal and national life. For the prophets, only a vital religion can give the guidance and motive power sufficient to bring social and economic

865 Skip Beli, "Learning, Changing, and Doing: A Model for Transformational Leadership Development in Religious and Non-Profit Organizations," *Journal of Religious Leadership* 9 (2010): 93.

866 Northouse, *Leadership: Theory and Practice,* 181.

867 John C. Maxwell, *The 21 Irrefutable Laws of Leadership* (Nashville: Thomas Nelson Publishers, 1998), 14.

868 Robert K. Martin, "Dwelling in the Divine Life: The Transformational Dimension of Leadership and Practical Theology," *Journal of Religious Leadership* 3 (2004): 99.

reforms into reality. Thus, for prophet Amos true religion should bring internal transformation.

Transformational Leadership inspires wholeness of being, so one's thoughts, feelings and actions are consistent. It is about leading with an integrity and authenticity that resonate with others and inspire them to follow. Not only does it inspire others to follow, but to become leaders themselves. Leaders inspire the followers "through motivation to become committed to and a part of the shared vision."[869] Transformational leadership can bring a commitment to strive toward a superlative excellence. In transforming leaderships, leaders champion and inspire followers. Followers might outstrip leaders. They might become leaders themselves. That is what makes transforming leadership participatory and democratic.

5.4. Visionary Leadership

Prophets were men and women of extra-ordinary vision, full of wisdom and the sense of urgency to accomplish the task of mission as commanded by Yahweh. They saw farther than others. This is clearly seen from the leadership of prophet Isaiah of Jereusalem. When Ahaz, the king of Judah could not see the possibility of having a peaceful nation, Isaiah saw a clear vision and advised Ahaz to heed the Word. It is proven by prophet that vision makes impossible possible and give hope to the hopeless. Where there is vision, people live.

A clear vision is essential to a leader, for without it a leader will be like the blind leading the blind, and failure will be the result. Vision is an act of seeing; it is an imaginative perception of things, combining insight and foresight. As noted in the previous chapter, when Hezekiah made a wrong decision Isaiah confronted with insightful thought/vision. Hezekiah did not see what is going to happen to his people in the future but he only thought about his fame and accomplishment. He was self-centred. Vision implies wisdom which is the faculty of making the best of knowledge, a combination of discernment, judgement, sagacity and similar power which create a sense of task in leaders to achieve the desired goals. Where there is no vision the people perish, but it is also true that where there is no vision the Church perishes, and where there is no vision the leader perishes. Therefore, the motivation factor of a leader should be the vision; people of vision, people of wisdom and people of task like prophets Amos, Isaiah, Hosea and Micah of the eighth century BCE Israel.

"What manner of man is the prophet?" asks Heschel in his work, *The Prophets*.[870] The answer lies in the true nature of the prophets' calling. He further puts it that a prophet is one who is called by God, and is one who has a vocation from God. Thus, the prophetic function encompasses far more than just predicting

869 Northouse, *Leadership: Theory and Practice,* 183.

870 Heschel, *The Prophets,* 3, 405.

the future, it is involved with confronting the culture with a word from God that may or may not contain an element of futurity.

Walter Brueggemann identifies the two key characteristics that make up what he calls the "prophetic imagination:" first of all it serves to *criticize* in dismantling the dominant or royal consciousness of a culture; and it seeks to energize an oppressed community against the dominant cultural consciousness. The concept of the royal consciousness is the key to Brueggeman's idea of what a prophet's calling actually is. He further remarks, the prophetic imagination must serve to *energize* persons and communities by its promise of another time and situation toward which the community of faith may move.[871] It is important to critique the royal consciousness but progress takes time. In the meantime, people must still live with the reality of present day oppression and it is part of the prophetic function to energize a community of hope. In such a context, a prophet must create the sense of new realities that can be trusted and relied upon just when the old realities had left us hopeless. A leader with vision has a clear, vivid picture of where to go, as well as a firm grasp on what success looks like and how to achieve it.

Throughout the books of the prophets in the OT, there are constant denunciations of human greed and economic injustice. The prophet Isaiah rails against those who oppress the poor (Isa 10:1-4). As Heschel writes, "prophecy is the voice that God had lent to the silent agony, a voice to the plundered poor, to the profaned riches of the world. It is a form of living, a crossing point of God and people. God is raging in the prophet's words."[872] God's logic is not human's logic, and he is eminently concerned with the well-being of the poor enough that he would speak especially on their behalf through the prophets. To the prophets, justice is not blind but has its eyes wide open.

The present ruin in the areas of relationship, unity, and vitality in the churches are not an eternal reality. With vision, there is a hope in hopelessness, unity in diversity, and peace in hatred. The churches today just need visionary leaders like Amos, Isaiah, Hosea and Micah. The churches need vision for the restoration of peace and unity, for the purpose of witnessing God by unique community of God. However, the problem of today's Churches is not the failure to have a vision as a Church but the failure of leaders to have a vision for the Church. Therefore, the time has come for today's church leaders to dream dreams of peace and see vision of godly community living godly lives in the midst of ungodly surrounding. Today's churches need leaders who have prophetic vision.

5.5. Humble Leaders

Humility is a mark of a spiritual life. Humility is a growing quality in an effective leader. The prophets grew in humility. The secret of greatness in prophets Amos,

871 Brueggemann, *The Prophetic Imagination*, 3, 14.

872 Heschel, *The Prophets*, 5.

Isaiah, Hosea and Micah was in their declaration of humility. Unless there is humility in leadership, there is likely to be an overbearing attitude, an attitude of domination and misuse of authority.

Patience is another fundamental qualification of an effective leader. An important leader, always hurrying about trying to do a great many things, desiring to move things rapidly will never succeed in anything. Rather that may create misunderstanding between leader and the group that he/she leads. As mentioned in the earlier chapters, we see this quality in the life and ministry of prophets. For instance prophet Hosea whose destiny was to witness God's faithfulness at a time of crisis and uncertainty. Hosea led the Israelites with humility and patience. Hosea's great success as a prophet lies in his quality of patience. It was his patience that gave him success in the midst of all discouraging criticism and violent opposition. Neither external criticism (priests) and opposition nor internal trouble (family) could displace him from his leadership. He was persistent in his vision and worked persistently.

5.6. Diligent Leaders

As discussed previously, the eighth century BCE Israelite's prophets lived during national crises. There were crises at all levels: political, social, economic, and religious life. The prophets as leaders played excellent roles, by facing crises as an opportunity for sacrificial service. They not only foresaw the future but also accepted the challenge for its change towards betterment. The prophets faced economic crisis. Among the classes affected by the economic crisis were the landless who were short of food. The greedy elite kept the poor on the edge of poverty. There was social crisis and many were forced to surrender their property to satisfy loans and pay in part the heavy tax levied by the Assyrian government. The prophets rebuked the exploiters. They appealed to their love by reminding them that they were robbing their own fellow Israelites. They also reminded them that the Law forbade Israelites to extract interest from one another. In the midst of all these crises, prophets diligently stood for the cost of the poor people in the society.

The prophets knew that God's judgement often meant destruction and ruin. However, they never reached the point where they tried to save their souls and let their world go to ruin. The prophets risked their lives time after time to bring their people back to God. They spoke to their day as if their people stood at the crossroads of human destiny and as if that destiny depended upon the choice made by their generation. They set before kings, royals, priests and the people the way of life and the way of death (Amos 5:14, 15; 7:10-17; Isa 7, 39). Today, the Church must involve in the social affairs such as the prophets did for effective participation in decision-making. The prophets clearly showed by their participation in political affairs that politics is not merely a matter of excising power but it is the matter of will and loyalty.

5.7. Faithful Leaders

Faithfulness is an indispensable qualification sought for in leadership. Faith is a religious term that expresses a person's commitment to the Ultimate. According to Paul Tillich, "faith is a total and cantered act of the personal self, the act of unconditional, infinite and ultimate concern."[873] In its broadest theological sense, faith may refer to one's commitment to things of the world or more narrowly limited to God in organised religion. Prophets of the ancient Israel's theological conviction show that they strove for God's liberation of victims from economic, social and political oppression. Their lives and ministries reflect faithfulness as reliability, loyalty, whole-heartedness, diligence, consistency, endurance and the like. More specifically as discussed in the preceding chapter, prophet Micah protested against rulers and leaders for failing to protect the rights of the poor. He proclaimed that the leaders were not faithful in their responsibilities and denied the rights of the poor by mean of violence and oppression.

Today, church leadership has increasingly assumed a "boss mentality." Leaders feel that they have to exercise "control" and "authority." In the process, leaders become insensitive to the needs of the individual and congregations. Prophets of the eighth century BCE Israel show good models for the churches today, i.e., their personal zeal, which was for the glory of Yahweh. When prophets saw the unjust society, they could not stay without confronting the reality. The prophets confronted the royal leaders and the elite and urged to stop oppressing their fellow Israelites. They were faithful in their duties. The success and failure of leaders is determined by their faithfulness to Yahweh, to fellow beings and to their faithfulness in words and deeds. Thus, we see here the prophets who demonstrated one of the greatest marks of leadership potentially.

5.8. Pastoral Leadership

One of the best models of leadership in today's church could be the model of pastoral leadership. People's daily experiences of insecurity, poverty and uncertainty demand pastoral care and concern. The churches need leaders with concern and care for the people. Restoration of unity and reconciliation among all people would be possible only by pastoral leadership. Leaders' presence among the people, living with them and sharing the life experiences with them is very much important in pastoral leadership. As discussed in the former chapters, it was true that during the time of Amos, Isaiah, Hosea and Micah leaders were challenged with various crises and problems but the leaders were not faithful in their duties and they abstained from the existing crises in the society. For instance, Amaziah, the priest was challenged with various issues in the society, namely, economic issue, class system (poor and rich), nominality of religion, and so on. However, as a religious leader, he failed to face the challenges. On the other hand, Amos never

---

873 Paul Tillich, *Dynamic of Faith* (New York: Harper's Torch Book, 1958), 8.

lived in isolation. He lived and spoke for the citizens of the land. Prophet Hosea nurtured the Israelite with his tragic family experienced. Micah lived among the poor people in the land and shared the same agony and sought for liberation from oppression. Isaiah continued to speak for political crisis.

It is a fact that the absence of leaders from the people for care and guidance is the root cause of all problems. Therefore, for the solution of this problem in the churches and to bring reformation and renewal, the leaders need to follow the model of pastoral leadership as seen in prophets.

5.9. Prophetic Heritage

The prophets of the eighth century BCE Israel were inescapable in the history of Israel. Patient and determined, they received the vision and led the way. They rapped persistently at the door of every leaders' hearts and challenge them to possess: (l) uncompromising loyalty to the kingship of God; (2) lives of blameless character; (3) unquestioned fidelity to the authority of the Torah/Scripture; (4) timeless commitment to the independence and interdependence of the religion that is founded in Yahweh/cult; (5) missions that share Yahweh with the whole world; (6) sacred respect for the simplicity and the meaning of the ordinances; (7) fairness in judging people and awarding honours.

Prophets were leaders who speak throughout the generations from the past, offering them their best experiences for the solving of our various problems. We should rediscover their best in ourselves and with their same confidence in Yahweh and we should press on to even greater victories.

Conclusion

Leading is not an easy task. It is true to say that following is cheap but leading is costly. True leadership always exacts a heavy toll on the whole being, and the more effective the leadership is, the higher the price to be paid. A leader has to pay the cost of loneliness. Throughout the time of leadership the prophets of the eighth century BCE Israel had gone through the lonely path. The prophets paid this price for their leadership. The prophets bore the cost of criticism. In fact, no leader is exempted from criticism and his/her humility will nowhere be seen more clearly than in the manner in which he/she accepts and reacts to it. They were self-sacrificing. Their secret of greatness lay in their sacrificial life. The prophets were faced with various issues and challenges. However, they could face each of the issues with great determination and without fear. They were fearless; they challenged the kings and rulers with courage because they had power and commission from Yahweh. Their leadership came from their calling and commission for a specific mission of Yahweh. Thus, they became a model for the people who desire to become a successful leader.

Conclusion

From the foregoing study of *Leadership in the Prophetic Literature with Special Reference to Eighth Century BCE Prophets*, the following conclusions can be drawn. The social and cultural life of Israel was governed primarily by three groups of leaders: the kings/royal officers, the priests, and the prophets. Of these, the kings and priests were by far the more prominent. Although, the prophets did not occupy a prominent position in the life of Israel as that of the other leaders, their popular style and genial manners attracted a large number of followers among the common people. They did not rule with the authority of the kings in secular world or the authority/piety of the priests in religious world; they were simply earnest seekers of the moral life and justice for the poor, and it was their aim to teach and advise their fellow common people on what that Yahweh wants from them and how good that good life is.

"The Emergence of Royal Leadership in Israel" formed the first chapter of the research. The history of Israel is one of the bases of the study of the OT which helps in understanding the biblical record more prominently. There are many ways in apprehending the facts of the history which can be based on the biblical evidences, or extra-biblical sources such as archaeological findings, socio-scientific aspects, and chronology, etc. In the history of Israel, the emergence of monarchy is marked as one of the most significant events because there were many changes brought in the social, political, economic, and spiritual realms among the people of Israel.

The period when the so called leaders as "judges," who exercised civil and military power in Israel came to an end with the career of Samuel, who served as the last judge (I Sam 7:15), a priest (I Sam 2:18; 7:9), and a prophet (II Chron 35:18). Under his leadership the Israelites had spiritual and material blessing, but as he grew older his people expressed concern for the future. The elders of Israel decided to ask Samuel for a king as their leader as they were conscious of continuing threat from the Philistines. Moreover, it is also illustrated that the population grew in size and the land was not enough to accommodate all the people with their increasing agricultural surpluses. It is clear that the need of a king for Israel was very essential. There was political unification of the hill country under Saul, followed by David's conquests and the creation of one powerful state throughout most of the country, which in effect changed the historical development of the entire region. It was for the first time where there was a local independent political entity in Palestine, a national ethnic state with a distinctive ideological and religious identity.

The type of government before monarchy was "theocracy" in which God ruled over His people. Though Israel welcomed monarchy, the concept of "theocracy" is still instilled in the hearts of the people. The understanding is that God is the supreme King, and He chose the king in Israel, to be His representative to the people. Thus, the king should rule the nation with truth, justice, and righteousness. The "kingship" in Israel is unique, in the sense that the "king" is not higher than the One who chose him, that is "God." He is the loyal servant of his master.

The second chapter "Leaders in Israel and Ancient West Asia: An Overview" briefly reviewed the three leadership offices: Royal leadership; Priestly leadership and Prophetic leadership.

The first section begins with the role of leaders from monarchical Israel. Prior to the institution of kingship in ancient Israel, the tribes of Israel were governed separately by charismatic leaders called judges who delivered the people from their enemies but were united under a common theocracy in their obedience to God. Then with the institution of monarchy in the structure or system of leadership changed from tribal leadership to the system of class-based society: consisting of royal family, recorders, scribes, priests, military commanders, and various other political appointments who were called bureaucrats; and the common people who served the royal officers and the kingdom. All these were essential to the daily lives of the people as well as to their collective existence.

The section also focused on the different functions of king in various fields, and the different positions and responsibilities (functions) held by the royal officials. The king functioned as a military leader who led his people into war, and as an administrator, he established justice and peace in the land. He is looked upon by the Israelites to be morally and ethically sound, because he was considered as a religious leader as well.

The next section focused on priestly leadership, extending the prior discussion of its origin, office and the responsibilities or functions. Priestly office in ancient Israel was one of the most ancient and essential aspects of the Hebrew people and their covenant with God. Thus, any proper understanding of the Israelites necessarily includes an investigation into the role of the priesthood. Before the Egyptian bondage (in the time of the patriarchs), the Hebrew people did not function by means of a special priesthood constituted of a divinely instituted family line. Usually the heads of the Hebrew household would perform what would later come to be recognized as properly priestly functions (i.e., such as the offering of sacrifice). This is easily seen through the familiarity with the patriarchs of Israel.

During the time of exodus, however, we see that God institutes a new covenant with Moses, and part of that covenant is a special priesthood with restrictions on who is included or can be admitted into that priesthood. Yahweh explicitly revealed His will regarding the conduct of the priests and His regulation of their varied ministries (Lev 21; Num 18). From this instruction, it is apparent that they were called into a high vocation and were expected to contribute to the development of the religious and civil life of the nation. However, a careful study of Leviticus 16:21 and Numbers 18 reveal that the priests were fallible men who had to strive for holiness in much the same way as their fellow Israelites. Priests were assigned to fulfill certain functions or responsibilities, namely, teaching of Torah, performing religious duties/rites, guardians of the temple or to keep the shrine and sacred things in order, meditate on behalf of the people, settled the dispute between parties whenever it is necessary, and so on.

The study also revealed that priestly office experienced much instability in the course of history of Israel. Priests also received prophetic criticism due to the unlovely characters such as the sons of Eli and Amaziah, the priest of Bethel. Prophets disapproved the attitude of worship and a mere cultic observance performed by priests. Prophetic criticism on priests was the failure to convey to the people the knowledge of God which it was their duty to teach.

The discussion of prophets, their experience of call, the messages that they received and their functions comprise third section. The understanding of the office of the prophet which we have found in prophets certainly is the result only of a long historical development. There is no doubt that the offices of prophet, priest, and king did not exist together as harmoniously as is often assumed. Especially the origin, tradition, historical development, and theological implications of the office of the prophet and of the king necessitate competition.

It is of fundamental importance to recognize that the concept of the kingship of Yahweh by no means has its presupposition in the earthly Davidic kingdom, but rather is linked with the prophet as his vizier. During monarchic era, particularly in the reign of David, prophets were given more freedom to exercise their function even in the royal court. It is important to notice that throughout the history of Israel, prophets gain more and more freedom in their role as prophets; they play a dialectical role in most of the occasions, like that performed by Nathan in judging the sin of King David.

Prophets dealt with the spiritual needs of the people, political, social, and religious conditions and affairs of the time. The prophet represented a voice independent of that kingly power, a voice from God to the power structures primarily, but also to and for the people. They also proposed and advocated such remedial measures and counsels as would bring the nation and people back into a proper relationship with God. All of the prophets understood their proclamation of God's Word in the context of the traditions of covenant community. They were interpreters of the community faith traditions. Prophets admonished, warned, directed, interceded, taught and counselled. Far more importantly they stood at the walls to see what Yahweh is doing that he may call the body to respond.

In short, the prophets model a pattern of leadership that finds its authority in God but its context in God's people. The study also revealed that though prophets did not hold any set-up or permanent office, they played important role in the lives of the people in general and monarchs in particular. One of their main tasks was to convey the message of Yahweh to the monarch and intervene in critical situation particularly political crisis.

The third chapter "Leadership challenges in the Eighth Century BCE Israel: A Historical Overview" introduced the problems or crises that arose because of the lack of proper leadership in the eighth century BCE Israel. Various issues related to political, social, economic, and religious overshadow the life of the people during the eighth century BCE Israel. All these issues brought political instability, social unrest, and religious nominalism. The political instability in South and North Israel caused a downfall of the kingdoms. As a nation, the Northern Israel was taken into captivity and the kingdom was torn into pieces and later the same happened to South Israel. Socially, the society has lost its moral and ethical values. The social sins, however, dispense justice, which had left bitterness behind and affected their relationship with Yahweh. Corruption, greed, oppression and exploitation crept into the just society. Religiously, the sacred cord of right relationship with Yahweh was broken. All these happened because of the lack of proper leadership and thus, the situation demanded leaders who can lead the people of Israel through the crises.

The fourth chapter discussed "Prophetic Leadership in the Eighth Century BCE Israel," the leadership model portrayed by the prophets. In the eighth century BCE Israel, prophets such as Amos, Hosea, Isaiah and Micah emerged with different characteristics to the earlier prophets. Although, the prophets certainly had spiritual experiences, they did not prophesy in a state of ecstasy and neither were they miracle-workers. They relied more on argument, reasoning and preaching. Their appearance created a great impact in the history of Israel.

Like the other prophets, they spoke out against social corruption and oppression of the poor. The concern for social justice was the genuine subject of the prophets' proclamation. They denounced injustice at all levels of Israelite society. Their prophetic social criticism was direct, vivid, and hard-hitting. While addressing the targeted groups about their responsibility in matters of injustice and corruption, for instance, Amos, Isaiah, and Micah highlighted the drastic consequences of their policies and practices for the underprivileged class of the society. Thus, they pointed out the privileged elite's (royal officers') failure to recognize that the effect of their conduct led to the ruin of the nation. In fact, corruption was so rampant that anyone who dared to act with integrity and dispense justice incurred the wrath and scorn of their colleagues.

They stood against the darkened conscience of the people and of the nation. They knew the ambitions of world conquerors like the Assyrian, the weakness of small nations like Israel and Judah, the petty intrigues that put personal gain before national welfare, and the shallow superficiality that made religion a hollow mockery. Theirs seems to be a hopeless cause. Their world did not seem to be worth saving. The people of their day seemed to be unfaithful beyond all hope. The prophets' hope for a genuine return of their people to God was repeatedly dashed in the dust. Yet in spite of it all, the prophets were right because they challenged to centre their thinking and their living in God and to speak their message from God.

The prophets displayed a good model of leadership through their life and ministry. Their concern was different from other leaders. They were the main critics of the monarchs, royal officials, religious leaders and society in general. Thus, one can conclude that without prophetic ministry, the executive or administrative role tends to revert to the kingly, the fallacy in which a human being or human structure becomes totalitarian and thus idolatrous.

The discussion of the personalities of these prophets, their activities, participation in political, religion and society as a whole revealed that the prophets portrayed different kind of leadership from that of royal and priestly leadership in ancient Israel.

The fifth chapter focused on "Patterns of Prophetic Leadership." The chapter discussed some challenges for the development of spiritual leaders for the churches today in the light of the eighth century BCE prophets. They were successful leaders. They are worthy examples for present day leaders, though they lived centuries back. They never considered themselves as great but yet their personalities and leadership qualities entitle them to be called a worthy minister model.

The prophets both taught and lived as though with God, there was always light ahead. The prophetic message delivered in their day is pertinent to us because the verdict of history is that the prophets saw clearly and lived impressively in a time when their world, like ours, was crumbling under its own terrific weight. The prophetic spirit demonstrated by the great prophets of eighth century BCE Israel is the spirit which is never overcome by the improper circumstances of life but which encourages leaders to make the choices that profoundly influence the destiny of the race. The prophets in their day gave the foundation for the belief that God controls the destiny of the nation.

Israelite prophets encouraged and challenged leaders to see history with the larger perspective out of which an adequate philosophy of history is born. Whatever the outcome of the historic battles of their world, the prophets called for decisions that would lead to heroic and abundant living. The prophets demanded that religion become the vital and controlling force, not only in personal living, but also in national growth and international statesmanship. One of their challenges was even though other nations put their faith in the sword, the faith of Israel and Judah need not be that of the sword. Rather, their mission was to demonstrate to the world a high moral integrity based on faith in God and obedience to God.

Leadership is God's given task for Israel. She was expected to lead the world community. The challenge of the day is the challenge of developing quality leadership who would be leading, guiding and encouraging people to achieve the goal, full of vision and a dedicated life for the cause of the one who called the leaders. The troublesome situation demands troubled leaders who would come forward and sacrifice their lives and restore peace and harmony in the church as well as in the society at large in the midst of vice and corruption.

It is essential to learn from history and find hope for future. Here, the lives and ministries of Amos, Isaiah, Hosea, and Micah stand as a living source of encouragement for the leaders. Their leadership style remains life giving source for the development of effective and spirit filled leadership. It calls for a visionary leader not imaginary, a godly leader not godless. It also calls for a leader who is prayerful, active, courageous and persistent in action and committed to God for selfless service. The Church is the witness to this prophetic leadership and has the divine obligation to pass it on.

Bibliography

Abe, G. O. "Yahwism and Priesthood in the Old Testament." *The Asia Journal of Theology* 8 (1994): 251-260.

Ackroyd, Peter R. "An Interpretation of the Babylonian Exile: A Study of 2 Kings 20, Isaiah 38-39." *Scottish Journal of Theology* 21 (1974): 329-52.

__________ "Hosea." In *Peake's Commentary on the Bible.* Edited by Matthew Black and H. H. Rowley. London: Thomas Nelson & Sons, 1962.

__________ *The People of the Old Testament.* Bangalore: The United Theological College, 1986.

__________ *The Second Book of* Samuel. London: Cambridge, 1977.

Adams, Robert Merrihew. "How Can I Give You Up, O Ephraim?" *Theology Today* 63 (2006): 88-93.

Aerathedathu, Thomas. "Social Teachings of Amos-Its Relevance to the Indian Situation." *Indian Journal of Spirituality* 4 (1991): 22-42.

Aharoni, Yohanan. *The Archaeology of the Land of Israel from the Prehistoric Beginning to the End of the First Temple Period.* Philadelphia: The Westminster Press, 1982.

Ahlstrom, G. W. *Royal Administration and National Religion in Ancient Palestine.* Vol. 1. Leiden: E. J. Brill, 1982.

Albertz, Rainer. *A History of Israelite Religion in the Old Testament Period. Vol. I: From the Beginning to the End of the Monarchy.* Louisville: Westminster Press, 1994.

Alden, Robert L. "Ecstasy and the Prophets." *Bulletin of the Evangelical Theological Society* 9 (1966): 149-156.

Alexander, T. D. *From Paradise to the Promised Land: An Introduction to the Pentateuch.* 2nd ed. Carlisle: Paternoster Press, 2002.

Alt, Albrecht. *Essays on Old Testament History and Religion*. Translated by R. A. Wilson. Oxford: Basil Blackwell, 1966.

Andersen, Francis I and David Noel Freedman. *Amos: A New Translation with Introduction and Commentary.* New York: Doubleday, 1989.

__________ *Hosea.* New York: Doubleday, 1980.

Armerding, Carl E. *The Old Testament and Criticism.* Michigan: W. B. Eerdmans Publishing Co, 1984.

Asen, A. Bernhard. "No, Yes and Perhaps in Amos and the Yahwist." *VT* XLIII (1993): 433-441.

Balasundaram, Franklyn J. *Prophetic Voices of Asia: Part I.* Sri Lanka: Centre for Society and Religion, 1992.

Barackman, Paul F. "Interpretation and Communication: Preaching from Amos." *Interpretation* 13 (1959): 296-315.

Barker, Margaret. "Hezekiah's Boil." *JSOT* 95 (2001): 31-42.

Barre, Michael L. "Restoring the 'Lost' Prayer in the Psalm of Hezekiah (Isaiah 38:16- 17b)." *JBL* 114 (1995): 385-399.

__________ "Textual and Rhetorical-Critical Observations on the Last Servant Song (Isaiah 52:13-53:12)." *CBQ* 62 (2000): 1-27.

Barstad, Hans M. "No Prophets? Recent Developments in Biblical Prophetic Research and Ancient Near Eastern Prophecy." *JSOT* 57 (1993): 39-60.

Barton, John. *Reading the Old Testament: Method in Biblical Study*. Sheffield: Sheffield Academic Press, 1984.

__________ *The Authority of the Old Testament.* Nashville: Abingdon Press, 1967.

Baudissin, Wolf. "Priests and Levites." In *A Dictionary of the Bible.* Vol. IV. Edited by James Hastings, et al. Edinburgh: T&T Clark, 1947.

Beli, Skip. "Learning, Changing, And Doing: A Model For Transformational Leadership Development In Religious And Non-Profit Organizations." *JRL* 9 (2010): 93-111.

Berry, Donald K. *An Introduction to Wisdom and Poetry of the Old Testament.* Nashville: Broadman & Holman, 1995.

Bewer, Julius A. *The Literature of the Old Testament in the Historical Development.* Massechetus: University press, 1962.

Bhushan, B. *Dictionary of Sociology*. New Delhi: Anmol Publications, 1997.

Birch, Bruce C. "Choosing of Saul at Mizpah." *CBQ* 37 (1975): 447-57.

__________ "Moral Agency, Community, and the Character of God in the Hebrew Bible." *Semeia* 66 (1995): 23-42.

__________ "Reclaiming Prophetic Leadership." *Ex auditu* 22 (2006): 10-25.

Blenkinsopp, Joseph. "The Social Roles of Prophets in Early Achaemenid Judah." *JSOT* 93 (2001): 39-58.

__________ *Isaiah 1-39.* New York: Doubleday, 2000.

__________ *Sage, Priest, Prophet.* Louisville: Westminster, 1995.

Boadt, Lawrence. "The Poetry of Prophetic Persuasion: Preserving the Prophet's Persona." *CBQ* 59 (1997): 1-27.

Bosma, J. Carl. "Creation in Jeopardy: A Warning to Priests (Hosea 4:1-3)." *Calvin Theological Journal* 34 (1999): 64-116.

Bramer, Stephen J. "Analysis of the Structure of Amos." *Bibliotheca Sacra* 156 (1999): 171-74.

__________ "The Literary Genre of the Book of Amos." *Bibliotheca Sacra* 156 (1999): 42-60.

Bright, John. *A History of Israel.* 3rd ed. Philadelphia: The Westminster Press, 1981.

Brotzman, Ellis R. *Old Testament.* Grand Rapids: Baker Books, 1994.

Brown, Sydney Lawrence. *The Book of Hosea.* London Methuen and Co, 1932.

Brueggemann, Walter. "Ancient Israel on Political leadership: Between the Book Ends." *Political Theology* 8 (2007): 455-469.

__________ "The 'Uncared For' Now Cared For (Jer. 30:12-17): A Methodological Consideration." *JBL* 104 (1985): 419-428.

__________ *A Social Reading of the Old Testament: Prophetic Approaches to Israel's Communal Life.* Edited by Miller, Patrick. Minneapolis: Fortress Press, 1994.

__________ *Texts Under Negotiation: The Bible and Post Modern Imagination.* Minneapolis: Fortress Press, 1993.

__________ *The Prophetic Imagination.* 2nd ed. Minneopolis: Fortress Press, 2001.

__________ *Worship in Ancient Israel.* Nashville: Abingdon Press, 2005.

__________ "That the World may be Redescribed." *Interpretation* 56 (2002): 359-367.

__________ "Prophetic Ministry in the National Security State." *Theology Today* 65 (2008): 285-311.

Budd, Philip John. "Priestly Instruction in Pre-Exilic." *VT* 23 (1973): 1-14.

Bullock, C. Hassel. *An Introduction to the Old Testament Poetic Books: The Wisdom and Sons of Israel.* Chicago: Moody Press, 1979.

Buttrick, George A. Ed. *Interpreter's Dictionary of the Bible.* Vol.1. New York: Abingdon Press, 1962.

Cahen, Chaim, et al. *Birkat Shalo: Studies in the Bible, Ancient Near eastern Literature, and Postbibilcal Judaism Presented to Shalom M. Paul on the Occasion of His Seventieth Birthday.* Winona Lake: Eisenbrauns, 2008.

Caldecott, W. Shaw. "Jeroboam II." In *The International Standard Bible Encyclopedia.* Vol. 3. Edited by James ORR, et al. Grand Rapids: Eerdmans Publishing, 1955.

Carroll R. Mark Daniel. "Imagining the Unthinkable: Exposing the Idolatry of National Security in Amos." *Ex auditu* 24 (2008): 37-54.

__________ *Context for Amos: Prophetic Poetics in Latin American Perspective,* JSOTSup 132. Sheffield: Sheffield Academic Press, 1992.

Carroll, R. P. *When Prophecy Failed.* London: SCM Press, 1979.

Case, Robert A. "Rehoboam: A Study in Failed leadership." *Presbterion* 14 (1988): 55-77.

Casto, R. Michael. "Conversing with the Text Application of Conversational Exegesis to Hosea 4:1-3." *Duke Divinity School Review* 40 (1975): 18-33.

Ceresko, Anthony R. "Poetry and the New Exodus." *CBQ* 56 (1994): 42-55.

__________ *The Old Testament: A Liberation Perspective*. Bangalore: St. Pauls, 2001.

Chalmers, R. Scott. *The Struggle of Yahweh and El for Hosea's Israel.* Sheffield: Sheffield Phoenix Press, 2008.

Chandran, J. Russell. "Justice in the Old Testament." In *Bible Speaks Today: Essay in Honour of Gnana Robinson.* Edited by Daniel Jones Muthunayagom. Delhi: ISPCK, 2000.

Chaney, M. L. "Systemic Study of the Israelite Monarchy." *Semeia* 37 (1986): 53-76.

Cherian, C. M. "People in the Prophetical Perspective." *Jeevadhara* 16 (1986).

Childs, Brevard S. *Introduction to the Old Testament as Scripture.* Philadelphia: Fortress, 1979.

__________ *Isaiah.* Louisville: Westminster John Knox Press, 2001.

Chinitz, Jacob. "Were the Prophets Opposed to Sacrifice?" *JBL* 36 (2008): 73-80.

Chisholm Jr., Robert B. *A Handbook on the Prophets.* Grand Rapids: Baker Academic, 2002.

Clements, Ronald E. *Isaiah 1-3*. Grand Rapids: Wm. B. Eerdmans Publication Company, 1980.

__________ *A Century of Old Testament Study*. London: Lutterworth Press, 1979.

Cliffprd, S. J. Richard J. "Prophetic Leader." *TBT* 39 (2001): 69-74.

Cobb, William Henry. "The Servant of Jahveh." *JBL* 14 (1895): 95-113.

Cogan, Mordechai and Haim Tadmor. "II Kings." *A New Translation with Introduction and Commentary*. New York: Doubleday & Company, 1988.

Coggins, Richard, Anthony Phillips and Michael Knibb. eds. *Israel's Prophetic Tradition: Essays in Honor of Peter R. Ackroyd.* Cambridge: Cambridge University press, 1982.

Coggins, R. J. and J. L. Houlden, eds. *A Dictionary of Biblical Interpretation.* London: SCM Press, 1990.

Coggins, Richard J. "History and Story in OT Study." *JSOT* 54 (1979): 36-46.

__________ "The Old Testament and the Poor." *The Expository Times* 99 (1987): 11-20.

Cohen, Martin A. "The Role of the Shilonite Priesthood in the United Monarchy of Ancient Israel." *Union College Annual* 36 (1965): 59-98.

Cohen, Simon. "Amos *Was* a Navi." *HUCA* 32 (1961): 175-178.

__________ "The Political Background of the Words of Amos." *HUCA* 36 (1965): 153-160.

Collins, J. J. "Proverbial Wisdom and the Yahwist Vision." *Semeia* 17 (1980): 1-17.

Colwell, Jill Carlson. "One Who Trusts Will Not Panic: Providence and The Prophet of Desecuritization." *EzAud* 24 (2008): 101-21.

Conard, Edgar W. *Reading Isaiah.* Minneapolis: Fortress Press, 1991.

Cook, Stephen L. and Ronald A. Simkins. "Introduction: Case Studies from the Second Wave of Research in the Social World of Hebrew Bible." *Semeia* 87 (1999): 1-14.

Coote, Robert B. *Amos Among the Prophets: Composition and Theology*. Philadelphia: Fortress Press, 1981.

Cormode, Scott. "Multi-Layered Leadership: The Christian Leader as Builder, Shepherd, and Gardener." *JRL* 1 (2002): 69-104.

Conrad, E. W. "The Royal Narratives and the Structure of the Book of Isaiah." *JSOT* 41 (1988): 67-81.

Couey, J. Blake. "Amos vii 10-17 and Royal Attitudes Toward Prophecy in the Ancient Near East." *VT* 58 (2008): 300-314.

Crenshaw James L. "Prolegomenon." In *Studies in Ancient Israelite Wisdom.* Edited by J. Crenshaw. New York: Ktav, 1976.

__________ "The Sage in Proverbs." In *The Sage in Israel and the Ancient Near East.* Edited by J. G. Gammie and L. G. Perdue. Winona Lake: Eisenbrauns, 1990.

__________ *Education in Ancient Israel.* Sydney: Doubleday, 1988.

__________ *Old Testament Wisdom-Introduction.* London: SCM Press, 1981.

__________ *Prophetic Conflict: Its Effect Upon Israelites Religion.* Atlanta: SBL, 1971.

Cross, Frank M. *Canaanite Myth and Hebrew Epic.* Cambridge: Harvard University Press, 1973.

Cuff, E. C., W. W. Sharrock and D. W. Farncis. *Perspectives in Sociology.* London: Routledge, 1992.

Dam, C. Van. "Priestly Clothing." In *Dictionary of the Old Testament Pentateuch.* Edited by T. Desmond Alexander and David W Baker. Illinois: InterVarsity Press, 2002.

Darr, Katheryn Pfisterer. *Isaiah's Vision and the Family of God.* Louisville: Westminster John Knox, 1994.

David L. Petersen, ed. *Prophecy in Israel: Search for an Identity.* Philadelphia: Fortress Press, 1987.

David M. Howard Jr. "The Case for Kingship in Deuteronomy and the Former Prophets." *Westminster Theological Journal* 52 (1990): 101-115.

David, Firth and H. G. M. Williamson, eds. *Interpreting Isaiah: Issues and Approaches.* Downers Grove: InterVarsity Press, 2009.

Davies, E. W. *Prophecy and Ethical tradition of Israel.* Sheffield: JSOT Press, 1981.

Davies, G. I. *Hosea.* Grand Rapids: Wm. B. Eerdmans, 1992.

Davies, Philip R. and John William Rogerson. "The Old Testament World." *Tyndale Bulletin* 17 (1966).

Delitzsch, F. *Commentary on the Old Testament in Ten Volumes.* Grand Rapids: Eerdmans, 1973.

Dempsey, Carol J. "Economic Injustice in Micah." *BT* (1994): 272-76.

__________ "Micah 2-3: Literary Artistry, Ethical Message and Some Considerations About the Image of Yahweh and Micah." *JSOT* 85 (1999): 117-128.

Dietrich, Walter. *The Early Monarchy in Israel: The Tenth Century B.C.E.* Translated by Joachim Vette. Atlanta: SBL, 2007.

Dommershausen, "כֹּהֵן." In *Theological Dictionary of the Old Testament.* Vol. 7. Edited by G. Johannes, et al. Translated by David E. Green. Grand Rapids; Michigan: William B. Eerdmans Publishing Company, 1995.

Donner, H. "The Separation State of Israel and Judah." In *Israelite and Judean History.* Edited by J. H. Hayes and J. M. Miller. Philadelphia: Westminster, 1977.

Dorsey, D. A. "Literary Architecture and Aural Structuring Techniques in Amos." *Bibloca* 73 (1992): 305-330.

Driver, Samuel R. *An Introduction to the Literature of the Old Testament.* 7th ed. Edinburgh: T&T Clark, 1907.

__________ *Isaiah: His Life and Times and the Writings Which Bears his Name* New York: Fleming H. Revell Co., n.y.

Durausungh, C. "Reflections on Theological Hermeneutics in the Indian Context." *Indian Journal of Theology* 31 (1982): 259-278.

Eaton, John H. "The Origin of the Book of Isaiah." *VT* 9 (1959): 138-157.

__________ *Mysterious Messengers: A Course on Hebrew Prophecy from Amos Onwards.* London: SCM Press, 1997.

Edward, J. Young. "Call of Moses." *Westminster Theological Journal* 30 (1967): 1-23.

Elliott, John H. *What is Social-Scientific Criticism?* Minneapolis: Fortress Press, 1993.

Escobar, Donoso S. "Social Justice in the Book of Arnos." *Review and Expositor* 92 (1995): 169-174.

Exum, J. C and D. J. A. Clines, eds. *The New Literary Criticism and the Hebrew Bible*, JSOTSup, 143. Sheffield: Sheffield Academic Press, 1993.

F. Cryer. *Divination in Ancient Israel and its Near Eastern Environment: A Socio-Historical Investigation,* JSOTSup 142. Sheffield: JSOT Press, 1994.

Farr, George. "The Language of Amos, Popular or Cultic?" *VT* 16 (1966): 312-324.

Fechter, Friedrich. "Priesthood in Exile According to the Book of Ezekiel." *SBLSP* 2000. Atlanta: SBL, 2000.

Fideles, Paul S. "The Cross of Hosea Revisited: The Meaning of Suffering in the Book of Hosea." *Review and Expositor* 90 (1993): 175-190.

Fiorenza, Elizabeth S. "Ethics of Biblical Interpretation Decentering Biblical Scholarship." *JBL* 107 (1988): 3-17.

Flanagan, J. W. "Chiefs in Israel." *JSOT* 20 (1981): 47-73.

Foster, Robert L. "Shepherds, Sticks, and Social Destabilization: A Fresh Look at Zechariah 11:4-17." *JBL* 126 (2007): 735-53.

Fox, Michael. *Proverbs 1-9.* New York: Doubleday, 2000.

Franco, F. "The structured Nature of Poverty in India." In *Poverty in India: Challenges and Response.* Edited by J. Murichan. Bangalore: A Xavier Board Pub. 1988.

Freedman, David Noel and Rebecca Frey. *Inspired Speech: Prophecy in the Ancient Near East: Essay in Honour of Herbert B. Huffmon*. JSOTSup 378. London: T&T Clark, 2004.

Freedman, David Noel, eds. *ABD.* 5 vols. New York: Doubleday, 1992.

Fretheim, T. E. "Source Criticism, OT." In *The Interpreter's Dictionary of the Bible, Supplementary Volume*. Edited by Keith Crim, et al. Nashville: Abingdon Press, 1982.

Frick, Frank S. "Social Science Methods and Theories of Significance for the Study of the Israelite Monarchy: A Critical Review Essay." *Semeia* 37 (1986): 9-52.

Gabel, John B. Charles B. Wheeler and Anthony D. York. *The Bible as Literature: An Introduction.* New York: Oxford University Press, 2000.

Gerbrandt, Gerald Eddie. *Kingship According to the Deuteronomistic History.* Atlanta: Scholar Press, 1986.

Gerstenberger, E. "כון." In *Theological Lexicon of the Old Testament*. Vol. 2. Edited by Ernest Jenni and Claus Westermann. Translated by Mark E. Biddle. Peabody: Hendrickson Publishers, Inc, 1997.

Gilbert, Pierre. "The Foundation of Imprecation in Israel's Eight-Century prophets." *Direction* 35 (2006): 44-58.

Giles, Terry. "A Note on the Vocation of Amos in 7:14." *JBL* 111 (1992): 690-69.

Giuseppe, Ricciotti. *The History of Israel.* Vol. I. Milwaukee: The Bruce Pub. Company, 1955.

Glenny, W. Edward. *Finding Meaning in the Text: Tradition and Theology in the Septuagint of Amos.* Boston: Brill, 2009.

Gluck, J. J. "Nagid-shepherd." *VT* 13 (1963): 144-150.

Goldingay, J. "Hermeneutics." In *Dictionary of the Old Testament Pentateuch.* Edited by T. D. Alexander & D. W. Baker. Illinois: InterVarsity Press, 2002.

Gordon, Cyrus H. *The Ancient Near East.* 3rd ed. New York: W. W. Norton & Company, 1965.

Gottwald, Norman K. "Social Class as an Analytic and Hermeneutical Category in Biblical Studies." *JBL* 112 (1993): 3-22.

__________ *A Light to the Nation: An Introduction to the Old Testament.* New York: Harper & Brothers, 1959.

__________ *The Hebrew Bible: A Socio-Literary Reading*. Philadelphia: Fortress Press, 1985.

__________ *The Tribes of Yahweh: A Sociology of the Religion of Liberated Israel, 1250-1050 BCE.* New York: Orbis Books, 1979.

__________ "Sociology." In *ABD*. Vol. 6. Edited by David Noel Freedman, et al. New York: Doubleday, 1992.

Grabbe, Lester L and Alice Odgen Bells, eds. *The Priests in the Latter Prophets: The Portrayal of Priest, Prophets and Other Religious Specialists in the Latter prophets.* JSOTSup 408. New York: T&T Clark, 2004.

Gray, G. B. *A Critical Commentary on the Book of Isaiah: 1-XXVII.* Edinburgh: T&T Clark, 1975.

Gray, Mark. *Rhetoric and Social Justice in Isaiah.* JSOTSup 432. New York: T&T Clark, 2006.

Gray, John .*1 & 11 Kings: A Commentary.* London: SCM Press Ltd, 1964.

Greenspoon, David. "The Prophet as Watcher." *JBL* 27 (1999): 29-35.

Grobel, K. "Form Criticism." In *The Interpreter's Dictionary of the Bible.* Vol. 2. Edited by George A. Buttrick, et al. Nashville: Abingdon Press, 1982.

Groves, J. W. *Actualization and Interpretation in the Old Testament.* SBLDS 86; Atlanta: Scholars Press, 1987.

Gunkel, Hermann. *The Legends of Genesis.* New York: Schocken, 1970.

__________ *The Psalms.* Philadelphia: Fortress Press, 1967.

Guyette, Fred W. "Amos the Prophet: A Meditation on the Richness of of 'Justice.'" *Jewish Bible Quarterly* 30 (2008): 15-21.

Hadjiev, Tchavdar S. *The Composition and Redaction of the Bible of Amos.* Berlin: W.de Cruyter, 2009.

Hahn, Herbert F. *Old Testament in Modern Research.* Philadelphia: Muhlenberg Press, 1954.

Hallo, William W. and William Kelly Simpson. *The Ancient Near East: A History.* New York: Harcourt Brace Jovanovich, Publishers, 1971.

Henson, Paul D. *The People Called: The Growth of Community in the Bible.* San Francisco: Harper & Row Publishers, 1986.

Harper, William Rainey. *A Critical and Exegetical Commentary on Amos and Hosea.* Edinburgh: T&T Clark, 1905.

Harrelson, Walter J. "Knowledge of God in the Church." *Interpretation* 30 (1976): 12-17.

Harrison, Roland K. *Introduction to the Old Testament.* Grand Rapids: Wm B Eerdmans Publishing Co, 1969.

Hasel, Gerhard F. *Understanding the Book of Amos: Basic Issues in Current Interpretations.* Grand Rapids: Baker Book House, 1991.

Hauer, Christian E. "Who was Zadok." *JBL* 82 (1963): 89-94.

Hayes, John H. "Prophetism at Mari and Old Testament Parallels." *Anglican Theological Review* 49 (1969): 397-409.

Hayes, John H. *Amos the Eighth Century Prophet: His Time and his Preaching.* Nashville: Abingdon Press, 1988.

__________ *An Introduction to Old Testament Study.* 1979, Reprint. Nashville: Abingdon Press, 1980.

__________ and Frederick Prussner. *Old Testament Theology: Its History and Development.* Atlanta: John Knox Press, 1985.

__________ and J. Maxwell Miller. *A History of Ancient Israel and Judah.* Westminster: John Knox, 1986.

Heicksen, Martin H. "Tekoa: Historical and Cultural Profile." *JETS* 13 (1970): 83-89.

Heschel, Abraham J. *The Prophets.* New York: Harper & Row, 1962.

Hester, H. I. *The Heart of Hebrew History.* Missouri: William Jewell Press, 1995.

Hillel, Daniel. *The Natural History of the Bible: An Environmental Exploration of the Hebrew Scriptures.* NY: Columbia University Press, 2006.

Himmelfarb, Martha. *A Kingdom of Priest: Ancestry and Merit in Ancient Judaism.* Philadelphia: University of Pennsylvania Press, 2006.

Hoffer, Vicki. "An Exegesis of Isaiah 38:21." *JSOT* 56 (1992): 68-84.

Hoffmeyer, Jeffrey H. "Covenant and Creation: Hosea 4:1-3." *Review and Expositor* 102 (2005): 143-151.

Holladay, William L. "Jeremiah and Moses: Further Observations." *JBL* 85 (1966): 17- 27.

Holladay, William L. "The Background of Jeremiah's Self-Understanding-Moses, Samuel, and Psalm 22." *JBL* 83 (1964): 153-164.

Horn, Siegfried H. "The Divided Monarchy." In *Ancient Israel: A Short History from Abraham to the Roman Destruction of the Temple.* Edited by Hershel Shanks. Washington: Biblical Archaeology Society, 1988.

Hornby, A. S., eds. *Oxford Advance Learner's Dictionary.* Oxford: Oxford University Press, 2010.

House, Paul R. "Amos and Literary Criticism." *Review and Expositor* 92 (1995):175-187.

__________ "Isaiah's Call and Its Context in Isaiah 1-6." *Criswell Theological Review* 6 (1993): 220-221.

Howington, Nolam P. "Towards an Ethical Understanding of Amos." *Review and Expositor* 63 (1966): 405-412.

Hubbard, David Allan. "The wisdom Movement and Israel's Covenant of Faith." *Tyndale Bulletin* 17 (1966): 3-33.

__________ *Joel and Amos: An Introduction and Commentary.* Leicester: IVP, 1989.

Huffmon, Herbert B. "The Expansion of Prophecy in the Mari Archives: New Texts, New Readings, New Information." In *Prophecy and Prophets: The Diversity of Contemporary Issues in Scholarship.* Edited by Y. Gitay. SBLSS; Atlanta: Scholars, 1997.

__________ et al. *The Quest for the Kingdom of God: Studies in Honor of G. E. Mendenhall.* Indiana: Eisenbrauns, 1983.

__________ "Prophecy in the Mari Letters." *Biblical Archaeologist* 31 (1968): 101-124.

Hyatt, J. Philip. "The Book of Amos." *Interpretation* 3 (1949): 338-348.

Ishida, T. "The Leaders of the Tribal League 'Israel' in the Pre-Monarchic Period." *RB* 80 (1973): 514-530.

Izu, Yoichi. "Theological Significance of the Hezekiah Narrative in Isaiah." *BV* 35 (2001): 77-86.

Jacob, Edmond. *Theology of the Old Testament.* Translated by Arthur W. Heathgote and Philip J. Allcogk. New York: Harper and Brothers Publishers, 1958.

Jacobs, Mignon R. *The Conceptual Coherence of the Book of Micah.* JSOTSup 322. Sheffield: Sheffield Academic Press, 2001.

Jacobson, Rolf A. "What Every Christian Should Know about Amos and Hosea." *Word & World* 28 (2008): 182-191.

James, Hauan, Michael. "The Background and Meaning of Amos 5:17." *Theological Review* 79 (1986): 337-348.

James, TGH. *An Introduction to Ancient Egypt.* New York: Farrar Straus Giroux, 1979.

Jang, Se-Hoon. *Particularism and Universalism in the Book of Isaiah: Isaiah's Implications for a Pluralistic World from a Korean Perspective.* Bern: Peter Lang Publishing, 2005.

Japhet, J. Sara . *I & II Chronicles: A Commentary.* London: SCM, 1993.

Jensen, Joseph. *Ethical Dimensions of the Prophets.* Collegeville, MN: Liturgical press, 2006.

Jenson, Philip. "כהן." In *New International Dictionary of Old Testament Theology & Exegesis.* Vol. 2. Edited by Willem A. VanGemeren, et al. Grand Rapids, Michigan: Zondervan, 1997.

Jeremias, Jörg. *The Book of Amos.* Westminster: John Knox, 1998.

Jesurathnam, K. "Thus says the Lord: The Dynamism of the Hebrew Prophetic Message and its Implications for the Contemporary Dalit Prophetic Discourse." *Bangalore Theological Forum* 41 (2009): 179-197.

Job, J. Anbalagan. *Prophecy*. New Delhi: ISPCK, 2005.

Johannes G., et al. *Theological Dictionary of the Old Testament.* Vol. VII. Translated by David E. Green. Grand Rapids, Michigan: William B. Eerdmans Publishing Company, 1995.

Johnson, Aubrey R. *The Cultic Prophet in Ancient IsraelI.* 2nd ed. Cardiff: University of Wales Press, 1962.

Jones, D. R. "Sacrifices and Holiness." In *Sacrifice and Redemption*. Edited by S. W. Sykes. Cambridge: Cambridge University Press, 1991.

Kaiser, Otto. *Isaiah 1-12:A Commentary. OTL*. London: SCM, 1983.

Kaiser, Walter C. *A History of Israel from the Bronze Age through the Jewish War.* Nashville: Boardman & Holman Publishers, 1998.

__________ *Toward Old Testament Ethics.* Grand Rapids: Zondervan, 1983.

Kallikuzhuppil, John. "Liberation in Amos and Micah." *Bible Bhashyam* 11 (1985): 215- 223.

Kautsky, John H. *The Politics of Aristocratic Empire*. Chapel Hill: The University of North Caroline Press, 1982.

Keil, Carl Friedrich and F.Delitzsch. "Amos." In *The Twelve Minor Prophets.* Vol. 1 Translated by James Martin. 2nd ed. Grand Rapids: Eerdmans, 1982.

Kelley, Page H. "Micah, Nahum, Habakkuk, Zephaniah, Haggai, Zecharaih, Malachi." *LBBC.* Vol. 14. Nashville: Broadman Press, 1994.

Kelly, Page H. "Contemporary Study of Amos and Prophetism." *Review and Expositor* 63 (1966): 375-385.

Kennedy, George D. *New Testament Interpretation Through Rhetorical Criticism.* Chapel Hill: The University of North Carolina Press, 1984.

Kennedy, James M. "Yahweh's Strongman? The Characterization of Hezekiah in the Book of Isaiah." *Perspectives in Religious Studies* 31 (2004): 383-397.

Keown, Gerald L. "The Prophet as Encourager." *Perspectives in Religious Studies* 35 (2008): 155-161.

Kettel, Bonnie. "Brevard Childs' Development of the Canonical Approach." *JSOT* 16 (1980): 2-11.

Killebrew, Ann E. *Biblical Peoples and Ethnicity: An Archaeological Study of Egyptians, Canaanites, Philistines, and Early Israel 1300-1100 B.C.E.* Atlanta: Society of Biblical Literature, 2005.

King, Philip J. *Amos, Hosea, Micah An Archaeological Commentary*. Philadelphia: The Westminster Press, 1988.

Kitz, Anne Marie. "The Hebrew Terminology of Lot Casting and its Ancient Near Eastern Context." *CBQ* 2 (2000): 207-214.

Klein, Ralph W. "Liberated Leadership: Masters and 'Lords' in Biblical Perspective."*Currents and Theology and Mission* 9 (1982): 282-290.

Klein, William W. et al. *Introduction to Biblical Interpretation.* Dallas: Word Publishers, 1993.

Klingbeil, Gerald A. and Klingbeil, Martin. "The Prophetic Voice of Amos as a Paradigm for Christian in the Public Square." *Tyndale Bulletin* 58 (2007): 161-182.

Knierim, Rolf. "Old Testament Form Criticism Reconsidered." *Interpretation* 27 (1973): 435-468.

Knight, Douglas A. "Political right and power in monarchic Israel." *Semeia* 60 (1994): 93-117.

Knight, George A. *Isaiah 40-55 Servant Theology*. Grand Rapids: W. B. Eerdmans Pub. Co., 1984.

Koch, Klaus. *The Growth of the Biblical Tradition: The Form-Critical Method.* 2nd ed. Translated by S. M. Cupitt. New York: Charles Scribner's Sons, 1969.

__________ *The Prophets: The Assyrian Period.* Vol. 1. London: SCM Press Ltd, 1982.

Kochuthara, Thomas. *Theology of Liberation and Ideology Critique*. New Delhi: Inter Cultural Publication, 1993.

Kumar, M. Chandra *Leadership Insights from Heroes of the Bible.* Secunderabad: Authentic Books, 2008.

Kruger, P. A. "Prophetic Imagery: On Metaphors and Similes in the Book Hosea." *Journal of Northwest Semitic Languages* 14 (1988): 143.

Laato, Antti. "Second Samuel 7 and Ancient Near Eastern Royal Ideology." *CBQ* 59 (1997): 244-269.

Laffey, Alice L. *An Introduction to the Old Testament: A Feminist Perspective.* Philadelphia: Fortress Press, 1985.

__________ *Wives, Harlots and Concubines: The Old Testament in Feminist Perspective*. London: SPCK, 1990.

Laney, J. Carl. "The Role of the Prophets in God's Case Against Israel." *Bibliotheca Sacra* 138 (1981): 313-325.

Levine, Nachman. "Twice as Much of Your Spirit: Pattern, Parallel and Paronomasia in the Miracles of Elijah and Elisha." *JSOT* 85 (1999): 25-46.

Leclerc, Thomas L. *Introduction to the Prophets: Their Stories, Sayings, and Scrolls.* New York: Paulist Press, 2007.

Leggett, Donald A. *Loving God and Disturbing Men Preaching from the Prophets.* Grand Rapids: Baker Book House, 1990.

Lemche, N. P. *Ancient Israel: A New History of Israelite Society.* Sheffield: Sheffield Academic Press, 1988.

Lessing, Reed. "Preaching like the Prophets: Using Rhetorical Criticism in the Appropriation of Old Testament Prophetic Literature."*Concordia Journal* 28 (2002): 391-408.

__________ "Upsetting the Status Quo: Preaching Like Amos." *Concordia Journal* 33 (2007): 285-298.

Lewis, Jack P. "A Prophet's Son (Amos 7:14) Reconsidered." *Restoration Quarterly* 49 (2007): 229-240.

Limburg, James. "Sevenfold Structure in the Book of Amos." *JBL* 106 (June 1987): 219-21.

Lindblom, Johannes. "Lot-casting in the Old Testament." *VT* 12 (1962): 164-78.

__________ *Prophecy in Ancient Israel.* Oxford: Blackwell, 1962.

Lieck, G. *The Babylonians: An Introduction.* London: Routledge, 2003.

Lochman, Shaull. "Ecumenical Theology of Revolution." *New Theology No. 6.* Edited by Martin E. Marty and Dean G. Perman. New York: Macmillan, 1969.

Long, Burke O. "Social Dimensions of Prophetic Conflict." *Semeia* 21 (1981): 31-53.

Longman III, Tremper. "Literary Approach to Old Testament Study." In *The Face of Old Testament Studies: A Survey of Contemporary Approach.* Edited by David W. Baker & Bill T. Arnold. Grand Rapids: Baker Books, 1999.

Love, Julian P. "Call of Isaiah: Exposition of Isaiah 6." *Interpretation* 11(1957): 291-294.

Lundbom, Jack R. "Contentious Priest and Contentious People in Hosea 4:1-10." *VT* 36 (1986): 52-70.

Lyn, Mehl. "The Call to Prophetic Ministry: Reflections on Jeremiah 1:4-10." *Currents in Theology and Mission* 8 (1981): 151-155.

Macintosh, A. A. *A Critical and Exegetical Commentary on Hosea.* Edinburgh: T&T Clark, 1997.

Maclean, Jennifer R. Berenson. "Micah 3: 5-12." *Interpretation* 56 (2002): 413-416.

Malina, Bruce J. "The Social Sciences and Biblical Interpretation." *Interpretation* 37 (1985): 229-245.

Manohar, Moses P. *Poverty and Human Rights: A Theological Perspective.* Delhi: ISPCK, 1997.

Marie, Kitz Anne. "Prophecy as Divination." *CBQ* 65 (2003): 22-42.

Marrs, Rick R. "Amos and the Power of Proclamation." *Restoration Quarterly* 40 (1998): 13-24.

__________ "Micah and the Task of Ministry." *Restoration Quarterly* 30 (1988): 1-16.

Martin, Robert K. "Dwelling in the Divine Life: The Transformational Dimension of Leadership and Practical Theology." *JRL* 3 (2004): 99-138.

Mason, Donald H. *Thus Saith the Lord: An Introduction to the Prophets of Israel.* Madras: Christian Literature Society, 1962.

Massey, James. *Communication and Community and Prophecy.* Delhi: Asia Region WACC, 1989.

Matthews, Victor H. *Social World of the Hebrew Prophets.* Peabody: Hendrickson Publication. Inc, 2001.

Maxwell, John C. *The 21 Irrefutable Laws of Leadership.* Nashville: Thomas Nelson Publishers, 1998.

__________ *Developing the Leader Within You.* New Delhi: Satyam Enterprises, n.y.

Maxwell, Miller J. "Saul's Rise to Power: Some Observations Concerning 1 Sam. 9:1-10:16; 10:26-11:15 and 13:2-14:46." *CBQ* 56 (1974): 157-174.

Mayes, Andrew. *The Old Testament in Sociological Perspective.* London: Marshall Pickering, 1989.

Mays, James Luther. "Words About the Words of Amos: Recent Study of the Book of Amos." *Interpretation* 13 (1959): 259-272.

__________ *Amos: A Commentary.* London: SCM Press, 1969.

__________ *Hosea. OTL.* Philadelphia: Westminster, 1969.

Maclean, Jennifer R. Berenson. "Micah 3:5-12." *Interpretation* 56 (2002): 413-416.

McCarter, P. Kyle. "The Historical David." *Interpretation* 40 (1986): 117-129.

McCarthy, Dannis J. "The Inauguration of Monarchy in Israel: A Form Critical Study of 1 Samuel 8-12." *Interpretation* 27 (1972): 401-412.

McComiskey and Thomas Edward. *The Minor Prophets: An Exegetical & Expository Commentary.* Grand Rapids: Baker, 1992.

McKeating, Henry. "Ezekiel 'Prophet like Moses'?" *JSOT* 61 (1994): 97-109.

__________ *Studying the Old Testament.* London: Epworth Press, 1979.

Mckenzie, Donald A. "Judge of Israel." *VT* 17 (1967): 118-121.

McKenzie, John L. *The World of the Judge*. Englewood Cliffs, NJ: prentice Hall, 1966.

__________ "Knowledge of God in Hosea." *Journal of Biblical Literature* 74 (1955): 22-27.

Mcnutt, Paula. *Reconstructing the History of Ancient Israel.* Louisville: Westminster John Knox Press, 1999.

Mendenhall, George E. *The Tenth Generation: The Origins of the Biblical Tradition.* London: The John Hopkins University Press, 1973.

__________ "The Monarchy." *Interpretation* 29 (1975): 155-170.

__________ "The Census Lists of Numbers 1 and 26." *JBL* 77 (1958): 52-66.

__________ "The Hebrew Conquest of Palestine." *Biblical Archaeologist* 25 (1962): 66-87.

Menezes, SJ Rui de. *The Cultural Context of the Old Testament.* Bangalore: Theological Publication in India, 2005.

Merrill, C. Tenney. "The Legitimate limits of Biblical Criticism." *Bulletin of the Evangelical Theological Study* 3 (1960): 89-92.

Mettinger, Tryggve N. D. *King and Messiah: The Civil and Sacral Legitimation of the Israelite Kings*. Lund: GWK Gleerup, 1976.

Meyers, C. L. and E. M. Meyers. *Zechariah 9-14: A New Translation with Introduction and Commentary.* New York: Doubleday, 1993.

Miller, Douglas B. "What the Preacher Forgot: The Rhetoric of Ecclesiastes." *CBQ* 62 (2000): 215-235.

Miller, Maxwell J. & John H. Hayes. *History of Ancient Israel and Judah*. 2nd ed. Louisville: Westminster John Knoz Press, 1982.

Miller, Patrick D. "The Prophetic Critique of Kings." *Ex auditu* 2 (1986): 82-95.

Mitchell, Eric A. "Micah-The Man and His Times." *Southwestern Journal of Theology* 46 (2003): 57-76.

Moberly, R.W. L. "'In God We Trust?' The Challenge of the Prophets." *ExAud* 24 (2008): 18-33.

Moore, Michael S. "Role Pre-Emption in the Israelite Priesthood." *VT* 46 (1996): 316- 329.

Moran, W. L. "New Evidence from Mari on the History of Prophecy." *Biblica* 50 (1969): 15-56.

Morgenstern, Julian. "Amos Studies IV: The Address of Amos-Text and Commentary." *HUCA* 32 (1961): 295-350.

Morlow, Hilary. *Biblical Prophets and Contemporary Environment Ethics: Re-Reading Amos, Hosea, and First Isaiah*. Oxford: Oxford University Press, 2009.

Motyer, J. Alec. *The Prophecy of Isaiah*. Leicester: InterVarsity Press, 1999.

__________ *The Day of the Lion: The Message of Amos.* London: Inter-Varsity, 1974.

Mowinckel, Sigmund. "Cult and Prophecy." In *Prophecy in Israel: Search for an Identity*. Edited by David L. Petersen. Philadelphia: Fortress Press, 1987.

__________ *The Psalms in Israel's Worship*. Oxford: University Press, 1962.

__________ *He That Cometh* Translated by G.W. Anderson. Oxford: Basil Blackwell, 1959.

Muilenberg, James. "Form Criticism and Beyond." *JBL* LXXXVII (1969): 1-18.

Mullins, Robert A. "Biblical Archaeology as a Social and Contextual Hermeneutic." *Didaskalia* 5 (1994): 66-82.

Murphy, Roland E. "Assumptions and Problems in Old Testament Wisdom Research." *CBQ* 29 (1967): 107-418.

__________ and O. Cram. *Wisdom Literature: Job, Proverbs, Ruth, Canticles, Ecclesiastes, and Esther*. Michigan: William B. Eerdmans, 1981.

__________ *Seven Books of Wisdom.* Milwaukee: Bruce Publishing Company, 1960.

__________ *The Tree of Life: An exploration of Biblical Wisdom Literature*. New York: Doubleday, 1990.

Muthunayagom, Daniel Jones. "Contemporary Approaches to Old Testament Interpretation." In *Interweaving Methodology and Praxis: Exploring Disciplinary Options in Today's world.* Edited by Indukuri John Mohan Razu. Bangalore: BTESSC/SATHRI, 2007.

__________ *The Relationship between Election and Israel's Attitude Towards the Nations in the Book of Isaiah.* Delhi: ISPCK, 2000.

Myer, C. F. "The Prophet: A Heavenly Messenger." *Restoration Quarterly* 9 (1966): 290- 294.

Nelson, R. *Raising Up a Faithful Priest: Community and Priesthood in Biblical Theology.* Louisville: Westminster John Knox Press, 1993.

Nelson, Jimmie L. "His Servants, the Prophets." *SJT* 24 (1981): 87-102.

Neusner, Jacob. *Amos in Tamud and Midrash: A Source Book.* Lanham, MD: University Press of America, 2007.

Nissinen, Martti and Peter Machinist. *Prophets and Prophecy in the Ancient Near East.* Atlanta: SBL, 2003.

__________ *Prophecy in its Ancient Near Eastern Context: Mesopotamia, Biblical and Arabian perspective*. Atlanta: SBL, 2000.

Noble, Paul R. "Amos and Amaziah in Context: Synchronic and Diachronic Approaches." *CBQ* 60 (1998): 423-439.

__________ "Amos' Absolute 'NO'." *VT* 47 (1997): 329-340.

Northouse, Peter G. *Leadership: Theory and Practice.* 4th ed. New Delhi: SAGE Publications India Pvt Ltd, 2007.

Noth, Martin. *The History of Israel.* Edinburgh: R. & R. Clark Ltd, 1958.

O'Connell, R. H. "Telescoping N+1 Patterns in the Book of Amos." *VT* 46 (1996): 56-79.

O'Kennedy, D. F. "Were the Prophets Really Intercessors?" *OTE* (2000): 329-47.

Obbink, Herman Theodorus. "The Forms of Prophetism." *HUCA* 14 (1939): 23-28.

O'Connell, Kevin G. "Those Lively Prophets Hosea–A Prophet of Passion." *Currents in Theology and Mission* 4 (1977): 104-108.

Oded, Bustenay. "The Historical Background of the Syro-Ephraimite War Reconsidered." *CBQ* 32 (1972): 153-154.

Ollenburger, Ben C., Elmer A. Martens and Gerhard F. Hasel, eds. *The Flowering of Old Testament Theology: A Reading in Twentieth-Century Old Testament Theology*, 1930-1900. Winona Lake: Eisenbrauns, 1992.

Olyan, Saul. "Zadok's Origins and the Tribal Politics of David." *JBL* 101 (1982): 177-193.

Oppenheim, A. L. "A Babylonian Diviner's Manual." *JNES* 33 (1974): 197-220.

Orlin, Louis Lawerence. *Life and Thought in the Ancient Near East.* Michigan: University of Michigan Press, 2007.

ORR, James, et al. *The International Standard Bible Encyclopedia.* Vol. 3. Grand Rapids: Eerdmans Publishing, 1955.

Oswalt, John N. *The Book of Isaiah: Chapters 1-39. NICOT.* Grand Rapids: Eerdmans, 1986.

Overholt, T. W. *Channels of Prophecy: The Social Dynamics of Prophetic Activity.* Minneapolis: Fortress, 1989.

Park, Aaron W. *The Book of Amos as Composed and Read in Antiquity.* New York/ Oxford: Lang, 2001.

Parker, Simon B. "Possession Trance and Prophecy in Preexilic Israel." *VT* 28 (1987): 271-85.

Partlow, Jonathan A. "Amos's Use of Rhetorical Entrapment as a Means for Climatic [*Sic*] Preaching in Amos 1:3-2:16." *Restoration Quarterly* 49 (2007): 23-32.

Patterson, Richard D. "Prophetic Satire as a Vehicle for Ethical Instruction." *JETS* 50 (2007): 47-69.

Patton, Corrine. "Priest, Prophet and Exile: Ezekiel as a Literary Construct." *SBLSP* 2000. Atlanta: SBL, 2000.

Paul, Shalom M. *Amos: A Commentary on the Book of Amos.* Minneapolis: Fortress Press, 1991.

Paul, W. Millhouse. *Enlisting and Developing Church Leaders.* Anderson: The Warner Press, 1947.

Paul S. Fideles. "The Cross of Hosea Revisited: The Meaning of Suffering in the Book of Hosea." *Review and Expositor* 90 (1993): 175-190.

Peacock, Kevin C. "Who is a God Like You?-Theological Themes in Micah." *Southwestern Journal of Theology* 46 (2003): 27-47.

Perrin, N. *What is Redaction Criticism*? Philadelphia: Fortress Press, 1969.

Petersen, David L. "Hebrew Bible Form Criticism." *Religious Studies Review* 29 (1992): 29-33.

__________ ed. *Prophecy in Israel: Search for an Identity.* Philadelphia: Fortress Press, 1987.

__________ *The Prophetic Literature: An Introduction.* Louisville/London: Westminster John Knox Press, 2002.

__________ *The Roles of Israel's Prophets.* JSOTSup 17. Sheffield: JSOT, 1981.

Pfeiffer, Charles F. *Old Testament History.* Washington, D.C.: Canon Press, 1973.

Phillips, Anthony. "David's Linen Ephod." *VT* 19 (1969): 485-487.

Pierce, Timothy M. "Micah as a Case Study for Preaching and Teaching the prophets." *Southwestern Journal of Theology* 46 (2003): 77-94.

Polan, Gregory J. "The Prophetic Voice as the Word of the Living God." *TBT* 46 (2008): 286-90.

Polley, Max E. *Amos & the Davidic Empire: A Socio-Historical Approach.* New York, Oxford: Oxford University Press, 1989.

Pollock, S. *Ancient Mesopotamia: The Eden that Never was.* Cambridge: Cambridge University Press, 1999.

Porter, Stanley E & Dennis L. Stamps, eds. *The Rhetorical Interpretation of Scripture.* Sheffield: Sheffield Academic Press, 1999.

Preez, J. Du. "Social Justice, a Motive for the Mission of the Church." *Journal of Theology for Southern Africa* 53 (1985): 36-46.

Premnath, D. N. "Amos and Hosea: Sociohistirocal Background and Prophetic Critique." *Word & World* 28 (2008): 125-132.

__________ *Eighth Century Prophets: A Social Analysis*. St. Louis: Chalice Press, 2003.

Pritchard, James B., ed. *Ancient Near Eastern Texts Relating to the Old Testament.* 3rd ed. Princeton: Princeton University Press, 1969.

Pui-lan, Kwok. *Discovering Bible in Non-Biblical World.* New York: Orbis, 1995.

Rad, Gerhard von. *Old Testament Theology Volume II: The Theology of Israel's Prophetic Traditions.* Translated by D. M. G Stalker. London: Oliver and Boyd, 1960.

Rad, Gerhard von. *The Message of the Prophets.* Translated by D. M. G. Stalker. London: SCM Press, 1962.

__________ *Wisdom in Israel.* Translated by James D. Martin. Nashville: Abingdon, London: SCM Press, 1972.

Raven, John Howard. *The History of the Religion of Israel: An Old Testament Theology*. Grand Rapids: Baker Book House, 1979.

Reinder, Joseph. "The Present State of Textual Criticism of the Old Testament." *Hebrew Union College Annual* 7 (1930): 285-315.

Rendtroff, Rolf. *The Old Testament: An Introduction.* London: SCM Press, 1985.

Robert, R. Wilson. "Prophecy in Crisis: The Call of Ezekiel." *Interpretation* 38 (1984): 117-130.

Roberts, J. J. M. "Recent Trends in the Study of Amos." *Restoration Quarterly* 13 (1970): 1-16.

__________ *The Bible and the Ancient Near East: Collected Essays*. Winona Lake: Eisenbrauns, 2002.

Roberts, Jimmy J. "A Note on Amos 7:14 and Its Context." *Restoration Quarterly* 8 (1965): 175-78.

Robertson, E. "The Urim and Tummim." *VT* 14 (1964): 67-74.

Robinson, Gnana. "The New Economic Order in the Light of the Message of the Pre-Exilic Prophets." *Bible Bhashyam* 22 (1996): 238-252.

Robinson, Theodore H. *Prophecy and the Prophets in Ancient Israel.* London: Gerald Duckworth & Co. Ltd, 1960.

__________ *A History of Israel.* Vol. 1. Oxford: Oxford University Press, 1948.

Romen, T. ed. *The Future of the Deuteronomistic History.* Leven: Leven University Press, 2000.

Rowland, C. & Mark Corner. "Liberating Exegesis: The Challenge of Liberation Theology to Biblical Studies." In *Biblical Foundation in Theology*. Edited by J. G. Dunn & J. P.Mackey. London: SCM Press, 1991.

Rosenbaum, Stanley N. *Amos of Israel: A New Interpretation.* Macon: Mercer University Press, 1990.

Rowley, Harold Henry. "The Nature of Prophecy in the Light of Recent Study." *The Harvard Theological Review* 38 (1945): 1-38.

__________ *Studies in Old Testament Prophecy.* New York: Scribner's Sons, 1950.

__________ *Worship in Ancient Israel: Its Forms and Meaning.* London: SPCK, 1967.

Ruffle, John. "The Teaching of Amenemope and its Connection with the Book of Proverbs." *Tyndale Bulletin* 28 (1977): 29-68.

Runions, Erin. *Changing Subject: Gender, Nation and Future in Micah.* New York: Sheffield Academic Press, 2002.

Ryken, Leland, James C. Wilhoit and Tremper Longman III, eds. *Dictionary of Biblical Imagery.* Illinois: IVP, 2002, 1998.

Sailhamer, John H. "The Canonical Approach to the OT: Its Effect on Understanding Prophecy." *JETS* 30 (1987): 307-315.

Sailhamer, John H. *Introduction to Old Testament Theology: A Canonical Approach.* Grand Rapids: Zondervan Publishing House, 1995.

Sanders, J. Oswald. *Spiritual Leadership.* London: Marshal, Morgan & Scott, 1967.

Sasson, Jack M. *Civilizations of the Ancient Near East.* New York: Scribner, 1995.

Sawyer, J. F. A. "A Change of Emphasis in the Study of the Prophets." In *Israel's Prophetic Tradition: Essays in Honour of Peter R. Ackroyd.* Edited by R.Coggins, A. Phillips and M. Knibb. Cambridge: Cambridge University Press, 1982.

Scaria, K. J. "Social Injustice in the Old Testament." *BB* 4 (1978): 163-192.

Schart, Aaron. *Thematic Threads in the Book of the Twelve.* Berlin, New York: de Gruyter, 2003.

Schieber, Paul L. "Priests Among Priests: The Office of the Ministry in the Light of the Old Testament." *Concordia Journal* 14 (1988): 215-228.

Schiffman, Lawrence. "Making the Bible Come to Life: Biblical Archaeology and the Teaching of Tanakh in Jewish Schools." *Tradition* 37 (2000): 38-49.

Schmidt, W. H. *Introduction to the Old Testament.* London: SCM, 1979.

Schultz, Samuel J. *The Old Testament Speaks.* New York: Harper & brothers, 1960.

Scott, R. B. Y. "Priesthood, Prophecy, Wisdom, and the Knowledge of God." *JBL* 80 (1961): 1-15.

__________ "The Study of Wisdom Literature." *Interpretation* 24 (1970): 20-45.

Segal, Michael. "The Responsibilities and Rewards of Joshua the High Priest According to Zechariah 3: 7." *JBL* 126 (2007): 717-34.

Segundo, Juan Luis. *The Liberation of Theology.* Translated by John Drury. New York: Orbis Books, 1977.

Seitz, Christopher R. *Prophecy and Hermeneutics: Towards a New Introduction to the Prophets*. Grand Rapids: Baker Academic, 2007.

__________ *Zion's Final Destiny: The Development of the Book of Isaiah: A Reassessment of Isaiah 36-39.* Minneapolis: Fortress, 1991.

Sell, Edward. *Prophets of the Exile*. Madras: Diocesan Press, 1923.

Seters, John Van. *The Pentateuch: A Social Science Commentary*. Sheffield: Sheffield Academic Press, 1999.

Sharp, Carolyn J. *Old Testament Prophets for Today.* Louisville: Westminster John Knox, 2009.

Silva, Charles H. "Literary Features in the Book of Hosea." *Bibliotheca Sacra* 164 (2007): 34-48.

Smith, Adam. *The Book of the Twelve Prophets*. Vol. 1. New York: Harper & Brothers Publishers, 1903.

Smith, G. V. *Amos*. Grand Rapids: Zondervan, 1988.

Smith, W. Robertson. *The Prophets of Israel and Their Place in History: To the Close of the Eighth Century BCE*. London: Adam and Charles Black, 1907.

Smith-Christopher, Daniel. "Of Swords and Plowshares: On Peace and the Hebrew Prophets." *TBT* 46 (2008): 154-59.

Smith, Ralph L. *Micah-Malachi.* WBC. Vol. 32. Edited by John D. W. Watts; Texas: Word Books, Publisher, 1984.

Sobosan, Jeffrey G. "Breaking the Circle of Humanity: On Political and Prophetic Authority." *Journal of the Interdenominational Theological Centre* 12 (1984-4): 78-82.

Soggin, J. Alberto. *Amos: The Prophet: A Translation and Commentary.* Translated by John Bowden. London: SCM Press, 1987.

__________ *An Introduction to the History of Israel and Judah*. 3rd ed. London: SCM Press, 1999.

__________ *Introduction to the Old Testament*. London: SCM Press, 1976.

Soulen, Richard N. *Handbook of Biblical Criticism*. London: Lutterworth Press, 1977.

Stanislaus, L. and Alwyn D'Souza. Eds. *Prophetic Dialogue: Prospects and Challenges in India*. Delhi: ISPCK, 2003.

Stanley, E. Porter and Thomas H. Olbricht. Eds. *The Rhetorical Analysis of Scripture*. Sheffield: Sheffield Academic Press, 1997.

Stansell, Gary. "The Gift in Ancient Israel." *Semeia* 87 (1999): 65-89.

Stuart, Douglas. *Hosea-Jonah. WBC.* Vol. 31. Edited by Bruce M. Metzger, et al. Nashville: Thomas Nelson Publishers, 1987.

Sweeney, Marvin A. "Resignifying A Prophetic Tradition: Redaction Criticism and the Book of Isaiah." *Voice of Tradition* (1984): 19-22.

__________ *Isaiah 1-39 with an Introduction to Prophetic Literature.* Grand Rapids: Eerdmans, 1996.

Sweeney, Marvin A. *Isaiah 1-4 and the Post-Exilic Understanding of the Isaianic Tradition, BZAW* 171. Berlin: de Gruyter, 1998.

Terrien, Samuel. "Amos and Wisdom." In *Israel's Prophetic Heritage: Essays in Honor of James Muilenburg*. Edited by B. W. Anderson and W. Harrelson. London: SCM Press LTD, 1962.

Thomas, J. A. *The Ancient Near Eastern Treaties and the Old Testament.* London: The Tyndale Press, 1963.

Thomas, P. P. *Jeroboam II the King and Amos the Prophet: A Social-Scientific Study on the Israelite Society During the 8th Century BCE.* Delhi: ISPCK, 2003.

Tidwell, Neville. "Linen Ephod: 1 Sam. 2:18 and 2 Sam. 6:14." *VT* 24 (1974): 505-507.

Tiemeyer, Lena-sofia. "The Watchman Metaphor in Isaiah LVI-LXVI." *VT* 55 (2005): 378-400.

Tillich, Paul. *Dynamic of Faith.* New York: Harper's Torch Book, 1958.

Tomes, Roger. "The Reason For The Syro-Ephraimite War." *JSOT* 59 (1993): 55-71.

Torrey, C. C. *The Second Isaiah: A New Interpretation.* New York: Scribner's, 1928.

Toy, C. H. *International Critical Commentary on Proverbs.* Edinburgh T&T Clarke, 1977.

Tucker, Gene M. "Prophetic Authenticity: A Form-Critical Study of Amos 7:10-17." *Interpretation* 27 (1973): 423-434.

Tull, P. K. "Methods of Interpretation." In *Dictionary of the Old Testament Historical Books.* Edited by Bill T Arnold & H. G. M. Williamson. Leicester: InterVarsity, 2005.

Van Gelder, Craig. "Defining the Issues Related to Power and Authority in Religious Leadership." *Journal of Religious Leadership* 6 (2007): 1-14.

Van Seters, J. *In Search of History: Historiography in the Ancient World and the Origins of Biblical History.* New Haven: Yale University Press, 1983.

Vanderkam, James C. "David Complicity in the deaths of Abner and Eshbaal." *JBL* 99 (1980): 532-33.

__________ *An Introduction to Early Judaism.* Grand Rapids, Michigan: William B. Eerdmans Publishing Company, 2001.

VanGemeren, William A. *Interpreting the Prophetic Word.* Grand Rapids: Zondervan Pub. House, 1990.

Vasholz, Robert I. "Isaiah and Ahaz: A Brief History of Crisis in Isaiah 7 and 8." *Presbyterion* 13 (1987): 79-84.

Viberg, Ake "Amos 7:14: A Case of Subtle Irony." *Tyndale Bulletin* 47 (1996): 90-114.

Wal, Adri van der. "The Structure of Amos." *JSOT* 26 (1983): 107-13.

Waltke, Bruce K. "The Book of Proverbs and Ancient Wisdom Literature." *Bibliotheca Sacra* (1979): 221-238.

__________ *An Old Testament Theology: An Exegetical, Canonical, and Thematic Approach.* Grand Rapids/Michigan: Zondervan, 2007.

Walton, John H. *Ancient Israelite Literature in Its Cultural Context.* Grand Rapids, Michigan: Zondervan Publishing House, 1989.

Wellhausen, J. *Prolegomena to the History of Israel.* Edinburgh, 1885.

Wanefsky, Rabbi David. *The Prophets Speaks to us Anew.* New York: Philosophical Library, 1952.

Ward, James M. *Hosea.* New York: Harper and Row, 1966.

Watts, John D. W. *Forming Prophetic Literature.* London: Sheed & Ward, 1996.

__________ *Vision and Prophecy in Amos.* Leiden: Brill, 1958.

Wayne, A. "The Causes of the Division of the Kingdom." *Bibliotheca Sacra* 141 (1984): 223-233.

Weiser, Artur. *The Old Testament: Its Formation and Development.* Translated by Dorothea M. Barton: New York Association, 1961.

Wenham, G. J. *The Book of Leviticus.* Grand Rapids: Eerdmans, 1979.

Wessels, W. J. "Engaging the Book of Haggai in Leadership Issues." *OTE* 16(2003): 767-84.

Westermann, Claus. *Basic Forms of Prophetic Speech.* Translated by H. C. White. Philadelphia: Westminster John Knox, 1967.

__________ *Hand Book to the Old Testament.* Minneapolis: Augsburg Publishing House, 1967.

Whitley, C. F. *The Genius of Ancient Israel.* Amsterdam: Philo Press, 1969.

Whitelam, Keith W. *The Just King: Monarchical Judicial Authority in Ancient Israel.* JOSTSup. 12, Sheffield: Sheffield Press, 1979.

Whybray, R. N. "The Making of the Pentateuch a Methodological Study: A Methodological Study." *JSOT* 53. David J. A. Clnes & Philip R. Davies, eds. Sheffield: Sheffield Academic Press, 1987.

__________ *The Intellectual Tradition of the Old Testament.* Berlin: Walter de Gruyter, 1974.

Wilcke, Claus. *Early Ancient Near Eastern Law: A History of Its Beginnings: The Early Dynastic and Sargonic Periods.* 2nd ed. Winona Lake, Indiana: Eisenbrauns: 2007.

Wildberger, Hans. *Isaiah 1-12. A Continental Commentary.* Minneapolis: Fortress Press, 1991.

Williams, James G. "Sacrifice and the Beginning of Kingship." *Semeia* 67 (1994): 73- 84.

Williamson, H. G. M. *Isaiah 1-5.* Maiden Lane, New York: T&T Clark International, 2006.

__________ *The Book Called Isaiah: Deutero-Isaiah's Role in Composition and Redaction.* Oxford: Clarendon, 1994.

Wilson, Robert R. *Prophecy and Society in Ancient Israel.* Philadelphia: Fortress Press, 1980.

Wilson, Robert R. "Prophecy and Ecstasy: A Reexamination." *Journal of Biblical Literature* 98 (1979): 321-37.

Wiwcharuck, Peter G. *Christian Leadership Development and Church Growth.* Manila: Christian Literature Crusade, 1973.

Wolff, Hans Walter. *Amos the Prophet: Man and His Background.* Philadelphia: Fortress Press, 1973.

__________ "Prophets and Institutions in the Old Testament." *Currents in Theology and Mission* 13 (1986): 5-12.

__________ *Hosea.* Translated by Gary Stansell. Edited by Paul D. Hanson. Philadelphia: Fortress Press, 1974.

__________ *Joel and Amos.* Edited by S. D. McBride Jr. Translated by W. S. D. Janzen, Mc Bride and C. A. Muenchow. Philadelphia: Fortress, 1977.

Wood, Joyce Rilett. *Amos in Song and Book Culture.* JSOTSup 337. London, New York: Sheffield Academic Press, 2002.

Wood, Leon J. "Ecstasy and Israel's Early Prophets." *Bulletin of the Evangelical Theological Society* 9 (1966): 125-37.

__________ *The Prophets of Israel.* Grand Rapids: Baker Book House, 1979.

__________ *Israel's United Monarchy.* Michigan: Baker Books House, 1979.

Wright, T. J. "Amos and the Sycamore Fig." *VT* 26 (1976): 362-368.

Young, Edward J. "Call of Moses." *Westminster Theological Journal* 30 (1967): 1-23.

Zalcman, Lawrence. "Piercing the Darkness at *Boqer* (Amos VII 14)." *VT* 30 (1980): 252-255.

Zevit, Ziony. "A Misunderstanding at Bethel Amos VII 12-17." *VT* 25 (1975): 783-90.

Zimmerli, Walther. *A Social Rewording of the Old Testament: Prophet's Approaches to Israel's Communal Life.* Edited by Patrick D. Miller. Minneapolis: Fortress Press, 1994.

__________ Old *Testament Theology in Outline.* Translated by David E. Green. Edinburgh: T&T Clark Ltd, 1978.

__________ *The Fiery Throne: The Prophets and Old Testament Theology.* Minneapolis: Fortress Press, 1989.

__________ *The Law and the Prophets.* Translated by R. E. Clements. New York: Harper & Row, Publishers, 1969.

__________ *Theology of Old Testament: Testimony, Dispute, Advocacy.* Minneapolis: Fortress Press, 1997.